Baltimore **'68**

Baltimore '68

Riots and Rebirth in an American City

EDITED BY

Jessica I. Elfenbein,
Thomas L. Hollowak,
and Elizabeth M. Nix

TEMPLE UNIVERSITY PRESS
Philadelphia

TEMPLE UNIVERSITY PRESS
Philadelphia, Pennsylvania 19122
www.temple.edu/tempress

Published 2011

Library of Congress Cataloging-in-Publication Data

Baltimore '68 : riots and rebirth in an American city / edited by Jessica I. Elfenbein, Thomas L. Hollowak, and Elizabeth M. Nix.
p. cm.
Includes bibliographical references and index.
ISBN 978-1-4399-0661-3 (cloth : alk. paper) —
ISBN 978-1-4399-0662-0 (pbk. : alk. paper) —
ISBN 978-1-4399-0663-7 (e-book)
1. Baltimore (Md.)—History—20th century. 2. Baltimore (Md.)—Social conditions—20th century. 3. Baltimore (Md.)—Race relations—History—20th century. 4. Race riots—Maryland—Baltimore—History—20th century. 5. African Americans—Maryland—Baltimore—Social conditions—20th century. I. Elfenbein, Jessica I. II. Hollowak, Thomas L. III. Nix, Elizabeth M. (Elizabeth Morrow), 1964–
F189.B157B336 2011
975.2′6—dc22

2010050108

♾ The paper used in this publication meets the requirements of the American National Standard for Information Sciences—Permanence of Paper for Printed Library Materials, ANSI Z39.48-1992

Printed in the United States of America

082311P

Contents

Foreword, by Howard F. Gillette, Jr. vii

Preface xv

Acknowledgments xxi

PART I: APRIL 1968

1 The Dream Deferred: The Assassination of Martin Luther King, Jr., and the Holy Week Uprisings of 1968 | by Peter B. Levy 3

2 Jewell Chambers: Oral History | edited by Linda Shopes 26

3 Why Was There No Rioting in Cherry Hill? | by John R. Breihan 39

PART II: THE POLITICAL, RELIGIOUS, AND URBAN PLANNING CONTEXT

4 "White Man's Lane": Hollowing Out the Highway Ghetto in Baltimore | by Emily Lieb 51

5 Spiro T. Agnew and the Burning of Baltimore | by Alex Csicsek 70

6 Thomas Carney: Oral History | edited by Linda Shopes 86

7 "Church People Work on the Integration Problem": The Brethren's Interracial Work in Baltimore, 1949–1972 | by Jessica I. Elfenbein 103

8 Convergences and Divergences: The Civil Rights and Antiwar Movements—Baltimore, 1968 | by W. Edward Orser and Joby Taylor 122

PART III: CONSEQUENCES FOR EDUCATION, BUSINESS, AND COMMUNITY ORGANIZING

9 The Pats Family: Oral History | edited by Linda Shopes 145

10 How the 1968 Riots Stopped School Desegregation in Baltimore | by Howell S. Baum 154

11 Pivot in Perception: The Impact of the 1968 Riots on Three Baltimore Business Districts | by Elizabeth M. Nix and Deborah R. Weiner 180

12 "Where We Live": Greater Homewood Community Corporation, 1967–1976 | by Francesca Gamber 208

13 Planning for the People: The Early Years of Baltimore's Neighborhood Design Center | by Mary Potorti 226

14 Robert Birt: Oral History | edited by Linda Shopes 246

Epilogue: History and Memory: Why It Matters That We Remember | by Clement Alexander Price 259

Contributors 265

Index 269

Foreword

Howard F. Gillette, Jr.

It's legitimate to ask why anyone would bother to open old wounds by revisiting the civic disorders that wracked our nation's cities a generation ago. Although some physical signs remain of that turbulence, for the most part the areas affected have been reconstructed, those who witnessed or participated in those events have largely moved on with their lives, and the urban issues that animated the period have, if not receded, been relegated to the periphery of civic discourse. At least that might appear to be the case. In fact, the riots live on in different form, through the power of negative association with the places that suffered and the people identified with them, whether by chance or by purpose. The term "rolling riots," referring to the breakdown of moral and civic rectitude associated with high levels of crime, especially drug use and other antisocial behavior, is used by social scientists as well as social critics to label inner-city areas as incubators of the pathology associated with the disorders of the 1960s.[1]

No such simple reading of the breakdown of civil order prevailed at the time of the riots themselves, though it would be a mistake to suggest that consensus reigned at the time. The single most important assessment of the widespread phenomenon of rioting, the report of the National Advisory Commission on Civil Disorders (also known as the Kerner Commission for its chair, Illinois governor Otto Kerner), issued in 1968, pointedly refused to blame the perpetrators alone for the consequences of their actions. Rather, the commission pointed to underlying social conditions, most notably the concentration of poverty and the sharp restrictions on opportunity that characterized the areas where order broke down. Most notably, the commission blamed an unrelieved national pattern of racism. In perhaps its most famous—and contested—statement, the commission declared, "The nation is moving towards two societies, one black, one white—separate and unequal. . . . Discrimination and segregation have long permeated much of American life; they now threaten the future of every American." These conclusions were echoed by a host of more specialized investigations, from California to New Jersey.[2]

The commission's conclusions have made their way into the vast social science literature on poverty and disinvestment frequently enough in subsequent years, even as they became the object of ridicule from conservative commentators. If the general public has been swayed at all by the exchange about a very difficult issue, it has shifted to the right and not to the left, and the tendency of policy initiatives to emphasize crime prevention over social uplift reflects that prevailing view.

The current situation is not unlike the one that emerged in the years following the abolition of slavery and the Reconstruction period that followed. While contemporary historians have demonstrated without doubt the essential purposes of Radical Reconstruction, providing freedmen rights under the law that had been closed to them as long as slavery existed,[3] they had to overturn a consensual belief prevailing over several generations that these efforts had been thoroughly corrupt and detrimental to the nation. Leading scholars, with the notable exception of W.E.B. DuBois, perpetuated such readings of the past, which northern as well as southern whites were quick to embrace. As the historian David Blight has demonstrated so convincingly, the victims of this prevailing collective memory were the freedmen themselves, whose voices were all but silenced in civil discourse, even as the liberties they had gained under Reconstruction were eliminated by Jim Crow segregation laws in the South and equally restrictive social practices in the North.[4]

The launch of a Second Reconstruction, as the civil rights movement of the post–World War II era is often called, challenged prevailing wisdom about the past and projected a very different future for civic life. Hard-won battles at the local level cumulated nationally in the civil rights acts of 1964 and 1965 as well as open housing legislation adopted in 1968. In law if not in practice, all citizens could expect equal treatment.

Some sort of backlash may well have been inevitable, but to be credible it had to find an object worthy of contempt. The riots of the 1960s proved a godsend to this cause, for the damage not just to property but to the very concept of what constitutes a stable democratic system was severe. Here was the chance, not to call for new investment in the ghetto, but to assert a powerful defense of established values without making the appeals overtly racial. Not insignificantly, calls for law and order dominated not just Republican discourse on the subject but that of third-party maverick George Wallace, whose popular image was burnished by his highly visible stand against federal efforts to integrate the University of Alabama in 1963. Significantly, the Republican position on inner-city blacks was neither uniform nor inevitable. In the months that Richard Nixon faced primary opposition from the more liberal Nelson Rockefeller for the 1968 presidential nomination, Nixon touted a plan to promote black enterprise. Modeled on the work of Philadelphia's Leon Sullivan, Nixon's proposal was complemented by GOP efforts to extend its reach into inner-city areas. With the encouragement of the Michigan Republican National Committee's chairwoman, Elly Peterson, Republicans opened storefronts in Detroit that were not touched by the rioting that broke out around them in 1967. Over time, however, these efforts were abandoned. With Nixon tested on Vietnam by critics on the left and a possible challenge to his next presidential run from George Wallace on the right, he chose to deal with both phenomena at once, by unleashing Vice President Spiro Agnew to shore up his standing among conservatives by attacking civil disobedience in any form.[5]

In recent years, scholars have begun to revisit the riots and their larger context. Most notably, Kevin Mumford and Max Herman have thoroughly investigated civil unrest in Newark and Detroit.[6] Their contributions are welcome and informative. It is possible that with time new readings will help overturn popular misconceptions of the riots, just as scholars of slavery and Reconstruction have altered national discourse. At the same time, university-based work has its limits, and that is why efforts to publicly commemorate the riots, and at the same time explore their meaning and consequences, are so important.

Issues that had simmered for years were confronted and brought to public attention by, first, an exhibit in Newark and then conferences on the subject both there and in Baltimore. The occasion, in both instances, was a fortieth anniversary, enough time it seems to distance the public from the searing emotions associated with the experiences but close enough to bring forth witness from those who lived through that trauma. Both commemorations generated a good deal of attention in the press, thus extending the public conversation. These events also coincided with an effort, initiated by the Milton S. Eisenhower Foundation, to revisit the findings of the Kerner Commission. Former U.S. senator Fred Harris, an original member of the commission, chaired the effort, which included public hearings in Detroit and Newark, among other places.[7] In short, the anniversary of the riots proved an opportunity both to assess their lasting damage and to interrogate their effect on popular opinion.

Initiating such conversations is never easy. Efforts to raise money for the exhibit at the New Jersey Historical Society dragged on for most of a decade. The exhibit's opening in November 2007 attracted a large audience, as did the conference that followed. Still, engagement did nothing to lift the

Store with "Soul Brother" sign. (Reprinted courtesy of the *Baltimore News American* Collection, University of Maryland–College Park.)

historical society's fortunes. When the effects of a deep recession hit a year later, the society had to close its doors to all visitors except by appointment.

The Baltimore experience behind this volume stands out. Built on a wide basis of civic engagement initiated at the University of Baltimore, the public program that emerged in April 2008, on the anniversary of the assassination of Dr. Martin Luther King, Jr., had enough breadth to it—performance, artistic representations, and readings, as well as scholarly papers—to ensure broad participation. Associated efforts to collect oral histories, some of which were published in time for the commemoration, as well as follow-up conversations sponsored by the Y of Central Maryland, generated additional participation. Conversations do not guarantee wide-scale revision of prevailing views as participants search for a higher truth. Such efforts would seem to be critical, however, not the least because an honest conversation needs to be entered into before past differences of knowledge and belief can even begin to be resolved.

How difficult that process might be has been illustrated over the past seven years in Philadelphia in the prolonged debate—much of it angry—that attended efforts to commemorate the presence of slavery at the President's House during George Washington's tenure as president. Only through a patient and dogged effort to bring U.S. National Park Service and

Burning building. (Reprinted courtesy of the Lt. James V. Kelly Baltimore City Police Department Collection.)

other government officials together with citizen groups and scholars was it possible to agree on a format and a design for a memorial commemorating this building and the full range of what had been experienced there.[8] The memorial, opened December 15, 2010, testifies to both the difficulties and the rewards of the effort.

The April 2008 conference that formed the basis for this volume recognized the importance of engagement before the presentation of findings and evaluation. By the time the program had been set, discussion of the riots and their legacy in the city had taken many forms in many forums. Starting with the premise that knowledge is power and that not everyone shared the same information, the program built from the ground up. As with the President's House controversy, scholars played a central role in conceiving the conference and enlisting participants to make scholarly presentations. But this was not done in isolation from the other work necessary to ensure a robust interchange of information and ideas among a wide range of interested parties.

Baltimore offers a valuable case study. Although damage to the city was almost as extensive as anywhere else, it has not received the same level of scrutiny as other affected areas. It was two days after Dr. King's death before disturbances broke out, and by that time a host of other cities had attracted national attention, not the least the nation's capital, just a short way down Interstate 95. Much of the research presented in this volume, then, is fresh, but it also has the advantage of being well informed by work on other cities. What emerges from the collection, then, is a set of observations that are new in particulars but begin to confirm larger truths about how the riots have been remembered and commented on generally.

In these chapters, and in the poignant memory of the Pats family especially, is confirmation of the searing pain that follows loss, not just of property but of trust. "These are not the people that I thought I knew," Sharon Pats Singer comments in Chapter 9 as she recalls the harsh words her black classmates directed at her. Her disturbing affirmation that "life as we knew it was over at that point" confirms the tragedy storeowners faced when their dreams literally went up in smoke. For those who left their homes and livelihoods behind in the aftermath of the riots, these memories live on as proof of a profound disrupture. Yet, put in context, the Patses' loss appears less typical than might be imagined. As Elizabeth Nix and Deborah Weiner point out in Chapter 11, the great majority of businesses in the area where the Pats pharmacy was located, as well as such important commercial strips as Pennsylvania Avenue, survived the riots. Those that closed in subsequent years did so for a variety of reasons, not all related to the riots. The loss of any business was quite clearly tragic, but Jewish commercial life did not come to an end when riots swept away some but not all of its presence in predominantly black areas of the city.

It has become common wisdom, confirmed by the decline of areas hardest hit by the civic disorder, to suggest that blacks living there brought the worst only on themselves. Yet if we recognize the full context of what led up to the disturbances, another picture emerges. The Pats family may have been among those welcoming urban renewal as an opportunity for reviving a decaying city. But not all plans were so benign as the one that promised an upgraded environment for their store. For those slated to leave their homes, not the least to make way for highways carrying commuters into and through the city, the effect was more threatening. Emily Lieb puts this most starkly in Chapter 4 where she writes, "In many ways, the highway plans and the riots were linked. To the people who lived in the neighborhoods slated for clearance, the expressway proposals made it clear that their homes and schools and luncheonettes and grocery stores were less important than an exit ramp. Public policy declared over and over again that Baltimore's black neighborhoods were disposable; in 1968 rioters treated them accordingly."

Even a cursory reading of testimonials to the effects of the riots confirms the suspicion that memories forged in different circumstances and nourished in communities that have since separated physically coexist but rarely merge. Without the opportunity for direct engagement, separate views prevail in separate societies. It only makes sense, if history is to be served and a fuller view of the past is to emerge, that conflicting views need to be brought into the same conversation.

To mediate differences requires a consensus builder, one who chooses to bridge the divide between the two worlds the Kerner Commission described as dangerously far apart. In a preview of what was to come, Alex Csicsek in Chapter 5 recounts the actions of Governor Spiro Agnew, known before the riots as a conciliatory moderate among Republicans who actively sought to advance civil rights legislation in Maryland. During and after the Baltimore disturbances, he was anything but conciliatory, blaming civil rights leaders for letting disorder get out of hand and rejecting any underlying social causes for the riots in his widely circulated contention that the riots were "caused in all too many cases by evil men and not evil conditions." Not without cause, Csicsek suggests that Agnew's comments, considered an outburst by black leaders who expected more of him at the time, sent a strong message to Richard Nixon of the kind of running mate he might be. The man Nixon had been considering for vice president because of his ability to attract traditionally Democratic white ethnic votes, Massachusetts governor John Volpe, was named secretary of transportation in the Nixon administration instead. He never gained the notoriety Agnew did stirring up resentments among fellow white ethnics by extending his post-riots position to all forms of civil disobedience.

Think of this volume, then, as part of a larger movement and conversation, one that started well before the Baltimore '68 conference and one that continues both formally in meetings sponsored by the Y of Central Maryland and informally across the country as we pass the anniversary of the riots and enter a period where a black man holds the highest office in the land. The wounds of discord cannot be wished away. They cannot be explained away. They need to be addressed across a divide that has kept many people apart socially, economically, and ideologically. Historians can provide context for discussions. They can identify, as the authors in this book do, the social and economic structures within which these events took place. With a larger picture before us, we can turn away from efforts to blame one group or another for ongoing problems associated with the areas hardest hit by rioting that continue to be devalued by trauma. We can bring value back by recognizing these areas and the events associated with them as part of a larger world we all inhabit. And we can recognize that our fate is tied up with theirs. And wouldn't it be a better world if we could finally put the riots behind us because we agreed on their root causes and knew just as well that we could address them to the benefit of all of us? The Kerner Commission asked us to do no less.

NOTES

1. Fred Siegel, *The Future Once Happened Here: New York, L.A., and the Fate of America's Big Cities* (New York: Free Press, 1997), 9.

2. *Report of the National Advisory Commission on Civil Disorders* (New York: Bantam, 1968), 1; U.S. Commission Governor's Select Commission on Civil Disorder, *Report for Action* (Trenton, NJ, 1968).

3. See especially, Eric Foner, *Reconstruction: America's Unfinished Revolution, 1863–1877* (New York: Harper and Row, 1988).

4. David Blight, *Race and Reunion: The Civil War and American Memory* (Cambridge: Belknap Press, 2001); Thomas J. Sugrue, *Sweet Land of Liberty: The Forgotten Struggle for Civil Rights in the North* (New York: Random House, 2008).

5. For more on the political context of the Kerner Commission report and Richard Nixon's determination to exploit its effect on disaffected whites, see Rick Perlstein, *Nixonland: The Rise of a President and the Fracturing of America* (New York: Scribner, 2008), 240–241.

6. Kevin Mumford, *Newark: A History of Race, Rights, and Riots in America* (New York: New York University Press, 2007); Max Herman's website http://www.67riots.rutgers.edu. Herman was the chief historical consultant to the New Jersey Historical Society's 2007 exhibit "What's Going On? Newark and the Legacy of the Sixties."

7. For information on this exercise, see the Eisenhower website, available at http://www.eisenhowerfoundation.org/kerner.php.

8. For updated information on the President's House controversy in Philadelphia, see http://www.ushistory.org/presidentshouse/index.htm.

Preface

It is hard to remember that, as recently as 2008, if one were to search for information on "Baltimore riots," actually or virtually, much more would come up for the unrest in 1861 than for the events of April 1968. The absence of materials for the latter belies its importance. Unlike the earlier turmoil, related to the Civil War, the events of April 1968 had no clear victors. The disorder that followed the assassination of the Reverend Martin Luther King, Jr., in Baltimore and scores of other American cities was, with the exception of contemporary news accounts, largely absent from both civic dialogue and the historical record because, even after forty years, the wounds festered and had not yet healed.

The editors of this volume—Elizabeth "Betsy" Nix and Jessica Elfenbein, Baltimore residents for their adult lives, and Tom Hollowak, a native Baltimorean—are proud of the role they have played in putting the causes and effects of April 1968 front and center for both civic discourse and historical research. This volume is the culmination of work that began in the fall of 2005. Jessica Elfenbein, an urban historian at the University of Baltimore (UB), and Tom Hollowak, head of Special Collections at UB's Langsdale Library, had collaborated for more than a decade. Together they had organized two public history conferences (1996 and 1999) that explored Baltimore history and had coedited *From Mobtown to Charm City*, a Baltimore anthology. This earlier work added to the scholarly understanding of this under-researched

East Coast industrial city and pointed up the absence of any scholarly exploration of the civic unrest that followed King's assassination and whose effects still marred the city. At lunch in downtown Baltimore, Tom and Jessica discussed that April 1968 week of destruction, with its mass arrests and widespread uncertainty, a topic about which they were keen to teach and learn but for which there was little material readily available.

Within the University of Baltimore community, the editors first found fodder for the project. Jessica mentioned her lunchtime conversation to Rosalind Terrell, then working as an administrative assistant, and asked what she had been doing during Holy Week of 1968. Rosalind replied, "I was young; I was poor; I was black. What do you think I was doing?" Linda Randall, then UB's associate provost, reported that her father, one of the first African American graduates of University of Maryland Medical School, had been defending his obstetrical practice with a shotgun. Eric Singer, an adjunct professor, said that his family, part of Baltimore's Jewish community, lost their business and their home during that week.

These brief conversations illuminated the complexity of this historical event and confirmed the editors' commitment to documenting and interpreting its causes and effects. They knew, too, that this topic required careful handling. Almost forty years later, these memories still prompted powerful visceral reactions among the citizens of Baltimore: "If it hadn't been for the riots, our family would have stayed in the city." "After the riots, we never went downtown any more." "Baltimore was wonderful before the riots, but it's been downhill since then." The forty-year cushion provided fertile ground for an oral history project. Witnesses to and participants in the events of April 1968 were still alive and well, but the passage of time allowed critical distance. Betsy Nix, an assistant professor of history at UB, volunteered to uncover and preserve the stories of individual Baltimoreans who had experienced the events. Over the course of several semesters, Betsy and her undergraduate students created an oral history archive that contains the memories of more than one hundred ordinary Baltimoreans, including looters, business owners, first responders, journalists, civil rights organizers, and National Guardsmen.

From the beginning, the project reached across the university, well beyond the history department and the archives. Law professors were interested in the legal ramifications of a city arresting thousands of its citizens. Understanding the impact the events had on mom-and-pop stores in Baltimore appealed to business school faculty. A playwright on campus saw the drama in the oral histories and started crafting an original play. Soon the project spread to a wide cross section of interested community stakeholders, including museums, cultural organizations, other colleges and universities, and K–12 schools. Together we planned a major convening for April 2008 to which scholars and citizens were invited to examine the uprisings' long-term causes and consequences in an effort to improve the quality of life in our city. Three days of panels, dramatic presentations, movie screenings, and discussion among more than four hundred scholars and Baltimore residents drew local and national media attention. The project continues with a series of civic dialogues, a community arts project, a K–12 curriculum project, a driving tour, and more.[1]

This anthology grew out of those activities. These chapters offer Baltimore as the prototypical American city: a scrappy factory and commercial center that had reached its productive height in the 1950s. In 1968 the city was home to a variety of ethnic, religious, and racial communities that, like those in many other American cities, were confronting a quickly declining industrial base. Baltimore sits distinctively on the nation's North–South divide and exhibits an unusual combination of the characteristics of each region. In addition, its proximity to the nation's capital made it a fertile testing ground for many Great Society programs.

Using April 1968 as the linchpin around which to detail the trends that shaped dozens of American urban places in the last third of the twentieth century, the scholars in this volume ask several questions: What actually happened, why did it happen, and what are the effects on American cities today? This project is strengthened by the range of contributors—from newly emerging voices bringing a new set of questions to well-established scholars drawing on decades of pathbreaking work. As a group, we argue that, although in popular understanding the disorders of April 1968 served as the trigger for middle-class flight from urban chaos and decay, in actuality the unrest punctuated trends already well under way.

Howard Gillette and Clement Price remind us of both the national context for this work and why it matters that we remember. Peter Levy of York College spent a sabbatical year at the University of Baltimore during the Baltimore '68 initiative, and his work goes a long way in answering the question of what actually happened here in Baltimore. His chapter works in combination with John Breihan's case study of Cherry Hill to establish the local context for the events, ferret out the facts of that week from popular memory, and establish the physical costs of the destruction. It may be news to some that the unrest came during a relatively healthy period of race relations in Baltimore. In 1967 a new white mayor had been elected on an integrationist ticket. The police department had recruited black officers, the city had formed the Community Action Committee, and the city administration had appointed African Americans to various municipal boards. Outside the local government, various nonprofit service and faith-based groups had been carefully building cross-race alliances, as Jessica Elfenbein outlines in her chapter, a case study of the work of the Church of the Brethren. Ironically, these advances fed heightened expectations at the same time that high rates of unemployment and widespread inferior housing affected more and more working-class Baltimoreans, both black and white. Government intervention in several cases apparently made the situation worse. Emily

Lieb's work reveals that many of the neighborhoods that went up in flames during the unrest had already been targeted by local urban renewal plans, often dependent on federal dollars. Looters and arsonists were just one step ahead of the city planners and their bulldozers. Scholars in this volume conclude that the lifting of despair in some areas highlighted the entrenched problems in others and led to the uprisings.

In that same vein, research indicates that the disturbances shifted the landscape along lines of race and class. After the disturbances, many blacks and whites retreated into protected enclaves, in ways both physical and metaphorical. Whole portions of city life, including the public schools, were ceded to African American interests. The violence, which had targeted property, underscored the deep class divisions within the African American community that the civil rights movement had in some ways obscured. Middle-class blacks now had additional reasons to join middle-class white Baltimoreans in their abandonment of older inner-city neighborhoods.

Baltimore's shift away from the rhetoric of race and toward the politics of law and order follows the pattern of many other cities during this period, as Alex Csicsek points out in his chapter. White Americans were exhausted and disappointed by the civil rights movement and confused by the insistent demands of the black underclass. Black Americans were discouraged by incremental gains in social and economic justice. Edward Orser and Joby Taylor discuss the ways that both parties pulled apart to pursue independent agendas against the backdrop of the Vietnam War. In his chapter Howell Baum argues that the unrest effectively stopped the muted attempts at full school desegregation in the city. In retrospect, Baltimore of the mid-1960s exemplifies boldly experimental attempts at interracial understanding and urban planning that were brought to a halt by an uprising of the very people those efforts intended to uplift.

While civil unrest affected scores of American cities, constituted the largest civil disturbance since the Civil War, and clearly had lasting political effects, other authors in this volume put the unrest into perspective. The initiative at UB was titled Baltimore '68: Riots and Rebirth, and many in the city interpreted the events as a wake-up call. As Elizabeth Nix and Deborah Weiner demonstrate, even some business districts hit hard during that week rebounded and continued to serve their customers for at least another decade. Mary Potorti and Francesca Gamber describe the formation of two new nonprofits, the Neighborhood Design Center—part of a national movement of grassroots initiatives undertaken by those in the built environment community—and Greater Homewood Community Corporation, fueled at least in part by the interests of Johns Hopkins University as an anchor institution. Forty years after their founding, these community organizing groups, shaped in the wake of the disturbances, still pursue social justice missions.

Interspersed among the chapters are four oral testimonies of Baltimore citizens who experienced April 1968 firsthand. The editors made these four selections because their narrators saw the events from very different perspectives. In addition, their wealth of detail and thoughtful observations illuminate our understanding of the events. Their stories were collected by University of Baltimore undergraduates and AmeriCorps volunteers and then rather significantly edited by Linda Shopes for both readability and space. Shopes, a past president of the Oral History Association, tried to remain true to the interviewees' voices and their understanding of the experience. Shopes also fact-checked the interviews, and her annotations point out inevitable discrepancies, not with the intention of correcting the narrators, but to highlight the differences between memory and history. Our work on Baltimore '68 has shown us that the memories people hold of events can mean more to a community than what actually happened.

The interviews can be found in their entirety on the project's prizewinning website, http://www.ubalt.edu/baltimore68, organized and maintained by Tom Hollowak. The oral histories contained in this volume represent a fraction of the testimony available on the site, which also contains scores of primary documents, photographs, a driving tour, a map, a retrospective calendar, television news footage, audio clips, official reports, and links to related archival collections. In many cases, the scholars in this anthology used the resources on the website for their research. We invite readers to consult the website as they work their way through the volume, just as we invite people everywhere to use this important and accessible resource for whatever purpose they find it to be useful.

We began this project as a way to examine a painful period in our city's history. We have reaped far more than we sowed. We believe that the manifold work that is Baltimore '68 has contributed to healing fair Baltimore. We urge readers to share with us new materials, new interpretations, and new questions that may be raised by reading this work.

NOTE

1. *Public Historian* published eight articles about the project in the November 2009 issue. *Public Historian: A Journal of Public History* 31, no. 4 (November 2009): 11–66.

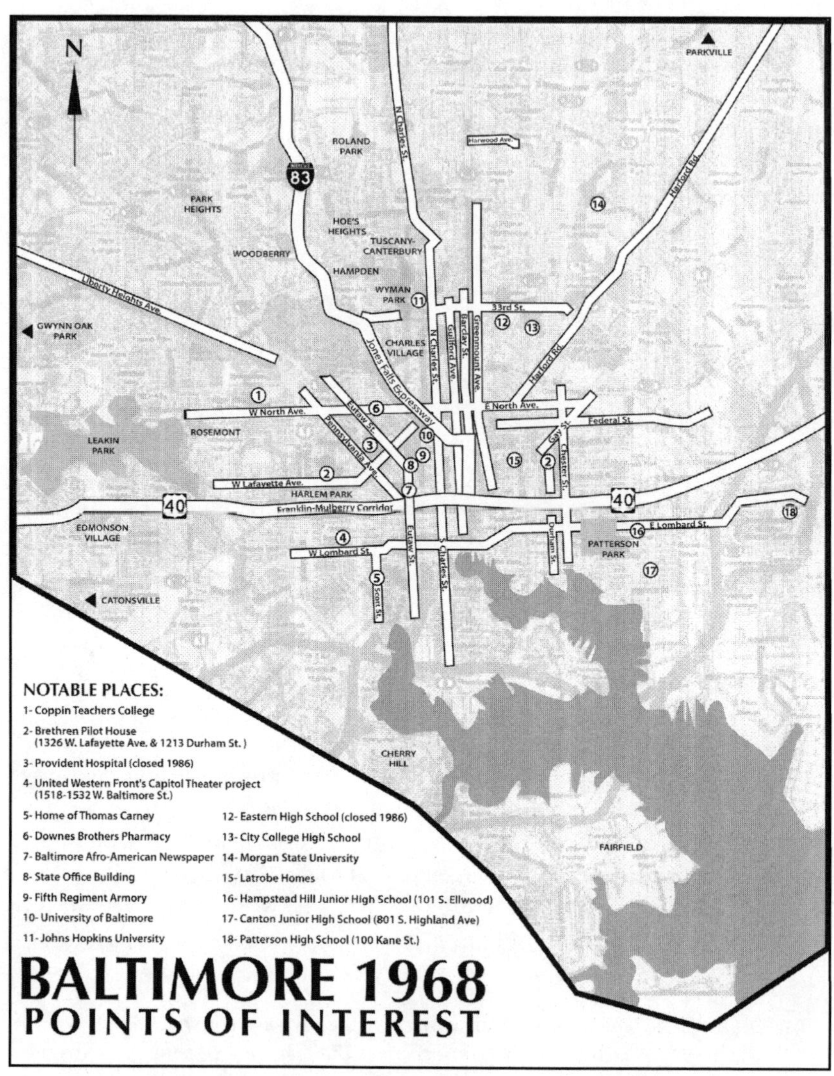

"*Baltimore 1968: Points of Interest.*" (Reprinted courtesy of Christina Ralls.)

Acknowledgments

An anthology, by definition, is a collaborative enterprise. The editors wish to thank all of the contributors to this volume, each of whom first presented or moderated at Baltimore '68: Riots and Rebirth, a pathbreaking public history conference held in April 2008 at the University of Baltimore. In addition to the authors of the chapters, we are indebted to many of our University of Baltimore and community-history colleagues who through their thoughtful contributions made possible the multifaceted enterprise known as Baltimore '68. From 2005 to 2009, as a steering committee, we learned together and then planned together the many activities that in turn spawned this volume. We are grateful to David Stevens, Linda Randall, Rachel Brubaker, Karen S. Brown, John Schwallenberg, Christina Ralls, Eric Singer, Linda Shopes, Kimberley Lynne, Chris Hart, Robert Shindle, Jim Kelly, Karla Shephard, Elaine Weiss, Lydia Woods, Anita Thomas, John Windmueller, and John Mealey.

The University of Baltimore's senior leadership made this work possible. Without the support of President Robert L. Bogomolny and former provost Wim Wiewel, this model university-engaged project would have been little more than a good idea. Their input, willingness to take on a risky topic, and financial support were instrumental to both the success of Baltimore '68 and this volume's creation. Provost Joseph S. Wood has continued the university's support in many important ways, including through funding to underwrite the publication of visual materials for this volume. We are also grateful to Lucy Holman, UB's Langsdale Library director, for her unwavering support for the creation, expansion, and ongoing commitment to the Baltimore '68 website (http://www.ubalt.edu/baltimore68) and to the related collections we've had the privilege to gather in Special Collections. To our students in more than a half-dozen classes at UB over five years, we say thank you. Your insights and enthusiasm for this project kept us moving forward.

We also thank the scores of people who came forward to offer their stories about the spring of 1968 and who allowed their oral histories to remain in our online archive. Their gracious contributions formed the foundation of our understanding of these events and constantly reminded us of the importance of including many perspectives in our historical investigation. We are grateful, too, to those from across the country who learned about our work and shared with us the stories of their families' experiences in Baltimore in April 1968. Our website features the transcribed oral histories as well as a number of collections of photographs, journal entries, and business records that have been generously shared.

Our work throughout the entire project was aided by the thoughtful guidance of Linda Shopes. A devoted steering committee member, she helped us in the early stages as we were building the oral history project and then spent countless hours editing and annotating the four oral histories that appear in this volume. We benefited immensely from her understanding of the vital role that oral history plays in the life of any community.

Mick Gusinde-Duffy has been a wonderful editor. He stayed with us even as he had to work extra hard to find peer reviewers who had not been directly touched by the multifaceted work that made up Baltimore '68. Our interactions with him and his colleagues at Temple University Press have been professional, productive, and fun. Authors can't ask for anything more.

In the end, in addition to our gratitude for the love and support of our families (thanks Robert, Nora, Susannah, Micah, Andy, Gareth, Nicholas, and Dave), we are truly thankful to have had the opportunity to work together on this enormously satisfying project. We now know what it means to call each other colleague and friend. We are clear, too, that the product is stronger because of the range of voices and views. It does indeed "take a village."

Part I

April 1968

1

The Dream Deferred

The Assassination of Martin Luther King, Jr., and the Holy Week Uprisings of 1968

PETER B. LEVY

If riots come, ask the question: Who is responsible—those who have been drawn to desperation or those who drive them to desperation?

—REV. HENRY J. OFFER
(qtd. in Paul Fairfax Evans, *City Life*)

As the sun began to set on Saturday, April 6, 1968, Robert Bradby, a twenty-one-year-old black steelworker, was relaxing at his girlfriend's house when a crowd of black men and women began to congregate about a mile away on Gay Street in East Baltimore. Two days earlier, Martin Luther King, Jr., had been assassinated in Memphis, Tennessee, and the black communities in Washington, D.C., and Chicago had erupted, but Baltimore, in the words of government officials, remained calm.

Concerned about the safety of his girlfriend's children, Bradby set out to find them. After learning that the children were safe, Bradby stopped for a beer at Club Federal, a local hangout at the corner of Federal and Gay. From the bar he could see a raucous crowd, which, when he left the bar, he did his best to avert. To his surprise, gunshots rang out, nearly hitting him. Presumably, the shots were fired by either the owner of Gabriel's Spaghetti House, John Novak, or by Clarence Baker, a forty-seven-year-old bartender, each white and each fearing the crowd was about to ransack his business.[1]

Bradby responded by concocting an improvised Molotov cocktail and throwing it into the restaurant. A small fire erupted. It was about to go out when another man threw a bigger firebomb into the building. As a result, the fire spread. By the time firemen arrived, much of the building had been destroyed. Unbeknownst to Bradby, Louis Albrecht, a fifty-eight-year-old white resident of Baltimore who had sought refuge in the restaurant, died in the blaze.[2] Around the corner another body, James Harrison, an eighteen-year-old black man, was later found. Albrecht and Harrison were two of Baltimore's six fatalities during the Holy Week uprisings of 1968.[3]

At about the same time that Bradby left to search for his girlfriend's children, Joe DiBlasi, a student at the University of Baltimore, was returning home from a National Guard drill session in Parkville, Maryland, one of the nearby suburbs. Though he witnessed a few kids throwing rocks at cars, he did not expect such juvenile pranks to escalate into a riot. However, he received a call from the National Guard ordering him to report to the federal armory as quickly as possible.[4]

Subsequently, DiBlasi was placed in charge of a squad of twelve men and given orders to take up a position at the corner of North and Pennsylvania avenues, near the historic center of the African American community in Baltimore. From his post, DiBlasi witnessed looting, burning buildings, and defiant crowds. By the time he returned to civilian life, five days later, Baltimore had suffered more than $12 million in damage and over ten thousand troops (Maryland National Guardsmen and federal forces) were encamped in the city. Looking back, DiBlasi emphasized the surreal nature of the event. "You would just look around and say, 'How can this be happening?'"[5]

The Pats sisters, Sharon and Betty, in their teens in 1968, together with their parents Sid and Ida, had gone to bed on the night of Saturday, April 6, just about the time that looting broke out on the corner of North and Pennsylvania avenues. Earlier in the day, a black woman from the neighborhood had warned their family that they "better get out." And Sharon Pats Singer later recalled that things had been tense in the neighborhood ever since King's assassination. Nonetheless, when the Pats girls awoke on Sunday morning, they felt secure enough to drive to Hebrew school and to go shopping. Not until Sharon steered her family's car down North Avenue did she realize that much of her neighborhood was in smoke. Winding her way around crowds of people, Sharon quickly picked up the rest of her family and drove away.[6]

Shortly afterward, the Patses' home and business were looted. A day later the building was burned to the ground. It was "the end of [our] life as [we] knew it." Her sister, Betty Pats Katzenelson elaborated: "My mom was out of her job and what she did. My dad was out of his job and what he did. . . . Nothing was right." Ironically, Sharon added, before the riots there had been a great deal of excitement about the prospect of renewing the neighborhood, with funds raised by the Mid-City Development Corporation. But, as Ida Pats put it, the redevelopment "never materialized."[7]

Louis Randall, one of the first African Americans to graduate from the University of Maryland Medical School, three years after the *Brown* decision, was delivering a baby at Provident Hospital, in West Baltimore,

U.S. Army encampment in Patterson Park. (Reprinted courtesy of the Lt. James V. Kelly Baltimore City Police Department Collection.)

when he heard the sounds of windows being broken. From the hospital he could smell the acrid smoke from burning stores. As soon as he could, Randall rushed home and then dashed off to his office building, which he had recently opened with several other black doctors. Like many other African American business owners, Randall placed a "Soul brother" sign on his door to make clear to would-be looters that his was a black-owned business. Still, not trusting the sign alone, Randall vigilantly stood guard, shotgun in hand, hoping he would not have to shoot anyone to preserve what he had worked so hard to achieve.[8]

These four stories provide a glimpse at the riots or uprisings that erupted across America in the wake of the assassination of Martin Luther King, Jr. Each one hints at the challenges historians face in trying to reconstruct the past. Whose story do we tell and which ones do we leave on the cutting board? How do these stories fit into established understanding of the time period? And what do these stories tell us about the causes and consequences of the urban or racial disorders of the 1960s?

While this chapter focuses on Baltimore, it is important to remember that the uprising was widespread. Between the evening of April 4, when James Earl Ray shot Martin Luther King, Jr., and Easter Sunday, April 14, 1968, cities in thirty-six states and the District of Columbia experienced looting, arson, or sniper fire.[9] Fifty-four cities suffered at least $100,000 in property damage, with the nation's capital and Baltimore topping the list at approximately $15 million and $12 million, respectively. Thousands of small shopkeepers saw their life savings go up in smoke. Combined, 43 men and women were killed, approximately 3,500 were injured, and 27,000 were arrested. Not until over 58,000 National Guardsmen and army troops joined local state and police forces did the uprisings cease.[10] Put somewhat differently, during Holy Week 1968, the United States experienced its greatest wave of social unrest since the Civil War.

In spite of the magnitude of the Holy Week uprisings, historians have virtually ignored them.[11] With the exception of *Ten Blocks from the White House*, collectively written by *Washington Post* reporters in the immediate wake of King's assassination, no comprehensive study of the events that followed King's death exists.[12] A survey of twenty texts on postwar America or the 1960s reveals scant discussion of the King-assassination uprising. In contrast, most of these same works spend a considerable amount of time and space on student-centered disturbances, such as those that took place at Columbia University and in Chicago during the Democratic Party's convention, in the spring and summer of 1968, respectively.[13]

Even before the spring of 1968, scholars and laypersons already had developed detailed analysis and theories as to why "rioting" or "disorders" were taking place. A large cluster of them concluded that the riots were rooted in the conditions of the ghetto. As the report of the National Advisory Commission on Civil Disorders (the Kerner Commission report) declared, the nation's failure "to make good the promises of American democracy to all citizens" stood as the central cause of the disorders.[14] Another cluster of scholars and laypersons strongly disagreed. They contended that the riots were the by-product of radical agitators, or "riot makers," to borrow the words of Eugene Methvin. In some cases, this school of analysis also blamed liberals for molly-coddling the militants, either directly or by promoting permissive values that allowed individuals to shirk their responsibilities.[15] Put somewhat differently, one school cast the disorders as rational political events, as a form of protest against unjust circumstances, while the other school contended that the riots represented the irrational actions of individuals who were "seeking the thrill and excitement occasioned by looting and burning."[16] In addition to providing a broad overview of the Baltimore uprising, the following analysis allows us to test both schools of thought.

On the basis of multiple sources, including police logs and the U.S. Army's "After Action Report," the "initial disturbance" took place in the 400 and 500 blocks of North Gay Street, in the heart of East Baltimore, between 5:15 and 5:20 P.M. on Saturday, April 6, two days after King's assassination. As orders were being issued for all off-duty police to report to their respective districts, crowds grew in size and a fire bomb was thrown into

Mayor Thomas D'Alesandro III at the scene of a building fire. (Reprinted courtesy of the Lt. James V. Kelly Baltimore City Police Department Collection.)

a vacant house. According to one source, policemen on the scene were commanded to withdraw rather than confront the crowd, but this claim cannot be confirmed. There is no question, however, that about an hour later two new fires broke out at the Ideal and Lewis furniture stores in the 700 block of North Gay Street and that crowds continued to gather in East Baltimore.[17]

By some reports, the crowd quickly grew to over one thousand men and women. Like a slow-moving wave, it rode its way up Gay Street and spilled over to Harford Road and Greenmount Avenue. Quickly, Police Commissioner Pomerleau ordered K-9 units to deploy downtown, and state police set up posts around the state office building. Just before 8:00 P.M. Governor Spiro Agnew declared a state of emergency. A couple of hours later he signed executive orders that established an 11:00 P.M. to 6:00 A.M. curfew and banned the sale and distribution of alcoholic beverages. In the same time period, Maryland National Guardsmen began to report for duty and to deploy around the city.[18]

Situation reports that flowed into the White House provided a keen sense of the speed with which circumstances changed in Baltimore. Whereas one report issued on the afternoon of April 6 reported that a peace rally had taken place in Baltimore "without incident," a separate report, issued about six hours later, stated that twenty fires had erupted, that "firemen [were being] pelted with bricks and stones," and that stores were being "ransacked."[19] By 4:00 A.M. on April 7, situation reports noted that Baltimore had recorded five deaths, 300 fires, and 404 arrests.[20]

Just as importantly, the uprising, which began in East Baltimore, began to spread to the Pennsylvania Avenue corridor in West Baltimore. Eventually, thirteen distinct neighborhoods and at least a half-dozen commercial districts experienced at least twenty incidences of looting, vandalism, or arson. Every major black section of the city, with the exception of Cherry Hill in southwest Baltimore, was affected. Areas that were predominantly white and the downtown business section remained relatively unaffected. Faced with this escalating situation, President Lyndon B. Johnson authorized the use of federal forces. Commanded by Lt. Gen. Robert York, the federal forces joined Maryland National Guard units that had already deployed. All told, 10,956 troops deployed in Baltimore.[21]

One tense moment occurred on the afternoon of April 9 due to miscommunications between federal, state, and local authorities. At midday about two hundred men and women began to assemble at Lafayette Square, in West Baltimore, for a peace rally. Unknown to federal officers, Maryland National Guard commander General George Gelston had given his approval for the rally. When General York instructed commanders that no permit to assemble had been issued, federal forces began to disperse the crowd. Local commanders requested the right to unsheathe their bayonets should the crowd resist. As the crowd proceeded to march down Pennsylvania Avenue, tensions and the chance for a confrontation peaked. Fortunately for all involved, Major William "Box" Harris, the top black police officer in the city, appeared. After fielding a barrage of jeers, Harris announced to cheers that the rally would be allowed to take place after all.[22] One other tense situation involved a white mob that assembled near Patterson Park. Vowing to have it out with blacks, it dispersed only after federal troops and National Guard units made clear they would not allow the whites to cross into the black section of town.

Some looting may have been augmented by organized crime. Intelligence sources reported that seasoned criminals paid children to help them steal valuable items. Young looters did this by creating diversions, serving as lookouts, and quickly fencing larger goods to adults who parked pickup trucks in back alleys behind appliance, furniture, and other stores. At the same time, one of Baltimore's best-known criminals, "Little Melvin" Williams, helped quell the uprising. With the permission of General Gelston, on April 8, Melvin, along with Clarence Mitchell III, called on people in the community to "cool it." As he recalled, "I . . . stood on a . . . car hood or roof and said that: You have taken all there is to take out of this black community. You've taken the heart out of your own area. But more importantly, I've been told by this General [Gelston] that in the event that

The "Soul Brother" sign—the apparent salvation of this beauty salon. The neighboring business did not fare as well. (Originally published in the *Baltimore Afro-American*, April 9, 1968. Reprinted courtesy of the *Afro-American Newspapers* Archives and Research Center.)

you cross Howard and Franklin Streets . . . they are going to kill you all."[23] Ironically, Melvin was arrested two weeks after helping to cool things down for allegedly pointing a machine gun at a police officer.[24]

The number of incidents dropped on April 9, allowing the Baltimore Orioles to play their opening game on April 10, one day later than originally scheduled. One final casualty of the uprising was a concert by the King of Soul, James Brown. Scheduled to perform at the Civic Center on Friday, April 12, Brown had to cancel his appearance in part because the venue was still being used to house an overflow crowd of riot-related arrestees. The decision to allow Brown to go ahead with his scheduled appearance in Boston on April 6 helped avert significant turmoil there.[25]

Even though the media called these events "race riots," there were only a couple of confirmed acts of violence between blacks and whites. Baltimore experienced few fatalities, especially in comparison to the "riots" of 1967 or to those earlier in the century. Six individuals were killed, five blacks and one white. In contrast, thirty-four and forty-three men and women were killed in Watts and Detroit, respectively. Somewhat along the same lines, even though they had to face large and unruly crowds, most often with unloaded weapons, few National Guardsmen or federal troops suffered serious injuries.[26] And while close to one thousand businesses were affected and hundreds were ransacked or torched, public and community buildings, including symbols of the establishment such as schools, government buildings, and churches, were largely spared.[27]

Indeed, the greatest difference between the riots that took place during Holy Week 1968 and those that took place between 1965 and 1967 was the substantial decrease in fatalities. This was not due to luck. Rather, the decrease in fatalities grew out of decisions that federal authorities made following their study of the disorders of the summer of 1967. More specifically, from recommendations put forth by Cyrus Vance, the federal government developed detailed procedures for responding to urban disorders and, building on these procedures, conducted intensive riot-training programs for law enforcement officials from across the nation. Branches of the military, including the National Guard and the army, did the same. The most significant change was to deploy troops with orders that they were not to load their weapons and that they were to refrain from shooting looters. This decision garnered much public wrath and, as we shall see, galvanized conservative attacks on liberalism. Conversely, it also saved hundreds of American lives.[28]

This analysis should not divert us from recalling the pain suffered by merchants, many of whom in Baltimore's case were Jewish. Close to 80 percent of all establishments that suffered damages were owned by whites, a disproportionate number by Jews. Some of these Jewish merchants were Holocaust survivors. Others had fled Russian pogroms earlier in the century or were descended from those who had. A number of commentators explicitly compared what had happened to Jewish merchants during the riots to what had happened during the Russian pogroms.[29] Still, those who vandalized, looted, and torched buildings did not, with rare exception, attack white men and women. Reports of sniper fire were vastly exaggerated, and no one was killed by the sniper fire that did take place.[30]

Over the course of the week, 5,512 men and women were arrested. Ninety-two percent of the arrestees were black; 85 percent were males. The plurality of arrestees were over the age of thirty. Sixty-three percent of all of the arrestees were charged with curfew violations and an additional 7 percent with disorderly conduct. Although 910 men and women were charged with larceny, many charges were later dropped because of the difficulty of proving them in a court of law. Only thirteen men (no women) were charged with arson, few of whom were convicted. Given its space constraints, this chapter will not survey the strains that the uprising put on the criminal justice system. Suffice it to say that authorities resorted to extraordinary measures, ranging from holding many of the arrestees in the city's main indoor arena to getting defendants to accept pleas to lesser charges in exchange for light sentences, during the crisis.[31]

Unlike riots in the early decades of the twentieth century, when whites attacked blacks in black neighborhoods, the Holy Week uprisings remained a very local affair. Surveys showed that the vast majority of those imprisoned

Baltimore police arresting suspected looters on Pennsylvania Avenue. (Reprinted courtesy of the *Baltimore News American* Collection, University of Maryland–College Park.)

were arrested within ten blocks of where they lived. Incidents of looting, arson, and vandalism took place almost exclusively in black neighborhoods. One reason this was the case, as suggested in the preceding by Little Melvin, was because state troopers quickly cordoned off downtown and blacks had reasons to believe that they would be shot if they ventured outside their own communities.[32]

If Martin Luther King, Jr., could come back to life, there is little doubt how he would answer the question, What caused the uprising? A year and half before his assassination, King appeared in Baltimore to receive the Baltimore Community Relations Commission's Man of the Decade prize. Upon receiving the award, King delivered a prescient speech, "The other America," in which he reflected on the social forces that had given rise to the riots that had already taken place. "One America," King explained, "is invested with enrapturing beauty. In it we can find many things that we can think about in noble terms. . . . This America is inhabited by millions of the fortunate whose dreams of life, liberty, and the pursuit of happiness are poured out in glorious fulfillment. . . . In this America," he continued, "little boys and little girls grow up in the sunlight of opportunity."[33]

In contrast, in the other America, "we see something that drains away the beauty that exists. . . . In this [other] America," King continued, "thousands of work-starved men walk the streets every day in search for jobs that do not exist. . . . In this America," King said, "people find themselves feeling that life is a long and desolate corridor with no exit signs. In this America, hopes unborn have died and radiant dreams of freedom have been deferred."[34]

As King easily could have gleaned from his visits to Baltimore, in housing, employment, education, and health care, the dreams of scores of Baltimore's black residents, like those in many of America's cities, had been deferred. Many of the city's black residents felt trapped in a "long and desolate corridor with no exit signs." Moreover, they felt trapped at a time of heightened expectations, and these heightened yet unfulfilled expectations amplified a widely held view that the American dream remained out of reach.[35]

One of the outstanding characteristics of Baltimore was the prevalence of residential segregation on which so many of the city's inequities were built. Between World War II and 1968, Baltimore's overall population remained fairly stable, yet its racial makeup changed dramatically. In 1950 over 700,000 whites lived in the city. Less than a generation later, fewer than 500,000 did. During the same time frame, the number of blacks rose from fewer than 220,000 to over 400,000.[36] When viewed from a metropolitan perspective, the magnitude of this demographic shift is even more apparent. In 1950 the entire population of Baltimore County, which surrounds Baltimore City in a horseshoe shape, stood at less than 250,000, approximately 20,000 of whom were black. Twenty years later the county's population had risen to over 600,000, all but 20,000 of whom were white.[37] Even within city limits, as documented by Edward Orser's fine study on blockbusting, Baltimore witnessed a racial sea change, as entire sections of the city went from being virtually all white to all black in a very short time. About the only change that did not take place was that whites did not move into predominantly black neighborhoods.[38]

Blacks and whites not only lived in separate neighborhoods but inhabited qualitatively unequal homes. Nearly 50 percent of homes in inner-city neighborhoods were rated as "very poor" quality. Nor did the postwar building boom alleviate the housing shortage faced by blacks. While housing construction skyrocketed in the largely white suburban Baltimore County during the 1960s, it came to a standstill in the city of Baltimore. Without new construction, older housing, especially older rental units in communities disproportionately inhabited by blacks, fell into increasing disrepair.[39]

Citywide, the infant mortality rate stood at 28.4 out of 1,000 live births in 1965. Yet in census tracts targeted by the Model Cities Program, which were largely black and poor, infant mortality rates often exceeded 50 per

From left to right: *Walter H. Lively of U-JOIN (Union for Jobs and Income Now) and also executive director of the newly formed Urban Coalition; David L. Glenn, director of the Baltimore Community Relations Commission; Robert Moore (*with his back to the camera*) of the Baltimore SNCC (Student Nonviolent Coordinating Committee); and Clarence Washington, assistant director of Dr. King's Poor People's Campaign Baltimore chapter holding a sidewalk note-comparing session during some of the tensest moments.* (Originally published in the *Baltimore Afro-American*, April 9, 1968. Reprinted courtesy of the *Afro-American Newspapers* Archives and Research Center.)

1,000. The same areas had twice the crime rate as the city as a whole, which was at least twice as high as the surrounding suburban communities.[40] While skyrocketing crime rates alarmed whites, leading conservatives to adopt "law and order" as one of their main demands and campaign slogans, we need to remember that blacks were victimized by crime at a far greater rate than whites, making it harder and harder for them to experience the American dream.[41]

Concomitantly, the city began to experience considerable economic pains. Long a blue-collar town, synonymous with work on the docks, garment shops, and steel mills, an increasing percentage of Baltimore's workforce found employment in the service sector, such as in the health care industry or the public sector. Since blacks in Baltimore were disproportionately represented in the manufacturing sector, this economic shift had a greater impact on them than it did on whites. During the 1960s, the number of men and women employed in manufacturing in Baltimore City declined by over 25 percent, in spite of heavy demand for defense-related goods due to the escalation of the Vietnam War. Looked at from a regional perspective, the transformation of the labor market took on even greater significance. Between 1945 and 1968 the total number of jobs in Baltimore City increased 11 percent, the vast majority in sectors of the economy with the lowest rates of black employment. During the same period, in Baltimore County, where few blacks lived, the number of jobs grew by a whopping 245 percent.[42]

Unemployment statistics illustrated the disparate worlds that blacks and whites of the Baltimore region occupied. Nationally, the unemployment rate in 1968 was less than 4 percent, suggesting a booming economy. Yet in Baltimore the rate for blacks was more than double this and in some inner-city census tracts unemployment hovered just below 30 percent, or at Great Depression rates.[43] Even in segments of the labor market where things looked bright for blacks on the surface, such as at Bethlehem Steel Corporation, they appeared gloomy beneath it. As a report by the U.S. Civil Rights Commission observed, blacks were "virtually unseen" in office work but were found abundantly in the most dangerous and worst-paying jobs.[44]

Although headline stories catalogued breakthroughs that blacks made in the public sector, from the first black police sergeant in 1947 and the first black housing inspector in 1951 to the "assignments" of 78 black firemen in 1954 and appointment of the first black judge in 1957, overall, blacks remained underrepresented in government jobs and even more underrepresented on construction sites paid for with federal, state, and city funds.[45] Whereas blacks made up over 40 percent of the city's population, less than 18 percent of the entire Baltimore government's workforce was black in 1966.[46]

Given that Baltimore's political leaders, unlike those throughout much of the nation south of the Mason-Dixon Line, chose to comply with rather than fight *Brown v. Board of Education*, one might expect that education stood out as a bright spot. Yet, even though de jure segregation died in Baltimore, de facto segregation and, perhaps just as importantly, unequal education remained the rule. In addition, achievement gaps between white and black schools remained large; even within racially balanced schools, significant gaps between blacks and whites existed. And glaring gaps between inner-city and suburban schools persisted. (For a detailed examination of school desegregation in Baltimore, see Chapter 10.)

This said, it needs to be remembered that in contrast to political leaders in the Deep South, where whites formed citizens councils to resist challenges to their way of life and rallied behind calls for "segregation forever," Baltimore's elite sought to address the racial divide. As I have noted,

*General George Gelston of the Maryland National Guard with his army of volunteers from the community (*third from the left: *Melvin "Little Melvin" Williams).* (Originally published in the *Baltimore Afro-American*, April 10, 1968. Reprinted courtesy of the *Baltimore News American* Collection, University of Maryland–College Park.)

Baltimore complied with the *Brown* decision. A decade later, it actively pursued various War on Poverty funds. (Indeed, the city's grant applications provide some of the best documentation on the distress of its inner-city neighborhoods.) One such program that won funding was Baltimore's Community Action Commission (CAC). Headed by Parren Mitchell, who went on to become Baltimore's first black congressman, CAC established job training and Head Start programs that sought to revive the dream of a better life.[47]

Moreover, there was some evidence that Baltimore's police department, unlike those in nearly all other cities, was making strides toward overcoming the racial divide. In March 1968 *Reader's Digest* specifically contrasted Baltimore's police to those in many of the nation's cities. The department had developed a "novel" form of policing, *Reader's Digest* reported. This included the "expansion of a biracial Community Relations Department" that had orders to "penetrate the Negro community, not with a gun and nightstick but with service." Baltimore's top black police officer, Major William "Box" Harris, the article continued, had become a folk hero in the black community. Under Harris's direction, the police even sought to open lines of communication with advocates of Black Power. "'We're going to have to deal with them, one way or another—either over the barricades with fire bombs falling about us," Harris explained, "or over a glass of beer in some gin mill. My department is trying the latter."[48]

Is it possible that these efforts along with Baltimore's willingness to comply with *Brown* further raised expectations that the racial divide would decline? Perhaps it was a pure coincidence that rioting first erupted in the Gay Street corridor of East Baltimore, a section of the city that was not simply poor but one that had been slated for urban renewal since 1963. Community members participated in over forty conferences on the plan to revive the neighborhood. "Militant civil rights leaders" and ordinary residents had "crowded into the City Council's chambers," in the fall of 1967, to get it to approve phase 1 of the plan. Yet as of April 1968, residents still awaited final approval of the plan by bureaucrats in Washington, D.C.[49]

For Baltimore's blacks, their expectations had been raised but left unfulfilled by everything from LBJ's promise of a Great Society to advertisements and television shows that consistently displayed Americans enjoying the "good life." That they earned more than their parents had or had more years of education mattered less to them than that, compared with whites, they earned less and had less access to quality education and good housing. The election of Thomas D'Alesandro as mayor, who won 93 percent of the black vote and quickly appointed blacks to top positions, including making George Russell the first black city solicitor, certainly reinforced the sense that things were getting better.

Of course, critics of the Kerner Commission, such as Spiro Agnew and William Buckley, claimed that the riots were not caused by "poverty or frustration" but rather by radicals, who incited the riots, and by individual men and women who of their own volition chose to violate the law. "It was no mere coincidence," Agnew proclaimed in the immediate wake of the uprising, "that a national disciple of violence, Mr. Stokely Carmichael, was observed meeting with local black power advocates and known criminals in Baltimore on April 3, 1968, three days before the Baltimore riots began." The leaders of the Student Nonviolent Coordinating Committee (SNCC), Congress of Racial Equality (CORE), and other black militant groups, Agnew continued, were "riot-inciting, burn-America-down" types who never did anything constructive.[50] And Agnew was hardly the only Baltimore official to accuse black militants of inciting the riot. Mayor D'Alesandro proclaimed that he was "an apostle of the view that this thing was planned and well-organized."[51] Similarly, Judge Liss, who oversaw the murder trial of Robert Bradby, blamed agitators for planning the riots and getting Bradby to do their dirty work. These people, Liss declared, made individuals such as Bradby "do things that [they] would never have done under normal circumstances." These people "planned" the riot; they

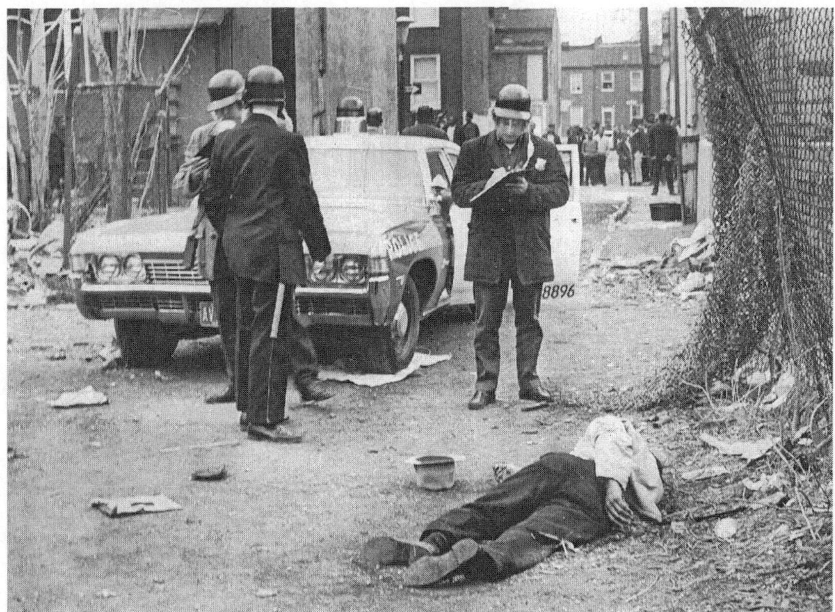

Suspected looter shot by police. (Reprinted courtesy of the *Baltimore News American* Collection, University of Maryland–College Park.)

"inflamed the community and got . . . damn fools like Bradby and others to do their dirty work for them"; and they, Liss indignantly concluded, "are walking away scot-free." (Nonetheless, lamenting that the law tied his hands, Liss sentenced Bradby to life in prison.)[52]

But if the "riots" were planned, why were authorities so unsuccessful in identifying and prosecuting a single instigator? Certainly not for lack of trying. Believing that militants hoped to cause riots, authorities carefully monitored their movements from the moment King was shot and quickly placed them under arrest whenever the slightest suspicion about their actions arose. For instance, Stuart Weschler and Danny Grant of CORE, Union for Jobs and Income Now (U-JOIN) leader Walter Lively, and SNCC activist Robert Moore were monitored or arrested during the uprising. All charges against them were subsequently dropped.[53]

Nor can those who contend that the uprising was planned explain how radicals knew King was going to be assassinated on April 4. Rather than acknowledge this flaw, some Federal Bureau of Investigation (FBI) officials, including J. Edgar Hoover, even followed up on a lead from an anonymous source that black radicals themselves had assassinated King so that they could foment a rebellion.[54] Moreover, the FBI and other government agencies had information that contradicted their own claims. Rather than organizing a riot, an FBI memorandum showed that Carmichael had come to Baltimore the day before King's assassination to help plan for his pending wedding.[55] Not surprisingly, authorities chose not to release such exculpatory evidence to the public.

But if the uprising was not instigated by radicals, what else explains it? One way to answer this question is to look at the one black community in Baltimore, namely, Cherry Hill, that did not experience looting or arson. Cherry Hill suffered only one isolated incident of vandalism and arson, none during the main wave of rioting that swept across the city from April 6 to April 9. None of the traditional variables highlighted by social scientists to explain the disorders of the era help us understand why this was the case. Put somewhat simply, Cherry Hill suffered from essentially all the same socioeconomic woes as did East and West Baltimore. It did not stand out in terms of educational achievement, family income, poverty rates, or homeownership.

While I cannot prove a counterfactual, in other words, why something did not take place, three key factors appear to explain why Cherry Hill did not, as Langston Hughes put it, "explode." First and foremost, the residents of Cherry Hill still felt that the American dream was in reach. Cherry Hill was established in the wake of World War II as a new enclave for blacks in Baltimore. Rather than build desegregated public housing in white communities, the government developed the previously largely uninhabited section known as Cherry Hill into an all-black neighborhood. It built public housing and nurtured the construction of private homes. As a result, by the mid-1950s, over twenty thousand African Americans lived there, in a mixture of public and private housing. In a short time a library, a shopping center, a movie theater, and recreational associations, all of which served to reinforce a sense of community or common destiny and helped keep alive the dream of a better life, arose. This common history, as well as a high level of community activism, led one resident to describe Cherry Hill as "the closest neighborhood I have ever lived in." This sense of pride, reinforced by a strong tradition of civil activism, persisted up to King's assassination.[56]

Second, Cherry Hill was cut off, isolated, from the rest of the city. This isolation acted as a buffer. Whereas looting and vandalism tended to spill over from one black neighborhood in the inner city to another, it could not spread to Cherry Hill because of its spatial isolation. To do so, it would have had to jump over the inner harbor or through adjacent white neighborhoods and physical barriers.[57]

Third, Cherry Hill's commercial establishments were spatially different from those in other sections of the city. In most of Baltimore's neighborhoods, merchants lined specific shopping ways or roads, such as Pennsylvania Avenue or Gay Street. In contrast, Cherry Hill's clothing stores, small supermarket, pool hall, and so on, were clustered in a shopping center. Up through at least the mid-1960s, Cherry Hill's residents gathered at this shopping center on Friday nights and perceived it as their village square. This perception of their shopping center as a sort of modern-day commons mitigated against vandalism and looting as well.[58]

Cherry Hill's actions or lack thereof during the uprising smash another parcel of conventional wisdom, that a firmer hand by the state, ranging from a stronger show of force to shooting looters, would have averted the turmoil. In the aftermath of the King uprisings a major debate erupted over whether authorities had responded properly to the rioting. Chicago Mayor Richard J. Daley's order to shoot to maim looters and kill arsonists had a good deal of support. In contrast, Attorney General Ramsay Clark's criticism of Daley and support for limited use of force earned him the venom of a large segment of the population.[59] Spiro Agnew's metamorphosis from a relatively unknown Rockefeller Republican to the second-highest public official in the land rested in large part on his get-tough persona. In a speech critical of the Kerner Commission report, Agnew proclaimed that it was not white racism but permissiveness that caused the riots. One example of this permissive climate, Agnew claimed, was the order to prohibit police officers from shooting looters. Agnew added that the federal government, not he, issued the command that limited the use of force.[60]

Yet as the case of Cherry Hill suggests, the use of force did not directly correlate to a lack of rioting. No federal troops or National Guardsmen were rushed into the neighborhood. Nor did police or state troopers increase their presence. On the contrary, off the beaten path, Cherry Hill remained out of sight and out of mind during the uprising. Community activism and engagement, not shotguns and bayonets, appear to have been the best defense against lawlessness.

What were the consequences of the uprising? According to conventional wisdom, the "riot" marked a turning point in Baltimore's history. One oral history after another, as well as most retrospective newspaper articles on the event, declares that the city was never the same again. Yet careful analysis suggests that the Holy Week uprisings had a much more nuanced impact on the local scene than often presumed.

For instance, in a comprehensive study of the Jewish business district on Lombard Street, Deb Weiner shows that merchants did *not* desert the area in the wake of the uprising, even though many suffered considerable damage at the time. Rather, Lombard Street's Jewish business district, known as Corned Beef Row, died a slower death. The district's demise was due in part to white suburban perceptions that the neighborhood was not safe; in part to the gradual rise of shopping malls and chain stores, which began before the uprising; and in part to a reconfiguration of Lombard Street that commenced in the early 1970s—its widening made the neighborhood less accessible because it was difficult to find parking, especially while road construction was taking place.[61]

Put somewhat differently, the Baltimore uprising was an extremely significant event in the city's history but more for what it symbolized than for what it did. It was both cause and effect, or perhaps more precisely effect and cause. Much of the social distress that we assume was the outcome of the uprising was well entrenched before April 1968, and its causes ranged from white flight to weaknesses in the traditional urban economy. The uprising consolidated these trends but it did not cause them. Or to borrow Howell Baum's words, the uprisings produced a "gestalt shift," whereby developments that had been in the background now appeared in the foreground. In turn, these changed perceptions reinforced shifts already taking place.[62]

But if the impact of the Holy Week uprisings on the local level has been exaggerated in the community's collective psyche, its effect on the national scene has been underappreciated—in part, as I suggested earlier, because historians have disproportionately focused on other major events of the year, such as student rebellions, suggesting that they were the most pivotal events in the watershed year of 1968. Yet there can be little doubt that the Holy Week uprisings shattered one of Lyndon Johnson's primary goals, namely, making American cities great; reinforced the dissipation of the liberal coalition; and boosted the fortunes of the New Right, particularly with respect to its "law and order" campaign.[63]

One way Baltimore effected this shift was through the rise of Spiro T. Agnew as a national spokesperson for the New Right. Agnew both symbolized the rightward shift of many moderate Republicans and urban ethnics away from liberalism and articulated the conservative attack on those who sought to keep alive the view that a great society depended on great cities. Agnew's metamorphosis from unknown moderate Republican to Richard Nixon's running mate rested on his reaction to the disorders of 1967 and 1968 and to the liberal response to them. On April 11, 1968, he gave a dressing-down to black moderates in Baltimore, accusing them of having not done enough to stop the riots and of having helped precipitate them by refusing to break with black militants and their incendiary rhetoric and demands. Agnew was well aware that his speech would alienate urban black voters, who had helped elect him to office in 1966 and whose votes still played a key role in electing other moderate Republicans.

As the 1968 campaign got under way, Republican leaders pondered how they could retake the White House. One option, long forgotten, was the idea of reaching out to black voters, to bring them back to the party of Lincoln. When Richard Nixon ran as Dwight Eisenhower's running mate, in fact, Republicans won about half the black vote. And one could interpret Johnson's landslide victory over Goldwater as proof that the Republicans could not win without regaining black support. Instead of trying to revive the party of Lincoln, Nixon chose to pursue the Southern Strategy. Rather than reaching out to blacks, he decided to try to convince Southern whites that their natural home was in the Grand Old Party. His nomination of

Agnew signaled this decision. That Agnew had been a moderate Republican and was from a border state legitimized the Republicans' turn away from blacks, the Great Society, and its commitment to urban America.[64]

Even if the Democrats had won the 1968 presidential election, the United States probably would have turned away from the ideals of the Great Society. Even before King's assassination, LBJ had refused to publicly endorse the findings of the Kerner Commission. Neither Jimmy Carter nor Bill Clinton placed urban affairs at the center of their agenda. Rather, Carter pledged to bring integrity back to the political arena, and Bill Clinton, empowerment zones notwithstanding, focused his agenda on the largely suburban middle class, represented by the so-called soccer moms. Nonetheless, it is important to remember that King's assassination played a pivotal role in these developments, by ending the life of one of the most, if not the most, prominent progressive spokesmen of the era and by sparking a nationwide uprising, which in turn gave a shot in the arm to the New Right. It is equally important to recognize that the Holy Week uprisings grew out of long-term urban ills and that our reexamination of them is an opportunity to refocus our attention on addressing them.

NOTES

1. "Stenographic Transcript in the Case of *State of Maryland vs. Robert Bradby*," Criminal Court of Baltimore, part 5, June 5, 1969, T495-1103, case 3330, Maryland State Archives (MSA), Annapolis. Also see *State v. Robert Bradby*, Postconviction files, 1972, Baltimore Criminal Court, 92105-2106, MSA.

2. "Stenographic Transcript in the Case of *State of Maryland vs. Robert Bradby*"; "Police Charge 2 in Arson Death," *Baltimore Sun*, April 26, 1968, C28.

3. "First Looter Shot to Death," *Baltimore News American*, April 8, 1968, p. 1; "Federal Troops Leaving the City, Order Restored, York Says," *Baltimore Evening Sun*, April 12, 1968, p. 1.

4. Interview with Joe DiBlasi, November 3, 2006, Baltimore '68: Riot and Rebirth project, available at http://www.ubalt.edu/bsr/oral-histories/transcripts/diblasi.pdf (accessed July 15, 2008).

5. Ibid.; "Federal Troops Leaving the City, Order Restored, York Says."

6. Interview with Sharon Pats Singer, Ida Pats, and Betty Pats Katzenelson, February 20, 2007, Baltimore '68: Riot and Rebirth project.

7. Ibid.

8. Interview with Louis D. Randall, November 30, 2006, Baltimore '68: Riot and Rebirth project.

9. Contemporary accounts employed various terms, from "riots" and "civil disorders" to "rebellions" and "revolts." I favor the term "uprising" because of the magnitude and widespread nature of the incidents.

10. Different sources arrive at different estimates of the number of disturbances. See Thomas F. Parker, ed., *Violence in America, 1968–72*, vol. 2 (New York: Facts on File, 1974), 15–29; "April Aftermath of the King Assassination," *Riot Data Review*, no. 2 (August 1968); Kevin Maroney to Ramsey Clark, April 15, 1968, "Riot Statistics, 1967–1968," Personal Papers of Ramsey Clark, box 75, LBJ Library,

Austin, TX; "Attachment A," Lyndon Johnson Papers, Aides: James Gaither, box 37, Riots 1968: Dr King, folder 2. Among other hard-hit cities were Washington, DC ($15 million in estimated damage); Chicago ($8.5 million); Pittsburgh, PA ($2 million); Kansas City, MO ($500,000); Trenton, NJ ($560,000); Wilmington, DE ($500,000); Newark, NJ ($500,000); Memphis, TN ($400,000); New Orleans ($400,000); Richmond, VA ($400,000); Nashville, TN ($300,000); Savannah, GA ($300,000); Cincinnati, OH ($200,000); Durham, NC ($100,000); Dallas, TX ($100,000); Raleigh, NC ($100,000); and High Point, NC ($100,000). Additional cities are listed in Warren Christopher Papers, Civil Disturbances, 1968 folder 3. Another way to measure the severity of the Holy Week uprisings is by the number of National Guardsmen called to duty. From 1945 to 1960, 33,539 troops were called into service to help restore order; from 1960 to 1965, 65,867 troops; in 1967, 43,300 troops; in 1968 a record 150,000 troops. See National Guard Association of the United States, "Use of National Guard during Civil Disorders in 1968," January 1, 1969, National Guard Files, Civil Disturbances, 1968 July/December.

11. One example of the limited nature of the coverage of the Holy Week uprisings can be found in the "comprehensive" two-volume *Encyclopedia of American Race Riots*. Though the encyclopedia contains a separate entry on King's assassination, this entry provides little detail on the riots and vastly underestimates the number of incidents. Only the riot in Washington, D.C., rated a separate entry, even though other riots at other times that were much less severe received far more coverage. This lack of coverage reflects the prevailing knowledge, or lack thereof, on the uprisings. See Walter Rucker and James Nathaniel Upton, eds., *Encyclopedia of American Race Riots* (Westport, CT: Greenwood Press, 2007). After I had written this chapter, a book devoted to the post-King riots was finally published. See Clay Risen, *A Nation on Fire: America in the Wake of the King Assassination* (Hoboken: NJ: Wiley, 2009).

12. Ben Gilbert and the staff of the *Washington Post*, *Ten Blocks from the White House: Anatomy of the Washington Riots of 1968* (New York: Praeger, 1968); Medrika Law-Womack, "A City Afire: The Baltimore City Riot of 1968: Antecedents, Causes and Impact" (master's thesis, Morgan State University, 2005).

13. For instance, in his popular text *The Sixties* (3rd ed. [New York: Pearson, 2007], 107), Terry Anderson writes that following King's murder "rioting swept the nation. Blacks poured out into the streets of over a hundred cities, venting their frustration. Sections of Boston, Detroit, and Harlem sank into chaos, but the worst was Washington, D.C. Over 700 fires turned the sky dark; smoke obscured the Capitol. Nationwide, officials called out more than 75,000 troops to patrol the streets, to keep the peace. . . . This because one violent white man slaughtered a nonviolent black man who called on America to live up to its promise." That's it. In contrast, Anderson spends four pages on Columbia, and five on the demonstrations in Chicago.

14. *Report of the National Advisory Commission on Civil Disorders* (Washington, DC: Government Printing Office, 1968); Robert Fogelson, *Violence as Protest: A Study of Riots and Ghettos* (Garden City, NY: Doubleday, 1971).

15. Eugene Methvin, *The Riot Makers: The Technology of Social Demolition* (New Rochelle, NY: Arlington House, 1970). Methvin's view that "riot makers" caused the riots was published in *Reader's Digest* and the *National Review*, and a film with the same title was widely distributed by the FBI to police departments across the nation.

16. Heather Ann Thompson, "Urban Uprisings: Riots or Rebellions," in *The Columbia Guide to America in the 1960s*, David Farber and Beth Bailey, eds., 111 (New York: Columbia University Press, 2001). The sociological literature on the rioting of the era is vast. Some studies incorporate data on those that took place after King's assassination. But these studies provide little description of the Holy Week uprisings. Instead, they use data from April 1968 to refine theories largely based on studies of the riots of 1965–1967. See Daniel J. Myers, "Racial Rioting in the1960s: An Event History Analysis of Local Conditions," *American Sociological Review* 62 (February 1997): 94–112; Greg Lee Carter, "In the Narrows of the 1960s U.S. Black Rioting," *Journal of Conflict Resolution* 30, no. 1 (March 1986): 115–127. For a brief review of the literature on the urban riots of the era, see Heather Ann Thompson, "Rethinking the Politics of White Flight in the Postwar City: Detroit, 1945–1980," *Journal of Urban History* 25, no. 2 (January 1999): 163–198. While little consensus exists on the causes of the urban riots or uprisings of the 1960s, scholars generally agree that they played a key, if not pivotal, role in altering the trajectory of the nation. See, for instance, William Chafe, *The Unfinished Journey: America since World War II* (New York: Oxford University Press, 2003), 366–368; and Irwin Unger, *Turning Point* (New York: Scribner, 1988).

17. Lt. Gen. Robert H. York, "After Action Report: Task Force Baltimore, April 7–13, 1968," Warren Christopher Papers, box 12, Civil Disturbances 1968 folder 2, LBJ Library, Austin, TX; "Action Reports," Emergency Headquarters Command Post, April 5–11, 1968, available at http://mysite.verizon.net/vzesdp09/baltimorepolicehistorybywmhackley2/id76.html (accessed July 30, 2007); City of Baltimore, "Report of Baltimore Committee on the Administration of Justice under Emergency Conditions," May 31, 1968.

18. "Action Reports," Emergency Headquarters Command Post, April 5–11, 1968, available at http://mysite.verizon.net/vzesdp09/baltimorepolicehistorybywmhackley2/id76.html (accessed July 30, 2007).

19. "Situation Reports," Ramsey Clark Papers, box 67, Summaries—Riots—April 8, 1968; City of Baltimore, "Report of Baltimore Committee on the Administration of Justice under Emergency Conditions," May 31, 1968; "Daily Staff Journal/Duty Officer's Log," April 5–10, 1968, National Guard Files, Fifth Regiment Armory, Baltimore, Maryland.

20. "Situation Reports."

21. York, "After Action Report"; "Executive Order: Providing for the Restoration of Law and Order in the State of Maryland," April 7, 1968, White House Central File, HU2-ST20-ST21, box 26, LBJ Library.

22. York, "After Action Report."

23. York, "After Action Report"; Ben Franklin, "Patrol of Negro Peacemakers Sent out in Baltimore," *New York Times*, April 10, 1968; interview with Melvin Douglas Williams, Baltimore '68: Riot and Rebirth project.

24. "'Little Melvin' Charged with Pointing Machine Gun at Officer," *Baltimore Afro-American*, April 27, 1968, p. 2.

25. National Public Radio, "The Night James Brown Saved Boston," available at http://www.npr.org/templates/story/story.php?storyId=89273314 (accessed July 15, 2008).

26. "April Aftermath of the King Assassination," *Riot Data Review*, no. 2 (August 1968); Thomas F. Parker, ed., *Violence in America, 1956–1967*, vol. 1 (New York: Facts on File, 1974); Thomas F. Parker, ed., *Violence in America,*

1968–1972, vol. 2; Morris Janowitz, "Social Control of Escalated Riots," University of Chicago Center for Policy Study, in White House Central File, HU2, box 7, folder March 1–April 7, 1968, LBJ Library.

27. Maryland Crime Investigating Committee, "A Report of the Baltimore Civil Disturbance of April, 1968," June 4, 1968.

28. Papers of Warren Christopher, box 11, Civil Disturbances 1968, folders 1 and 2 of 2, LBJ Library.

29. See *Baltimore Jewish Times*, April 12 and 19, 1968.

30. "Situation Reports."

31. The Maryland Crime Investigating Committee, "A Report of the Baltimore Civil Disturbance of April, 1968," June 4, 1968; Jane Motz, "Report on Baltimore Civil Disorders, April 1968," (Baltimore: Middle Atlantic Region, American Friends Service Committee, 1968).

32. Stephen J. Lynton, "Arrests Present a Profile of City Rioters," *Baltimore Sun*, April 22, 1968, C1.

33. King's "The other America" speech is quoted at length in Baltimore Community Relations Commission, "Tenth Annual Report, 1966: A Decade of Progress," pp. 39–42.

34. Ibid.

35. H. D. Davis and T. R. Gurr, eds., *Violence in America: Historical and Comparative Perspectives*, vol. 2 (Washington, DC: Government Printing Office, 1969); James Patterson, *Grand Expectations: The United States, 1945–1974* (New York: Oxford University Press, 1996), ch. 21.

36. U.S. Commission on Civil Rights, "Staff Report: Demographic, Economic, Social and Political Characteristics of Baltimore City and Baltimore County," August 1970 (Washington, DC: Government Printing Office, 1970).

37. U.S. Commission on Civil Rights, "Staff Report."

38. W. Edward Orser, "Flight to the Suburbs: Suburbanization and Racial Change on Baltimore's West Side," *The Baltimore Book: New Views of Local History*, Elizabeth Fee, Linda Shopes, and Linda Zeidman, eds. (Philadelphia, PA: Temple University Press, 1991), 203–226; W. Edward Orser, *Blockbusting in Baltimore: The Edmondson Village Story* (Lexington: University Press of Kentucky, 1994).

39. U.S. Commission on Civil Rights, "Staff Report"; City of Baltimore, "Baltimore Model Cities Neighborhoods: Application to the Department of Housing and Urban Development," n.d.

40. City of Baltimore, "Baltimore Model Cities Neighborhoods."

41. International Association of Chiefs of Police, "A Survey of the Police Department, Baltimore, Maryland," 1965; Police Department, City of Baltimore, "Annual Report," 1966; Herbert Lee West, Jr., "Urban Life and Spatial Distribution of Blacks in Baltimore, Maryland" (Ph.D. diss., University of Minnesota, 1973).

42. U.S. Commission on Civil Rights, "Staff Report"; City of Baltimore, "Baltimore Model Cities Neighborhood"; Kenneth Durr, *Behind the Backlash: White Working-Class Politics in Baltimore* (Chapel Hill: University of North Carolina Press, 2003), 199.

43. U.S. Commission on Civil Rights, "Staff Report."

44. Maryland Commission on Human Relations, "Systematic Discrimination: A Report on Patterns of Discrimination at the Bethlehem Steel Corporation, Sparrows Point, Maryland" (1970); "Negro Workers Picket Steel Firm," *Washington Post*, January 20, 1968, C5.

45. On strides made by blacks, see *Toward Equality: Baltimore's Progress Report* (Baltimore: Sidney Hollander Foundation, 1960).

46. Baltimore Community Relations Commission, "Annual Reports" (1965, 1966, and 1967); Gilbert Ware to Spiro Agnew, September 17, 1967, Governor Spiro T. Agnew, General File, 1967–68, S1041-1713, box 14, "Civil Rights: Re: Dr. King's Assassination."

47. City of Baltimore, "Baltimore Model Cities Neighborhood: Application to the Department of HUD" (1966).

48. Floyd Miller, "How Baltimore Fends off Riots," *Reader's Digest*, March 1968, pp. 109–113.

49. *Baltimore Sun*, April 9, 1968, pp. 9, 10.

50. Spiro T. Agnew, "Statement at Conference with Civil Rights Leaders and Community Leaders, State Office Building, Baltimore," April 11, 1968, in *Is Baltimore Burning? Maryland State Archives: Documents for the Classroom* (Annapolis: Maryland State Archives, n.d.), available at http://teachingamericanhistorymd.net/000001/000000/000061/html/t61.html (accessed August 24, 2007).

51. "Riot Planned in Advance Mayor Says," *Baltimore Evening Sun*, April 10, 1968, p. 1.

52. "Stenographic Transcript in the Case of *State of Maryland vs. Robert Bradby.*"

53. James Dilts, "The Fire This Time," April 14, 1968, "Riots," Vertical File, Enoch Pratt Free Library; "Selected Racial Developments and Disturbances," April 9, 1968, White House Confidential File, HU2, box 56, folder 1 of 2, file (1967–) 3 of 5, LBJ Library.

54. "Memo: Assassination of Martin Luther King, Jr.," April 10, 1968, Mildred Stegall Papers, Martin Luther King, 1966–1967, folder 2 of 2, LBJ Library.

55. SAC, Baltimore (80-720), to FBI director, April 17, 1968; W. C. Sullivan, "Memorandum: Stokely Carmichael," May 8, 1968, J. Edgar Hoover to *Baltimore Evening Sun*, April 24, 1968, and *Baltimore Evening Sun* to J. Edgar Hoover, April 17, 1968, all in Cointelpro: Black Nationalist Hate Groups, file 100-448006, reel 1, Scholarly Resources.

56. "Cherry Hill: Oral History Project Interviews, April–May, 2000" (copy in author's possession); DeWayne Wickham, *Woodholme: A Black Man's Story of Growing Up Alone* (Baltimore: Johns Hopkins University Press, 1995).

57. John R. Breihan, "Why No Rioting in Cherry Hill?" Paper presented at Baltimore '68: Riots and Rebirth conference, April 4, 1968.

58. John R. Breihan, "Why Was There No Rioting in Cherry Hill?" (Chapter 3 in this collection).

59. On the Daley-Clark dispute, see Ramsey Clark Papers, especially boxes 50 and 60, LBJ Library.

60. Richard Harrison, "Riot Study Criticized by Agnew," *Washington Post*, July 31, 1968, C1; "General Quits after Street Riots," *Chicago Tribune*, July 6, 1968, S10; "Curb on Riot Troops Denied in Maryland," *New York Times*, July 9, 1968, 21.

61. See Chapter 11 in this volume.

62. See Howell Baum, "How the 1968 Riots Stopped School Desegregation in Baltimore," Chapter 10 in this collection.

63. Michael Flamm, *Law and Order* (New York: Columbia University Press, 2005).

64. Rick Perlstein, *Nixonland: The Rise of a President and the Fracturing of America* (New York: Scribner, 2008).

2

Jewell Chambers

Oral History

Jewell Chambers was a young reporter on the staff of the Baltimore Afro-American *newspaper at the time of the 1968 riot. Assigned to cover "on the street stuff," as she puts it, her interview recalls the carnivalesque quality of the riot, as well as some of its more destructive and frightening moments. Chambers also provides a thoughtful assessment of who rioted and why they did so and of the changes in Baltimore since 1968. Typical of oral history, her narrative demonstrates the interplay between the remembered past and the past as it actually happened. Chambers left the* Afro *in 1968, worked for the U.S. Department of Education, left the area for several years, and then returned to Baltimore, where she taught English and humanities at Morgan State University.*

Duane Howard and John Schwallenberg conducted the interview on February 7, 2008. Both were University of Baltimore students at the time of the interview.

At the time we're speaking of, in 1968, I was a reporter for the *Baltimore Afro-American*. I had started work in September of '67 and I would leave the *Afro* in May of '68 and go to the U.S. Office of Education.[1] But I couldn't have picked a better year in which to be a reporter. Even though I was new, the staff at the *Afro* was so small that you don't stay a cub reporter long, only until they're sure you can read and write. I was twenty-five; I was living in northwest Baltimore, on Mount Holly Street—just off of Garrison Boulevard, so I was in the Garrison and Liberty Heights area.

I had been involved in the civil rights movement prior to '68. Actually I was arrested in 1960 for sitting-in. That's the first year of CIG, Civic Interest Group, and I was a part of it. And then I had been at Morgan in 1962 when Morgan took over the Northwood Shopping Center, because here was a school and here was this shopping center; you had Hochschild's that had a tearoom in which you couldn't eat, you had the Northwood Theater, to which you couldn't go. So we stacked the jails and desegregated the place and that was a totally student movement.[2] One of our biggest supporters was a white guy named Augie Meier, whom you'd probably know as Dr. August Meier, who has written several seminal books on black-white relationships. I think he just recently died. But at that time he was a professor of history at Morgan State University, which wasn't Morgan State University. It was Morgan State College because it doesn't become a university until '75.[3]

What you need to realize is at that time Baltimore was a segregated town. The segregation, having grown up in it, was there. It wasn't in your face every minute of the day. You lived in a colored neighborhood; you went to a colored school; you had colored teachers; you went to a colored church; the pastor was colored; everybody else in that school, in that church [was colored]. So when you went downtown, you had to deal with white people, and how they reacted ran the gamut. I can remember going downtown to shop. In some stores people were very nasty and in other stores they were very pleasant. But it didn't hit you in the face the way it would have when you go to school and you have to deal with white teachers calling you a "nigger." Our teachers said, "Be the best you can. This is what you must do and what you can do."

And Baltimore did not spend the same for black education, colored education, as it did for whites, but it wasn't Alabama. So that if programs came to the schools, there would be one in some black school, and you might have four in white schools. Case in point: when I tell people I went to prekindergarten in a public school they are dumbfounded because this is the forties. But the city had started prekindergartens so that women could go to work during the war. And one of those programs was at P.S. 112, in my neighborhood, so we started school at age three, all day. In a segregated school, in a segregated city south of the Mason-Dixon Line.

I am in no ways apologizing—you had nasty bus drivers. You did not see black people driving buses. Milk was delivered by either Cloverland Dairy or Greenspring Dairy; there were no black milkmen. Bread was delivered by whites. Even the Good Humor man was white.

As to my interactions with people of other races around the time of the riots, because I was working for a newspaper I interacted professionally.

You know, I might have to interview somebody white as well as somebody black even though I was working for a black newspaper. Socially? No. I had two [white] friends from Morgan. One had actually been my roommate. She was the only homegrown white living in the dorm. And the reason that I have to say "homegrown" is there was another group of white students, but they were Greek. I mean, Greek from the Aegean.

I would say that the racial mood in the city before the riots was—tense is not the word that I want to use. I think the idea was that things are changing, times they are a'changin'. It's a cliché, but I think that's where it was—that if we keep on going we are changing the status quo. Any number of the overt measures of segregation had been lifted—i.e., shopping; i.e., movies; i.e., to some extent, restaurants. There were several that closed rather than integrate. There were others—the larger restaurants, the more expensive ones, would take your money. I remember I was with a friend who was a reporter and we were over on the East Side in Bohunkville. Do you know what I mean by Bohunkville? It was where you had a number of people from Bohemia, white folks of Eastern Europe persuasion—Highlandtown, in that neighborhood. And we got run out of a couple of places, small, where we went in to get a sandwich or a hot drink, that kind of thing. You were definitely not wanted. And my friend would grab me, "Come on, Jewell. Shut your mouth before we both get hit upside the head." But we were seeing how far we could go.

And you had to remember 1968 was an election year, and in 1968 you're just beginning to get the growth of the antiwar demonstrations. By the time of King's assassination Lyndon Johnson had said he would not run again. Bobby begins to run. Bobby Kennedy. So, you have a lot of people who are interested: "Hey, hey, hey, Bobby Kennedy, Bobby Kennedy, Bobby Kennedy."[4] And as I said, to my memory things were not calm, things were changing. Everything was stirred up. But, to say that things were stirred up does not say that it's tense and tight. And particularly since the Voter Registration Act, what you'd been dealing with has been this idea of "Hey, we're getting a vote." This is really going to be the big election because the Voting Rights Act is '65. It didn't make too much of a difference in '66, but '68—this is going to be it. So you're interested in not only who's running in Baltimore but who's going to run throughout the South.[5]

I was in the food store when I heard that Dr. King had been assassinated. Let me go back. Sunday, Saturday, Friday, Thursday . . . it was Thursday, it was a Thursday. As a reporter, my week was Sunday to Thursday because the paper went to bed on Thursday because it came out on Friday. So by that time I finished my stories. I was off and I had a girlfriend who was sick and I had taken her mother shopping—food shopping—at Mondawmin Mall. And the notice went through that King had been shot. And of course I went home to listen to the radio and listen to the television and find out what had happened. They began to play the "I've been to the mountaintop" speech—"I may not be there with you. . . ."[6] And of course that just sent cold chills down you and then all the visuals, the images of them out pointing on the balcony.[7]

And then the question was "What's going to happen?" That was Thursday, and by Friday there was a riot in D.C.[8] The reason that I am very well aware of the fact that there was a riot in D.C.—remember I said that I went to work for the Office of Education. The *Afro* didn't pay that well, and I wanted to go back into education. So I had taken the standard test to enter the federal government at a grade five; then if you pass it, they call you in for interviews; and if you pass that, then you went. To make a long story short, I had come through the test and I was interviewing on Fridays at various and sundry agencies. And on this Friday I had two interviews, one at the Office of Education, which is in Southwest D.C. The second one was at USIA [U.S. Information Agency], where I really wanted to go, which was up on the 1700 block of Pennsylvania Avenue.

When Washington started burning, the federal government said, "Go out, dismissed." And even though there were only half as many cars on the road as there are now, it was an absolute gridlock. And I walked from 400 Maryland Avenue, which is basically around Seventh and D streets, up to the 1700 block of Pennsylvania Avenue. I walked up. It was astonishing because all of these people moving, cars tied up—and in D.C. intersections jam very easily—it was silent. What was so surprising was the silence because what everybody wanted to do was get the hell out of Dodge. So when I got up to USIA, I got greeted with great disdain: "What did I come up there for, didn't I know the agency was closed? Didn't I know D.C. was in a riot situation?" "Yes, but I had an interview." Well, there was nobody there.

So now I have to walk back to Fourth Street and Independence Avenue Southwest to get to my car. You know it's funny, I had no trouble doing that walk. I put my sneakers back on and walked. When I come to Seventh Street—this is Seventh Northwest—I go up, I walked a long ways up Seventh Street and there were burning buildings. When the fire trucks came up, they had chicken wire over them. At that time some fire engines were open, and I very quickly found out why they had chicken wire over them. Because they were throwing rocks and bottles. It suddenly dawned on me, "Whoops, let me go stand on the other side of the street, to stand with the throwers rather than the throwees." So I went over and then I found a telephone and called the *Washington Afro* and told them, "Hey, I'm in the middle of all this." "Sorry, we've gone to bed." All right. So I got back in my car and came on back to Baltimore.

Baltimore was fairly quiet, fairly quiet. But evidently they were beginning to make moves as to what they were going to do. Saturday the trouble started and they started burning. First reports were on Gay Street in East Baltimore and it's moving. And it's also moving west—this is Saturday. Then the announcement comes through: The police aren't dealing with it. The

National Guard's forming. And either Saturday or Sunday, we were under martial law, which we'd be under for the next week or so. So on Sunday when I went to work, they had been told the first thing we had to do was to report to the Fifth Regiment Armory and get press passes. And in the meantime, the situation intensified. And that's when they called in the regular army. So my initial reaction was "Oh my God, what's about to happen?"[9]

Sunday, we went down and got our credentials, two or three of us from the *Afro*. I was the only woman on City Desk. So I went home—and this seems funny but back in the day I wore dresses and stockings to work every day. So I went home and I changed my clothes. And I even remember what I had on. I had on corduroy pants. I had on penny loafers, wool socks, and a multistriped sweater, and a shirt—a button-down shirt. You know, oxford cloth. I was together. But the thing about that was my press pass would fit in my back pocket. My notebook would fit in my back pocket and I could carry my pass and my keys, and I didn't have to have a pocketbook, so I'm good to go everywhere.

A coworker of mine, Roger Nissly, was covering the City Desk, and he wanted me to come down and cover the desk so he could go out in the street. And when I talked to my editor, he said, "Stay home and leave that white boy in the building." Nissly was white. "He does not need to be running the street." There was also a lot of concern about sending a woman out during the riot times. George Collins[10] had sent this fellow Al out with me at first, and then I lost him because I was happy wandering around on my own. As long as I was in West Baltimore, I was secure. And I ran into a black homicide detective whom I knew. And he told me somebody had just killed somebody over on Preston Street. So I go zipping over there. It was a lot easier then, you didn't have police lines when somebody killed somebody. The lady was in the house. I walked right in the house with all this blood in the stairway, all this blood, she's standing there—little lady. I asked, "Why did you kill him?" And she said, "Doggone, he hit me once too often." This was during the riots. So life went on.

And I just started riding around. I was doing the "on-the-street" stuff—that's the bottom of the pile stuff—rather than the "What's the man saying and what's the governor saying?" I saw one place down on Division Street. They had broken into a warehouse, and I was seeing some of the same things now that I had seen in D.C. You know, people taking stuff. When you watch people carry stuff, some of it is really, really funny. Remember, television sets came in eight-foot boxes. Somebody's getting somebody to help him put it on his shoulders so he can go up the street with an eight-foot television. And then here are these two ladies. They had this tussle, but then they decided there was one for each. You just stand there and you watch because the thing was "I'm going to get something."

One of the most interesting vignettes though—this one has stuck with me forever—was I was up on Thomas Avenue between North Avenue and Baker Street, the black section—middle, lower-middle class. And on one corner there is a corner bar, and they had already trashed it. So I'm in there and there's this black guy telling people what you can take, but there's nothing here unless you want a variation on Thunderbird. The good stuff is gone. And he's saying, "And don't be lighting no matches, don't be lighting no matches 'cause I live upstairs. So take whatever is here, only thing here is cheap, but don't be lighting." And I remember the words, "Don't be lighting no matches 'cause I live upstairs." And he probably saved the building; they didn't light any matches.

Then I went across the street and that was a corner store; it was a mom-and-pop store. Well, they had done a job: there were corn flakes and flour all over the floor, stuff all over the floor. But what got me—this is the thing that sticks with me—there was this older woman doing her shopping. In the mom-and-pop stores, to this day, you do not have to buy a pound of butter, you know, you can buy a stick. And she fished around and somewhere found two sticks of margarine—two sticks, not a whole pound. She was taking exactly what she would have shopped for. It was weird. At one point I said, "Don't you want a big box of cereal?" "Oh no, dear." She didn't want a big box of cereal. And then I went along, because I was told, "Observe, but don't get too close where you're going to get yourself hurt."

And I came upon these guys who had broken into the back of a larger store on Fulton Avenue. They had gone in the meat locker and one guy had a Cadillac. And they are loading sides of meat into somebody's Cadillac! Once they had gotten the meat and stuff, they stood there and yelled, "Y'all can go in now." And then other people went in. I'm standing in the middle of it. Because if you are in the middle of them, nobody's going to say anything to you. I didn't have to go in, but it was quite, it was interesting.

That was Sunday. But the next day George [Collins] said that he did not want me running the streets. So I had to go down to the West Baltimore command post, down at Lafayette Market on Pennsylvania Avenue, and figure out what was going on there. That's the night I had the one story I never wrote. I got tired of just sitting around, so I went out with the police. I wasn't supposed to be in a cop car but I was. And then when somebody came close, I'd put a riot helmet on and slide down the seat and just would say, "We're patrolling, I'm just going out on patrol in a police car." Then there was this group of soldiers from out of town getting ready to go on patrol. And they're looking at this map. They don't know anything, and like I said, I didn't have anything to do. So I told them, which was true, that I had gone to school in that area, which meant I knew the whole area. So I hop in the jeep and go out riding with three fully armed sergeants from Fort Bragg.[11] Now they had men stationed on the corners. So as we went by, they had to pass out these dry packs of sandwiches and stuff. But we stopped in the liquor store and found some little half-pint bottles of wine. When we passed out the sandwiches they didn't know about it. But it was the truth!

We were riding down Carey Street, the block of Carey between Presstman and Laurens streets. Three-story houses . . . and it was weird, because all the lights were on. And somebody yells out, "You all right, sister? Have they arrested you?" So I said, "No, no, brother. I'm fine. I'm fine. I'm with them voluntarily." Lord, that was fun. That was fun.

Then somewhere in there, one of those days, I went to court. That was interesting, because one of the issues was who could arrest people. This is when the soldiers were out. Could the soldiers arrest people? Or could they not arrest them? They were supposed to, I believe, hand them over to a policeman to be arrested.[12] A whole bunch of folks got turned in. I think they had set up court in the basement of the Municipal Building. And it was an absolute madhouse because they were bringing people down by the school bus-full. And some people didn't have identification papers. I think the majority of the people, unless they were there for actually stealing, if they were just there for violation of curfew, they were in and out the door, just in and out the door. If somebody said they were stealing and they hadn't been caught with the stuff on them, they were in and out of the door. If they got caught, you know, then they were subject to a little more justice. But the basic thing was that the courts were sensible, and what you wanted to do was get people off the streets.[13] One thing I do remember is that Gelston very clearly said that he would not issue ammunition to the National Guard. Because by this time there had been incidents where National Guards would just kill people, and he said that it wasn't going to happen in Baltimore. So they didn't have any ammunition.[14]

In fact, one of the scariest things that happened to me during that whole riot happened on Sunday night. I was coming back home, I lived on Mount Holly Street off Garrison Boulevard. Oh yes, and I drove a blue Mustang. I came on up McCulloh Street through Druid Hill Park. The fun thing about that was—and you gotta be kind of kiddie to do this and enjoy it—I ran every red light. Just went through. I got up to Walbrook Junction. Walbrook Junction was a little staging point for the National Guard. So I slowed down very nicely, and here come these two little National Guard boys. You know, white. White. And this one goes, "Why are you out?" So I tell him that I'm a reporter, and he has something smart to say. Because I don't think he had seen too many . . . you know, he's from the wilds of Baltimore County someplace. Oh, he wants my identification. So what do I have to do? The car has stopped but I have to go [gestures reaching into her back pocket to retrieve identification]. When I did this, he jammed the bayonet in the window. Scared the absolute [pause] out of me.

And what I can now see in retrospect is how people get shot so fast. Because he figured I'm going for a weapon. What I'm doing is to go into my back pocket. But where he is, he can't tell whether I'm going down into the seat. He doesn't have ammunition. So he jams the bayonet. Of course, he didn't try to cut me with it. He just scared me. And I'm stupid enough to get irate. I also know he didn't have any bullets, wasn't supposed to have any bullets, anyway. So I told him, "Get that goddamned thing out of my face, I'm getting your identification." And I think we were both scared of each other. And he said, "Well, give it here." Then he said, "All right, are you really a reporter?" "Uh-huh." "All right." "Thank you, officer." So then I went home. I never did tell my mother that. But you talk about somebody really peeing in their pants right then and there. 'Cause, ooh, that was scary. That was the scariest thing of the whole thing, because that's how people get killed.

It didn't take long to begin to hear the whole bunch of conspiracy theories. One of them was that the killing of King was from the federal government, the CIA [Central Intelligence Agency], you know, take your choice. I picked up really, really fast that as long as King was fighting for civil rights and just let us desegregate this place, that was all right. But he was one of the first blacks to take an anti–Vietnam [War] stance. People focused on his being in Tennessee, in Memphis, when he was killed. But they forget that what he was really working on was a Poor People's March that was going to bring a gazillion poor people, not just black poor people, but poor people, to that whole strip between the Capitol and the [Washington] Monument in Washington, D.C. So, all of this is going around, and when you are working for a newspaper, you see more and you hear more.[15]

Personally, I love conspiracy theories because I was well into the whole thing about John F. Kennedy's death having been a conspiracy. My favorite was J. Edgar Hoover, because anything I could put on J. Edgar Hoover—he's a bad man. He was a really, really bad man.[16] So, did I think it was a conspiracy? Uh-huh, because they captured James Earl Ray too fast. And to the day he died, he never divulged what had truly motivated him and how he had done it.[17] As I say, I like conspiracy theories. And it was all brewing then. It would brew more in the coming months. Remember, you don't have too much longer before Bobby Kennedy is killed, and then you can spill theories all over the place because there's all this, all of this.[18] This kind of thinking certainly was one of the aftermaths of the riot.

Looking back and trying to understand why the crowds were doing these things—if you looked at them, any human reason that is good for the getting worked. There are those who had animosity toward the food bank. I'm sure there was somebody who said that if I do it, then I could get rid of my book, you know. Do you know what "my book" is? It was a little notebook—it was basically the ability to buy food on credit. We were moving more and more into bigger food stores, but that depended on your money. You may go to a supermarket when you have money. When you run short you're going to go down the street to the corner store, and "I need a half a pound of hamburger." My favorite is a quarter pound of ham bologna and a quarter pound of cheese and a half a loaf of bread. And you could put it on your book. Then at the end of the week, "How much do I owe you?" Pay off or pay what I'm going to pay. The book kept people afloat. A storekeeper could make money by running a book. Most of them ran the books honestly, and most of the people paid it because they realized it worked to your advantage. But if I owe you five dollars and if your book gets burned up, I'm sure that there are—just like the woman who was shopping—I am sure that when that store burned up and the owner showed up, there were some people who went in and paid him his money. As much as there were people who stuffed their fingers in their nose.

Lots of places burned. And most of them did not reopen. So, did they burn them out of spite? I don't know, I don't know. I have a hard time sorting out what I knew then and what I know now. But I think it's the same kind of mood that made white people lynch black people. That crowd mentality, once it gets going, was the same thing that made black people burn. That crowd mentality, which is a very human reaction, not necessarily a positive one, but a very human reaction. You know, "Once it's done, let's toss the matches." I don't think people stopped to think, "How are we reacting?" I don't know. I don't think people in a group stopped to think that much. I think if it's one thing that characterizes group reactions, it's a total lack of thought.

But the mood in my area—my neighbors and people around there were thinking, "People are crazy, some people are crazy. They're crazy. What's going on?" The older folks were all, you know, "Hey, you're burning up where you have to live. This is wrong, this is not what you should do. This doesn't prove anything, it just doesn't prove anything." My grandmother said, "Well, if white people wanted to think we were crazy animals, there are some of us who are acting like it now." So I think many thought that it was wrong. You're not proving anything, and in the long run you are going to hurt yourself.

There's a question you haven't asked, and that's about the class status among black folks in the riots. Because you have gotten me thinking about the whole issue of class. I'm putting pieces together about where did I live, where did I shop. You know. I'm implicitly saying something about class. I think that the question becomes "Who rioted?" Well, I don't know, but my sense is—I'm not going to say that there weren't people who were out there getting their little "gimme." They may have been the ones to buy stuff because after the riots, stuff was selling. A half gallon of J&B, five bucks, because somebody had gotten into a liquor store and wanted to sell it. But basically your black middle-class population was not the basic rioter.

At that particular time I didn't evaluate press coverage of the riots. Certainly from the beginnings of the civil rights movement, there was press coverage. All of that's a part of a visual history. So riots, yes. If you are going to show a riot, you are going to show burning buildings and you are going to show people stealing and running. So when I saw it, I didn't say that this was one sided. I didn't say that this was trying to put black people in a bad light. There's a line in journalism that says, "If it bleeds, it leads"—that's not new. So if it bleeds it leads, if it burns it leads, and if I'm visual, burning is a strong visual image. So I did not particularly look at it as necessarily biased in one way or the other. I think that later, when we look at it in a perspective, the bias comes in, because you say, "Well, I can always find pictures of black people doing bad, and if they are not black, then they're Latino now. But I don't find the pictures of people doing good." But then again, good is going to be below the fold of a newspaper. It's not going to be up here, at the top of the page.

Thinking about how Baltimore has changed since the riots, remember I left in '68 and I didn't come back until '84. Unfortunately, I think I have seen a lot more changes since I have been back, since '84, than happened during the years that I was gone. And that's not a good thing. Somewhere in that period of time, public schools lost the interest or the information to educate the children. It's a damn shame. The kids cannot, they don't read. I was at Morgan, teaching English and humanities. They can follow words, but the idea of reading, getting what it says, not just reading to find the answer, they don't know. And then the worst thing, the absolute worst thing is this change in young people—that to be educated is to be white. That goes against the grain of every black person who's over the age of forty, because education is a way to succeed and get ahead. It may make you better than me, it may not. But it will give you some skills.

The other thing is that there are some changes in Baltimore that are happening throughout the country. One is the loss of a manufacturing base. Where do people work? Because if you don't work, what happens? Look at small things. Forty years ago there were two bakeries on a block of Laurens Street that sold bread throughout the city, cakes throughout the city. Bread and cakes are still baked. Bread and cakes are going to be local. They are not coming in from California. Where are the bakeries? Or are they so automated that they don't need people? That's a very, very small thing, but that's part of the problem.

And if you take it even further, you begin to get into issues of who benefited from the rebirth. What I see now is there's a group of Baltimoreans who are just as bad off today as their grandparents were forty years ago, in fairly relative terms. Of course you may have more money, but things are relative. That's scary. And now the entire city is pretty much identified as being the ghetto. And then there's Canton and a little pocket of redevelopment.[19] By and large, wherever there's a whole bunch of black folks, it's all [thought to be] ghetto. But Kurt Schmoke lives in Ashburton and there's none of that.[20] And that's scary. That's scary. We are so prone to look at that. The police react accordingly. Police had to come to my house, I forgot why. First thing he said when he walked in the door, "What a lovely house." Because I live on Lafayette Avenue, implicit in that statement was "I would never expect it in this neighborhood." We are too busy drawing assumptions, and we do it at all levels. And it's scary, it's really scary. And it doesn't speak to an opportunity for goodwill, for positive relations. I could say I would not be twenty-five today for all my money. That's an awful indictment, isn't it?

Edited by Linda Shopes

NOTES

1. In 1968 what was then the Office of Education was part of the U.S. Department of Health, Education and Welfare (HEW). It became an independent department in 1979, and HEW became the Department of Health and Human Services.

2. The CIG was a local direct-action civil rights organization formed in 1955 by students at what was then Morgan State College, a historically black school. While Morgan students always dominated CIG, it also involved both black and white students from other Baltimore-area colleges and universities, sympathetic community members, and later, high school students. Initially, CIG focused on integrating facilities at the Northwood Shopping Center near the Morgan campus: the Arundel Ice Cream store was integrated in 1959 and the Rooftop Restaurant at the Hecht-May Company (not Hochschild-Kohn, as Chambers remembers) department store in 1960. However, it took eight years to integrate the Northwood Theater, which finally removed the color bar in 1963, after a protest at which about 350 students were arrested. By 1960 CIG had expanded its activities beyond Northwood: it protested, with considerable success, segregation at other local lunch counters, restaurants, and department store dining rooms; joined with other Baltimore civil rights groups in support of voter registration; and became active in protest and community development programs elsewhere in Maryland. See Robert M. Palumbos, "Student Involvement in the Baltimore Civil Rights Movement, 1953–63," *Maryland Historical Magazine* 94, no. 4 (Winter 1999): 449–491.

3. August Meier (1923–2003) was a notable scholar of African American history and a pioneer in that emergent field. He taught at Morgan State College from 1957 to 1963.

4. President Lyndon Johnson announced he would not seek reelection on March 31, 1968, largely because of escalating protest to his pursuit of the war in Vietnam. On March 16, New York senator Robert Kennedy had announced his candidacy for president.

5. President Johnson signed the Voting Rights Act of 1965 into law on August 6 of that year. It prohibited discrimination in the exercise of voting rights and included strict enforcement procedures, thus ending decades of black disenfranchisement.

6. King delivered his "I've been to the mountaintop" speech on April 3, 1968, the day before he was killed, at the Mason Temple in Memphis, Tennessee. He was

speaking in support of the city's striking sanitation workers, whose cause he had come to Memphis to support.

7. The images Chambers is referring to are likely the post-assassination photographs of King's aides on the balcony of his room at the Lorraine Motel, where he was standing when he was shot; they are pointing toward the direction of the shots.

8. Rioting had broken out in Washington, D.C., on Thursday, April 4, the night of King's death, and continued through Monday, April 8.

9. On Friday, April 5, Governor Spiro Agnew had placed the Maryland National Guard on standby and also signed into law an emergency measure empowering him to take a variety of actions to meet the impending crisis. He activated the Guard, headquartered at the Fifth Regiment Armory, shortly after 10:00 P.M. on Saturday, April 6, two hours after he had declared an official state of emergency. On Sunday, April 7, President Lyndon Johnson authorized the use of federal forces to join the National Guard. In all, nearly eleven thousand troops were deployed in the city over a period of approximately one week.

10. George Collins (1925–) worked at the *Baltimore Afro-American* from 1950 to 1968, starting as a reporter and rising to editor in chief. He subsequently worked for WMAR-TV in Baltimore.

11. Among the federal troops sent to Baltimore were members of the Eighty-second Airborne Division, stationed at Fort Bragg, North Carolina.

12. There was some initial confusion about the National Guardsmen's authority to arrest people. On Saturday evening, April 6, Governor Agnew issued a statement that the Guard would not have the power to arrest, and the order was not rescinded.

13. While most cases were tried in municipal court, the Supreme Bench of Baltimore also held special sessions to expedite trials of the more than 5,500 people arrested. The majority were charged with curfew violations. Charges of larceny were often dropped because of insufficient evidence. While the courts did adopt extraordinary measures to move those arrested through the system quickly, they did so by ignoring certain legal rights of the accused, e.g., advising them to waive the right to hear the testimony of the accuser, to cross-examine opposing witnesses, and to present witnesses in their own defense.

14. Major General George Gelston, the adjutant general of Maryland, commanded the Maryland National Guard. To avert the large number of fatalities that had occurred during race riots in Detroit and Newark the previous year, federal troops in Baltimore and elsewhere had been ordered not to load their weapons and to refrain from shooting looters.

15. In the last years of his life, King moved toward a broader politic, opposing the United States' involvement in the Vietnam War and speaking out against economic inequality. In 1968 he and the Southern Christian Leadership Conference, a powerful civil rights organization, initiated the Poor People's Campaign to address issues of economic injustice. The campaign culminated in May and June of that year, when thousands converged on Washington, D.C., to demonstrate and lobby the federal government for economic reforms. During this time campaigners created an impromptu settlement on the Mall called Resurrection City, where they slept, ate, talked, and mingled with supporters and tourists.

16. J. Edgar Hoover (1896–1972) served as director of the Federal Bureau of Investigation (FBI) from its founding in 1935 to his death. During his tenure he used the power of his office to harass political activists, sometimes using illegal methods.

Beginning in 1957, the FBI began to track King; subsequently, it tapped his home and office telephones and bugged his hotel telephones.

17. James Earl Ray (1928–1998) was captured two months after King's assassination and convicted of his murder without trial. Initially he confessed to the murder, presumably to avoid a jury trail and hence a possible death sentence. Three days later, however, he recanted his confession and spent the rest of his life trying unsuccessfully to secure a jury trial. He also hinted at a conspiracy to assassinate King, and though some credence has been given to this claim, no conspiracy has ever been proved convincingly.

18. Democratic presidential candidate Robert Kennedy was assassinated on June 5, 1968, shortly after claiming victory in the California primary. Sirhan Sirhan was convicted of his murder and as of this writing is serving a life sentence at a California state prison. Various theories about the assassination have circulated over the years, but none has convincingly replaced Sirhan as the lone gunman.

19. Canton is one of several neighborhoods along the Baltimore waterfront that has experienced redevelopment—and the accompanying gentrification and displacement—since 1968.

20. Kurt Schmoke (1949–), currently dean of the Howard University School of Law, served as Baltimore's first elected black mayor from 1987 to 1999 and as state's attorney for Baltimore City from 1982 to 1987. Since the mid-twentieth century, Ashburton has been home to many middle- and upper-class black Baltimoreans.

3

Why Was There No Rioting in Cherry Hill?

John R. Breihan

The Cherry Hill neighborhood on the south side of Baltimore was constructed in the 1940s and 1950s as a racially segregated "planned suburb" for African Americans. By the time of the rioting that followed the assassination of Dr. Martin Luther King, Jr., in 1968, Cherry Hill was home to fourteen thousand to forty thousand African Americans, 3 to 10 percent of Baltimore's black population at the time.[1] Yet, aside from a small fire set in the Cherry Hill Shopping Center two days before the real rioting began, the neighborhood remained calm during the dramatic events that gripped much of the rest of the city, particularly its other African American neighborhoods.[2] Why? It is not possible to prove a counterfactual, but this chapter puts forward several possible explanations that will possibly stimulate thinking about just what prevented—and what caused—civil violence in the Baltimore of 1968.

Explanation 1: Isolation from the Rest of the City

Cherry Hill lies on the south side of the Middle Branch of the Baltimore Harbor, which separates it from most of the city. To the east, another body of water—the mouth of the Patapsco River—separates Cherry Hill from the adjacent Brooklyn neighborhood. To the west and south, an industrial area alongside the Curtis Bay branch of the B&O Railroad divides Cherry Hill from Westport and Anne Arundel County. This isolation was no accident. The site was chosen for African American housing during World War II, when the influx of in-migrant war workers overwhelmed the already crowded black neighborhoods of segregated Baltimore. Seeking to maintain war production, federal officials promised $8 million to Baltimore—on condition that it be spent on new permanent housing for African Americans beyond the boundaries of existing ghettos. Two proposed sites on the city's eastern boundary generated fierce opposition from white neighbors. Eventually, the choice—over the opposition of the Urban League and NAACP—fell on Cherry Hill.[3] Aside from the city's potter's field, an incinerator, and a few small farms, there was nothing on the site and there were few white neighbors to object.

Cherry Hill's isolation remained attractive when location decisions again became contentious after the passage of the 1949 Housing Act. Once again, Cherry Hill became the sole site in Baltimore for peripheral public housing projects built specifically for African Americans. During the 1950s, the original Cherry Hill Homes public housing project of 600 units was expanded by three extensions, adding nearly 1,200 more units, almost all inhabited by black residents. Cherry Hill was often referred to as the largest public housing project east of Chicago.

Only three streets led into or out of this peripheral site—the Hanover Street Bridge to South Baltimore, which became the divided highway Maryland Route 2 leading to Glen Burnie, and Waterview Avenue and Cherry Hill Road leading to Westport. In terms of social geography, these routes led into mostly white neighborhoods in 1968. The disorder in other parts of the city could not easily spill over into (or from) Cherry Hill.

Explanation 2: Mix of Private and Public Housing

Cherry Hill was never only a public housing project. Even before it was selected for the Housing Authority's Cherry Hill Homes, three white Jewish development companies had purchased land there to build houses for sale. Edward and Julius Myerberg built Cherry Hill Village; Jerome Kahn built DuPont Manor (on the site of a cemetery of that name); and the Welsh Construction Company, controlled by Morris and Morton Macht, built Cherrywood. Nearly seven hundred houses were built in 1944 and 1945, with several hundred more after the war.[4] This too was an innovation, as before this, fewer than two hundred new houses had ever been built for black Baltimoreans to purchase.[5] The new construction was a source of pride for Cherry Hill residents. Mrs. Estella Collins, a pioneer resident, declared, "This was the first time in our lives that we moved into a house that people hadn't lived in for hundreds of years before. A brand new home."[6] Initially, about 30 percent of Cherry Hill's dwelling units were owner occupied, far higher than the 8 percent homeownership rate for African Americans recorded in the 1940 census of Baltimore.

Could a higher proportion of proud homeowners have prevented civil disorder in Cherry Hill? Probably not. By the 1960s, the citywide homeownership rate for Baltimore African Americans had risen to nearly 34 percent. Meanwhile, owner-occupied dwellings in Cherry Hill actually decreased, to 23 percent in 1960 and 16 percent in 1970. There were several reasons for the fall. The small two-bedroom row houses that were the sole products of Cherry Hill's private builders gave prosperous families no space to expand.[7] A few bought houses in two small sections of larger bungalows built during the early 1950s, but others moved away to larger houses elsewhere. This was particularly true after the bonds of segregation in the rest of the city began to loosen, opening up a wider range of housing choices for African Americans.[8] Responding to this, Cherry Hill's private builders stopped constructing single-family houses in the mid-1950s and instead turned to building garden-apartment complexes that differed little from the public projects in appearance or density.

Explanation 3: Cherry Hill's Suburban Plan

With its combination of public and private housing on a nearly vacant site, Cherry Hill was more than a subdivision or project; it was a whole planned community. The new infrastructure of streets and sewers and utility connections was paid for jointly by the federal government, the city, and the private developers, and it was laid out according to a master plan supplied by the city's Commission on the City Plan.[9] The commission in turn employed the Boston-based Olmsted Brothers landscape architecture firm to design the new community. Since 1901 the Olmsted firm had been involved in the design of the pioneer Baltimore "garden suburb" of Roland Park; since 1904 the firm had served as consultants to the city with regard to parks and parkways.[10] Henry Hubbard, an Olmsted associate, envisioned another garden suburb in Cherry Hill, with curving streets and parkland—an arrangement more like that of upper-class Roland Park than the rectilinear street grid of the rest of Baltimore. Indeed, the Roland Park Company did some of the site engineering for Cherry Hill.[11]

Both Roland Park and Cherry Hill featured short blocks and curving streets—considered both safer, as they slowed automobile traffic, and more picturesque.[12] As at Roland Park, the principal streets followed topographical lines, curving around the hilltop oval that was the site of the neighborhood's first public school. The master plan designated sites for two more schools, a firehouse, shopping center, police substation, health center, swimming pool, playgrounds, and even churches. Hubbard's site plan shows extensive landscaping.

Cherry Hill Homes, designed for the Housing Authority of Baltimore City by the architecture firm of Whitman, Edmunds, and Wright, occupied a ridge to the south of the central hilltop. Besides curving streets, the project included two short dead-end "courts," an early appearance of the cul-de-sacs that were to be a popular feature of postwar middle-class suburbia. Basic building design resembled the traditional Baltimore row house, though in fact units were not individual dwellings but "stacked apartments." Rows were set back from the streets, allowing green lawns in front. Because of the curving streets, no single building was more than six units long. When it came to extending Cherry Hill Homes in the 1950s, the Housing Authority followed the same pattern of low-rise housing, curving streets, and cul-de-sacs, with rows of two- and three-story houses facing away from the streets into internal grassy courtyards.[13] By contrast, this was at the same time the Housing Authority was erecting now-notorious high-rise towers at other sites in Baltimore. The private developers active in Cherry Hill preferred a more traditional pattern of rectilinear blocks of row houses with traditional alleys in back. They were made "suburban," however, by the use of short blocks and the addition of grassy yards between front doors and street.

When the new housing became available in 1945 and 1946, the war had ended, and with it the need to house in-migrant war workers. Of the first 250 families to move in to Cherry Hill Homes, 136 were veterans (who received a priority), 43 were families of men still in the service, and 69 came from overcrowded segregated neighborhoods of Baltimore. The pioneer residents' reactions to Cherry Hill and its suburban setting were very positive. According to Mrs. Cleoda Walker, who, in 1945, moved in,

> I can remember earlier on when some of my cousins would come from the City of Baltimore into Cherry Hill. They were surprised and amazed at the green grass. They really didn't have grass—all you saw were streets and paved sidewalks and really no trees, plant life, or open air space. . . . [In Cherry Hill] there would be cherry trees, and we would pick blackberries, and they would make blackberry pie.

Mrs. Collins had a similar recollection: "Every weekend my family members that still lived in the city would come out, they'd sleep on the floor, they'd do everything. It was just like the country, you know, and it was just a happy time."[14] Did this degree of "customer satisfaction" decrease the inclination toward civil violence? It is difficult to say.

Explanation 4: Small Retail Sector

This factor is more clear-cut. Cherry Hill lacked appliance and furniture stores with the high-value merchandise that attracted looters in April 1968. Moreover, local activists had prevented the establishment of a liquor store—another riot target—in the community. Again, this was no accident.

Garden-suburb planners tended to dislike garish commercial buildings and to minimize their number. At both upper-class Roland Park and Cherry Hill, liquor stores were prohibited, and the few essential shops allowed were grouped in small "strip" shopping centers. Cherry Hill's included only a supermarket, men's and women's clothing stores, a hardware store, a barbershop and beauty parlor, a dry cleaners and laundromat, a pool hall, and the Hill movie theater, all facing a large parking lot along Cherry Hill Road. Most were owned by white businessmen, though at least one store was not: the dry cleaners was owned by Mrs. Lavinia Booth, an African American resident of the community.[15] Other businesses, mostly automobile related, occupied peripheral sites.

DeWayne Wickham, a writer who grew up in Cherry Hill in the 1960s, recalled the crowds that gathered at the shopping center on Friday nights, making it "Cherry Hill's village square, a gathering place for young and old, . . . as much the social hub of the community as its economic center, a place to see and be seen." Youngsters with home-built wagons clustered outside the A&P supermarket, available to carry customers' groceries home and earn pocket money. Teenagers patronized the hardware store, which apparently also sold the latest records; older people went to the cleaners and barbershop to look their best on dates.[16]

In 1968, when much of the violence took place in the context of breaking store windows and looting their contents, there was simply less to loot in Cherry Hill—and perhaps residents' affection for the shopping center as their "village square" prevented attacks on it.

Explanation 5: Community Organizations

All of the previous four explanations have to do with the physical layout of Cherry Hill. Less visible but perhaps more important were the activities of individuals involved in neighborhood civic affairs in 1968. Since Cherry Hill was established on a previously vacant site, isolated from surrounding neighborhoods, all sorts of civic organizations were needed. The federal housing project included a handsome community building, and Cherry Hill's pioneers used it extensively. By the time of the first anniversary of Cherry Hill Homes in December 1946, seven volunteer groups had begun to serve the community, including the Ladies Club and the Cub Scouts.[17] Catholic and Presbyterian congregations began worshipping in the assembly room of the community building before their own structures were built.[18] Eventually, Cherry Hill was home to fourteen church congregations.

Civic activism began early. In 1945 the Cherry Hill Protective Association took on the Myerberg Company for shoddy workmanship in some of its Cherry Hill houses, employing William Murphy, a young lawyer then living in the public housing project, to bring a class action suit on behalf of the homeowners—ending in the conviction of the builders.

Over subsequent years, Cherry Hill residents successfully lobbied for more schools, bus service, better street lighting, more sidewalks, a public-library branch, public swimming pools, and restrictions on liquor sales in the community. Madeline Murphy, William Murphy's wife, was involved in many of these efforts.[19] She characterized 1966 as the "zenith" of Cherry Hill's neighborhood activism. That year saw local residents' success in staving off a new and larger city incinerator. Later came the replacement of the old city park by a new one.[20]

It was just two years after this zenith of civic activism that the riots came to other parts of Baltimore. Although oral histories of the neighborhood conducted in 2000 encountered no stories of neighborhood activists walking the streets of Cherry Hill in April 1968, it seems likely that the strong civic leadership and community cohesiveness of those days played a role in preventing violence. In June 1968 the Maryland Crime Investigating Commission issued a report on the April 1968 civil disturbance. The commission noted that "Cherry Hill, a community of 40,000 Negroes, did not have a single window broken nor a single looting occurrence during the general disturbance. This is interesting in lieu of the fact that no soldiers from the National Guard or the Army were on duty in the area. There were over 30 places of business in the Cherry Hill area and all were spared."[21]

Forty-two years later, Cathy Brown McClain, a second-generation activist in Cherry Hill, used almost exactly the same language in speaking to an oral history interviewer: "I think it was interesting [that] during the riot in the 60's, there was not a single window broken, not a single incident of looting."[22] This is indicative of deeply ingrained pride in community leadership in Cherry Hill.

Sadly, the community's fortunes declined sharply after April 1968. In September 1968, only five months after the riot in the rest of Baltimore, Cherry Hill saw its own violent disturbance, when the Supreme Food Market was burned out in a nighttime firebomb attack. The store had previously been picketed by local activists complaining of high prices and low-quality goods.[23] Other developments were more insidious. Fair housing laws and blockbusting continued to open other neighborhoods in Baltimore to African Americans, including more-affluent Cherry Hill residents who outgrew the small houses there. The proportion of owner-occupied dwellings, originally 30 percent, fell by about half in the 1970, 1980, and 1990 federal censuses. There were problems in the Housing Authority buildings, and a perception, at least, of crime. Coverage in the local press, once uniformly positive, became overwhelmingly negative during the early 1970s. Instead of admiring Cherry Hill's "suburban" layout in articles with titles such as "Air, Space, Cleanliness—That's Life in Cherry Hill," reporters focused on poverty, crime, guns, and drug addiction, portraying the planned suburb as a "troubled," "inner-city" neighborhood.[24] This was most evident at one of the community's main focal points, the shopping center.

Once considered Cherry Hill's "village square," it was depicted by *Baltimore Sun* investigative reporters Matthew Seiden and Michael Olesker as a no-man's land where gun-toting gang members extorted "protection money" and sold drugs.[25] Cherry Hill's still-active community organizations responded with frustration born of wounded pride but were unable to halt the bad publicity.[26] Not until the later 1990s did the negative perceptions of Cherry Hill begin to change.[27] Even at this distance in time, though, Cathy Brown McClain's recollection of "not a single window broken" establishes the ongoing importance of the question: Why was there no rioting in Cherry Hill?

NOTES

1. The figure fourteen thousand is from the 1970 U.S. Census and is not accepted by all. Sheldon Smith of the *Baltimore Evening Sun* put Cherry Hill's population at twenty-two thousand in 1961 ("Cherry Hill Section Gives 22,000 Suburban Living," May 16, 1961). The Maryland Crime Investigating Commission's "Report of the Baltimore Civil Disturbance of April, 1969," issued June 4, 1968, put Cherry Hill's population at forty thousand (1). The *Baltimore Afro-American* guessed higher still: "90,000 Persons Compose This Unique 'Little Town,'" September 4, 1976. Every source agrees, however, that since the construction of the planned suburb in the late 1940s, Cherry Hill's population has been over 99 percent African American.

2. "Arsonists Set Series of Blazes," *Baltimore Evening Sun*, April 5, 1968.

3. "Urban League Hits Sites as Unsatisfactory," *Baltimore Afro-American*, October 26, 1943; "War Homes Sites Dubbed Undesirable," *Baltimore Afro-American*, October 30, 1943. For an account of the whole controversy, see John R. Breihan, "Wings of Democracy? African Americans in Baltimore's World War II Aviation Industry," in Jessica I. Elfenbein, John R. Breihan, and Thomas L. Hollowak, eds., *From Mobtown to Charm City: New Perspectives on Baltimore History* (Baltimore: Maryland Historical Society, 2002), 170–195; and Peter H. Henderson, "Suburban Visions and the Landscape of Power: Public Housing, Suburban Diversity, and Participation in Metropolitan Baltimore, 1930s–1950s," in Marc L. Silver and Martin Melkonian, eds., *Contested Terrain: Power, Politics, and Participation in Suburbia* (Westport, CT: Greenwood, 1995), 195–210.

4. See deed of March 8, 1943, to Lincoln Village, a corporate title used by Edward and Julius Myerberg, Baltimore City Land Records, Liber MLP 6431, folio 51. The Myerbergs eventually marketed their first subdivision in Cherry Hill as Cherry Hill Village. The Machts initially used "Carver Housing Corporation" as a corporate title (see sewer agreement, August 28, 1944, Baltimore City Land Records, L. MLP 6639, f. 582). Jerome Kahn built DuPont Manor, after initially calling it "Race Manor" (deed from Joseph Castranada, May 9, 1945, Baltimore City Land Records, L. MLP 6741, f. 321. See also Citizens Planning and Housing Association (CPHA), Mrs. Charles C. Killingworth, "Memorandum on Cherry Hill," n.d. (probably April 1946), untitled memo, CPHA Papers series 1, box 7, folder 2, University of Baltimore Archives.

5. C. W. Barnett and T. J. S. Waxter, "Negro Housing," report prepared for the Governor's Sub-Committee Studying Negro Housing, June 6, 1942, p. 2. CPHA Papers series 1, box 19, folder 1.

6. Transcript of oral history interview with E. Collins, Cherry Hill Oral History Project (CHOHP), 2000, tapes and transcripts on file at the Maryland Historical Trust, Crownsville, CH00/KAER/EC, pp. 2–3.

7. Transcript of oral history interview with R. McCoy, CHOHP, CH00/DGJG/RM, pp. 9, 14.

8. W. Edward Orser, *Blockbusting in Baltimore: The Edmondson Village Story* (Lexington: University Press of Kentucky, 1994).

9. Clark S. Hobbs, "Cherry Hill's Possibilities," *Baltimore Evening Sun*, April 13, 1945; CPHA, Mrs. Charles C. Killingworth, "Memorandum on Cherry Hill," n.d. (probably April 1946), untitled memo, CPHA Papers series 1, box 7, folder 2.

10. Olmsted Brothers Landscape Architects, "Report to the Commission on City Plan," 1945, CPHA Papers, series 1, box 22; Duncan Stuart and Eric Holcomb, "Baltimore City Planning the Critical Role of the Olmsted Firm," *Olmstedian*, vol. 17 (Summer 2008).

11. Edwin Wells et al., deed to Hanover Realty, July 28, 1944, New Annex Blocks, Baltimore City Land Records.

12. For the pedigree of the curvilinear suburb, see Kenneth Jackson, *Crabgrass Frontier: The Suburbanization of the United States* (New York: Oxford University Press, 1985); Roy Lubove, *Community Planning in the 1920s* (Pittsburgh, PA: University of Pittsburgh Press, 1963); Clarence Stein, *Toward New Towns for America* (Cambridge MA: MIT Press, 1973); Daniel Shaffer, *Garden Cities for America* (Philadelphia, PA: Temple University Press, 1982).

13. Unsigned memorandum by Citizens Planning and Housing Association, April 23, 1946, CPHA Papers, series 1, box 7, folder 2, University of Baltimore Archives. Plans for the later phases of Cherry Hill public housing may be found in Maryland Project Files, Records of the Federal Public Housing Administration, RG196, National Archives and Records Administration.

14. Transcript of oral history interviews with E. Collins, CHOHP, CH00/KAER/EC, pp. 2–3; L. Booth, CH00/KAER/LBBC, pp. 1–2; and C. Walker, CH00/PDAB/CW, pp. 3–4.

15. Transcript of oral history interview with L. Booth, et al., CHOHP, CH00/KAER/LB-BC, pp. 1–3.

16. DeWayne Wickham, *Woodholme: A Black Man's Story of Growing Up Alone* (New York: Farrar Straus, 1995), 31, 86–97, 143–144.

17. "Cherry Hill Homes to Hold Anniversary Ball Tonight," *Baltimore Evening Sun*, December 13, 1946.

18. "Baltimore MD St. Veronica's" I-073, Josephite Archives, Baltimore; Report on Cherry Hill, Metropolitan Council of Churches, April 10, 1946. Metropolitan Council of Churches papers, MCC-1 38/25, University of Baltimore Archives.

19. Reddi Sumathy and Laura Vozzella, "Activist Dedicated to Racial Justice, the Poor; Columnist; TV Personality Inspired Family, City to Action; Madeline W. Murphy, 1922–2007," *Baltimore Sun*, July 10, 2007.

20. Transcript of oral history interview with M. Murphy, CHOHP, CH00/DMBM/MM, pp. 2–3 (lawsuit against builders), p. 3 (buses); pp. 7–8 (schools); "Four Give Bond in Housing Cases," *Baltimore Sun*, October 22, 1948; "Housing Firms Found Guilty," *Baltimore Sun*, May 7, 1949; Odell M. Smith, "Negro Unit Calls School a 'Violation of Rights,'" *Baltimore Evening Sun*, October 14, 1946; "Cherry Hill Seeks School Space Aid," *Baltimore Sun*, September 14, 1947; Madeline Wheeler Murphy, "Cherry Hill," in Joan Netherwood, Leslie Rehbein, Kate Peterson, eds.,

Beyond White Marble Steps (Baltimore: Citizens Planning and Housing Association Livelier Baltimore Committee, 1979), 68–69.

21. Maryland Crime Investigating Commission, "Report of the Baltimore Civil Disturbance," 1968, p. 1.

22. Transcript of oral history interview with C. Brown [McClain], CHOHP, CH00/PDAB/CB, p. 16.

23. "Cherry Hill Fire Seen as Work of Outsiders," *Baltimore Afro-American*, September 7, 1968.

24. Jane Bedell, "A Contrast in Housing as It Is—And Might Be," *Baltimore Evening Sun*, July 18, 1945; Lois Felder, "Air, Space, Cleanliness—That's Life in Cherry Hill," *Baltimore Sun*, May 1, 1946; "Cherry Hill Stirs Debates over Housing Policies," *Baltimore Sun*, May 2, 1946; Sheldon Smith, "Cherry Hill Section Gives 22,000 Suburban Living," *Baltimore Evening Sun*, May 16, 1961. The reference to Cherry Hill as an "inner-city" neighborhood appears in Laurie Willis, "Ex-Clinton Speech Writer Makes Cherry Hill Return," *Baltimore Evening Sun*, March 25, 2001.

25. Seiden and Olesker later reflected on their earlier coverage. Matthew Seiden, "Guns: Seven Years Later," *Baltimore Sun*, July 9, 1978; Michael Olesker, "A Grand Gesture in Cherry Hill," *Baltimore Sun*, January 28, 1997.

26. The *Baltimore News-American* and *Baltimore Afro-American* provided a stream of offsetting hopeful publicity, but still the *Baltimore Sun*'s portrayal caused rancor. Larry Lewis, "Cherry Hill: Its Leaders Work for a Good Image," *Baltimore News-American, Maryland Living* magazine, March 30, 1969; "Cherry Hill Fighting to Believe in Itself," *Baltimore News-American, Maryland Living* magazine, May 16, 1976; "No Fanfare, Just Progress in Cherry Hill," *Baltimore News-American, Maryland Living* magazine, December 2, 1979; "90,000 Persons Compose This Unique 'Little Town,'" *Baltimore Afro-American*, September 4, 1976; Eddie King, "Cherry Hill Is Vibrant, Innovative," *Baltimore Afro-American*, February 25, 1984; John C. White, "Cherry Hill Project Residents Resent Description of Frustration," *Baltimore Evening Sun*, August 20, 1971; Weldon Wallace, "Cherry Hill's Drive," *Baltimore Sun*, July 9, 1973; "Despite Group Achievement in Cherry Hill, There Is an Abiding Frustration," *Baltimore Sun*, July 16, 1973; "The New Image Cherry Hill Strives for Becomes Streaked in the Rain," *Baltimore Sun*, April 12, 1979.

27. Joe Matthews, "Baltimore Finds Hope in Newark," *Baltimore Sun*, October 23, 1996; Michael Olesker, "A Grand Gesture in Cherry Hill," *Baltimore Sun*, January 20, 1997; Sharon Crews Hare, "Cherry Hill Is Blossoming," *Baltimore Catholic Review*, July 26, 1998; Ginger Williams, "Cherry Hill Apartment Community 'Revitalized,'" *Baltimore Times*, May 14–20, 1999; three articles by Antero Pietila in the *Baltimore Sun*: "Community Waits for a Second Chance," December 26, 2003; "Leader Pushes for a Revival," February 5, 2004; "Cherry Hill Sees Hope for Revival in Proposed Condominiums," July 16, 2004.

Part II

The Political, Religious, and Urban Planning Context

4

"White Man's Lane"

Hollowing Out the Highway Ghetto in Baltimore

EMILY LIEB

"The coming of violence to Baltimore's ghetto," began the American Friends Service Committee's "Report on Baltimore Civil Disorders, April 1968," "was no surprise." Baltimore's African Americans were subject to the same abuses and indignities that had sparked riots in other American cities: in Baltimore, just as in Watts and Harlem and Newark and Louisville and Detroit, white children went to better schools than black children, played in cleaner parks and community centers, and rarely had to watch as police officers harassed their parents for no good reason. Many of Baltimore's African Americans lived in overcrowded, fetid apartments in run-down neighborhoods where zoning and housing ordinances were barely enforced, good jobs did not exist, and white merchants and landlords exploited their customers without restraint. "When one accumulates a list of the complaints of Baltimoreans," the Quakers concluded, "one tends to wonder why the retaliation was not worse."[1]

In *its* report on the riots, the Maryland Crime Investigating Commission took a more expansive view: "The finger is pointed to the white, middle class man who, knowingly or not, establishes barriers of racism," the commission declared. "Not flagrant racism or violent racism, but a sort of 'cold-shoulderism' toward the Negro that excludes their feelings and their rights."[2]

Baltimore's cold shoulders were made of concrete: the highways, or prospective highways, that planners had been mapping over and over since the 1940s. They hoped that these roads would make downtown more convenient and accessible; they also hoped that these roads would replace the city's most troublesome neighborhoods. Instead, those lines on the expressway maps had the opposite effect: they carried disinvestment and decay wherever they went. That most of the roads were never built hardly mattered: as the *Baltimore Sun* reporter James Dilts pointed out, "Plans for highways, if they are around long enough, become self-fulfilling prophecies."[3] The neighborhoods in their path rotted so thoroughly that they were unsuited to any other use.

In many ways, the highway plans and the riots were linked. To the people who lived in the neighborhoods slated for clearance, the expressway proposals made it clear that their homes and schools and luncheonettes and grocery stores were less important than an exit ramp. Public policy declared over and over again that Baltimore's black neighborhoods were disposable; in 1968 rioters treated them accordingly.

However, it was the highways, not the riots, that made a ghetto out of black Baltimore—for instance, in places like Rosemont, a middle-class community of African American homeowners on Baltimore's west side. In the early 1960s, Rosemont was emphatically not a slum; on the contrary, it was the kind of place that, said one reporter, "every explosive . . . city would most like to have: a highly stable and cohesive [black] neighborhood."[4] At the end of the decade, after years of quibbling over an expressway route through its middle, Rosemont had become exactly the kind of blighted neighborhood that the roads were supposed to be eliminating. The threat of urban renewal had forced disinvestment and neglect even onto homes and communities whose residents cared very deeply about them.

By the middle of the 1970s, Baltimore's highway ghettoes were indistinguishable from its riot ghettoes. The riots were a symptom, and not the cause, of the epidemic of abandonment that was spreading through the city's residential neighborhoods. These places were casualties of ham-fisted and poisonous urban-renewal and transportation policies that undermined the city they were supposed to be saving.

Magic Motorways

By the early 1940s, the idea that express highways were the solution to the problems facing aging cities was a popular one in urban-planning circles. Some people believed that traffic was choking cities to death. "It has caused congestion," according to the Baltimore Planning Commission, "made our streets dangerous . . . and created blight."[5] At the same time, the highway builders embraced a knock-it-down-and-build-it-over ethos of urban renewal: to eliminate the "obsolete buildings and lowered property values" that plagued the inner city, all the city had to do was pave them over. This, in turn, would make people *want* to come downtown again, and more efficient roads—the "convenient access now found only in suburban centers," as one federal highway official put it—would make it easy for workers, shoppers, and sightseers to do just that.[6]

Many historians trace the rise of this expressway mania to the 1939 World's Fair in Queens—and in particular to its most celebrated exhibit, the Futurama. The Futurama, sponsored by General Motors, imagined a utopian metropolis that was defined not by blight and traffic jams but by the sublime flow of automobile traffic through and around it, via roads that the exhibit's mastermind, the industrial and set designer Norman Bel Geddes, called "Magic Motorways." These were sleek, wide, jam-proof superhighways that soared above the city's archaic surface streets.

To Bel Geddes and GM, "Magic Motorways" were the warp and woof of the American city of the future. "The people who conduct polls to find out why other people do things, and the editorial writers, newspapermen and columnists who report daily on the doings of the human race, all had their theory as to why the Futurama was the most popular show of any Fair in history," Bel Geddes wrote in his 1940 book *Magic Motorways*. "And most of them agreed that the explanation was really very simple: All of these thousands of people who stood in line ride in motor cars and therefore are harassed by the daily task of getting from one place to another, by the nuisances of intersectional jams, narrow, congested bottlenecks, dangerous night driving, annoying policemen's whistles, honking horns, blinking traffic lights, confusing highway signs, and irritating traffic regulations; they are appalled by the daily toll of highway accidents and deaths; and they are eager to find a sensible way out of this planless, suicidal mess."[7]

Though Norman Bel Geddes was a set designer—a man whose life's work was rendering fantasies in plastic and particleboard—by the end of the 1930s he was not the only person who thought that the key to the city of the future lay in the bulldozer and the cement mixer. The vision at the Futurama's core, that replanning and rebuilding the city went hand in hand with—indeed, depended on—highway building, was widely shared.

The same year the Futurama debuted in Queens, the federal Bureau of Public Roads published a report called *Toll Roads and Free Roads*. The report cited Baltimore in particular—"an old City, growing by the coalescence of numerous ancestral villages, [where] the irregular and discontinuous street plan is the despair of the stranger and the daily inconvenience of its own citizens"—and made explicit the connection between traffic congestion and urban obsolescence. "The old residential section of the City clustered closely about the central business section, which has grown little in size in the last fifty years," the engineers explained. "But, since 1900, the more well-to-do families that formerly lived in the older sections have moved in large numbers to outlying suburban areas. . . . The old homes, vacated by this movement, have descended to the less well-to-do, and by stages large areas have finally reached a critical stage of decay. *It is apparent that the whole interior of the city is ripe for the major change that it must undergo in order to afford the necessary relief to pressures generated by the effort to force the stream of twentieth-century traffic through the arteries of the early nineteenth century.*"[8] Reviving these decayed neighborhoods was hardly the point; to the federal road builders, urban highways could simply clear out the old city and build a new one in its place.

To many Baltimoreans concerned about the future of their "old City," this was an appealing prescription. In 1941 a group of businessmen formed the Downtown Committee and sent a representative, a vice president at the Industrial Corporation of Baltimore named G. Harvey Porter, on a grand tour of American downtowns to find out what made them thrive. Porter came to a familiar conclusion: in every one of the cities he visited, he wrote the committee, "*accessibility*"—via private automobile, on a high-speed expressway—"was the key to the well-being of downtown."[9]

Inspired by Porter's findings, the Baltimore Planning Commission hired a group of engineers to design a freeway system that would carry the nineteenth-century city into the future. To draw traffic around instead of through the already clogged downtown, the engineers recommended the construction of a bypass highway, or beltway, around the top of the city and a harbor tunnel across its bottom.[10] And to draw traffic into and out of the city center, they proposed an east–west expressway between Franklin and Mulberry streets at the edge of downtown, slicing the western half of the city neatly in two.

These plans yoked highway building to slum clearance. As they approached downtown, Franklin and Mulberry streets ran through an old part of Baltimore, where they had been crowded with shops and taverns and houses for almost as long as they had existed. Traffic had always been a problem there. According to Letitia Stockett's 1928 history of the city, even at the end of the eighteenth century "Franklin Street was so thronged with wagons bivouacked for the night that citizens complained to the city fathers for relief from the congested traffic."[11] More recently, the wagons had given way to a concentration of poor black Baltimoreans: the corridor along Franklin and Mulberry streets formed a band of slums across the southern border of Old West Baltimore, Baltimore's first predominantly African American neighborhood. But the highway planners were confident that, once they made those slums disappear under a ribbon of pristine blacktop, the rest of the neighborhood could shake off their deleterious influence—becoming, somehow, less old, less poor, and less black.

In part, transportation planners targeted the neighborhood just because it was all of those things. Also, as one Johns Hopkins sociologist pointed out in 1974, it lay along the border between two election districts, and was "a kind of political 'no man's land' . . . leaving some question as to who [was] responsible for the welfare of the people living there."[12] Other neighborhoods had someone to speak up on their behalf, but this one did not.

Almost immediately, the highway proposal won a handful of powerful allies. Porter's Downtown Committee trilled that the Franklin Street route was "OF FIRST INTEREST TO THE CITIZENS AND BUSINESS INSTITUTIONS OF BALTIMORE." An expressway through the Franklin Street slums would be the best way to "attack [the] rehabilitation of the old central city," the businessmen argued.[13] The Association of Commerce spoke up in its favor as well: "If the right of way takes full city blocks and does not leave the scars of blank walls," it declared in 1943, the freeway would be far more attractive than the "congested districts" it replaced. In March 1944 the city's planning commission officially approved the Franklin-Mulberry route, giving Mayor McKeldin the go-ahead to "take the necessary steps" to get the highway built as soon as possible.[14]

To strengthen their case for the road, the mayor and the Downtown Committee asked Robert Moses, New York City's legendary champion of highway building and slum clearance, for his advice. In October 1944 Moses and his consulting engineers published the "Baltimore Arterial Report," which corroborated the expressway route that the city's highway engineers had mapped out two years before.

It also defended city living in an age when, the report said, "some of our more glittering theoretical planners" had decided that "urbanism must be discarded." The authors of the arterial report, unlike the "Ivory-Tower Remote-Control Planners" who "called for the abandonment of most of the town," offered a blueprint for a city that was more magnetic than any suburb.[15] The "city car" might have been an "intrusive and in many respects disquieting gadget," Moses said, but it was the only thing that could make in-town places "accessible, not abandoned." Good roads would bring good people downtown: it was as simple as that. To the planners who preached that "large cities should be completely decentralized or done away with entirely," Moses thumbed his nose: his expressways were proof that the city was more viable than any suburb.[16]

But one tiny detail betrayed all this feel-good talk about the preservation and promise of urban living. Baltimore was not the Futurama, and Moses's magnificently city-friendly expressway would not just hover beatifically overhead, complementing the streets and sidewalks below. On this, the arterial report was candid: in "[this] solidly built town [that] has no continuous opening through which to lay down an expressway," some part of the city would have to be sacrificed to make room for the road.

Moses was not a sentimental man—he was quite comfortable with the idea that you needed to break an egg or two to make an omelet—and his plan kept the broken eggs on either side of Franklin Street.[17] "The slum areas through which the Franklin Expressway passes are a disgrace to the community," he wrote. "Merely as a matter of local pride . . . business leaders as well as citizens sensitive about the appearance and reputation of their city should be unwilling any longer to tolerate this close juxtaposition of civic center and slum. We do not propose to tear down familiar and cherished landmarks which cannot be replaced, nor will the Franklin Expressway make the town unrecognizable. Nothing which we propose to remove will constitute any loss to Baltimore." Loss to Baltimore or not, Moses's list of buildings to be demolished was alarmingly long: two hundred blocks of shops, hotels, taverns, factories, schools, and churches; an ice-storage facility, a tinsmith, an awning company, the local headquarters of the American Relief for France, and the brand-new School for Handicapped Colored Children; and the homes of nineteen thousand people, mostly black. But Moses turned this problem into a virtue. "The more of them that are wiped out," he said, "the healthier Baltimore will be in the long run."[18] Wiping out poor black neighborhoods was the primary benefit of the road.

At the same time, as far as Moses was concerned, the road was more than just a road. It came with sleek new public-housing towers and plenty of "incidental recreation areas" such as playgrounds, sports fields, and promenades. The arterial report emphasized over and over again that the Franklin Expressway was not just a high-speed, high-priced funnel for commuters; the incidental improvements—the slum clearance along the way—would be the road's real "lasting benefit to the rest of the city" and especially to "those living within walking distance of the development." This was an important caveat, since only a very few residents of Old West Baltimore, and fewer in the Franklin-Mulberry neighborhood, even owned a car.[19]

The planning commission, the Downtown Committee, and other boosters cheered the Moses plan, but it failed to convince many other Baltimoreans. Some objected to the road's $26 million price tag. For example, at one hearing, a city councilman rebuked his colleagues for their failure to tell Mr. Moses just where he could shove his "excessive taxes for building a fantastic project" that would take Baltimore's citizens "and their children and their grandchildren many years to pay for." Others protested that it was unfair to toss twenty thousand citizens out of homes that, as another councilman put it, might not have been "good enough for some members of the [city council]" but were "palaces" to the people who lived in them.[20]

Two days after the Moses committee issued its plan for the Franklin Expressway, an opinionated Baltimore lawyer and civic activist named Herbert M. Brune took the podium at a meeting of the city council's Harbor Crossing–Freeway Committee and ripped the arterial report to shreds. The Franklin Expressway was nothing but "a mountain of human misery," Brune said. It contained "no specific or adequate provision for the 19,000 to be removed from their homes" other than a smattering of "vague suggestions involving 'subsidized housing projects.'" Also, it removed $15 million in assessable property from the city's tax rolls. Brune was a crank, but he was a perceptive one: instead of the "genuine slum clearance" and "municipal improvement of wide scope" that Moses pledged to build, he predicted "the Freeway will become a wilderness of trash and weeds."[21]

As time passed, the Moses route grew more and more unpopular. It was easy enough to ignore the objections of the low-income black people who lived in the slums of the Franklin-Mulberry corridor, but it was harder to ignore the white people who lived in the newer neighborhoods to the west who were unwilling to sacrifice their homes for the well-being of a few downtown fat cats who lived in the suburbs. At the same time, white people who lived near, but not in, the path of the road despised any plan that might send displaced African Americans into their neighborhoods in search of someplace to live.

In March 1945 the city council held a public meeting on the Moses highway at the Polytechnic High School—the first, as the *Sun* reporter James Dilts pointed out, "of the raucous highway hearings that became a Baltimore tradition in later decades." Fifteen hundred people were there, most horrified by the Franklin Expressway plan (although the *Sun*'s correspondent did spot a few Build the Expressway placards bobbing defensively above the crowd). Speaker after speaker stood up and denounced the road. "Cheers, boos, and other interruptions were so frequent," the *Sun* reported, that the meeting's moderator fled the podium in despair, taking the mayor's representative with him. And a Mrs. Rufus Gibbs read a letter from H. L. Mencken in which he insisted that the expressway would almost certainly be adopted because "it has everything in its favor, including the fact that it is a completely idiotic undertaking." On that note—another prescient glimpse into Baltimore's future—the meeting adjourned.[22]

That first Moses road might have been a flop—all of the hoopla over its route had spooked the state general assembly, which refused to authorize its construction—but highway engineers and city officials kept at it. For the next decade, they churned out plan after plan, hoping to find one that some government agency would agree to pay for. The $26 billion Federal-Aid Highway Act of 1956, which paid 90 percent of the cost of road construction, transformed Baltimore's enthusiasm for slum-clearing highways into a mania for highway building for its own sake, regardless of the actual effect the roads had or did not have on the city. The purpose of the highway began to change: from a means to an end, the road became an end in itself. "With such mouthwatering subsidies," one reporter noted later, "it was hardly worth *not* building expressways."[23]

What all these plans had in common was the uncertainty they created for the citizens of West (and East) Baltimore, who on any given day might or might not have been living in the expressway's path. As the white citizens of the west side migrated to the suburbs—driven, at least in part, by the threat and the promise of the road—black Baltimoreans migrated away from Old West Baltimore and into neighborhoods like Edmonson Village and Rosemont that had been predominantly white at the beginning of the 1950s. As Baltimore grew blacker, highway builders grew more cavalier. Highway building for its own sake was less troublesome when there were fewer politically influential people around to object to it.

"My Home's No Slum"

In 1961 Mayor J. Harold Grady used $600,000 in federal highway funds to buy a new plan from a group of engineers who called themselves Expressway Consultants. These consultants were to take all of the city's highway plans, master plans, and commission reports and distill them into one überhighway system that could wring every available ten-cent dollar from the highway trust fund.

In October Expressway Consultants gave the city a comprehensive plan for two highways and a harbor crossing that they called the 10-D alignment. It entered Baltimore through Leakin Park on the west and connected with the Moses road through the Franklin-Mulberry corridor by barging for the first time through middle-class Rosemont.

Rosemont, to the west of Old West Baltimore, was one of a handful of row house neighborhoods near the Gwynns Falls and Leakin parks on the city's west side that had grown up, in the early decades of the twentieth century, as modest suburban subdivisions filled with tidy "daylight" or "sunlight" row houses.[24]

When these new daylight-row-house neighborhoods were built in the 1910s and 1920s, they were segregated (white), and the people who lived in them were young families headed by salesmen, skilled craftsmen and factory workers, and clerks who commuted to downtown offices each day.[25] But after World War II, suburban opportunities—brand-new developments with detached houses and real lawns and driveways—expanded for the white homeowners on Baltimore's west side. Meanwhile, the city's color line, pushed by an expanding inner-city black population and pulled by unscrupulous real estate blockbusters who preyed on white racism and black desperation for decent housing, inched westward.[26]

By the early 1960s the neighborhoods clustered around the west-end parks were becoming—and in Rosemont's case, had become—mostly black.[27] And since Expressway Consultants claimed to be as devoted as Robert Moses had been to the idea that the whole point of their road was to clear blight out of Baltimore, not simply to connect the city to its suburbs or to shake down the federal government, they emphasized that their route would snake from slum to slum, trading crumbling old heaps for ribbons of blacktop. There was only one problem: like all the planners who had come before, the consultants had not bothered to differentiate between black neighborhoods and blighted ones.

In fact, even in the face of the highway threat, Rosemont was a lovely neighborhood. The black people who lived there were very much like the white people who had fled: gainfully employed homeowners who wanted to raise their families in a stable, secure neighborhood. They were, as one resident put it, "citizens, voters, employed Americans in search of better housing, street maintenance, better equipped schools . . . and open spaces where we could breathe cleaner air and enjoy the blessings of nature." In short, like most Americans in the postwar era, the Rosemonters wanted "all the amenities of suburban living."[28] A 1968 study bore out this claim: it found that that the neighborhood had a substantially higher rate of homeownership than did Baltimore as a whole (72 percent, compared to 55 percent), that 80 percent of its residents had been living in their homes for more than ten years, that 57 percent of homeowners had done some remodeling (most spending more than $1,000) since 1960, and that, in general, "[Rosemont's] people have great pride and respect for their property and the appearance of their houses."[29]

This concern radiated into the community as well. In 1952 the small but growing handful of black Rosemonters organized a Neighborhood Improvement Association. In 1957 they united in passionate protest against the construction of a box factory nearby and the demolition of twenty-six neighborhood houses to build an elementary school. Shortly after that, a group of Rosemonters formed the We Workers Civic and Social Club. "Working together," wrote local historian Mary Rosemond, "the men of this organization cut lawns, trimmed shrubbery, painted homes, and made minor plumbing and electrical repairs for their families and for the families of non-members as well." They cleared vacant lots, picked up litter, and whitewashed trees to protect them from sunscald in the winter. They built a flagpole and took turns raising and lowering the American flag every day. (They were typical suburbanites in other ways, too: "After work was over," Rosemond explained, "the wives provided refreshment for their industrious husbands.")[30] Despite all this, when the road builders looked at Rosemont, they did not see a leafy, middle-class, in-town suburb; they saw a black neighborhood and therefore a slum, and their map plowed a highway right through it.

After Expressway Consultants' 10-D road passed through Rosemont and headed downtown, the neighborhoods in its path became noticeably older, poorer, and more crowded—thanks in large part to the decades of road plans that had pledged to do away with them altogether. The route overlapped with Moses's until, for no clear reason, it turned south toward downtown a few blocks sooner than the earlier route had. To the highway engineers, this made no difference—they were just moving pieces around on a chessboard. But, in fact, this change of plans condemned a whole new area and left the city with no road where for decades there was supposed to be one. The new plan did not hint at what should be done with all of the buildings the road now bypassed, many of which had not been maintained since the Moses connector had effectively condemned them twenty years earlier.

The 10-D plan was supposed to draw shoppers and businesspeople back downtown by creating an easy expressway commute from Charles Center to the suburbs and reducing surface congestion once they arrived.

However, a 1962 evaluation of the route made clear that the road passed too far from the city center to do much good in this regard. It would, the report said, "require traffic to and from the CBD [central business district] to travel for some distance on already congested access streets" and "promote the further spreading out of the CBD over a larger area than it now occupies and the weakening of its economy which depends to a large extent on concentration of business activities."[31]

Expressway Consultants' highway was bad for the neighborhoods and bad for downtown. The people who embraced the plan anyway—mostly booster groups like the Downtown Committee, the Greater Baltimore Committee, the Association of Commerce, and the Retail Merchants Association—did so because, for them, any road was better than no road at all. If Baltimore did not take that almost-free federal money, they reasoned, some other city would. But for more and more people, the road's rationale was flimsy and unconvincing: the city, they believed, simply did not need it.

And so the antiroad protests returned. According to the *Sun*, at one 1962 planning meeting,

> an aroused crowd of about 1,300 persons gave the proposed new East–West Expressway route a rough reception last night. East Baltimore steel workers [whose homes were threatened at the road's other end] and West Baltimore housewives heckled a small band of city officials and business leaders who generally backed the route at a hearing in the auditorium of Eastern High School. . . . The most vigorous demonstration of the three-hour session came when Bruce A. Herman, a spokesman for the consultants who drew the route, said: "Many of the neighborhoods affected have already been earmarked for slum clearance." A chorus of boos greeted this remark, interspersed with shouts of "Who says?" and "My home's no slum."[32]

Slum or not, it did not matter: in October 1963 city and state officials approved the $230 million 10-D route alignment. Federal officials endorsed the plan early in 1965. At last, it seemed, Baltimore would get its road.

To build it, though, the city first needed to get its hands on the land that the lines on all those planners' maps represented. Thanks to a quirk of Baltimore's home rule charter, only the city council had the power to condemn land; since its members were elected by district, they were beholden to voters who were not, generally speaking, pleased about trading their homes for a highway. This neighborhood resistance might have been overcome but for another idiosyncrasy in the Baltimore condemnation process: instead of considering and voting on the entire expressway system as one unit, the city council held a separate hearing for each segment.[33]

Each one of these was, as Mayor McKeldin put it, "a real bloodbath." The first one was held July 1965, and 550 furious citizens turned up—far more than anyone expected and enough to ensure that, by the *Sun*'s account, the meeting "ended in a fashion similar to the city's entire expressway program—a shambles." First, a chamber of commerce representative politely read letters of support from General Motors, the Maryland Petroleum Association, the Automotive Club of Maryland, and the Greater Baltimore Committee. Then, one by one, expressway opponents marched to the microphone and "shouted into [it] so loudly that the words could not be understood as they bounced back and forth off the marble walls." They so irritated the meeting's chair, Councilman William Donald Schaefer, that he went home halfway through the meeting, shouting, "To hell with it all!" as he stormed out of the auditorium.[34]

Nevertheless, by the end of 1965, the city council had managed to condemn the land in the proposed path of the eastern leg of the highway, now officially called the East–West Expressway, and in February 1966, by an almost unanimous vote, they condemned the Franklin-Mulberry-to-Rosemont corridor.[35] This was in part because, as Johns Hopkins political scientist Robert Loevy pointed out in 1967, councilmembers tended to be particularly indifferent to the concerns of the black people in the path of the highway. Since the city council was essentially elected in the Democratic primary, and since "the people who get out and vote in the Democratic primary are lower-middle-class white voters"—Baltimore's blacks joined wealthy whites and voted Republican—the councilmembers were not beholden to those losing their homes because they were not constituents.[36]

The threat of the road destroyed Rosemont. Not a single bulldozer had started rolling, a local antihighway group called the Relocation Action Movement protested, and still the Department of Sanitation had stopped picking up the trash; the police dawdled when they were called; the Baltimore Bureau of Inspection refused to issue repair permits for any house in the neighborhood; and the city's "negligent method of condemnation . . . often left one or two families stranded in a block of vacated, boarded-up, garbage-infested, city owned houses causing increased problems of vandalism, rats and an unreasonably large amount of additional upkeep on their own homes."[37] Years before the road was scheduled to be completed, highway engineers were nailing shut Rosemont's coffin.

The community organized in protest. Members of the neighborhood's improvement association joined the citywide antihighway group Movement against Destruction.[38] They wrote angry letters and clogged city council meetings.

At first, highway officials treated the Rosemont protestors as obstreperous children, ignoring them in hopes that they would go away, but when that proved unsuccessful the officials took a new tack. They hired a handful of consultants to expedite the building of the highways simply by making the road more attractive: to “blend the expressway into the city fabric.”[39] The road builders were working for their clients—“the people who were signing the checks for the highways,” as one reporter put it.[40] The new Urban Design Concept Team (UDCT), by contrast, was working on behalf of Baltimore’s citizens (at least in theory) to make the road more palatable: to “weave tubes of traffic through [Rosemont’s] vital parts without unduly disturbing the living organism of the city.”[41]

But such an enterprise would be impossible in Rosemont, where the expressway route was so wantonly destructive that it made a joke out of everything the team was supposed to be doing. The UDCT research team found that the 10-D road would displace more than eight hundred households and sixty-eight businesses that employed nearly five hundred neighborhood residents. It would separate the surviving part of residential Rosemont from the neighborhood’s three supermarkets, complicating errand-running for the 40 percent of Rosemonters who did not own cars. Their report quoted neighborhood residents: “We keep up our property and take pride in it.” “We hope to be all paid for soon and it’s awful to leave when you’re used to things.” “We want to send the children to college; the money would go to a house if we had to move.” “People around here are letting their property go down—landlord keeps saying no use to do anything because of highway.” “Expressways are for people who have cars.”[42]

Even if they had wanted to leave, many Rosemonters were stuck. The city government was offering what it called “fair value”—that is, market value—for the houses inside the condemnation lines, but the market value of a condemned house is like that of a crashed car or a half-eaten sandwich: certainly not enough to buy an equivalent home in a neighborhood not about to be bulldozed. The city’s housing authority estimated in 1967 that replacement houses typically cost about double what the city was paying black Rosemonters.[43] At the same time, there were not many “equivalent” homes left in Baltimore—especially not for black people. A house in the city could be had for $4,000, but it would likely be located in a neighborhood such as Franklin-Mulberry: riddled with vacant houses, populated by teenaged criminals, ignored by police and city services. That none of these things was the fault of the people who lived in such neighborhoods did not make them any more appealing to the middle-class Rosemonters who wanted to spend their retirements puttering in their gardens and drinking lemonade with their neighbors. They had never lived in the ghetto, and they had no interest in doing so now.

This last problem only got worse two days after Martin Luther King, Jr., was killed, when someone lobbed a brick through a store window east of downtown and the riots that Baltimore had been fending off for three years finally arrived. On that first day, the unrest stayed mostly on the city’s east side, and the chaos lent a sort of bacchanalian atmosphere to the neighborhood. Teenagers milled around, smashing store windows and grabbing whatever merchandise—armloads of clothing, bottles of liquor, color television sets, matched pairs of lamps—they could. Police officers tried to shoo people back into their houses but did not make much progress: they were, the newspaper reported, "pelted with stones and bottles" and "met with jeers and oaths whenever they came upon crowds."[44]

The next day, along a spine formed in part by the old expressway corridors, the disturbances made their way to West Baltimore via the Franklin-Mulberry corridor (but not as far west as Rosemont). There, the scene was familiar: smoldering shops, looters, young people tossing rocks and bricks at policemen red-eyed from sleeplessness and tear gas. By Monday, April 8, the *Sun* informed its spellbound readers that "to drive through West Baltimore . . . was to enter an ugly no-man's land in which throngs of Negro youths roamed unchecked by airborne troops, National Guard soldiers or city police."[45] But, of course, thanks to the 10-D condemnations and their ripple effect on surrounding areas, many of the places the rioters targeted were on their way to becoming ugly no-man's lands to begin with. Indifference to these landscapes had been public policy in Baltimore for nearly thirty years.

Many causes were at the root of 1968's unrest, just as in the disturbances in other cities, but in Baltimore the baleful highway plans went a long way toward explaining its context. Perhaps mindful of this lesson, city officials turned their attention to neighborhoods such as Rosemont that the riots, if not the highways, had spared. In August the Expressway Conference Committee summarized the grievances of the neighborhoods in the path of the road: "the lack of housing for purposes of relocation and the absence of plans for providing such housing was cited as one of the principal deterrents to considering the proposal seriously; e.g. roughly 27,000 housing units are to be destroyed by 1974 and less than 1/10 of this number are on the drawing board as replacements plus the displacement of 500 businesses with a net loss of 6,500 jobs." The report continued, "Perhaps the most violent opposition to the proposal is based upon the fact that the black and the poor are victimized by what is apparently a political rather than a technical decision. . . . The proposed expressway proves to be of no benefit to the residents; but rather an expedient to facilitate the travel of suburbanites and to garner interstate highway funds that serve the needs of trucking and highway interests."[46]

The Interstate Division for Baltimore City (the joint city-state agency responsible for designing, planning, and building the highways) came up with a series of bribes for the Rosemonters: "schools, playgrounds, industrial sites, and air rights if they went along"; a floodlit playground under the highway; and, for the displaced homeowners to live in, a set of high-rise apartment buildings that straddled the road. (Highway officials were genuinely surprised when the Rosemonters rejected the apartment-building idea, apparently unable to understand why someone might be reluctant to trade her own home in the suburbs for a high-rise apartment on top of an eight-lane expressway.)[47]

To keep Rosemonters where they were, and to keep Rosemont from becoming a slum, the UDCT devised a route for the road that ran through the Western Cemetery instead of through Rosemont. The mayor, panicked by the riots and exhausted by the bickering, approved the new alignment. However, the officials in the build-the-road-at-all-costs camp believed that the original 10-D alignment—for which condemnations had already been approved and federal money allocated—offered their best shot at actually getting the road built. They leaned on the mayor, and in 1969 he reversed his decision: the road, he declared, would run through Rosemont yet. "It looks," one resident told a reporter, "as if dead white bodies mean more to the city than live black families after all."[48] Then, in 1970, the mayor reversed his reversal and announced he had changed his mind entirely: there would be no east–west road through Baltimore at all.[49]

Through all those months of uncertainty, Mayor D'Alesandro refused to lift the 10-D condemnation lines. His justifications for this were vague: "It is not feasible or politically possible to remove the existing condemnation ordinance," he said. "This is a matter of practical necessity and therefore administration policy at this time." Over and over again, neighborhood activists tried to point out how destructive this policy was—"Since the people living under the condemnation of the old 10D route, where it is in excess of what will be needed for the proposed new route cannot get repair permits or negotiate loans to fix up their property, wouldn't they tend to decide to leave the city and no longer *be* city tax payers?" one asked. "How much *more* money will it cost the city to restore houses left vacant by unnecessary condemnation after they have been vandalized as in Rosemont?"[50]—but their efforts were in vain. "The city has forced blight on this neighborhood," one anti-expressway leaflet fumed. "As long as the condemnation line was not lifted, no one wanted to risk living there, the empty houses attracted vandals, the abandoned areas were highly hazardous to the children of the neighborhood." A "viable area" had been made into a "blighted scar." The *Sun* agreed: in Rosemont, the newspaper said, "the state has created chaos."[51]

Indeed, the city had turned a neighborhood of middle-class homeowners into a slum in less than ten years. In 1942 Baltimore's expressway engineers had imagined that their roads would create a whole new city, and they were right. By 1970 just the threat of the highway had practically destroyed residential Baltimore.

The Highway and the Permanent Slum

Government action had created the problems in Rosemont, and so it fell to the government to try to breathe new life into the neighborhood after the mayor agreed to lift the condemnation lines in December 1970. The next year, with a confidence that was perhaps unwarranted under the circumstances, the municipal Department of Housing and Community Development announced a campaign that officials swore would re-create a "sound, safe, decent, and sanitary . . . *normal* city residential environment" in Rosemont: a Vacant Housing Program that would restore 425 city-owned houses to their pre-expressway condition and then sell them to deserving families. Ads for the program promised that the houses would be a good investment, since city contractors were rebuilding them "from cellar to roof." They would have new plumbing and electrical systems along with new walls and fixtures, sleek contemporary appliances, and fashionable carpeting.[52]

In theory, this housing-rehabilitation and homeownership offensive was meant to bring back the old Rosemont by bringing back the old Rosemonters. In practice, it attracted an entirely new group of people, mostly first-time homebuyers hovering just above the poverty line, by offering to sell the renovated houses to anyone with a $200 down payment. In this way, the Department of Housing and Community Development hitched its antivacancy campaign to a broader crusade in favor of "Home Ownership for the Poor," the centerpiece of the federal Housing Act of 1968. That law, the first federal antipoverty measure passed after that year's riots, had made mortgage loans more available and affordable to low-income people in inner cities: under section 235 of the act, for just $200 and 20 percent of his or her income each month, a low-income homebuyer could own a house approved by the Federal Housing Administration (FHA). For many of its champions, this was a pragmatic response to the claim that it was federal disinvestment in urban areas that was to blame for the decade's turmoil. For others, it was a prophylactic measure: "People," one Republican senator said, "won't burn down houses that they own."[53]

However, just as highway officials had failed to differentiate between black neighborhoods and blighted ones, housing officials failed to differentiate between the old Rosemont homeowners and the new: it was as if the concept of homeownership alone, no matter the details, had some magical, neighborhood-saving quality. Though the section 235 mortgages made it possible for many working-class African Americans to own their own homes for the first time, they were not an unalloyed good: they were hard to understand and frequently exploitative, even abusive.

Meanwhile, the Rosemont vacant-housing and ownership campaign itself unwittingly encouraged low-income people to assume expensive responsibilities that they could not quite afford. Under section 235, home *buying* was (relatively) cheap; home *ownership*, however, was not. Predatory lending was epidemic: FHA policy ensured that even bad mortgage loans could make a profit for unscrupulous lenders. And even people who were consistently able to pay the mortgage struggled to pay for upkeep on their supposedly rehabilitated houses.

This was because most of the Rosemont rehabs were lemons. Contractors, working as quickly as they could to discourage squatters and vandals from wrecking half-finished houses, routinely cut corners. The *Baltimore Afro-American* warned buyers repeatedly to "take a good, critical look at houses being offered for sale in the Rosemont area." In 1972 Congressman Parren Mitchell launched an investigation of his own and was shocked by what he found. He noted that the supposedly top-of-the-line appliances in the remodeled homes were "the cheapest models you can get," for instance, and a child could accidentally knock a hole in the flimsy walls "in no time." The new Rosemonters were in real danger, he said, of buying "a home with a 30-year mortgage only to have it fall apart in 10."[54] Taken as a whole, this did not do much to change the by-now-commonplace impression that Rosemont was simply too far gone to bother investing in.

After just a few years, as costs escalated with nothing to show for them, and as Rosemont's struggling new homeowners began to default on their mortgages, the city gave up and withdrew from the neighborhood. Housing officials swapped their optimism for cynicism: instead of acquiring new properties or nagging contractors to improve the quality of their work, they initiated a makeshift Home Care Services Program, designed to combat the "lack of interest or pride in the home and community which may result in deteriorated, neglected properties." In other words, they blamed the homeowners themselves for the low quality of the Rosemont rehabs. They sponsored courses in home beautification and decoration (lessons included "color coordination," "furniture arrangement," and "window dressing, flower and shrubbery planting, and creating decorative accessories with needle point and crocheting"), property maintenance, and home management. Volunteers taught do-it-yourself seminars that encouraged the new Rosemonters to "make the most of your creative genius!"[55] City workers installed window boxes to disguise the neighborhood's growing complement of abandoned homes, and mortgage lenders cut their losses since, as one memo put it, "the collection staff was afraid to enter the neighborhood."[56]

In Rosemont, failure begot failure. By the middle of the 1970s, when outsiders looked at the neighborhood, they did not see the "peaceful, clean, safe, attractive area of Baltimore" that had nurtured family and community life for decades.[57] They did not see the "stable, cohesive" hamlet that two generations of activists had worked so hard to preserve. Instead, they saw a hopeless ghetto—just what they had been expecting to see all along.

NOTES

1. Jane Motz, "Report on Baltimore Civil Disorders, April 1968" (Middle Atlantic Region, American Friends Service Committee, 1968), 1 and 26, available at http://www.ubalt.edu/baltimore68, Archival Resources tab.

2. Maryland Crime Investigating Commission, "The April, 1968 Civil Disturbances," *Maryland Crime Report* 68-2 (July 1968): 4, available at http://www.ubalt.edu/baltimore68, Archival Resources tab.

3. James Dilts, "How Not to Run a Roadway" in MAD [Movement against Destruction] Expressway Conference Committee Report, "History, Facts, and Opinions on Expressway" (August 1968), University of Baltimore (UB), MAD, series 6, box 1.

4. "Roads: In Baltimore, New Options Are Opened and New Alliances Formed" *CITY*, 1968, UB, Baltimore Heritage Collection (BHC), series 9, box 1.

5. Planning Commission of Baltimore, *Traffic and You*, 7, pamphlet, n.d. [1954?], Temple University Urban Archive, 100–109.

6. Lawrence I. Hewes, Western Operations chief of the Public Roads Administration, qtd. in Mark H. Rose, *Interstate: Express Highway Politics, 1939–1989*, 2nd ed. (Knoxville: University of Tennessee Press, 1990), 60.

7. Norman Bel Geddes, *Magic Motorways* (New York: Random House, 1940).

8. *Toll Roads and Free Roads* (Washington, DC: U.S. Government Printing Office, 1939). Emphasis in original.

9. Qtd. in Robert M. Fogelson, *Downtown: Its Rise and Fall, 1880–1950* (New Haven, CT: Yale University Press, 2001), 249.

10. City of Baltimore Planning Commission, *Study for East-West Expressway* (1958).

11. Letitia Stockett, *Baltimore: A Not Too Serious History* (1928; Baltimore: Johns Hopkins University Press, 1997), 112.

12. Douglas H. Hauber, *The Baltimore Expressway Controversy: A Study of the Political Decision-Making Process* (Baltimore: Johns Hopkins University Center for Metropolitan Planning and Research, 1974), 5.

13. Downtown Committee, *The Weight of Evidence: For Baltimore's Post-War Project Number One* (March 20, 1944). UB, MAD, series 7A, box 1. See also letter from the Downtown Committee to Hon. Herbert R. O'Conor, April 8, 1944. UB, MAD, series 7A, box 1.

14. Downtown Committee, *The Weight of Evidence.*

15. Robert Moses et al., "Baltimore Arterial Report" (October 9, 1944), 5.

16. Ibid., 5–6.

17. As he told Congress a few years later, "When you're operating in an overbuilt metropolis you have to hack your way with a meat axe." Qtd. in Raymond A. Mohl, "The Interstates and the Cities: Highways, Housing and the Freeway Revolt" (Research Report: Poverty and Race Research Action Council, 2002), 27.

18. Moses, "Baltimore Arterial Report," 9; "Expressway Would Raze 200 Blocks," *Baltimore Sun*, October 16, 1944, p. 20.

19. Moses, "Baltimore Arterial Report," 30.

20. Qtd. in Jon C. Teaford, *The Rough Road to Renaissance: Urban Revitalization in America, 1940–1985* (Baltimore: Johns Hopkins University Press, 1990), 41–42.

21. Herbert M. Brune, Jr., "Analysis of Freeway Proposal: Statement of Herbert M. Brune, Jr., to Harbor Crossing–Freeway Committee, October 11, 1944; as supplemented by Statement of October 13, 1944," UB, MAD, series 7, box 1.

22. James Dilts, "A Brief History of Baltimore's Transportation Planning" (1977), 2, UB, MAD, series 7A, box 1.

23. Mark Reutter, "Before the City Council," (master's thesis, University of Baltimore, 1972), MAD, series 7, box A, p. 13.

24. See W. Edward Orser, "The Making of a Baltimore Rowhouse Community: The Edmonson Avenue Area, 1915–1945," *Maryland Historical Magazine* 80 (Fall 1985): 3; Orser, "Flight to the Suburbs: Suburbanization and Racial Change on Baltimore's West Side," in Elizabeth Fee, Linda Shopes, and Linda Zeidman, eds., *The Baltimore Book: New Views of Local History* (Philadelphia: Temple University Press, 1991), 203–225; and Roderick Ryon, *West Baltimore Neighborhoods: Sketches of Their History, 1840–1960* (Baltimore: University of Baltimore Press, 1993).

25. Orser, "The Making of a Baltimore Rowhouse Community."

26. See W. Edward Orser, *Blockbusting in Baltimore: The Edmondson Village Story* (Lexington: University Press of Kentucky, 1994).

27. As the local historian Michael McCarthy has pointed out, it would have been nearly impossible for highway planners "to pick any route through the west side . . . that avoided black neighborhoods." Michael P. McCarthy, "Baltimore's Highway Wars Revisited," *Maryland Historical Magazine* 93, no. 2 (Summer 1998): 144.

28. Rosemont Neighborhood Improvement Association, "Letter of Philosophy," n.d. UB, BHC, series 9, box 5: Rosemont Community.

29. C. W. Grier, "Preliminary Conclusions on Social Impact of the Official Interstate Expressway Route upon the Rosemont Area," in Urban Design Concept Associates, *Rosemont Area Studies* (February 1968), UB, Greater Baltimore Committee, unprocessed materials, series 2, box 5.

30. "We Workers" (n.d.) UB, BHC, series 9: Community Histories, box 1: Rosemont Neighborhood Improvement Association. See also "Roads: In Baltimore, New Options Are Opened and New Alliances Formed."

31. In particular, the 10-D route passed about a dozen blocks from the brand-new Charles Center urban renewal project. *Socio-Economic Impacts of the East-West and Southwest Expressways on the City of Baltimore* (Washington, DC: Blair and Stein Associates, 1962), 9.

32. Qtd. in Dilts, "A Brief History of Baltimore's Transportation Planning," 2–3.

33. See Louise Campbell, "Transport: A Concept Team for Baltimore," *CITY*, November 1967, p. 15.

34. "Expressway Hearing Ends in Shambles: D'Alesandro Presides after Schaefer Quits at Midpoint," *Baltimore Sun*, July 21, 1965.

35. Scott Sullivan, "Expressway East Leg Is Near Accord," *Baltimore Sun*, November 30, 1965; "Expressway Leg Okayed," *Baltimore Sun*, February 22, 1966.

36. See Campbell, "Transport," 15.

37. "A History of the Relocation Action Movement," *Relocation Action Movement*, June 19, 1968, p. 2, UB, MAD, series 7A, box 1.

38. This merger created what activists called "the first alliance between Blacks and Whites in the history of Baltimore." Mary M. Rosemond, "Our Neighborhood," March 28, 2004, UB, BHC, series 9, box 5: Rosemont Community.

39. Campbell, "Transport"; Dilts, "A Brief History of Baltimore's Transportation Planning," 3.

40. David Allison, "The Battle Lines of Baltimore," *Innovation Magazine*, July 1969, p. 10, UB, MAD, series 7A, box 1.

41. Nathaniel Owings, "Baltimore—Its Concept Team and Environment," in *The American Aesthetic*, Nathaniel Owings, ed. (New York: Harper and Row, 1969), 2.

42. C. W. Grier, "Preliminary Conclusions on Social Impact of the Official Interstate Expressway Route upon the Rosemont Area," in Urban Design Concept

Associates, *Rosemont Area Studies* (February 1968), UB, GBC, unprocessed materials, series 2, box 5.

43. The Relocation Action Movement noted that whatever "market value" was, it could not begin to compensate for the losses, financial and otherwise, that the neighborhood residents suffered: "They cannot indicate the loss that a man undergoes after purchasing a house in 1948 for $6,500 and skimping and slaving for 20 years to make the mortgage only to have the state offer a pitiful $4,000 for it in 1968, [or paying] $6,950 in 1949, the actual sum of money paid on the mortgage amounted to over $13,999 and now the state is coming up with the 'munificient' [*sic*] sum of $5,200 to take his home." The activists went on: "What do these figures mean in children deprived of education, in 'dreams deferred,' in the quickening erosion of the belief that America is a land of opportunity? By stealing our homes you also steal our faith in America." "A History of the Relocation Action Movement," 2.

44. "Guard Called Out in Baltimore Riot," *Baltimore Sun*, April 7, 1968, p. 10.

45. Richard Basoco, "West Baltimore Is an Ugly No-Man's Land," *Baltimore Sun*, April 9, 1968.

46. Expressway Conference Committee, "Final Statement," August 3, 1968, UB, MAD, series 6, box 1.

47. Joan Wrights and Jeff Stansbury, "The Planned Destruction of Baltimore—Part 1," *Conservation News* 4, no. 12 (March 23, 1973): 3, UB, MAD, series 3A, box 2.

48. "Neighborhood Busters," *Baltimore Evening Sun*, December 24, 1969.

49. Dilts, "A Brief History of Baltimore's Transportation Planning."

50. N.d., in UB, BHC, series 9: Community Histories, box 1: Rosemont Neighborhood Improvement Association.

51. "Movement against Destruction Statement of December 10, 1969," UB, MAD, series 1, box 4, Rosemont Community; Dilts, "A Brief History of Baltimore's Transportation Planning."

52. "A Home for You in Rosemont!" Baltimore City Archive (BCA), call number RG 48, series 40, box 6, Rosemont Sales Program (1972); "Rosemont," in *The Settler: A Chronicle of Home Ownership in Baltimore* (March 1975), UB, BHC, series 9: Community Histories, box 1: Rosemont Neighborhood Improvement Association, folder September 1970–June 1971.

53. Qtd. in John McClaughry, "The Troubled Dream: The Life and Times of Section 235 of the National Housing Act," *Loyola University Law Journal* 6, no. 1 (Winter 1975): 11.

54. "Residents Warned on Rosemont," *Baltimore Afro-American*, January 25, 1972; "*Afro* Victory: City Spends $744,000 More in Rosemont Area," *Baltimore Afro-American*, June 17, 1972.

55. HCD Rosemont Home Care Catalog, "Rosemont Is Now," BCA, RG 48, series 40, box 2.

56. Memo from Home Ownership Development Program to Hugh Coyle, vice president of James Rouse Company, February 20, 1974, BCA, RG 48, series 40, box 2.

57. Rosemont Neighborhood Improvement Association, "Let's Talk about Our Neighborhood," June 2004, UB, BHC, series 9, box 5.

5

Spiro T. Agnew and the Burning of Baltimore

Alex Csicsek

Around 5:00 P.M. on Saturday, April 6, 1968, a black teenager tossed a brick through a store window in East Baltimore, setting off a riot that consumed the city for days. When order was restored, 6 people were dead, 4,474 had been arrested, and over a thousand fires had swept through the city.[1] The riot served as a test for Maryland governor Spiro T. Agnew, who responded aggressively and mercilessly. Many interpreted the governor's harsh response, particularly an infamous speech in which he blamed moderate black leaders for failing to stop the violence, as a shift from his reputed liberalism to hard-line conservatism.[2] However, a comparison of Agnew's actions and rhetoric before and following the riot reveals that the governor was not transformed by the violence in Baltimore but had always held conservative views on civil disobedience, regardless of his stance on civil rights. The Baltimore incident merely provided the opportunity to show his true colors.

In *White Knight: The Rise of Spiro T. Agnew*, Jules Witcover documents the widely held view that the Baltimore riot and related events transformed Agnew from a liberal to a law-and-order conservative. He quotes observers such as state senator Clarence Mitchell, who remarked, "I was shocked primarily because it had not been his pattern as governor."[3] Those who saw Agnew's actions and rhetoric as indicative of a transformation noted that Agnew was a product of liberal Maryland and claimed a list of civil rights accomplishments, such as the creation of a human relations commission and support for open housing legislation. The riot, they argued, shattered Agnew's affinity for the black community and the movement, and so he responded in a harsh manner. This view, however, fails to distinguish between the ends and the means; the governor was comfortable supporting the goals of civil rights while deploring the radical tactics that were later used to reach them.

Law-and-order conservatism is a political philosophy that places a premium on social order. Adherents believe that threats to the established political or social systems must be repressed. Progress should be accomplished only through established means, such as the democratic process; other avenues of effecting change are not worth the disruption to society. Agnew himself articulated the concept when he asked, "What good are revolutions if we are devoured by them?"[4] Law-and-order conservatism finds its origins in the writings of political theorists such as Thomas Hobbes, who wrote that humans can enjoy their lives only if they are in an environment in which they are free from threats. This stability, Hobbes argued in *Leviathan*, is maintained by the state's imposition of law and order.

Baltimore Burns

When civil rights leader Martin Luther King, Jr., was assassinated on April 4, 1968, racial tensions escalated throughout the United States. Unrest broke out in over 130 cities and towns across the nation, resulting in widespread physical destruction and at least forty-three deaths. Few immediately took to the streets in Baltimore, however, creating an eerie sense of calm before the storm.

The storm broke two days later, on Saturday, April 6, when Baltimore erupted in flames. Initial disturbances were reported in the "Gay street ghetto area about 5:30 P.M." when a teenager broke a window at Gay and Eden streets. Within an hour, a serious fire had been set at the Sun Cleaners a few blocks away at the intersection of Gay and Monument. Fires crawled through the area and gangs of youths roamed the streets, throwing stones and looting businesses. Two people died in a blaze at Federal and Chester streets and "a dry cleaning establishment, a candy factory and another smaller building" were consumed by fire at Harford Avenue and Federal Street.[5] The unrest was not confined to the east side. Less than three hours after the first blaze, a fire was set in north central Baltimore in the 2300 block of Greenmount Avenue. From there, destruction spread across the city. In a recap of the events, the *Baltimore Sun* reported the violence was "concentrated in the East Baltimore area, but there were sporadic reports of fires, looting and gangs on the streets in other parts on the city."[6] By 10:00 P.M., the city police declared the situation out of control.[7]

Calm was restored within days. By Thursday, the curfew had been lifted and rioters were off the streets, but fires still smoldered and glass carpeted the sidewalks along abandoned storefronts. The *Baltimore Afro-American* reported that between Saturday morning and Thursday evening, there had been 1,987 lootings, 1,206 fires, and nearly 6,000 arrests.[8]

The Governor Responds

Maryland governor Spiro T. Agnew responded aggressively, holding "to his lawyerly concern for community order and due process."[9] In a private letter discussing his response to the riot, he wrote, "My claws are honed to a razor sharpness."[10] On Sunday, April 7, the governor made a primetime television address intended to reassure Marylanders that "the situation is under control."[11] He informed the public of the forceful steps his administration had taken to quell the violence, including proclamations of a state of emergency in Baltimore City and Baltimore County; imposition of extensive curfews, prohibitions on "the sale of alcoholic beverages, firearms, ammunition, flammable materials and liquids"; and requests for federal reinforcements. The next evening, in an update address, he announced that the Maryland National Guard had been federalized.[12] Local police joined National Guard and federal troops in patrolling the streets. Agnew handed control of the forces to General George M. Gelston, a tough National Guard commander who harbored no sympathy for those causing trouble on the streets, not even for those out for legitimate reasons.[13] Gelston used his men to intimidate everyone to stay in their homes and arrest those who remained in public, as instructed by Agnew.

Moderating Actions

This tough, aggressive response on the ground was tempered by efforts to restore quality of life to those harmed by the riots. Agnew developed a ten-point plan to assist the recovery effort. He directed his staff to draft "legislation to create a new agency that would use state and private funds to aid in the speedy rebuilding of areas ravaged by riots."[14] He asked the state's welfare services to "use all possible resources to meet the needs of the victims of the recent civil disorders"[15] and instructed the director of the Federal Manpower Coordination for Maryland, Christian H. Kahl, to reexamine social service programs and determine if they were effective in attaining employment for poor blacks.[16] In addition, Agnew created two task forces. One was charged with a review of the events of the riot.[17] The other, the Governor's Youth Council comprising black college men and returning Vietnam veterans, was formed to advise the government "on the particular problems of the ghetto child."[18]

Rhetoric of a Conservative

Despite the governor's social welfare initiatives and task forces, his response was widely viewed as tough and merciless. In November of that year, days after a successful bid for the vice presidency with Richard M. Nixon on the 1968 Republican ticket, the *New York Times* characterized Agnew's response to the Baltimore riot as "authoritarian."[19] This impression, based on measures such as extensive curfews and no-nonsense troop patrols, was reinforced by the governor's tough rhetoric. Agnew was harsh and often inflammatory in comments about the riot. He strongly condemned the rioters and, tellingly, rejected socioeconomic or political explanations for their behavior.

In one of the executive orders, Agnew made clear his belief that riots were "caused in all too many cases by evil men and not evil conditions."[20] In a public address, he blamed much of the lawlessness on "unruly and unsupervised youth."[21] This view refused to acknowledge the social and economic conditions that led to the riot. In 1970, less than two years after the disturbance, 5 percent of black homes in urban Maryland still "lacked some or all plumbing," compared with only 2 percent among the larger population. Blacks were also much less likely than the rest of the population to own their homes, forcing many black Baltimoreans to pay high rents for low-quality housing.[22] Standards of education and medical care for blacks were lower than those for whites.[23] Agnew was well aware of these conditions and supported policies intended to correct them but refused to draw a connection between the conditions and the unrest on the street. Instead, he saw the riot simply as a criminal matter.[24] Agnew countered this supposed breakdown of society with "law and order." He proclaimed May 1, 1968 "Law Day USA" throughout the state.[25] More concretely, he vowed "to those few who loot and burn we shall show no sympathy, nor will we tolerate those few who would take the law into their own hands" and promised "to confront force with force."[26] In late July, he even suggested that it was morally permissible shoot looters.[27]

Agnew spoke of the riots with grandeur, at times waxing philosophical on the nature of civil unrest, never failing to emphasize the ultimate importance of law and order. In his address to the state on the Sunday after the riot broke out, he argued that social disturbances presented a threat to the liberty of all citizens: "We know now as never before how vital is the law to our liberty. We know now as never before that violence is no friend to freedom, and that the mob is no ally of civil rights. . . . We know now that to move ahead we must never stand still. We must not stand for a violation of our laws."[28] It was clear to most Marylanders that Agnew saw the riot as a battle between Good and Evil, and that he certainly saw himself on the side of Good.

Speech to Moderate Black Leaders

Most shocking was Agnew's April 11 speech that blamed moderate black leaders for failing to stop the violence for fear they would be labeled "Uncle

*Governor Spiro T. Agnew holding a press conference with General George Gelston during disturbances following the assassination of Dr. Martin Luther King, Jr. (*Far left: *Max Johnson, political analyst for the* Afro-American. Standing behind Johnson: *Dr. Gilbert Ware, aide to Agnew.)* (Originally published in the *Baltimore Afro-American.* Reprinted courtesy of the *Afro-American Newspapers* Archives and Research Center.)

Toms."[29] The address mounted suspicions in the black community "about the depth of his [Agnew's] understanding of the civil rights cause and his commitment to it" and cemented the public perception that the riot transformed Agnew from a liberal to a law-and-order conservative.[30] It was also, unbeknownst to Agnew himself, the first time the Maryland governor showed up on Richard Nixon's radar.[31]

Moderate black leaders, including local black lawyers and NAACP members, gathered in the governor's downtown Baltimore office on the afternoon of Thursday, April 11. Although the event had been scheduled before the outbreak of violence, attendees went with the expectation that they, as the leaders of black political establishment, would be provided an assessment of the situation on the ground and Agnew's plans for dealing with the unrest. Instead, they were treated to accusations and attacks.

The meeting was held in the legislative chambers, a cold, imposing room more suited for a trial than a constructive dialogue. State police frisked the attendees as they entered. Agnew was late. Although he was

Governor Spiro Agnew meeting with civil rights leaders. (Reprinted courtesy of the *Baltimore News American* Collection, University of Maryland–College Park.)

detained by legitimate business, the attendees were not informed of the delay, an unfortunate circumstance that many would later interpret as a prelude to the disrespectful tone of the event. As time went by and the governor failed to appear, his aide Charlie Bresler took the floor. The address went unrecorded but many of those present described it as a shocking interpretation of the riot and its causes that was at best patronizing and at worst racist. He compared the experience of European immigrants with those who were shipped to America in slavery and insinuated that since he and the governor's immigrant parents were able to control their families, black Baltimoreans should have been better able to deal with theirs.[32]

A confrontational tone had been set. After the unexplained delay and Bresler's offensive rant, the governor finally arrived. He made no apologies for being late but strode up to the stage with a group of dour whites.[33] Among them was National Guard commander Gelston, wearing his fatigues. It was clear that this was not going to be the constructive meeting the moderate black leaders had been expecting.

Agnew opened the speech by declaring his purpose was not to assign blame, but he then immediately proceeded to blame the leaders for their failure to stop the riot. He first implied that the riots were incited by "a reckless stranger to this city," an apparent reference to an April 3 visit to Baltimore by Stokely Carmichael during which the activist praised

Civil rights leaders meeting at Douglass Memorial Church after walking out of their meeting with Agnew. (Reprinted courtesy of the *Baltimore News American* Collection, University of Maryland–College Park.)

violence.[34] The governor then accused the moderate black leaders assembled in the room of complicity in the riots because they failed to stop the destruction. Agnew went on at length about meetings between some of those present, including a prominent state senator, and more radical elements he called "advocates of violence"; the implication was that they had given their stamp of approval to the use of violence, when in reality the meetings had been attempts to bridge the widening gaps in the black political community. As if to prove his point, the governor called on the crowd "to publicly repudiate all black racists" and, without waiting for an answer, declared, "This, so far, you have been unwilling to do." He told them they refused to stand up to the militant elements in the civil rights movement for fear of being "stung by insinuations that you were Mr. Charlie's boy, by epithets like 'Uncle Tom.'"[35]

The faces of the audience showed their offense.[36] As Agnew digressed into mocking quotations from militants and scolding blacks for losing sight of the goals of the civil rights movement, fifty of the eighty who had originally gathered got up and left.[37] They felt they had been duped into taking part in an effort to divide their community and compared the situation to a slave master scolding the "good negroes" for failing to keep the rest of the slaves in line. Troy Bailey, a black member of the state house of delegates who was among those who walked out, told a journalist, "He's got to be out of his mind."[38]

When Agnew reached the end of his written comments, he opened the floor to questions and continued to express his anger in his answers.[39] At one point during the nearly two-hour discussion that followed, Juanita Jackson Mitchell[40] attempted to engage Agnew by reminding him of the socioeconomic and political conditions that fomented the unrest. "The government have made . . . our children hunters and looters," she argued. Agnew utterly ignored the substance of the argument, instead repeatedly asking Mitchell if she repudiated H. Rap Brown and Stokely Carmichael—two men who in Agnew's view epitomized the dangerous outside agitator. When Mitchell continued to say her piece, Agnew interrupted and began to taunt her, insistently asking, "Do you? Do you?"[41] He also yelled at Mitchell's elderly mother, Lillie May Jackson, the beloved civil rights pioneer who founded Baltimore's branch of the NAACP and matriarch of the Mitchell family.[42] The exchange made clear that Agnew had no intention of genuinely engaging moderate black leaders but instead sought only to scold them for failing to stop the riot. "We were talked to like children," summarized state senator Verda Welcome.[43] The meeting had been so hostile that Agnew canceled plans to repeat his speech on television later that evening. Media reports noted that those in attendance came away from the meeting with the impression that Agnew had shed his liberal reputation and embraced law-and-order conservatism.[44]

The public, particularly black leaders, interpreted Agnew's actions as a transformation because of the general perception that the governor had a strong civil rights record. Yet Agnew's previous support for moderate advances in civil rights should not be confused with toleration of the radical tactics that were later associated with the movement. Agnew loathed civil unrest, a position that was not at all diminished by his views on civil rights.

The Suburban Strategy

While Agnew's sincere ideological commitment to preserving law and order largely accounts for his response to the riot, it would be naive to suggest political calculation had no role in motivating his actions. The governor was in constant communication with the public and made numerous appearances on television, a medium with growing significance in American political life.[45] Agnew was a sincere man but also an ambitious one, and he would certainly have seen the political opportunities afforded by the riot.

Considered through this political prism, Agnew's actions and remarks could have been taken straight out of *The Emerging Republican Majority*, Kevin Phillips's 1969 book detailing the Southern Strategy.[46] Phillips argued that changes in racial and social demographics polarized the country and that politicians could exploit this divisiveness to their electoral advantage.[47] Agnew's public comments regarding the riot seem almost designed to contrive friction with the black community. These statements bear the hallmarks of the Southern Strategy as it was developing in the late 1960s, yet that was not their inspiration. Agnew's political strategies are better understood as a Suburban Strategy.

The governor lived in a suburban county and embodied its ethos in both his private and public life. As a private individual, Agnew epitomized the midcentury suburban male: born and bred in a dense urban neighborhood, he took advantage of the GI bill to buy a home outside the city in Loch Raven. He immersed himself in his neighborhood's suburban culture, joining the Kiwanis, taking up golf, and getting a family dog.[48] The cleanliness and orderliness of the cut lawns, tidy homes, and paved driveways of Loch Raven held an innate appeal for Agnew and reflected what he understood to be the proper function of society.

As a public figure, Agnew was essentially suburban as well. He became one of the first in a new wave of suburban politicians.[49] His political views and career are best understood within the framework of the increasing political clout of American suburbs. His path to Government House led exclusively through Baltimore County, first as a member and then chairman of the Board of Zoning Appeals and later as county executive, just as the county was completing its transition from rolling farmland to cul-de-sacs and strip malls. By 1960, 48 percent of the metropolitan population was suburban.[50] This demographic shift resulted in profound changes for the region's politics as the suburban middle class rapidly replaced urban white ethnic voters as the decisive political category. Spiro Agnew emerged as the voice of this new political bloc.[51]

Within this context, it becomes apparent that the political calculations behind Agnew's response to the riot reflected not a Southern Strategy but rather a Suburban Strategy. He did not see the dividing line as between white and black but between suburb and city.[52] As the new suburban politician, there was no question which side the governor came down on. His public remarks were designed to reassure suburban residents that the situation would remain contained in the recesses of deepest, darkest Baltimore.

The urban-suburban divide at the heart of Agnew's strategy is reflected in the responses to the April 11 meeting with moderate black leaders. Politicians from Baltimore City, including the white mayor, rejected Agnew's views and behavior, while most of the governor's suburban counterparts remained relatively quiet. Support was evident in the suburban media, however, with newspapers such as the *Bethesda–Chevy Chase Tribune* and the *Suburban Record* praising the governor. Suburban Marylanders wrote to Agnew to congratulate him for "standing up for the average middle-class [suburbanite]."[53] Agnew's actions and statements were designed to win over the suburban voter, and in this he was wildly successful.

Agnew: Maryland's Civil Rights Politician?

The Suburban Strategy required Agnew to take a hard line. This response to the riots signified a transformation to many because it appeared to sharply contrast with his previous record on civil rights. Agnew's reputation as a progressive dated back to his tenure as Baltimore County executive[54] and was reinforced by his early actions as governor.

In 1963, shortly after his election to the top post in Baltimore County, Agnew created a human relations commission designed to speed up desegregation in public life, including at a park. In October of that year, he received a Helping Hand Award from the Metropolitan Civic Association for his civil rights accomplishments. In August 1964 he submitted to the county council "an administration civil rights bill covering several major areas of complaint—swimming pools, amusement parks and employment opportunities."[55]

Agnew brought his decidedly pro–civil rights platform to Annapolis when he became governor. His 1968 agenda's top priority was the creation of expansive community mental health programs. He also called for creating "a State authority to provide financial and technical assistance for low and middle income housing projects" and expanding higher education services to low-income students.[56] Agnew followed through on these promises in his requests for the 1969 capital budget.[57] He started an employment program in impoverished areas of Baltimore in 1967,[58] publicly toyed with issuing an executive order to end discrimination in state jobs,[59] and allowed state employees to take paid time off work to attend memorial services for Martin Luther King, Jr.[60] He signed several civil rights bills, including an open housing law[61] and legislation that legalized interracial marriage.[62] Finally, Agnew used the governorship as a bully pulpit for civil rights, condemning racial slurs used by a circuit court judge[63] and urging the state's congressional delegation to support federal legislation to outlaw housing discrimination.[64]

Although his commitment to civil rights served a political purpose in liberal Maryland, some evidence indicates Agnew was a true believer. *Time* magazine suggested his disposition toward support for economic opportunities was likely influenced by his childhood experience as the son of a struggling Greek immigrant.[65] In an interoffice communication not meant for public consumption, Agnew disparaged the racial slurs of circuit judge William B. Bowie.[66] In another private communiqué, he expressed deep regret over racist killings of blacks in Baltimore.[67] In a private conversation while on vacation in Ocean City, Agnew told Gilbert Ware that he fully intended "to do all [he] could to put an end to school segregation."[68]

Agnew's civil rights record initially won him the support of the black community. In the 1966 gubernatorial race, he received the endorsement of the Interdenominational Ministerial Alliance, a powerful group of black ministers based in Baltimore. He won the urban black vote in that election. Agnew also maintained relatively good, although at times strained, relations with black leaders until the riot. For example, he met NAACP leader Roy Wilkins in July 1967 and "announced he was considering an executive order ending all discrimination in state jobs."[69]

Despite these accomplishments, Agnew's civil rights record is not as impressive as could be expected from the governor of a liberal state with one of the largest proportions of blacks in the population outside the Deep South. He supported reform only on his own terms. For example, the Baltimore County Human Relations Commission, whose formation was a welcomed gesture, was designed by Agnew to remain a toothless body.[70] In addition, Agnew's civil rights actions were carefully calculated political balancing acts: just enough to placate the demands of the important white-liberal and black voting constituency but not enough to anger the conservatives who were beginning to fill the ranks of Maryland's Republican Party.

Agnew: The Law-and-Order Conservative

In light of this record, black leaders and the larger Maryland public were shocked by Agnew's hard-line response to the Baltimore riot. They concluded that the contrast was explained by a shift from liberal to conservative. A review of Agnew's rhetoric and actions before the 1968 incident, however, reveals the governor was not transformed by the violence in Baltimore but rather had always held conservative views on civil disobedience and did not believe it to be a legitimate form of political protest.

Agnew's aversion to civil disobedience was based on his deep reverence for law and order. Speaking to the *Annapolis Evening Capital*, he explained that civil disobedience "leads inevitably to riots and riots condoned lead inevitably to revolution."[71] When the National Advisory Commission on Civil Disorders, commonly known as the Kerner Commission, released the findings of its investigation into the causes of race riots, Agnew rejected it as "a searing indictment of the American mainstream" that was pervaded by "masochistic group guilt for white racism." He disputed the report's findings that blacks were acting out of frustration with unequal economic opportunity. He instead claimed, "If one wants to pinpoint the cause of riots, it would be this permissive climate and the misguided compassion of public opinion. It is not the racism and deprivation that have built to an explosive crescendo but the fact that lawbreaking has become a socially fashionable and occasionally stylish form of dissent."[72]

Agnew also held firm to the belief, more commonly associated with opponents of civil rights, that riots and other forms of civil disobedience were not genuine popular uprisings but rather were the results of a few black militants persuading the ignorant masses to violent dissent. In a statement to the Baltimore County Human Relations Commission more than three years before the Baltimore riot, Agnew posited that outside agitators manipulate "average citizens, mentally fatigued after a day in the arena of private sector." He argued that government has "an obligation" to "protect our Negro community against exploitation by politically motivated opportunists."[73]

Agnew's attitude is evident in not only his words but also his actions as demonstrated in his response to the Bowie State affair. In March 1968 the student body president of Maryland's historically black Bowie State College, Roland Smith, wrote Agnew a letter asking the governor to fix the school's dilapidated dorms and classrooms. Agnew never responded. Later that month, Smith led the student body in a peaceful boycott of classes to protest the refusal of tenure to a young history professor. The students demanded that Agnew visit, but the governor only sent aide Charlie Bresler, whose handling of the situation aggravated tensions. On April 4 a false rumor that Agnew had decided to visit a white college to address student grievances motivated hundreds of Bowie State students to descend on the statehouse in Annapolis and demand to see Agnew. The governor refused to meet with the students, and a showdown ensued.[74]

As with his reaction to the Baltimore riot, Agnew responded harshly to the Bowie State affairs. Late in the evening, as students continued to refuse to vacate the statehouse, the governor gave the go-ahead to have 227 arrested. He immediately ordered a temporary shutdown of Bowie State, forcing even those students who were entirely uninvolved in the protest to move out of their dorms in the midst of a torrential rainstorm. The governor matched his actions with strong rhetoric that reflected his intolerance of civil disobedience and his belief that outside agitators were to blame for all unrest. "Today's events at Bowie State College should amply demonstrate that this Administration has no intention of yielding to the demand and threats of those who would take matters into their own hands," he said in a statement. "It is unfortunate that students, who no doubt have legitimate grievances, came under the spell of outside agitators."[75]

Agnew was always against civil disobedience in all its incarnations, from peaceful sit-ins to violent riots. For example, Agnew refused to give in to the demands of integrationists at Gwynn Oak Park because they picketed.[76] Agnew's view was a principled rejection of disobedience as a legitimate political activity because it disrupted the social order that he saw as the foundation of freedom.[77] This philosophical foundation is evident in other Agnew policies, such as his strong support for the suburbanization of Maryland.[78] Agnew balked at any political goal that was attempted through means other than established, de jure political channels.

Conclusion

The riot that consumed Baltimore for a few days in April 1968 did not transform Maryland governor Spiro T. Agnew from a liberal into a conservative.

Agnew had always held conservative views on civil disobedience, as demonstrated by his reaction to the Kerner Commission, his statement to the Baltimore County Human Relations Commission, and his aggressive response to the Bowie State affair. The Baltimore riot did not create Agnew's positions but simply provided an opportunity to show his true colors.

Agnew's response to the riot propelled him onto the national scene in a way few could have predicted. The April 11 fiasco made national news and spread his reputation as a defender of suburbia.[79] Agnew's office reported receiving 7,588 pieces of correspondence from across the country, with most thanking the governor for standing up for safety and security in the face of an unsettling urban threat.[80] His views were endorsed by the conservative publication *Human Events*, and the *Washington Post* even ran a letter to the editor calling for someone like Agnew to take the reins in the White House. Taking advantage of his newfound popularity, Agnew cultivated his credentials as a bona fide conservative with increasingly conservative statements made in a series of speeches throughout the nation.[81] Within weeks, he had attracted the attention of Nixon aide Pat Buchanan, eventually becoming Nixon's running mate and then the only U.S. vice president from Maryland, a result based on a decision that was made "largely from his April 11 performance and what came after."[82]

NOTES

1. Robert Marsh, *Agnew: The Unexamined Man: A Political Profile* (New York: M. Evans, 1971), 91.

2. Jules Witcover, *White Knight: The Rise of Spiro T. Agnew* (New York: Random House, 1972), 28.

3. Ibid., 28.

4. John R. Coyne, Jr., *The Impudent Snobs: Agnew vs. the Intellectual Establishment* (New Rochelle, NY: Arlington House, 1972), 164.

5. "City Curfew Imposed; Agnew Sends Troops as Unrest Spreads," *Baltimore Sun*, April 8, 1968, A1, A10.

6. Ibid., A10.

7. Ibid., A1.

8. Jewell Chambers, "Baltimore Begins Road Back after Four Days," *Baltimore Afro-American*, April 13, 1968, p. 3.

9. Marsh, *Agnew*, 47–48.

10. Spiro T. Agnew, letter to state senator Jervis S. Finney, April 18, 1968, University of Maryland, Hornbake Library, Maryland Room, Papers of Spiro T. Agnew, sec. 2.1, box 1, folder 11.

11. Spiro T. Agnew, "Address to Citizens of Maryland on Burning and Looting," April 7, 1968, University of Maryland, Hornbake Library, Maryland Room, Papers of Spiro T. Agnew, sec. 2.3, box 1, folder 111.

12. Spiro T. Agnew, "Address to Citizens of Maryland on Burning and Looting," April 8, 1968, archives of Maryland Online, vol. 83, pp. 755–756, available at http://www.mdarchives.state.md.us/megafile/msa/speccol/sc2900/sc2908/000001/000083/html/am83—755.html.

13. Marsh, *Agnew*, 89.

14. *Baltimore Sun*, April 21, 1968.

15. *Baltimore Sun*, April 23, 1968.

16. Spiro T. Agnew, "Request to Negro Youth to Assist in Solving Ghetto Problem," April 25, 1968, University of Maryland, Hornbake Library, Maryland Room, Papers of Spiro T. Agnew, sec. 2.3, box 3, folder 116.

17. Spiro T. Agnew, "News Release on the Creation of Baltimore Riot Task Force," August 14, 1968, University of Maryland, Hornbake Library, Maryland Room, Papers of Spiro T. Agnew, sec. 2.3, box 3, folder 195.

18. Agnew, "Request to Negro Youth."

19. "Vice President Spiro T. Agnew," *New York Times*, November 1968, A21.

20. Spiro T. Agnew, "Proclamation of Executive Order Concerning Baltimore Riot, April 1968," University of Maryland, Hornbake Library, Maryland Room, Papers of Spiro T. Agnew, sec. 2.3, box 3, folder 85.

In *Agnew: The Unexamined Man*, Robert Marsh argued that Agnew fell victim to one of the "two white myths" that followed the civil rights movement since its inception: "No matter what the issue or where the confrontation with the establishment, 'a few agitators' provoke a problem where none existed" (97–98).

21. Agnew, "Address," April 7, 1968.

22. U.S. Department of Commerce, *1970 Census of Population and Housing: General Demographic Trends for Metropolitan Areas, 1960 to 1970: Maryland: Final Report* (Washington, DC: U.S. Government Printing Office, 1971), 6–7.

23. Ernest M. Kahn, "Universities and Urban Affairs: Case Studies of the Colleges and Universities in the Baltimore Area in the 1960's" (Ph.D. diss., University of Maryland, College Park, 1972).

24. In a 1992 feature in the *Washington Post*, Howard Schneider observed that, while blacks interpreted the civil disturbances of 1960s Maryland as "a fight for equality," whites saw the same events as senseless violence and destruction. Schneider argued that segregation prevented the two communities from empathizing with one another. "Summer of Fire," *Washington Post*, July 26, 1992, W14.

25. Spiro T. Agnew, "Announcement of Proclamation—Law Day USA," April 1968, University of Maryland, Hornbake Library, Maryland Room, Papers of Spiro T. Agnew, sec. 2.3, box 3, folder 109.

26. Agnew, "Address," April 7, 1968.

27. "Shooting of Riot Looters Gets Approval of Agnew," *Baltimore News American*, July 31, 1968, B2.

28. Agnew, "Address," April 7, 1968.

29. Spiro T. Agnew, "Speech to Prominent Black Leaders in Baltimore," April 11, 1968, University of Maryland, Hornbake Library, Maryland Room, Papers of Spiro T. Agnew, sec. 2.3, box 3, folder 106.

30. Witcover, *White Knight*, 159.

31. Influential Nixon aide Pat Buchanan was so impressed with Agnew's performance that he clipped a newspaper article about the speech and gave it to his boss. Theo Lippman, Jr., *Spiro Agnew's America* (New York: Norton, 1972), 113.

32. Marsh, *Agnew*, 98.

33. Witcover, *White Knight*, 20.

34. Ibid., 17.

35. Agnew, "Speech to Prominent Black Leaders."

36. Marsh, *Agnew*, 101.

37. Witcover, *White Knight*, 27.

38. "Agnew Angers Negroes," *New York Times*, April 12, 1968, p. 20.

39. Witcover, *White Knight*, 25.

40. Mitchell was a member of a family prominent in the black political establishment. She was married to NAACP lobbyist Clarence M. Mitchell, Jr., who was instrumental in national civil rights accomplishments in the 1950s and 1960s, and is the mother of two Maryland state senators. Mitchell was also a respected civil rights advocate in her own right and was the first black woman to practice law in Maryland; the NAACP awards an honor in her name each year.

41. Lippman, *Spiro Agnew's America*, 111–112.

42. Witcover, *White Knight*, 25.

43. "Agnew Raps Top Negroes for Silence," *Washington Post*, April 12, 1968, p. 1.

44. Witcover, *White Knight*, 28.

45. Austin Ranney, *Channels of Power: The Impact of Television on American Politics* (New York: Basic Books, 1983).

46. New Rochelle, NY: Arlington House.

47. Theodore Rosenof, *Realignment: The Theory that Changed the Way We Think about American Politics* (Lanham, MD: Rowman and Littlefield, 2003), 116.

48. Garry Wills, *Nixon Agonistes: The Crisis of the Self-Made Man* (New York: Houghton Mifflin, 2002), 277–281.

49. Kenneth Jackson called Agnew "the first suburban politician to rise to national office." Kenneth T. Jackson, *Crabgrass Frontier: The Suburbanization of the United States* (Oxford: Oxford University Press, 1985), 283.

50. Kenneth D. Durr, *Behind the Backlash: White Working-Class Politics in Baltimore, 1940–1980* (Chapel Hill: University of North Carolina Press, 2003), 68.

51. Clay Risen, *A Nation on Fire: America in the Wake of the King Assassination* (Hoboken, NJ: Wiley, 2009), 175.

52. In his April 7 television address, Agnew made a point of explicitly noting that a majority of black Marylanders "have remained calm in these hours of crisis." Agnew, "Address," April 8, 1968.

53. Risen, *A Nation on Fire*, 225.

54. Jim G. Lucas, *Agnew: Profile in Conflict* (New York: Award Books, 1970), 35–36.

55. Marsh, *Agnew*, 37–47.

56. Spiro T. Agnew, "Release of Governor's 1968 Legislative Program in Brief," January 2, 1968, University of Maryland, Hornbake Library, Maryland Room, Papers of Spiro T. Agnew, sec. 2.3, box 3, folder 2.

57. Spiro T. Agnew, "Announcement of Requests Included in '69 Capital Budget," January 8, 1968, University of Maryland, Hornbake Library, Maryland Room, Papers of Spiro T. Agnew, sec. 2.3, box 3, folder 7.

58. Marsh, *Agnew*, 67.

59. Witcover, *White Knight*, 159.

60. Spiro T. Agnew, "Statement on King Memorial Services," April 6, 1968, University of Maryland, Hornbake Library, Maryland Room, Papers of Spiro T. Agnew, sec. 2.3, box 3, folder 83.

61. Oswald Johnson, "Agnew Signs, Praises Open Housing Bill," *Baltimore Sun*, April 22, 1967, B1.

62. Richard Homan, "Agnew Signs Far-Reaching Bills on Constitution, Racial Marriage," *Washington Post*, March 25, 1967.

63. Witcover, *White Knight*, 162–163.

64. Spiro T. Agnew, letters to Congressmen Harvey Machen and Edward Gormatz concerning HR 1100, April 4, 1968, University of Maryland, Hornbake Library, Maryland Room, Papers of Spiro T. Agnew, sec. 2.1, box 1, folder 11.

65. "Unlikely No. 2," *Time*, August 16, 1968, pp. 19–20.

66. Spiro T. Agnew, interoffice communications on Judge Bowie matter, January 1968, University of Maryland, Hornbake Library, Maryland Room, Papers of Spiro T. Agnew, sec. 2.1, box 2, folder 21.

67. Spiro T. Agnew, "Gov's Telegram to Lally and Pomerleau re: Negro Shooting," July 15, 1968, University of Maryland, Hornbake Library, Maryland Room, Papers of Spiro T. Agnew, sec 2.3, box 3, folder 188.

68. Gilbert Ware, confidential interoffice memo, "Sensenbaught and School Desegregation: Reaction rather than Action at the Top," August 24, 1967, University of Maryland, Hornbake Library, Maryland Room, Papers of Spiro T. Agnew, sec. 2.1, box 2, folder 20.

69. Witcover, *White Knight*, 159.

70. Marsh, *Agnew*, 27.

71. "Agnew Criticizes Disobedience," *Annapolis Evening Capital*, July 31, 1968.

72. Ibid.

73. Spiro T. Agnew, "Statement to Baltimore County Human Relations Commission," December 9, 1963, University of Maryland, Hornbake Library, Maryland Room, Papers of Spiro T. Agnew, sec 1.3, box 1, folder 13.

74. Witcover, *White Knight*, 10–16.

75. Spiro T. Agnew, "Statement on Bowie State College," March 30, 1968, University of Maryland, Hornbake Library, Maryland Room, Papers of Spiro T. Agnew, sec. 2.3, box 3, folder 74.

76. Marsh, *Agnew*, 43.

77. "Shooting of Riot Looters Gets Approval of Agnew," *Baltimore News American*, 1968.

78. Particularly following the King riots, the urban-suburban divide was enhanced by powerful representations of the city as chaotic and dangerous space that sharply contrasted with the orderliness and idyllic space of the suburb. Security and safety were integral to the mid-twentieth-century suburban concept, and thus policies that can encourage suburbanization, such as zoning and highway expansion, can be understood as efforts to create a securer and safer society.

79. Risen, *A Nation on Fire*, 241.

80. Ibid., 225.

81. A helpful selection of the statements Agnew made to cultivate this image is *Frankly Speaking: A Collection of Extraordinary Speeches* (Washington: Public Affairs Press, 1969).

82. Risen, *A Nation on Fire*, 241.

6
Thomas Carney
Oral History

Thomas Carney, who currently works in public health and bioinformatics, was a freshman at the University of Maryland–Baltimore County and living with his family in southwest Baltimore at the time of the 1968 riots. His interview richly describes life in this white working-class neighborhood in mid-twentieth-century Baltimore and the impact of the riot and its aftermath, as well as the broader social changes of the 1960s, on the neighborhood. Carney is an especially thoughtful narrator: focusing on the riot as a moment that "changes you forever," he carefully juxtaposes a description of his experiences coming of age in the 1960s with his mature assessment of those experiences.

Shannon Chorba, a student at the University of Baltimore at the time of the interview, and Alison Carney, also a UB student and Carney's wife, interviewed him on October 28 and December 5, 2006.

I grew up in a row home in the middle of the 600 block of Scott Street, with my sister, my father, and my mother, in an area that is known colloquially as Pigtown. It was an area of the community with a lot of factories. My father, my uncles all worked in factories. The people who lived there lived there to be close to work. It was a racially divided area, not integrated, as we describe integration. There were certain streets where blacks lived, and there were certain streets where whites lived. The [white] area was divided by Catholics, non-Catholics, Germans, Italians, and Irish. The different areas were all self-contained; the stores you would shop in met the criteria of your ethnic background. Every little neighborhood had a saloon on the corner of some main street; and inside that saloon members of the same religion and same ethnic background communed every evening. All day on Fridays and Saturdays, when the paychecks came in. I lived in the Irish sector of Pigtown, bounded on the west by Route 1, which was Washington Boulevard. Route 1 was a major access route in and out of the city prior to the building of Interstate 95. On the west side it was bounded by another large street, Monroe Street. Our backs were against the harbor, which is now the center of downtown Baltimore.

As with most families, ours was very close. My mother was one of ten children; my father was one of three children. My aunt, who was my father's sister, lived five minutes away, three streets away. My mother's youngest sister lived at the end of the same street that we lived on, probably four blocks away. Another sister lived two streets away at the other end of the same street. We saw each other almost daily. We all went to the same church. Many of my other aunts and uncles had moved from the area, but they moved to other areas of the city close to where those that they had chosen to marry had lived. They still worked inside of our community, still worked inside the same factory where they had worked as teenagers and young adults, so they had never really left the area. My cousins and aunts and uncles were always coming through our house; in fact, we lived in the house that was my grandfather's and grandmother's, so it became the meeting place, the stopping place on a daily basis for all the extended family.

Everyone went to separate schools. There was a Catholic school for each neighborhood. The German community had their Catholic school if they were Catholic and their public school if they were non-Catholic. There were no blacks in the Catholic schools.[1]

On many occasions, being a white child, a white teenager, I saw members of the African American community but never interacted with them. They lived on streets that we bypassed; and we bypassed by direction. Their fathers and mothers were those who did the cleaning chores, the sweeping, the trash removal in the factories. They also worked in some of the stores in the neighborhood doing some of the same activities. In fact, there was a grocer that my mother frequented, that my cousin worked for, called Jake's. Jake Franz, who was a butcher and a grocer, was out of the German Catholic community, and his delivery service was provided by a young black male by the name of Reggie. And my interaction with Reggie was letting him in and out of the door and giving him his tip when he delivered our groceries on Saturday. For the most part we did not wave, we did not speak, we did not have any social or communal action with the members of the opposite race at all. In fact we rarely, if ever, spoke to non-Catholics. It was a very ethnically controlled community, and you tried to date, meet, greet, and socialize, as you were asked to do, by your heritage.

My memories for the most part are of being very happy as a child. I liked the fact that I could have a hundred friends in a three-block area. You could play any sport, play cowboys and Indians. There was a very large park, Carroll Park, which housed the Carroll Mansion, named after one of the founders of the country, if you believe history. In that park we could swim, we could play baseball, we could play basketball, we could play any game that we wanted. The interesting thing about the park was that even though it was given to the city, it was not given to all the occupants of the city. It was a strictly white-used park. The time frame of this was the early to mid-1950s when legislation was being talked about but not being enacted.[2]

The path to the park took us past black streets. Again, we did not walk down those streets; we walked past those streets, and those individuals did not greet us, and we did not greet them. Knowing what streets not to go down was handed down much like the secrets of families. It is part of what we do in America. It is part of the unspoken racism rather than the outspoken, blatant racism. As you were leaving the house you were asked where you were going. When you delivered the response, you were asked, "Do you know how to get there?" "Do you know how to get there?" was not a question that sought out whether you knew the directions; it sought that you knew the path. And the path was [making your way around] those streets where nonwhites lived and in many cases, non-Catholics. It was passed down in the secret way when you observed behaviors, when you took walks as a child with your parents and you observed the streets that they took, the directions that they took.

My father was very adamant about doing things his way. There was no second way. He was less than open, he was less than agreeable about socializing with members of the opposite communities, meaning the black communities or even the non-Catholic communities. If he heard, saw, that you had such communications, such socializing, to use the words of the day, you were grounded. Our community, much like many communities, had its own little network. Relatives lived in close proximity, and they saw your behavior, friends of theirs saw your behavior, members of the church saw your behavior; the eyes and ears were out and about. So if you happened to have a conversation or engaged in a game with someone other than a white Irishman or a white German—because my family is a little bit of both—your parents knew about it before you got home, and there was questioning; there was a reckoning. The reckoning was usually my father telling you to "knock it off." And if you did not "knock it off," there was punishment to follow, which was usually physical.

And the hordes of relatives and friends in the neighborhood were there to keep the process in place. They expected our family to do the same for them. The networking was essential to keeping it white, keeping it Catholic, and keeping it safe. And my mother was really the mayor of the neighborhood. She was the one with the eyes and the ears that controlled the traffic, directed the responses, and ran a very elegant and efficient network. She had the phone lines going, simply because she knew everything going on in the neighborhood. She worked at the school library, she worked at the parish house for the priests, and she worked inside the church. There was probably no one in the community that she didn't know, whose parents she didn't know, whose ethnic background she didn't know, who they were seeing, why they were there, what streets they walked down. She was the master of the communications network.

This is how they lived. This is the way they sought to control their environment. No matter how restrictive it was, this is what made sense to them. They had no alternatives. They lived out of fear. They were not well-educated people. My father at fourteen was forced to quit high school; he went out to work to earn a living to pay for his mother and his two siblings. In fact, at some point, due to the lack of money, he had to move in with another family a few blocks away from where his mother lived. In a very true sense, he was entirely angry at the world and at the hand he was dealt. He was angry at everyone who got a place in front of him; be it white, black, male, or female. He was very outgoing and very generous to my cousins and to anyone who did not have what we had, which was not a lot. But for the children inside of the family, and for his own wife, he was extremely, extremely controlling; and would only allow those things that he approved to ever enter their front door. It was the only way he—and others in the neighborhood—could control their environment and not allow those outside, who they feared would take their jobs and bypass them, to gain a foothold in their community.

Then, in the late 1950s and early 1960s, as the war spending had run its course,[3] the neighborhood started to change. What happens is two things. There were two major factories. There was Koppers Company, which was a company that my father worked for; it supplied mostly parts for trains and wheels, large assemblies called couplings, which connect trains, car to car. The other company was Revere Copper and Brass. At some point after the war, there was less military spending, fewer guns, fewer tanks, all those things. This created a loss of jobs inside those factories, and they start laying people off. They go elsewhere for jobs, and they pick up and they move out of that neighborhood to wherever their job is. What happens then is more black families start moving in to the neighborhood. Where they were restricted by the community to one street, now they are on multiple streets, now they're on the street that we're in. The neighborhood became more and more racially mixed, not really racially integrated but racially mixed. It evolved slowly over time, until blacks came to predominate. And their families sought jobs in the area also. One of the things that happened is that that the factories started laying off people who had many years of experience and vacations built up and sought to hire behind them people who would work for less money and poorer wages and poorer conditions—which in many cases meant black males and black females were taken advantage of.

With that began a set of behaviors in our neighborhood which were adversarial at best. Blacks now emerged onto the streets that were white. They would walk those streets as if they were the owners of those streets in the eyes of the white person. They were gaining a voice. Martin Luther King was out there. The civil rights movement was active. And with his marches, they marched. They marched down the streets that before they could not walk down. That was their demonstration. White people fled back inside their homes.

As the neighborhood began to change racially, it also started to change philosophically. The "Old Joes," who were my father and the white males who were in charge of all the activities and all the community events, were being bypassed by their sons and their daughters. Their world had changed—the culture of the paternal white father was gone. Their cooks, their cleaners, and their sweepers were now out on the streets saying, "No more. We are not doing this anymore. We are not going down this road ever again." And their sons and their daughters had heard and seen the president get shot, had seen Lee Harvey Oswald get murdered on TV.[4] Their white children were being drafted and sent off to Vietnam to die. [Their sons and daughters] had started to hear a different history by getting away from the local schools and going to high schools outside the neighborhood. They had seen people who were still Catholic, in my case, but who had other ideas and other ways of describing the events that were in front of them. In essence we stopped believing in the ways of our fathers. We stopped believing that it was only good if it was white and was only good if it was Irish, if you will.

I had Italian friends, I had German friends, I had friends of many different ethnic backgrounds at my high school.[5] Unfortunately, we had only one black student. But I was very lucky. His last name was Brown, and my last name was Carney, and he sat in front of me for four years in every class because we were arranged alphabetically. So we became friends. He had told me stories about his family that did two things: One, I realized that they were just like my family. They had the same fears, the same hopes, the same dreams. And two, he had the same imagination and the same mental capacity, he had the same learning instincts [as the white students]. And with that, the world of the white master, in my case my father, began to shatter.

Through all this, I wasn't really concerned. Honestly, I really wasn't afraid because I thought, "I didn't do anything to them." I had this white amnesty thing going on. I started UMBC[6] the fall of 1967, and that was the beginning of an eye-opening experience for me that probably has never stopped. It was the first time I had been with a diverse population of kids my age, many of whom were not Catholic. I saw my first hippie, saw the first large group of black students. There were antiwar protesters; there were students who were part of the civil rights movement. I saw mixed professors; some tall, some short, not dressed uniformly; some black, some white, females, males; any combination. Not nuns or brothers, no one of the cloth, as we say. And that was an eye-opening experience. I remember the first day of college I showed up in a shirt and a tie, a sports coat, a pair of slacks, and dress shoes, like I would have every day in high school. People looked at me like I was from Mars. They didn't get me and I didn't get them. Later on, I certainly understood more and more as I listened, as I went to classes and had conversations with different students why they were the way they were, why they dressed the way they dressed, and why they believed the way they believed. But in the beginning it was very disconcerting to me, and it was a fearful experience. Simply because they were different, they were alien. They were saying words that I never said, thoughts that I never heard, and they were listening to a vastly different music than I ever listened to.

By the time of King's assassination, there were many forces at play, coming out of the roots of an America that I had never heard of: NAACP [National Association for the Advancement of Colored People], CORE [Congress of Racial Equality], the Student Nonviolent Coordinating Committee [SNCC]. Names like Rap Brown. I had heard of Martin Luther King, but Eldridge Cleaver, the Black Panthers, Jerry Garcia, Jimi Hendrix were people that I knew nothing about because those waves of information had never made it into my neighborhood.[7] So I was almost an infant again. I was learning about a culture that had begun to exist with a passion in the mid-1960s and was beginning to grow into a fury.

I remember a number of things about King's assassination and then when the riots first broke out. I remember being in school, and I remember coming home. My sister, who was still living at home at the time, was working in a department store in downtown Baltimore after school, and she came home and said turn on the TV, that Martin Luther King had been shot. My father, who owned the only TV, said, "What station? What station?" We turned it on and the riots had not started yet. But the news of the shooting was sweeping across the country. A few hours later it was confirmed that he had died.

I didn't know what to expect. The next day was Friday and it's not to be insensitive, but I had school. So I went off to school, and it started to strike me there. There was a group of black students that I actually had become friends with and had spent a lot of time with. They had taught me to play a card game called tonk, and I used to sit down between classes in the student union—it was the only building on campus at the time, other than the classroom building—and just mess around and play this game.

But they were all crying, they were all upset. I didn't know why they were upset. I didn't understand, I didn't feel it at that time. I went over and asked them what was wrong, and they told me that Martin Luther King had been killed, and didn't I understand. I didn't understand, and I went and sat down at another table. It was the last time I ever sat with them.

Half the campus was crying and very upset, and the other part of the campus was like me. They didn't understand, they were there to go to classes. Since it was only the second year that that college was formed and having classes, there was no organized anything. People knew each other but were drifting from class to class. There was nothing the college was doing, there was nothing anybody was doing, to have a sounding board for feelings. There were no microphones, there were no rallies. It was just a bunch of people who were upset with good reason and people who didn't understand why they were upset. It was even more chaotic for me than normal because I sort of understood why people were upset, but I didn't understand the alien feeling that they had, which was don't talk to me, get away, stay away.

The neighborhood was as it was before. It was still asleep. People came and went to work; cars drove up and down the street. Every now and then you would hear a police car, a fire engine. But the church, which was down the street, had its normal services. It was the beginning of Holy Week, I remember, so there was a lot of bustle about the grocery stores. And people shopping for the food for the week. Things like that. There was nothing that was odd that day—I speak of the day afterwards [Friday, April 5]. I'm sure people were talking about it all over the place. But the paper was delivered; the milk was there. In many cases it was just another day.

It was about to change obviously, with the riots, which had probably already begun in at least Washington, D.C., Detroit.[8] But probably as those reports started on the news and people thought about it—especially people inside the black community thought about it, understood, and started to move from sorrow to anger—it began to change. Phone calls, I remember the phone ringing in our house almost constantly. Someone who was a relative who was in an area that started to see problems would call and say, "Be careful," would give us warnings. My aunt Ellen called my mother and told her, "Take your stockings out and tie them to the antenna of your car and no one will touch it, no one will fire bomb your car." She and my uncle George lived in an area that was just north and west of Johns Hopkins Hospital, over where there was beginning to be a problem, where mostly people from the black community were beginning to get out on the street and demonstrate their anger, their sorrow, their own fears, if you will. So, that is where probably one of the earliest "Get out of your house! Show your anger; show your sorrow!" demonstrations started. And my aunt probably had heard it in the stores, on the streets, that if you tie a stocking, a silk stocking, a nylon stocking to your antenna of your car, they would not burn it, they would not destroy it. So she was passing it on. And my own mother, as I said, being the mayor, started calling people and then she would get calls back. The communication network started.

When things came to a head it was like being in a room with a stereo and someone turns up the volume higher and higher and higher and higher and higher until it starts reverberating on you. There were so many reports on the radio. There were so many reports on television, so many phone calls. People coming to the house saying, "They're rioting and it's close." And it was physically close, but it was never physically in our neighborhood. We know that there was rioting and demonstrating as close as Fremont Avenue, but that was a predominately black community street. We didn't go up that street, as I spoke before. And it had traveled across parts of Monroe Street, which bounded us on one side. It was on the other side of downtown Baltimore, on Gay Street, which was a very, very involved area in the beginning. So it was very close. It wasn't in our neighborhood, but it was very close.[9] There was a calm but also a sense of foreboding that something big and something very bad was about to happen. Or was beginning to happen and the place to be was inside. So pretty much we stayed inside. We received a call from our aunt Betty who lived down the street from us. She told us that her son, my cousin, Joseph's National Guard unit had been called up, and he had been told to report at the Fifth Regiment Armory, where all the National Guards were being deployed from.[10] So when it starts getting inside of your family like that, the tension does build. So it had already hit my uncle George and aunt Ellen, and my cousin had been called up, and it was in our area. What I remember is just endless phone calls, endless sirens, endless noises of fire engines.

You could smell it in the air. You could just smell it—all the burning, all the smoke in the air. No matter where you were, it was wafting across the city. I remember it being a very windy, windy evening. I remember looking out and seeing all the nylon stockings that people had tied to their antennas blowing in the wind. And probably the biggest thing I remember the most is just being scared. Not being able to come to grips with the issues that made so many people so angry. I was ignorant to it; I was completely ignorant to it. But I knew they were angry. And you started seeing some live reports of buildings burning. I remember seeing the reports, and then a few hours later national TV started picking up the things that were going on in Detroit, Washington, D.C., and Baltimore. It's funny but I think my fear turned to embarrassment at that point because your city is on national TV for something like this. It's crazy the way a teenager's mind works, but two years before, the Orioles had won the World Series, and I was thinking, "Boy, that was great!" And here we are two years later and our cities are burning. So, it was a lot of feelings, but mostly you sit and hope that it goes past you and it doesn't hang around very long. You don't know what it is and how angry these people are, but you know it's something you can't touch. It's almost a helpless feeling.

On Monday, believe it or not, schools were opened. Factories were opened. I don't know if state or local office buildings were open. But I do know that my father went to work—wasn't no damn rioter stopping him from going anywhere. And I went to school. But there was almost no one there. There weren't many transit buses—I took a transit bus because I didn't have a license—and I know there was nobody on it. And I thought, "Wow, this is weird." And there was almost no one on campus, so I turned around and went home.[11]

The stores in my neighborhood pretty much stayed open. Most of the people who owned them lived in my neighborhood. The National Guard and my cousin had the easternmost boundary of Washington Boulevard, where it butts up against Camden Yards now. He was down there with his National Guard group keeping that road open. There were National Guardsmen all the way across the Boulevard, all the way to Monroe Street, keeping anybody from coming down any of the other side streets. I was about two blocks away from where the National Guardsmen with bayonets were. I think in that environment the shop owners felt safe. They knew that nobody was going to attack them there, that they would have had to get past the National Guardsmen, and they were blocking access.

I think my mother felt better knowing the National Guard was present. And I'll tell you a funny story about my mother. She wanted me to walk with her on Sunday afternoon because she was going up to where my cousin was positioned to take him lunch, which you can't quite do because they are in the army. She was fine, she wasn't scared, and she wasn't afraid. I think she made a point of talking to as many of the National Guardsmen as she could, reminding them that we lived at 603 Scott Street, two blocks down and in the middle of the block. Things like that, making small talk with them, hoping that they are okay. I think it was good for her to see that she was protected, if you will. Not that they could have stopped them if the rioters had decided to come down our way, but at least it gave her some sense of safety. And again, it was more for the communication network and the phone calls she could make when she returned home about what she saw, and who was out there, and all the troop trucks that were parked at the end out our street, and that they were letting off National Guardsmen, and they were tall, and things like that.

There were points in time where I thought the neighborhood wasn't going to be safe. It comes from nothing that I saw firsthand. It comes from the news reports and the phone calls. It comes from all those things, where you just don't think that you are going to be spared. Let me go back and give you a time when I had a similar feeling. During the Cuban missile crisis[12] we were pulled out of classes more than once in a day. All of a sudden we were told to line up—the bell would ring and we would all hustle over to the basement of the church. We knew it was about the Cuban missile crisis, but we never found out what triggered these things. As we were walking across this long school yard to the church, planes were flying overhead and I thought they were going to bomb us. I thought they were the attack planes from somewhere, from Russia, from Cuba, who knew? This was it—we're done. I think the same was true with the riots. I think they were getting closer and closer, the smell, the smoke was all that you could smell at that time, there was no fresh air. It was in your clothes. The sirens, of course, the bayonets, of course. I thought this was war. I thought at any moment thousands of angry black rioters were going to be coming down our streets. I don't think you could avoid feeling that way unless you were totally removed from the city. The voices were angrier and the voices on television were angrier. The politicians were pleading and getting no result. When it seems like all authority has lost control, what then would stop them? I don't know of anything that would've stopped them had they decided to come down our street. But they didn't. So it was a helpless feeling, an alone feeling even inside of your house.

The National Guard probably was effective in that they allowed the rioters to see some level of law enforcement on the streets that was not the police. It's okay to look back and say, "Yeah, they hated the police," but in those days I didn't understand the hate, I didn't understand the abuse the black community went through at the hands of the police. Looking back—the National Guard was placed at places that said, "You don't go past this line because there are white homes on the other side of this line. You want to burn your own stuff, you have a great time." Sort of the racist basis of the city and the state at that time. But I don't think they were armed with anything other than bayonets.[13] I think their effectiveness was only that they created an aura of "we mean business," and there was some crowd control, but the riots went on at least forty-eight hours after they deployed the National Guardsmen. So what effect they had is they were able to guard the policemen and guard the firemen who were putting out the fires. But as far as being able to control the rioters, the black communities, to quell the anger, no, they were useless. There was no power in this country at that time that would've been effective. I know this now but did not know this then. I am speaking with some separation and some experience—I would never have ever thought this in the middle of this situation. The anger of being a second-class citizen and the anger of being pushed into a ghetto economically severed from the rest of the country is an anger that bullets don't stop, and guns don't stop, and bayonets don't stop. Even though Congress had passed the Civil Rights Act of 1965 stating that everyone was equal in this country,[14] everyone had the same rights, and everyone had the same rights to education, the world of the Orval Faubuses and the George Wallaces still was in place.[15]

The National Guard stood in a place and said, "Don't come down this road!" and whether or not the humans came down that road the anger did, the outrage did. Nor do I think the police made a difference. Not that they didn't go out there and try, not that they weren't brave, not that they didn't go out there when they were shot at and having things thrown at them.[16]

I'm not a fan of Governor Agnew. I never was. But I think what his response to the riots demonstrated to me is an unfailing desire to blame somebody else for that which he didn't take care of. He called the black leaders into his office and went after them with some very belligerent language: This is all your fault for not being able to control your people. You are responsible for the deaths and you are responsible for this.[17] The fact is who was responsible for it—again a fact I know now that I didn't know back then—was all the white people who didn't include black people in the government, in society, in just the mix of this country. But Agnew certainly profited by his response, because he became vice president. Without understanding the divide that was already there, he widened it.

The media at the time was biased. There were three major black radio stations in the Baltimore area. I listened to them because I like soul music. I listened to Motown and Southern soul music a lot. And it was an interesting difference between WBAL, which is probably the flagship station of Baltimore, and the black stations. The black stations were trying to calm their populations. They really were. They were talking about "Let's focus on what Martin Luther King meant. He was a non-violent man, and we are not honoring his legacy by doing this." I think the typical white station was saying, "We are reporting the news here. Angry Negro mobs." And angry this and angry that and talking about—when I say this I don't mean to slight the police—the brave police. And the overwhelming job they had to do, and the overwhelming responsibility of the mayor, Thomas D'Alesandro.[18] The overwhelming responsibility of Governor Agnew. They were a part of the power elite. They were going to speak to who was in charge and say they did the right stuff.

As for the national news, it was just reporting the riots as a five- to ten-minute blip along with all of the other news it had to report—what was going on in Moscow, what was going on in East Germany and West Germany, and all those other things you get into an hour's news. But the local news was all over it. Local news, I remember, would cut in to all of the TV programs. Every half hour there would be news, this is going on, this is going on, as if it were a blizzard or a nuclear attack. They would have spot reports come on, especially when they called up the National Guard and then the federal troops—those kinds of things. And I think most of the story from the national side was on the assassination of Dr. King, the potential identification of who the assassin was, where it was, what time of day it was. The focus was on this enormous human inside the country who had just been killed. But locally the riots were everything. They probably talked two hours about the riots and ten minutes actually about Dr. King. Because King's not the story, your city is burning is the story.

Immediately after the riots, everything just calmed down. Everybody just tried to go about their way of life and sort of forget that it happened. Myself, I was finishing out my last semester of my first year of college. I had my own ideas about what I was going to do and where I was going to do it. I think the biggest thing I was looking forward to was getting out of the neighborhood, getting out of the area. I didn't know where I was going. But I was ready to leave it all behind. I found out that I had erred in the process of dropping a class, which made me not a full-time student, at which point I was in receipt of letter congratulating me on the fact that I was able to serve in the United States military. I got drafted and exercised my right not to join them in their party going on in Southeast Asia. So with that I left my parents' home and proceeded to spend the summer in Ocean City, which was a place where many of the locals went for the summer. I then went to Loyola College and never looked back.

I don't think my parents' lives changed at all after the riots. St. Jerome's, their church, didn't change immediately, but it changed over time. What changed in my case and the case of many of my parents' friends was many of the people who went to St. Jerome's, the children of the people who were the cornerstone of that church, of that neighborhood, left the neighborhood, so as the parents passed away there was no legacy left. There was no one left in the city that was their child, their cousin, their nephew; they were all gone. I returned to the neighborhood after I was married, and my wife and I moved to an area very close by to where my parents lived. It had changed absolutely radically. In that time period, which spanned twenty to twenty-five years, the factories had not only closed, they were no longer there. The population had become predominately African American as the whites who were there moved out to follow the jobs. The houses were sold for very little money. My parents' house was sold in the early nineties, after they passed away, for a few thousand dollars. The neighborhood had gone down economically. There was a lot of crime in the area. At the time I went back with my wife, I think it was probably five to ten minutes between sirens. There was a lot of vandalism, a lot of boarded-up homes. It had been a lower-middle-class neighborhood and stable. Businesses in my childhood enjoyed being open. They enjoyed the clientele and they obviously did enough business to stay in business. The people who inhabited the neighborhood enjoyed going to those businesses. There was not a recognizable face when I went back; any store that had been there was not there any more. They were all gone.

But I don't believe that simply looking at the effects of what happened on the neighborhood tells the whole story. A neighborhood shows the symptoms and shows the injuries and the bruises and the scars of everything that happens when the business owner, the man in charge, the white guy, if you will, decides he is going to take his chips and move somewhere else. All those people who depend on that business, who depend on that income, who depend on that revenue must follow the business if the business leaves, unless another business comes in. Post-1968, that didn't happen.

The angriness and the outrage calmed down over time, but it was allowed to grow anew. It became a splintered country. It was a splintered country around women's rights; it was splintered around equality of African Americans and other minorities. It was about the Vietnam War. As a result, the majority of white voters went to the polls and elected Richard Nixon president.[19] So as Nixon becomes president, you have an extended period of continued white power, of continued white interest—it just keeps going and going.

All we do is move around the inequality. We continue to maneuver and manipulate around the system that does not give equality. We've never to this day said, "You're an equal. Come be part of us." Until we do that, I don't think we'll ever make any inroads into the inequalities that we have created simply because we riot or simply because we burn some buildings. Until we get the opportunity to share in the wealth and share in the power, it won't happen.

The riots absolutely affected me personally. I think it's one of those things you don't know at the time but it changes you forever. Prior to the riots, as I said earlier, life was great. It was about being white. It was about being Catholic. It was about living in a neighborhood, going to the church that was five minutes away. It was about going to the school that was five minutes away, surrounded by my friends and my family. For probably fifteen years, this is what I thought life was all about. Then with the assassination of President Kennedy, followed by seeing a human shot live on TV—Lee Harvey Oswald. And Vietnam is going on. All of these things weren't supposed to happen. Your childhood is supposed to be calm and peaceful and caring. I began to realize there was a different world out there. Life wasn't bounded by the little streets I walked down and the little streets that I played on. There was another world out there that I was completely and utterly ignorant of.

I think that what the riots did, more than anything, is got my attention and got inside of my psyche and my fear and made me pay attention to a lot of things. From the time of the riots, which was sometime in April, to the point where I had been drafted by the United States military, my ideas and my sensibilities and my passions all changed. I realized that there was a lot of wrong going on. I didn't know how to stop it. I didn't know where to begin, but I knew I wanted to be part of stopping it. It was just dead wrong. And so, I changed my outlook. I changed my views. I realized that many of the people we revered as politicians were actually telling us other than the truth. Many of the people that we believed in as good and holy people were telling us other than the truth. Whole systems we had set up in the country were doing that which the powers wanted them to do as opposed to what they were supposed to do or needed to do. They were paying lip service to equality. They were paying lip service to helping. The people in charge made it appear that we are concerned, and we are doing something about this problem. In fact, the opposite was true.

I once said to a professor in college that probably the most insidious thing that happened during this whole period was all these things not only got inside of your head but they got inside of your family; they got inside of your heart and your soul; and you were making determinations for the rest of your life of what's right, what's wrong, what's correct, what's not correct. You grow up to believe that authority is good, the police are good, the army is good, that they are your safety net, they are looking out for you. And then you realize there is a whole population in this country that they are not looking out for, that they don't care one whit about. And those things come to a reckoning when you see something like the riot happen. You realize subliminally but you realize it nevertheless, what I said before: how can somebody be so angry, what did somebody do to make them so angry? Because that number of people just don't walk around that angry, that's just not going to happen [without some reason]. So it triggered in me to go find out why. What happened? What really happened? What is this all about? Who are these people? Who is Medgar Evers?[20] Who is Martin Luther King? Who are these people who are getting shot in front of their homes or getting shot in front of their hotel rooms? And who's shooting them? Why are they shooting them? Why do we just decide one day, if I don't agree with someone I get to shoot them? I thought for a long time the country was going to split, fall apart. Civil war. So it did, it changed me forever, absolutely.

Edited by Linda Shopes

NOTES

1. Baltimore's Catholic schools were officially desegregated in the early 1960s, and it seems that some schools had already been accepting black students. Given the racial patterns of his neighborhood, however, Carney's recollection that the local Catholic schools were all white is probably correct.

2. Carroll Park was originally part of the Mount Clare estate of John Carroll; upon his death, his brother Charles Carroll, known as "the barrister," inherited the property. John and Charles Carroll were distant relatives of the Charles Carroll who signed the Declaration of Independence. In 1890 the city of Baltimore purchased the Mount Clare mansion and twenty acres of the estate from Carroll heirs for use as a public park; it expanded the park through purchase of additional parcels of land

through 1901. Racial practices and policies governing use of park facilities had a long and complicated history. Blacks and whites both used the park's open spaces, though blacks generally kept to the park's eastern areas. Ball fields and tennis courts were open to all on a first come, first serve basis regardless of race, but racially mixed play was not allowed. The wading pool and children's playground were restricted to whites. The park's golf course, established in 1924, was designated for whites only; black golfers and their allies challenged this restriction repeatedly from the 1930s to the 1950s, with mixed results. In the wake of the Supreme Court's landmark *Brown v. Board of Education* decision in 1954, outlawing racial segregation in public schools, the Supreme Court upheld the Fourth Circuit Court of Appeals ruling that Baltimore desegregate its public swimming pools. In 1963 the Maryland General Assembly enacted an open accommodations law, outlawing race-based segregation in restaurants, hotels, theaters, stores, beaches, and recreational facilities in Baltimore and twelve of the state's twenty-three counties. The following year open accommodations were extended to the rest of the state. See James E. Wells, Geoffrey L. Buckley, and Christopher G. Boone, "Separate but Equal? Carroll Park and the Campaign to Desegregate Baltimore's Golf Courses, *Geographical Review* 98, no. 2 (April 2008): 151–170. While Carney's memories of the park as "strictly white-used" are thus not strictly accurate, they probably do reflect quite accurately his perceptions and experience.

3. Military spending for World War II had been particularly pronounced in Baltimore with Glenn L. Martin's Middle River aircraft manufacturing complex and Bethlehem Steel's Sparrows Point plant in production around the clock. Smaller industrial operations such as those in Pigtown would have benefited from the war production and would have suffered when operations wound down.

4. President John F. Kennedy was shot and killed on November 22, 1963, while riding in a motorcade in Dallas, Texas. His alleged assassin, Lee Harvey Oswald, was murdered by Dallas nightclub owner Jack Ruby as he was being escorted to a car for transfer from a Dallas police station to the Dallas County Jail. Oswald's transfer was broadcast live on national television; hence millions watched his murder as it happened. Here Carney is implying that these two events were profoundly disillusioning to young Americans, including Kennedy's fellow Catholics, who had been inspired by his youth, energy, and glamour.

5. Carney attended Mount Saint Joseph High School in Baltimore.

6. UMBC is the initialism for the University of Maryland–Baltimore County, founded in 1966 as part of the University System of Maryland.

7. H. Rap Brown (1943–) and Eldridge Cleaver (1935–1995) were well-known black activists of the 1960s, associated with the militant Black Panther Party. Brown served as chair of the SNCC in 1967–1968 and then became justice minister of the party. Cleaver, author of *Soul on Ice*, served as the party's minister of information. Jerry Garcia (1942–1995) and Jimi Hendrix (1942–1970), both guitarists, were among the most popular rock musicians of the era. Garcia is best known for his long-time association with the band The Grateful Dead; Hendrix is recognized as among the greatest electric guitarists of all time.

8. Rioting broke out in Washington, D.C., on Thursday night, April 4, the day of King's assassination. By the next day, rioting was taking place in dozens of cities around the country, including Detroit.

9. In this and the previous paragraph, Carney's chronology and locations are not entirely accurate. No significant incidents of rioting or other social disorder

occurred in Baltimore on "the evening after the death of Martin Luther King"—that is, on Friday, April 5. Unrest began in earnest in the late afternoon of the next day, Saturday, April 6. While Carney is correct in stating that these early disturbances were centered along Gay Street in the eastern part of the city, which is where Johns Hopkins Hospital is located, significant unrest did not move to the west side of the city, where Carney lived, until Sunday, April 7. Rioting along Fremont Avenue was not reported until Monday, April 8.

10. Maryland governor Spiro Agnew placed the Maryland National Guard on standby on Friday, April 5. He activated the Guard, headquartered at the Fifth Regiment Armory, shortly after 10:00 P.M. on Saturday, April 6, two hours after he had declared an official state of emergency.

11. Declaring Monday, April 8, an official day of mourning for Martin Luther King, Mayor Thomas D'Alesandro III ordered Baltimore city schools and city offices closed on that day. Schools and offices reopened on Tuesday, though many students and workers remained home a few days. Whether UMBC remained open throughout is unclear.

12. The Cuban missile crisis, occurring in the fall of 1962, was a Cold War confrontation between the United States and the Soviet Union after U.S. intelligence learned the Soviets were constructing missile bases in Cuba, within striking distance of the United States. Expecting military confrontation, the United States blocked delivery of Soviet weapons to Cuba and demanded that existing missile bases be dismantled and all offensive weapons removed. The crisis was resolved peacefully when the Soviets agreed to U.S. demands in return for certain concessions. The crisis is generally recognized as the time when Cold War tensions came closest to erupting into nuclear war.

13. Although federal troops carried live ammunition, they had been ordered not to load their weapons and to refrain from shooting looters in order to avert the large number of fatalities that had occurred during riots in Detroit and Newark the previous year.

14. Carney seems to be conflating two pieces of federal legislation. The Civil Rights Act of 1964 outlawed unequal application of voter registration requirements, racial segregation in schools and public accommodations, and employment discrimination by race (and sex). The National Voting Rights Act of 1965 prohibited discrimination in the exercise of voting rights.

15. Orval Faubus (1910–1994) and George Wallace (1919–1998) were nationally prominent segregationist Southern governors during the 1950s and 1960s. Faubus, who served as governor of Arkansas from 1955 to 1967, is best known for (unsuccessfully) defying court-ordered desegregation of Little Rock's Central High School in 1957. Wallace, who governed Alabama from 1963 to 1967, again from 1971 to 1979, and again from 1983 to 1987, made his famous stand in front of the doorway to Foster Auditorium at the University of Alabama in 1963 in an (also unsuccessful) attempt to prevent integration at the university. He also ran unsuccessfully for president of the United States four times. Both men came to moderate their racial views in later life.

16. According to the "Report on Baltimore Civil Disorders, April 1968," issued by the Middle Atlantic Region American Friends Service Committee in September 1968, "a policy of preventive deployment [of law enforcement personnel] might have reduced the toll of property damage and arrests." The report goes on to say that "there were well over 10,000 men in Baltimore, who could have been deployed

in such a way as to guard all the ghetto business sections, particularly protecting against looting where windows or doors had been breached" (30). As it was, the police and National Guard tended to operate in groups and aimed to contain looting and arson in areas where they had occurred, not protect areas where they had not.

17. Spiro Agnew (1919–1986) served as governor of Maryland from 1967 to 1969. His harsh and critical words to the one hundred moderate black leaders he had summoned to his office the week after King's assassination both angered and alienated the black community. However, his "law and order" stance also catapulted him into national office: he became Richard Nixon's running mate in both the 1968 and 1972 presidential elections; when the ticket won, he served as vice president from 1969 to 1973. He resigned from the office in 1973, just before pleading no contest to charges of tax evasion.

18. Thomas D'Alesandro III (1929–) served as mayor of Baltimore from 1967 to 1971. He chose not to run for a second term.

19. Richard Nixon was elected president of the United States in 1968 and 1972. He served from 1969 to 1974, when he resigned in the face of nearly certain impeachment as a result of his participation in the cover-up of Republican operatives' effort to break into Democratic Party headquarters at the Watergate Hotel in Washington, D.C. See note 17.

20. Medgar Evers (1925–1963) was a World War II veteran, civil rights activist, and the NAACP's first Mississippi field secretary. He was murdered outside his home in Jackson, Mississippi, by Byron De La Beckwith (1920–2001), a member of the White Citizens' Council and the Ku Klux Klan. Twice all-white juries failed to reach a verdict in De La Beckwith's murder trials. In 1994 new evidence led to a third trial and De La Beckwith's conviction of first-degree murder and subsequent sentence of life imprisonment.

7

"Church People Work on the Integration Problem"

The Brethren's Interracial Work in Baltimore, 1949–1972

Jessica I. Elfenbein

While the 1950s and 1960s are not always remembered as the golden age of interracial and interfaith work in American urban history,[1] this chapter shows how the Church of the Brethren, a small, historically white, rural, and pacifist Protestant denomination, helped lead innovative interracial and faith-based work in Baltimore during those critical years. The Brethren undertook bold and progressive faith-based efforts in Baltimore. Their work from 1949 to 1972 provides a case study of the ways growing social movements, including Black Power, and the civil unrest that followed the assassination of Martin Luther King, Jr., in April 1968, affected urban, integrated, faith-based initiatives. Despite barriers of many kinds, the Brethren's work persisted for more than two decades before it became a direct casualty of the rising tide of racial self-awareness and increasing unwelcome and self-doubt that they and other predominantly white groups working in American inner cities in the late 1960s and early 1970s experienced. To achieve an understanding of the subtleties and nuance of the urban landscape in the second half of the twentieth century, it is critical to examine the role of groups such as the Brethren before, during, and after the jarring events of April 1968. Doing so helps readers understand earlier efforts at addressing urban ills that existed in places such as Baltimore and emanated from faith communities during the modern civil rights era.

The Church of the Brethren began in Germany in the early 1700s. Most followers came to America as religious dissenters by 1740.[2]

Notable for their belief in pacifism, simplicity, and adult baptism, Brethren maintained an antiwar stance until Americans' nearly universal approval of World War II caused them to recast their opposition to war into a more positive propeace stance. In 1947–1948, out of their belief that "a negative stand against war was not enough—that positive Christian action on a world-wide basis could be the only possible foundation for world peace"—the Brethren created the innovative Brethren Volunteer Service (BVS). BVS evolved from the Brethren's war relief work. Designed to offer young people an opportunity to serve humanity for at least a year, BVS volunteers (BVSers) worked on international and domestic projects.[3]

As the national BVS program began, the men's group at Baltimore's First Church of the Brethren (located in the then all-white suburban neighborhood of Liberty Heights in the northwest section of the city) studied the issues and crafted an action plan to help alleviate the effects of systemic racism in inner-city Baltimore. Their awareness, like that of many other middle-class Baltimoreans of the midcentury, was aroused at least in part by a series of articles written by cub reporter Martin Millspaugh that ran in the *Baltimore Evening Sun* in the late 1940s and early 1950s, "What Is Urban Renewal?"[4]

Even as the muckraking articles on aspects of inner-city life were published, a comprehensive and aggressive antiblight program was beginning in Baltimore. G. Yates Cook, a housing inspector who would become the city's leader of housing law enforcement, led a committee of city agencies appointed by the mayor in organizing the Baltimore Plan. It featured legislation that set forth minimum living standards and created the required enforcement agencies, including an independent Housing Court established in 1947 to hear only housing cases.[5] The city assigned a score of police officers to a Sanitation Squad to find outdoor violations. Still, by 1950, even with those extraordinary efforts, the Baltimore Plan and its street level enforcement covered only 5 percent, or 100, of 2,000 blighted city blocks. Slum growth outstripped rehabilitation.

Housing inspector Cook served with a young Jim Rouse on the Mayor's Advisory Committee on Housing Law Enforcement.[6] Here, Rouse suggested a pilot program for the Baltimore Plan, with the goal of eliminating substandard living conditions in a targeted twenty-seven-block area of East Baltimore that had "not yet degenerated into a hopeless slum but in which most of the structures now standing can be made livable and attractive without excessive expense."[7] On the theory that "in neighborhoods where living conditions have been allowed to drop below acceptable standards, every area of municipal government and civic interest is needed in its maximum capacity," the pilot program brought those "Municipal Functions and Public and Private social services together in a single team for the enforcement of their laws and the establishment of their policies." Called the Pilot Program because planners believed it would be "the program that will show the way towards the eventual elimination of the cause of slums," it attracted national attention.[8]

A truly cooperative venture, the Pilot Program featured not only the coordinated efforts of local and federal governments but also the work of nonprofits, most notably citizen groups and faith-based organizations, with Baltimore's First Church of the Brethren at the helm. The men's group at First Church, led by Frank Rittenhouse, conceived Brotherhood Pilot House out of their conviction that "people should not have to live in degrading circumstances in the midst of plenty."[9]

In 1949 members of Baltimore's First Church of the Brethren "decided to do something constructive to help the people who lived in sub-standard housing areas" and formed a nonprofit organization called Brotherhood Service that secured $1,200 for the purchase of a derelict house at 1213 Durham Street, an alley in the heart of the Pilot Program area in East Baltimore. Brotherhood Service had a three-part purpose: "to engage in various forms of social service and religious training in the greater Baltimore area; to help build a better community by the elimination of slums and other unwholesome conditions; [and] to attempt *to minimize racial and religious discrimination, and make the brotherhood of man a reality in community life*."[10] Through Pilot House (as their Durham Street property came to be known), the Brethren offered a variety of programs and services to their neighbors, including Brotherhood Services, a Fresh Air program, and work camps.

Brethren church members and the Maryland Home Builders Association rehabilitated the house as a demonstration project, changing it from a "dilapidated unsanitary four room house" to a "neat modernized six room dwelling" that exceeded housing codes. Pilot House quickly emerged as a model for low-cost housing rehabilitation and modernization efforts.[11] From 1951 until 1954, the Pilot Program was championed as a model of what could happen when a comprehensive effort at urban revitalization was mounted. Not only was the story highlighted in Baltimore; it was carried by newspapers around the country. Fight Blight, Inc., a nonprofit group of Baltimore business leaders, and the Ford Foundation underwrote the cost of a study of the effect of the Pilot Program.[12] As a project of the BVS, Pilot House was staffed by both a paid Brethren director and BVSers coming from throughout the United States. Because Brethren are pacifists and thus (usually) conscientious objectors, Pilot House served as living quarters for young people interested in giving a year or two of service to those in need, as well as for those volunteering in lieu of military service.

Volunteers and staff from the Church of the Brethren locally and nationally worked with community leaders at Pilot House and throughout East Baltimore's Pilot Program area. Viola Jackson, the African American principal of a nearby elementary school and an area resident, chaired the Neighborhood Committee. A program teaching children about the Pilot

Program was promoted at Jackson's school. When a first grader was asked, "Where is the Pilot House?" she answered, "The Pilot House is at 1213 Durham Street. It is the place where you go for any help you need."[13]

The Work

Sociologist Vernon Hoffman and his wife Elsie Hoffman, Brethren professional staffers, led Pilot House for four years, starting in December 1951. As directors, the Hoffmans supervised young BVSers and worked with the community. City inspectors used Pilot House to carry out the city's housing code enforcement program, meeting with homeowners and explaining how housing repairs would improve the neighborhood. Pilot House was nerve central for the referral service that the Hoffmans and the BVSers provided. Area residents were invited to bring their problems to Pilot House. The Hoffmans and the young Brethren volunteers arranged appointments with social agencies or city bureaus and assisted local residents with home repairs and yard work. Proactive and holistic in their approach, the Brethren organized recreational programs including camping trips and "street showers" (sprinklers) for neighborhood children and renovated a community center at Knox Presbyterian, a large African American church in the area.[14]

For the first half of the 1950s, the Brethren remained in East Baltimore. Their contributions were central to the success of the Pilot Program. They spurred positive change in the quality of life in this poor and increasingly African American part of town. Championed as a model of what could happen when a comprehensive effort at urban revitalization was mounted, the success of the Pilot Program was repeatedly touted in articles in the *Evening Sun* and also in stories carried by newspapers around the country. In 1953 Encyclopedia Britannica produced a twenty-two-minute short film, *The Baltimore Plan*, shown in countless movie theaters across the nation before feature films. *The Baltimore Plan* focused largely on the Pilot Program as a replicable model for American cities from coast to coast. Even a decade later, the film was used as a springboard for discussion about fair and decent housing.[15]

Despite all the good intentions of the parties involved, in reality the Pilot Program tried to address the problems of a twenty-seven-square-block area while largely ignoring powerful national policy issues such as the federal government's insidious support of housing segregation through discriminatory highway building, veterans' benefits, and mortgage lending (including redlining), which all harmed established inner-city neighborhoods and favored new suburbs.[16] By 1953, although the Pilot Program area had become "a pleasanter place in which to live, the tendency to run downhill was still there." Despite the good work of the Brethren and others, "the underlying cause[s] of blight—the traffic hazards, overcrowding, zoning exceptions and commercialization—were not changed."[17] The problems the Pilot Program attempted to address at the neighborhood level were not, in fact, endemic. Instead, in East Baltimore, as in other neighborhoods, the attempt at rehabilitation in the 1950s ignored macro forces much bigger than the immediate community. In East Baltimore, as long as the external support provided by the concentration of governmental and nonprofit services (such as the Brethren) existed, the problems of blight—though not solved—were held at bay. Removing those external supports allowed quick neighborhood decline.

The vagaries of federal policy together with the peculiarities of local partisanship caused a change in focus and relocation of blight-fighting activities from East to West Baltimore. The city's response to the new Urban Renewal Administration, established by the federal Housing Act of 1954, effectively killed the Pilot Program. In lieu of continuing efforts on the East side, a mayor's committee selected Harlem Park, an area on the city's west side with two "natural neighborhoods" as the site for Baltimore's first federally funded urban renewal project. In 1956 the Brethren, following the city's lead, refocused their work there, selling the old Durham Street Pilot House and establishing a new one at 1326 West Lafayette Avenue in Harlem Park.

From the start, Brotherhood Pilot House leaders imagined their East Baltimore involvement as temporary. In his first report as president of Brotherhood Service in 1951, Frank Rittenhouse wrote, "When the work in this area has been completed we can retain the house as a low cost rental unit to continue to serve as a model and try another similar dwelling elsewhere in our city."[18] That next move came before the work in East Baltimore was done.

Fresh Air Program

In 1954 just as Pilot House activities on the east side began to wind down, the Brethren in Baltimore began a Fresh Air program called the Hospitality Project to enhance the experience of urban children and to provide the opportunity "*for church people to work on the integration problem.*"[19] The Brethren's rhetoric describing the purposes of their Fresh Air program evolved over time. By 1966 their goal was to make "an underprivileged child part of a rural Christian family life with its ordinary activities of work, recreation and worship. *We believe this program can be effective as a long-range attempt at bridge-building in the area of race relations on a family to family basis.*"[20]

The Fresh Air program (and the work camps that followed) grew out of a historically conservative movement, but in the Brethren's hands it became an unabashedly radical tool for interracial cooperation. The Brethren built on the formula that by the 1960s had been part of the American urban experience for decades. Reflecting the "growing respect for the sacredness of childhood," in the 1870s Fresh Air charities began offering poor urban

Baltimore Pilot House, 1326 West Lafayette Avenue. (Reprinted courtesy of the Brethren Historical Library and Archives.)

children the chance to temporarily escape the "unhealthy" city by providing brief stays in the countryside.[21] Soon there were hundreds of similar programs in northeastern and Midwestern cities.[22] These programs, often sponsored by local newspapers, partnered rural citizens willing to open their homes to "disadvantaged" city children (often at the urging of clergy), urban social service providers who screened children for public health readiness, newspaper readers who provided the requisite financial support, and railroads that transported children from the city to the hinterlands, often at a reduced fare.

The goal of early Fresh Air charities was child saving in the form of the "physical improvement of the poor": it was believed (and early public health research demonstrated) that a fortnight in the countryside had ameliorative effects on poor city children. The hope was that "bodies diseased, enfeebled by poor and insufficient food and foul air" would be benefited by a stay in "better surroundings." Children who participated gained enough weight to protect them from disease through the winter ahead.[23] The children who were placed by most Fresh Air operations between the 1870s and the 1930s were ethnic Europeans, either first- or second-generation immigrants, who then represented "other" in American culture.[24]

By the 1950s it was poor African American children who were the target for the Brethren's Fresh Air program in Baltimore, which greatly deemphasized the old public-health-inspired "child saving" motive and instead

Baltimore Pilot House Project. (Reprinted courtesy of the Brethren Historical Library and Archives.)

focused intensely on building interracial understanding. As was much of the work at Brotherhood Pilot House, organizing the Fresh Air program was done largely by church volunteers through BVS. Brethren volunteers recruited both the urban children *and* rural and suburban host families who for a week invited into their homes "children from Baltimore's Inner City," who "have no place to play that is free from broken bottles and trash. During this week the children become acquainted with life outside the crowded city in clean, happy homes."[25]

BVSers worked with ministers of white, rural congregations (mostly but not exclusively Brethren) and Harlem Park neighborhood children and their parents to find host families and guests. The numbers of both increased over time. In 1961, 97 children visited 74 families, all of whom were located in central, southern, and eastern Pennsylvania.[26] By 1963 the program had grown to 134 children visiting 105 families from 43 different churches. Host families were located in Pennsylvania and on Maryland's Eastern Shore.[27] In 1965, 156 children were sponsored by 118 host families from 47 Brethren congregations.[28] By 1970 more than 200 children (110 of whom were repeaters) went to 135 host families, more than half of whom had hosted previously. That year, though the host families were predominantly Brethren (99), the Brethren coordinated the host families of other faiths, of which twelve were Roman Catholic, six Presbyterian, five Episcopal, and two or three each Quaker, Methodist, Baptist, Lutheran, and other.[29]

Given the Pilot House's 1956 relocation to Harlem Park, not surprisingly most of the Pilot House Fresh Air program's children hailed from West Baltimore. Although the program was open to children ages seven to fourteen, the majority were nine to twelve. A child's parent or guardian made a written application to participate in the Fresh Air program. A twenty-minute home visit, conducted by "interested laymen" was also required. Pilot House provided medical examinations, ensuring that all participating children were in good health. The Brethren carried accident and sickness insurance on all children in the program. Bus transportation was provided early on, waxing and waning over the years. In 1963 host families came to the city to pick up and drop off their young charges at home, after first stopping at Pilot House. In 1970 bus service was provided from Baltimore to York and Lititz, Pennsylvania, for 66 kids and their 53 host families who were "most grateful."[30]

Besides having to trust unknown host families and pass medical exams, many children had to find clothing sufficient for the sojourn away from home. Brethren organizers solicited the involvement of city churches whose job it became to send clothes and shoes to distribute to those in need.[31]

While we know that Fresh Air children corresponded with their families in the city and with their host families after their return home, none of those letters have been located. There is, however, an article written by an eleven-year-old boy, Edward Reeves, a Pilot House Fresh Air child in 1964, in which he chronicles his bus trip and his week on a farm. His perspective is useful. Though he concludes that "the farm is better than the city" and that "when I get old enough and get married and all that, I am going to move to a farm or to the country, somewhere out of Baltimore," he is not entirely taken with rural life and sees some advantages to city life. Though Edward and the other Fresh Air children had had different experiences from their hosts, they did not see themselves or their families as "disadvantaged"; nor did they perceive host families as privileged. For example, Edward's host family lacked a television set, something that was then common in his city neighborhood. His desire was to save enough money to get his host family a TV. On the topic of church, Edward found that the country service was much like his own, "except that it was shorter. The preacher got right to the point. He didn't waste a lot of time."[32] Another host family reported overhearing the prayers of a Fresh Air child: "Dear Lord, these white folk are just like us colored folk."[33]

It is easier to find host family testimonials. Heidi Hershey of Manheim, Pennsylvania, wrote of her family's experience hosting nine-year-old Pam in 1961 and Pam and her seven-year-old brother Joseph the following year. The first summer, Pam arrived with a shopping bag of new clothes. Still, her clothing supply was inadequate. Hershey lent Pam her daughters' clothes and "even made 3 blouses all alike so they could look like *sisters*!"[34] The topic of race relations comes up in many of the families' testimonials. For Heidi Hershey the issue was broached even as the family weighed participation in the program, which they learned about through their church bulletin's request for host families. In response, the Hershey family discussed how "a Negro [would] be treated in a totally white community . . . [and whether] a Negro [could] blend in" with their family life. What they found was that their Fresh Air child and their own children learned from each other. The Hershey children were interested in Pam's skin color and hair texture. Heidi Hershey told her children, "That was the way God wanted them to be." She found that Pam envied her children's straight hair and the Hershey children envied Pam's curly hair.[35]

The second year the Hersheys went to Pam and Joseph's Harlem Park home to pick them up. When the children's family invited them in for cake and iced tea, the Hersheys found the home "surprisingly clean" while "still very shabby," overcrowded, and lacking window screens.[36]

The response of host family neighbors to Fresh Air children is also telling. In the case of the Hersheys in Manheim, Pennsylvania, there was great change between their first and second years as hosts in the early 1960s because a new housing development was built across the fields from their home. The new development had "Greek, Jewish, Catholic, Puerto Rican, and Protestant all on one street, which of course all put together creates many opinions and ideals." Mrs. Hershey had concerns about how the guest children would be received. In fact, their neighbors were all welcoming. In Manheim, the community pool accepted the Fresh Air kids free of charge, as members of the family. Many local people asked the Hersheys, "How can we have a cute Negro child at our home next year?" Many local people were surprised that Pam and her brother came from Baltimore, as most Fresh Air children came from New York City.[37]

Clyde Nafzinger's family in Earlville on Maryland's Eastern Shore had a very different community response to hosting Willie, a boy participating in the Pilot House Fresh Air program. The Nafzingers lived on a block in "an all-white 'restricted' community" on which four families' children played often with their children. When Willie visited, "three of the families kept their children in their houses or on their own lawns and did not allow them to come to our house to play." The fourth family allowed their ten-year-old son to play with the guest "all the time, with no hint of hostile feelings." According to Nafzinger, the three families who "rejected Will's friendship all attended Sunday School with their children every Sunday. The one who accepted him do not attend anywhere regularly." In addition to the disapproval of their neighbors, the community association "held meetings to discuss this 'intrusion' but nothing happened." The Nafzingers ran a produce business, and "some people talked of the town boycotting" it. That did not happen, and in time the Nafzingers "found favorable support" for their actions and their business "gradually improved." When Willie took swimming lessons, there was one family that forbade their child to take lessons "with a colored person." Still, another local resident stated, "I'm glad of the stand you took. You have done Hacks Point a great favor!"[38]

Reflecting on the Nafzingers' experience, Wilbur E. Mullen, the Brethren's national director of social welfare, wrote, "The Fresh Air program as carried out in the last several years has challenged members of the Church of the Brethren to witness to their Christian faith." Though difficult, Mullen believed the program was "a testimony to our faith in Jesus Christ."[39]

The swimming pool issue was often a hot-button topic for Fresh Air host families. While the Hersheys in Manheim, Pennsylvania, found welcome there, the Nafzingers on Maryland's Eastern Shore found some resistance. Other host families avoided community pools entirely. One family reported, "Our town is still segregated so there were places we couldn't go. . . . We wanted very much to go swimming but there was no pool in this vicinity to which we could take her." This reality proved a teachable moment for the host family. "In a very small way, not being able to take her to a local swimming pool helps us to feel what is like to be a Negro today."[40] In contrast, another family reported that their Fresh Air child was well accepted. "Neighbors invited her to swim in the children's little pools" and the family took her to a community pool "without comment."[41]

The Brethren's rhetoric describing the Fresh Air program's purposes evolved over time. After the assassination of Martin Luther King, Jr., and the riots that ensued in April 1968, the Brethren dropped the Fresh Air name and called the program the Baltimore Inter-Cultural Exchange. In 1970 "direct communication, understanding and acceptance between persons of different racial and cultural backgrounds" were the program's goals. Host families still welcomed "guest" children, and "because of the area that we service, the majority of the guest children are 'Black.'"[42] In 1970 the Brethren's brochure featured a quote from the Kerner Commission's 1968 *Report of the National Advisory Commission on Civil Disorders*. "What white Americans have never fully understood—but what the Negro can never forget—is that white society is deeply implicated in the ghetto. White institutions created it, white institutions maintain it, and white society condones it."[43] The Brethren's own language in describing this program lagged behind—or only slowly caught up with—their progressive, purposeful, quiet interracial actions.

Work Camps

Though the Brethren took pride in their Fresh Air work, they realized early on that without home-and-away experiences, the model would lack reciprocity for both the guest and host families and would be one sided and thus flawed. Forgoing bus transportation and instead requiring Fresh Air host families to transport their own visitors was an effort to bridge the racial divide. A more radical initiative was the Brethren's creation of, and ongoing commitment to, work camps, in which white rural and suburban young people came to Pilot House to perform building tasks and other work needed in the neighborhood. Work camps were a Brethren tradition in Baltimore that went back all the way to the creation of the first Pilot House in 1951 and that quietly presaged the work of Habitat for Humanity.[44]

In 1955 a young person involved in the BVS work camp creating the new westside Pilot House reflected, "Sound houses are not the complete answer to all the problems caused by city dwelling. Building sound children matters, too." BVSer Eve Cameron noted, "Sweat, laughter, and prayer are great dissolvers of barriers of all sorts; they open many windows for the soul."[45] In 1960, just as Fresh Air siblings Pam and Joseph were visiting Manheim, forty-one young people from five churches near Manheim participated in a Pilot House work camp in Baltimore. They removed wallpaper and painted four homes and the Lafayette Square Community Center. Pilot House's director pronounced the results "most satisfactory."[46]

Work camps featured both white "outsiders" and black "indigenous" young people. For example, in 1962 a Brethren work camp in West Baltimore included joint programming with Union Baptist Church Center, a nearby community center. Rev. Vernon Dobson, the center's director, an African American parole officer with insights into the challenges facing Baltimore youth, was formerly minister of Knox Presbyterian Center, Pilot House's partner on the east side. Pilot House director Robert Cain described Dobson as "especially effective in bringing out community reactions in work evaluation sessions." Brethren work campers responded well to the evening spent at the Baptist Center, as reflected by their statement in their final gathering: "The discussion Saturday evening was worth the whole weekend."[47]

During the school year, Pilot House hosted about ten weekend work camps. In the summer the format was extended, with work camps ranging from a week to three weeks. Work campers assisted with housing rehabilitation projects, and many also led youth activities such as arts and crafts classes, Bible camps (in local black Methodist and Baptist congregations), and playground recreation. Ten to fifteen white young people (often church youth group members ages sixteen and older) with an advisor worked with black Harlem Park teenagers, in the belief that "this makes the experience richer educationally and spiritually to the work camper, and also makes the work camp more meaningful and beneficial to the community." In the evenings, groups studied race relations and aspects of the inner city, using "films, local persons, discussion leaders, work camp leadership from within the group, and much reading material." Work campers transported themselves and paid a modest fee to cover food. Often, West Baltimore neighbors generously provided housing through home stays in the community. Sometimes work campers slept at Pilot House.[48] Work camps included time for reflection and discussion, worship in local churches, and interaction with residents and stakeholders.

Summer work campers contributed to the fabric of the community. A 1964 census of summer work camp activities reveals that volunteers contributed 122 work days of housing rehabilitation and days more of playground supervision, Bible school teaching, day camp counseling, and domestic and clerical work for Pilot House.[49] Work camp participants ranged from all female and all Brethren to "interracial, interdenominational, interfaith and international."[50] Priming the pump with volunteers required effort. In correspondence with Brethren churches, Pilot House's leadership suggested hooks that might attract participants:

1. It's an opportunity to learn about people. We work in an area of Baltimore where housing is not always adequate. Your group may be interested in such questions as—What kind of people live there? Why do they remain? How do they feel about it?
2. It's a chance to live with other volunteers who may come from different racial, social or religious backgrounds from your own, and who may help you to understand new and different points of view.
3. It means a full day of physical work and the satisfaction of having done something useful.
4. It is giving of oneself in service as an expression of our love for humanity and of our concern for those who may not have enjoyed the same advantages and opportunities that we have known.
5. It's fun! Ask those who have done it.[51]

Pilot House leaders also imagined a "family exchange visitation program" in which white Brethren families would host and then visit black families in the urban core. That initiative, first broached in 1963, was a follow-up to the race relations work of Baltimore's First Church of the Brethren that included a pulpit exchange with a "Negro church."[52] The family exchange program never got the traction of the Fresh Air program or work camps.

As the years passed, new groups of Brethren young people came to Pilot House as BVSers, prepared to do a year or two of service. Dozens of BVSers together with a few paid staff members worked to keep the Brethren's Fresh Air program and work camps going strong throughout the changeful 1960s. Their agenda was religious rather than political. They attempted to imitate Jesus by serving those in need and helping where they saw an opportunity. Yet, as the Brethren promoted interracial and interfaith understanding, their policy of tolerance and inclusion tested in-group norms. For example, in 1960 a white BVSer, Marion Poff, was dating a black Morgan College student who worked part time at the Lafayette Square Community Center. According to Richard W. Edwards, then Pilot House's director, "The unit feels it is all right for Marion to date Bill and we have given our approval. In the BVS Handbook it specifically says that BVSers are not to date residents of the community where they serve. Bill, however, does not live in this area and really is a co-worker.

I cannot in conscience interpret the handbook as establishing a racial standard."[53] Church headquarters responded from Elgin, Illinois: "From our office we have no direction on Marion's dating a Morgan College student (Negro). While there is specific policy statement on this from the standpoint of BVS, we recognize it is entirely up to the unit and the unit director to determine application of the statement to the local situation. We are not passing the buck, but are not giving any policy statement on it."[54]

Although most of their work was local, the Brethren involved in Pilot House were keenly aware of and tied to national events and concerns. In 1963 Pilot House BVSers attended the March on Washington. For the Poor People's Campaign in 1968, they took their extensive construction experience and built the infirmary on the National Mall. Not surprisingly, the Vietnam War received the attention of the Brethren in Baltimore and nationally. As a pacifist church, BVSers were actively involved in the antiwar movement.

The End

The April 1968 assassination of Reverend Martin Luther King, Jr., proved to be a turning point in the history of the Brethren's Pilot House. Although the house and its occupants were protected during the unrest (loyal neighbors festooned the house with "Soul Brother" signs and black scarves even as Max Katz Grocery down the block at 1341 West Lafayette Street was looted and damaged), the riots shook Pilot House's leaders, causing them to question their role in a changing social justice landscape.[55] They did not then end the work, but their profound concerns, together with the United Church of the Brethren's concomitant shift to indigenous leadership (meaning that the local people had charge) of both their international missionary work and Brethren Services, changed the direction of the efforts of Pilot House. Warren E. "Sam" Miller, Pilot House's last director, from 1966 to 1972, took ownership of some of the concepts presented by both the Brethren's interest in local leadership and in the federal government's 1968 Kerner Commission report. In early 1969 Miller proposed a careful reexamination of the work:

> The time has come to seriously question the role of an all-white church-related, volunteer-staffed "service" agency in the West Baltimore inner city.
>
> Nineteen years of experience, involvement, and expended energy need not be considered wasted for Brotherhood Pilot House. Those years have left their mark on both the volunteers and the lives they have touched.
>
> But the scene has changed. The mood and tempo of the predominately Black inner city requires new attitudes and new structures. . . .

> The present staff of Pilot House has come to the painful conclusion that white involvement in a Black community *can* be detrimental to the people themselves when it is primarily service oriented. The service function of any agency too easily becomes a type of paternalism which denies the people any sense of self-determination. White paternalism creates and maintains Black dependency.[56]

Still, Pilot House continued and evolved. In concert with their neighbors, BVSers began Your Community Food House (YCFH) in January 1968 when "a group of Harlem Park residents met at the Brotherhood Pilot House." With grants, loans, and private donations totaling more than $30,000 from sources as diverse as the Archdiocese of Baltimore, the national Church of the Brethren, the National Council of Churches, the University Park Church of the Brethren, and the federal Office of Economic Opportunity, the store at 1729 West Lanvale Street opened in March 1969. "Designed to help neighboring residents in consumer problems and business management as well as offering good quality, low-cost food," it was a "resident-owned corporation." Sam Miller, a Brethren minister and director of Pilot House, was treasurer.[57] YCFH carried meats, soda and cakes, and staples such as salt, sugar, and lard.[58]

Although a "needed service," YCFH, "a cooperative non-profit effort" the primary aim of which was "to provide quality foods at the lowest prices consistent with a sound business operation," turned out to be fraught with challenges for Pilot House. A 1970 report describes the effort as educational "concerning the trials and errors of inner-city organizing" and talks of its "difficulties and disappointments." Still, despite the complications, YCFH "expanded its range of merchandise" and provided workers with "technical assistance and training." Weekly sales flyers identified "best buys and educate[d] the residents with consumer information news on how to get better food value per purchasing dollar." In addition, store employees received training in "cash handling, accounting controls, receiving procedures and controls, work habits, merchandising and buying."[59]

The good intentions of the Brethren and their partners were not enough and the short-lived YCFH experiment died on May 25, 1970, following "a series of robberies" and threats to the two BVSers. "The store never was able to operate on a practical basis and suffered from poor community support."[60]

Meanwhile, Pilot House changed course. In 1969 it restructured "around an emphasis upon racial/urban problems from the perspective of the ex-urban community, and the knowledge that racial/urban problems can be solved only to the extent that the majority community is exposed and sensitized, both individually and institutionally, to these problems and develops a commitment to take actions to solve them."[61] In November 1970 Pilot House's future was debated, with two distinct proposals under consideration. The first was to make it an interfaith urban training center. The second proposed a regional training center for the Church of the Brethren Fund for the Americas in the United States run by Pilot House.[62] The first won out: branding themselves BPH Associates, the social entrepreneurs then in charge began to sell their services as consultants. Business was good enough that an incentive pay model for Sam Miller, executive director, and P. Jeanette Williams, administrator, was approved by Pilot House's executive committee in April 1971, retroactive to October 1, 1970.[63] Not everyone was happy with the new direction. When the executive committee discussed the Pilot House program, some thought the enterprise should have a "new focus, such as housing" and others were concerned the effort would turn into "big business" and lose touch with the traditional partners: "churches, civic and volunteer groups."[64]

By mid-1972, Pilot House was gone. The rise of the Black Power movement, the Brethren's national commitment to local or indigenous leadership, and the 1968 riots that followed the death of Martin Luther King together raised thorny issues about leadership, mission, and strategy. Financial hardship, caused by a national economic downturn and a forgery incident, was an additional nail in the coffin.[65] Still, in trying to understand the landscape of Baltimore in the third quarter of the twentieth century, it is instructive to consider the efforts of the nonprofit Church of the Brethren through its breadth of place-based programs emanating from Pilot House. This multifaceted, well-intentioned, historically significant, but, by 1970, uncomfortable social justice effort organized and sustained by the Church of the Brethren in Baltimore bears continued exploration as it illustrates some of the contradictions and complications of not-for-profit, interracial, faith-based work in American cities in the 1950s and 1960s.

NOTES

1. For an overview of the national scene, see Taylor Branch, *Parting the Waters: America in the King Years* (New York: Simon and Schuster, 1988), 695–696, 738–743.

2. Available at http://www.brethren.org/site/PageServer?pagename=visitor_about_history (accessed July 21, 2010).

3. Richard L. Rowe and David Eiler, "The Background of Brethren Volunteer Service," [1951?], Citizens Planning and Housing Association (CPHA) Papers, series 2, box 14, file 15, University of Baltimore Archives (UBA).

4. Millspaugh, a Baltimore native, collected his articles in a twenty-seven-page pamphlet, "What Is Urban Renewal?" (Reprinted from the *Baltimore Evening Sun*, 1955). He went on to write with Gurney Breckenfeld *The Human Side of Urban Renewal: A Study of the Attitude Changes Produced by Neighborhood Rehabilitation* (Baltimore: Fight-Blight, 1958). Millspaugh then spent nearly a quarter of a century as president and chief executive of Charles Center Inner Harbor Management overseeing the rebuilding of Charles Center and the Inner Harbor.

5. Program for the Pilot House Dedication Ceremony, July 19, 1951, Pilot House Files, First Church of the Brethren, Baltimore, MD.

6. Joshua Olsen, *Better Places, Better Lives: A Biography of James Rouse* (Washington, DC: Urban Land Institute, 2003), 32–36.

7. "Why Not Drive By and See?" undated and unattributed editorial (July 1951?), Pilot House Files, First Church of the Brethren, Baltimore, MD.

8. Program for the Pilot House Dedication Ceremony, July 19, 1951, Pilot House Files, First Church of the Brethren, Baltimore, MD.

9. Foreword by Frank Rittenhouse, September 1952, CPHA series 2, box 14, file 15, UBA.

10. Ibid. Emphasis added.

11. "Pilot House Opens in Anti-slum Fight," undated, unattributed article (July 1951?), Pilot House Files, First Church of the Brethren, Baltimore, MD. The Pilot House stood "as an example of what astonishing things can be done with a superficially unpromising property at relatively slight expense." Purchased for $1,200, and with improvements of $2,941, the total cost of the house with improvements was about $4,100, with $500 coming from the Maryland Home Builders Association and more than $3,500 from Brotherhood Service. "Why Not Drive By and See?"; and *Rehabilitation of the Brotherhood Pilot House, Summary of Origin, Functions, and Itemized Statement of Costs* (Baltimore: Baltimore City Health Department, Housing Bureau, issued November 1, 1952, revised April 1953).

12. The work resulting from the study is Millspaugh and Breckenfeld, *The Human Side of Urban Renewal*.

13. Eleanor Johnson, "Pilot Plan Focuses Needs of Baltimore," undated (July 1951?), Pilot House Files, First Church of the Brethren, Baltimore, MD.

14. Martin Millspaugh, "Old Pilot House Closing Doors, but Blight Work to Continue," *Baltimore Evening Sun*, February 13, 1956.

15. In 1963 a Pilot House work camp group met with the Metropolitan Methodist Church to view *The Baltimore Plan*. Promotional material for that work group describes the film (mistakenly calling it *The Baltimore Story*) as "a practical approach to the problem of slum housing, showing how a blighted area in Baltimore was reclaimed through co-operative efforts of owners and tenants, and systematic, legal enforcement of existing housing codes." Schedule for Week-End Work Camp, January 18–20, 1963, Brethren Service Commission, director of Race Relations and Social Welfare, 1957–1968, box 1, Baltimore Pilot House, 1962–1964, Brethren Historical Library and Archives, Elgin, IL.

16. The examination of the effect of federal policy on the development of postwar suburbs and the challenges posed to inner-city neighborhoods is discussed by Kenneth T. Jackson in his now-classic *Crabgrass Frontier: The Suburbanization of the United States* (New York: Oxford University Press, 1985) and by others.

17. Letter from Dale Ulrich to BVS Alumni, undated (1957?), Collection of Dale Ulrich, Bridgewater, VA. It is interesting to note that employment was not listed among the factors then causing blight. In the 1950s there was still significant industrial employment opportunity throughout downtown Baltimore.

18. Brotherhood Service, Inc., Report of the President, 1951, Pilot House Files, First Church of the Brethren, Baltimore, MD.

19. Millspaugh, "What Is Urban Renewal?" 17; and *Gospel Messenger*, November 9, 1957, p. 20. The program formally changed its name to the Fresh Air program in 1961. Emphasis added.

20. Letter from Arthur F. Shive, acting director, Pilot House, to Church of the Brethren Pastors, March 2, 1966. Brethren Service Commission, director of Race Relations and Social Welfare, box 1, Fresh Air Program.

21. The *New York Tribune*'s Fresh Air Fund that began in New York City in 1877 was the model for many of these programs. The Reverend Willard Parsons, a Union Theological Seminary graduate who worked in Manhattan's notorious Five Points district before securing a rural pulpit in Sherman, Pennsylvania, began the *Tribune*'s Fresh Air Fund. Walter Shepard Ufford, *Fresh Air Charity in the United States* (New York, 1897), 1.

22. Peter L. Schmitt, *Back to Nature: The Arcadian Myth in Urban America* (New York: Oxford University Press, 1969), 96–98. In Baltimore, the Children's Fresh Air Society of Baltimore City began operations in 1903. The Enoch Pratt Free Library has a scrapbook of newspaper clippings related to the Fresh Air Fund for the years from 1903 to 1907. The *Baltimore News* was the local sponsor.

23. Willard Parsons, "The Story of the Fresh-Air Fund," in Robert Archey Woods, ed., *The Poor in Great Cities: Their Problems and What Is Doing to Solve Them* (New York: Scribner, 1895), 1, 144.

24. Notably, "Church of the Brethren involvement in fresh air programs for Negro children dates back to the 1920's" when "the Hasting's Street Church of the Brethren in Chicago operated a program for several years, involving between 200 and 300 children annually." Letter from Wilbur E. Mullen to Rev. Wm. Smith, July 17, 1962, Brethren Service Commission, director of Race Relations and Social Welfare, box 1, Fresh Air Program, Brethren Historical Library and Archives, Elgin, IL.

25. Letter from Dale Ulrich to BVS Alumni, undated (1957?), Collection of Dale Ulrich, Bridgewater, VA.

26. Letter from Wilma Leaverton and Marianne Senff to "Sir," March 21, 1962, Brethren Service Commission, director of Race Relations and Social Welfare, box 1, Fresh Air Program, Brethren Historical Library and Archives, Elgin, IL.

27. Letter from Robert D. Cain, Jr., to Wilbur E. Mullen, September 13, 1963. Brethren Service Commission, director of Race Relations and Social Welfare, box 1, Elgin, IL.

28. Ibid., August 3, 1965. News of the Brethren's Fresh Air program spurred interest from other Baltimore churches. In 1962 the pastor of the Chestnut Grove Presbyterian Church in rural Phoenix, Maryland, asked the Brethren for help in starting a Fresh Air program in his church, which, in its first year, placed twelve African American children from Baltimore's Knox Presbyterian and the Church of Our Savior at McKim Community Center in East Baltimore for a two-week period. The city children participated in the church's Bible school while visiting and living with families. Letter from Robert D. Cain to Wilbur E. Mullen, September 30, 1963, Brethren Service Commission, director of Race Relations and Social Welfare, box 1, Elgin, IL.

29. Director's Report, Pilot House, November 1970. Brethren Service Commission, director of Race Relations and Social Welfare, box 1, Fresh Air Program, Elgin, IL.

30. Fresh Air program brochure, 1963, Brethren Service Commission, director of Race Relations and Social Welfare, box 1, Fresh Air Program. Memorandum from Robert Cain, director, Pilot House, to Baltimore Area Church of the Brethren ministers, May 7, 1965. Brethren Service Commission, director of Race Relations and Social Welfare, box 1, Elgin, IL; Brotherhood Pilot House, director's report from Warren E. Miller, executive director, November 1970.

31. "The Fresh Air Program—1961," a report by Wilma Leaverton and Marianne Senff, Brethren Service Commission, director of Race Relations and Social Welfare, box 1, Fresh Air Program, Brethren Historical Library and Archives, Elgin, IL.

32. Edward Reeves, "I Liked It an Awful Lot," *Gospel Messenger*, July 11, 1964.

33. Fresh Air brochure, June 1964, Brethren Service Commission, director of Race Relations and Social Welfare, box 1, Pilot House General Correspondence, 1964, Elgin, IL.

34. Testimonial from Heidi R. Hershey, 1962, Brethren Service Commission, director of Race Relations and Social Welfare, box 1, Pilot House General Correspondence, 1964, Elgin, IL.

35. Ibid.

36. Ibid.

37. Ibid.

38. Letter from Robert D. Cain, Jr., to Wilbur E. Mullen, August 15, 1963, Brethren Service Commission, director of Race Relations and Social Welfare, box 1, Pilot House General, Elgin, IL.

39. Letter from Wilbur E. Mullen to Robert D. Cain, Jr., September 9, 1963, Brethren Service Commission, director of Race Relations and Social Welfare, box 1, Pilot House General, Elgin, IL.

40. Fresh Air brochure, June 1964, Brethren Service Commission, director of Race Relations and Social Welfare, box 1, Pilot House General, Elgin, IL.

41. "We Opened Our Hearts and Homes," *Gospel Messenger*, July 11, 1964.

42. Letter from Pearl Moulton, exchange coordinator, to all former host families, 1971, Brethren Service Commission, director of Race Relations and Social Welfare, box 1, Fresh Air Program. Elgin, IL. The quotes around "Black" signify a change in language from "Negro," which had earlier been used.

43. Baltimore Inter-Cultural Exchange program brochure, 1971. Brethren Service Commission, director of Race Relations and Social Welfare, box 1, Fresh Air Program, Elgin, IL.

44. From the records of Robert Cain, Pilot House's director in the early 1960s, we know that Clarence Jordan visited Pilot House in Harlem Park *before* Habitat began its housing work. Jordan founded Koinonia Farm, an interracial community near Americus, Georgia, in 1942 and was the spiritual founder of Habitat for Humanity, working with Millard Fuller, in the late 1960s.

45. Eve Cameron, "Baltimore Work Camp," *Gospel Messenger*, October 22, 1955, pp. 20–21.

46. Letter from Richard W. Edwards, Jr., to James E. Renz, director, Social Welfare Department, Brethren Service Commission, July 27, 1960, Ralph E. Smeltzer office files, circa 1960–1970, box 5, Pilot House General, 1959, p. 60, Elgin, IL.

47. Letter from Robert D. Cain, Jr., to Wilber E. Mullen, Brethren Service Commission, December 3, 1962, director of Race Relations and Social Welfare, 1957–1958, box 1, Baltimore Pilot House General, Brethren Historical Library and Archives, Elgin, IL.

48. Flyer on Baltimore Weekend Work Camp, 1964–1965, Brethren Service Commission, director of Race Relations and Social Welfare, 1957–1968, box 1, Baltimore Pilot House, 1962–1964; and Letter from Robert D. Cain, Jr., to Wilbur E. Mullen, director Social Welfare, BSC, September 16, 1963, director of Race Relations and Social Welfare, 1957–1968, box 1, Baltimore Pilot House General Brethren Historical Library and Archives, Elgin, IL.

49. Brotherhood Pilot House, Breakdown of Summer Work Camp Activities by Man Days and Hours of Involvement, July 1–August 24, 1964, Brethren Service Commission, director of Race Relations and Social Welfare, 1957–68,

box 1, Baltimore Pilot House, 1962–64, Brethren Historical Library and Archives, Elgin, IL.

50. Letter from Robert D. Cain, Jr., to Wilbur E. Mullen, director Social Welfare, BSC, September 16, 1963, director of Race Relations and Social Welfare, 1957–68, box 1, Baltimore Pilot House General, Brethren Historical Library and Archives, Elgin, IL.

51. Flyer on Baltimore Weekend Work Camp, 1964–1965, Brethren Service Commission, director of Race Relations and Social Welfare, 1957–1968, box 1 Baltimore Pilot House, 1962–1964, Brethren Historical Library and Archives, Elgin, IL.

52. Letters from Robert D. Cain, Jr., to Wilbur E. Mullen, May 7 and July 2, 1963, Brethren Service Commission, director of Race Relations and Social Welfare, box 1, Pilot House General, Elgin, IL.

53. Letter from Richard W. Edwards, Jr., to James E. Renz, director, Social Welfare Department, Brethren Service Commission, June 24, 1960, Ralph E. Smeltzer office files, circa 1960–1970, box 5, Pilot House General, 1959, p. 60, CBA, Elgin, IL.

54. Letter from James E. Renz, director, Social Welfare Department, Brethren Service Commission, to Mr. and Mrs. Richard Edwards, Brethren Service Unit, July 8, 1960, Ralph E. Smeltzer office files, circa 1960–1970, box 5, Pilot House General, 1959, 60, CBA, Elgin, IL.

55. Peter Levy, "Buildings Damaged during Riots Database," available at http://archives.ubalt.edu/bsr/%20buildings%20damaged%20during%20riots%20e.xls (accessed March 1, 2009).

56. Brotherhood Pilot House, Program Proposal, February 8, 1969.

57. "Your Community Food House," *Baltimore Catholic Review*, August 15, 1969, A20.

58. Flyer, Your Community Food Store, April 1969; and "Where the Action Is," May 1969, Brethren Service Commission, director of Race Relations and Social Welfare, box 2, Baltimore Pilot House, Brethren Historical Library and Archives, Elgin, IL.

59. "Food Store Report," by Dwight Taylor, in Pilot House Happenings, January–February 1970, Brethren Service Commission, director of Race Relations and Social Welfare, box 2, Baltimore Pilot House, Brethren Historical Library and Archives, Elgin, IL.

60. Brotherhood Pilot House, minutes, executive committee meeting, June 5, 1970, Brethren Service Commission, director of Race Relations and Social Welfare, box 2, Baltimore Pilot House, Brethren Historical Library and Archives, Elgin, IL.

61. Brotherhood Pilot House, Inter-Faith Urban Training Proposal for Baltimore, n.d., Brotherhood Service, Inc., Baltimore First Church of the Brethren Pilot House Collection.

62. Brotherhood Pilot House, director's report from Warren E. Miller, executive director, November 1970, Baltimore First Church of the Brethren Pilot House Collection.

63. Brotherhood Pilot House, minutes, executive committee meeting, April 2, 1971, F. Rittenhouse Files. This discussion did not end the matter. In September and October 1971, the executive committee again took up the issue of compensation.

64. Brotherhood Pilot House, minutes, executive committee meeting, June 11, 1971. Baltimore First Church of the Brethren, Pilot House Collection.

65. Brotherhood Pilot House, minutes, executive committee meeting, December 3, 1971. F. Rittenhouse Files.

8

Convergences and Divergences

The Civil Rights and Antiwar Movements—Baltimore, 1968

W. Edward Orser and Joby Taylor

At the time of the assassination of Martin Luther King, Jr., in April 1968, King represented the most notable example of an American social activist whose perspective on the social ills of America—indeed of the world—explicitly and vocally linked both civil rights and opposition to war. Exactly one year before his assassination, in a major speech before religious leaders at New York's Riverside Church, King broke his relative silence on the Vietnam War by insisting that racial injustice, war, and poverty were inextricably linked. And on March 31, 1968, only a few days before he was killed, he reaffirmed his position on the connections between peace and freedom in what was tragically his final Sunday sermon. Speaking at the National Cathedral in Washington, D.C., in the address "Remaining awake through a great revolution," King served notice of the Poor People's Campaign in the nation's capital that summer. His central message criticized America's involvement in the Vietnam War as the action of an "arrogant nation" and explained why he could no longer avoid speaking out in opposition. By taking this stand, of course, he had reached the point of breaking with an administration that had supported important and historic civil rights legislation.[1]

For many social activists, civil rights and opposition to the Vietnam War stemmed from similar convictions, representing considerable convergence. However, what is striking is the degree to which one cause often took primacy over the other, resulting in significant divergence as well. In the crisis atmosphere of the period, tensions over goals and tactics often produced division, and competing priorities took precedence. This chapter considers convergences and divergences between the civil rights and peace movements in Baltimore in the period immediately before and after the assassination of Martin Luther King, Jr., focusing on two illustrative case studies: the experience of the local chapter of the Congress of Racial Equality (CORE), among the most active of the city's civil rights organizations at the time, and the example of those who destroyed draft records in the suburban Baltimore community of Catonsville in May 1968, who became known as the "Catonsville Nine."

Peace and Freedom

Participants from the period, and scholars in retrospect, see the civil rights and antiwar movements of the 1960s as among the most significant social movements of the twentieth century. The degree of convergence between the two was considerable in terms of ideology, and indeed, the links in the lives of participants was complex and compelling. Yet as much as they had in common, they did speak in important ways to differing ideas about goals and strategies.

Simon Hall, a British scholar of American culture, has examined the two movements in his 2005 book, *Peace and Freedom: The Civil Rights and Antiwar Movements in the 1960s*, and he contends that "the years between 1960 and 1972 saw the emergence of two of the most significant social movements in American history—the American freedom struggle and the movement to end the war in Vietnam."[2] However, he concludes, "for a variety of reasons . . . a meaningful coalition was never constructed [between them]." Hall goes on to say of the antiwar movement, "Despite widespread opposition to the war within the civil rights movement, and the peace movement's consistent attempts to attract black support, the mostly white antiwar leadership was discussing the lack of black participation in 1972, just as it had been in 1965."[3]

The reasons for the divide were complex, of course, but Hall especially focuses on the circumstances for African American leaders, divided between those he calls "black moderates," including the leaders of major mainstream civil rights organizations, and those he calls "Black Power advocates," typically younger, leading newer groups challenging the mainstream, and often working closer to the grassroots. For both, the overriding question was one of priorities. Moderates as well as radicals worried about the hazards of linking what in some ways seemed two issues, rather than keeping a laser focus on civil rights. Many Black Power advocates moved to overt hostility toward the American policy on Vietnam, whether because of the disproportionate brunt borne by African American draftees, the irony of being asked to die abroad while being denied full rights at home, or the broader concern for an American war policy that victimized racially "other" third-world peoples. But, at the same time, as they turned ideologically to insistence on black empowerment, they found it increasingly difficult to forge an alliance with the white-dominated peace movement.[4]

For black moderates, the conflict was equally acute. Long outside the political mainstream, they found themselves a key constituency in Lyndon Johnson's Great Society coalition, consulted for the first time on policy and witnessing political victories they had worked all their lives to achieve—civil rights acts, immigration reform, the appointment of African Americans to high positions within the government. For those such as Roy Wilkens of the NAACP and Whitney Young of the Urban League, the ties were too close to risk breaking. And for Martin Luther King, Jr., the tension was agonizing. When in 1965 he began to link his vision of civil rights and nonviolence at home with his concerns for the Vietnam War abroad, he immediately was reminded of the threat to civil rights gains and took a step back. It was not until 1967 that he felt he could no longer hold his relative silence and made the public statement at Riverside Church. He continued to speak out right up to the very moment of his untimely death.

Hall's view that those for whom opposition to the war was primary were predominantly white may be an overstatement of the case. However, he is right to point out that this appeared to be true for those leading and participating in the major antiwar rallies and that in the various moratorium and mobilization coalitions, whites tended to play the most prominent roles. As we have noted, strains within the civil rights movement made cooperation with the peace movement problematic for many African American leaders. In considering the role of whites, however, Hall—and indeed other retrospective analysts—may not fully take account of the degree to which the social activism of many white antiwar advocates had its roots in the civil rights and antipoverty campaigns and for whom these commitments remained strong. As the case study that follows makes clear, there had been considerable interaction between civil rights and peace activists in Baltimore, though even in the local setting, issues of priorities and focus tended to produce divergence.

The Baltimore Civil Rights Movement: The Case of CORE

> Housing remains as one of the most important areas of discrimination. And this barrier will be swept away. It will go because it is wrong. Fair-minded whites know it is wrong. . . . The question is "How will it go?" Will it require the familiar sequence of protest, strife and the resulting disruption of all citizens? . . . Colored citizens have too long suffered from this wrong. . . . Signed, Walter Carter and Barbara Mills.[5]

In late 1960s the Baltimore CORE chapter stood out as one of the most active civil rights groups in the city. Yet this heightened visibility was occurring at a moment when the organization was experiencing considerable turmoil, the result of conflicting tendencies—within the local chapter, between the local and national leadership, and indeed within the hearts and minds of individual members. Before the late 1960s a number of social activists who later became more identified with the antiwar movement worked closely with CORE, but increasingly the war issue took primacy for them. Moreover, even though the coalition against the Vietnam War was mounting, Baltimore's CORE chapter seldom made explicit positions on the war part of its public agenda.

Nationally, CORE had its origins in the early 1940s as an outgrowth of the Fellowship of Reconciliation, a group that grounded its pacifist and social justice positions in religious principles. CORE was interracial, and it practiced tactics of nonviolent direct action. From an early point, James Farmer, who originally had planned to enter the ministry, headed the organization, and until 1965 he was its most recognizable voice.[6]

Baltimore's chapter of CORE got its start in the early 1950s as an interracial group committed to nonviolent direct action. Barbara Mills attributes the role of convener to Herbert Kelman, whom she identifies as a "white psychologist at the Phipps Psychiatric Clinic" who was drawn to "CORE's Gandhian nonviolent social action."[7] The racially mixed organizers included teachers, attorneys, clergy, and trade unionists. Mills also says that the group hoped to forge links with activist students from Morgan State College, some of whom might have participated in the chapter's founding. With its integrationist composition and mission, CORE soon became one of the most visible civil rights groups in the city. During the 1950s it spearheaded challenges to racial segregation at lunch counters, theaters, and department stores in Baltimore, and in the 1960s it took its protest actions statewide—from freedom rides along Route 40 to sites in Annapolis and along Route 50 on the Eastern Shore. In many ways its high-water mark may have been in the early 1960s, before the series of national civil rights acts in the second half of the decade that upended de jure racial discrimination but left far from finished the more complex de facto goal of changing hearts and minds.

During this period Baltimore CORE was headed by an interracial team of Walter Carter, an African American who also organized Maryland's participation in the March on Washington in 1963 and came to be known as "Baltimore's Mr. Civil Rights," and white American Civil Liberties Union (ACLU) official John Roemer. The chapter relentlessly organized, staged pickets and sit-ins, and after much struggle, counted numerous victories in settlements that led to desegregation of public accommodations, gains that were ratified in federal law in 1964 with the first of the civil rights acts. One of the most visible local campaigns challenged segregation at Gwynn Oak

Amusement Park, just outside the city limits in Woodlawn, in actions that culminated in 1963 with national attention and a desegregation agreement. Each year on the ironically titled "All Nation's Day," CORE-led pickets demonstrated outside the privately owned park and on several occasions were arrested, as Carter and Roemer were in 1962. In 1963 large-scale protests, with nationally prominent religious leaders participating, initially led to massive arrests but eventually to an agreement by the owner to desegregate. The result proved a somewhat hollow victory, since the park limped along until it finally closed following hurricane-caused flooding in 1972.[8]

Walter Carter resigned as chairman of the Baltimore CORE chapter in 1963, but in the mid-1960s he redirected his commitment and became head of the new CORE Housing Committee. Of all the civil rights targets, segregation in housing had proved to be among the most resistant. As Carter and Barbara Mills put it in the letter to the Baltimore Home Builders Association quoted at the beginning of this section: "Housing remains as one of the most important areas of discrimination. And this barrier will be swept away. It will go because it is wrong. Fair-minded whites know it is wrong. . . . The question is 'How will it go?'"[9] In 1965 the CORE Housing Committee, not satisfied with the response to its public appeals, decided to challenge discrimination in apartment rentals directly. Adhering to CORE's tradition, it first employed testing to establish discrimination and then proceeded with pickets and sit-ins, resulting in arrests and publicity, with the goal of reaching settlements with owners. The actions were also intended to bring attention to the need for fair housing legislation at the city, state, and federal level. In August interracial testing teams from the committee established clear instances of discrimination in new apartment complexes in northern Baltimore. In one of the tests, at Edward Myerberg's Chartley II Apartments in suburban Reisterstown, white tester Fred Nass was offered an apartment and African American Walter Carter was refused. Picketing and sit-ins followed, leading to arrest warrants against the protesters. Participants in the actions were interracial, and among the other young whites taking part were David Eberhardt and Tom Lewis, both later involved in prominent antidraft actions of the peace movement in the Baltimore area.[10]

As American involvement in the war escalated, the national CORE organization took a more antiwar stance than some of the other traditional civil rights organizations, notably the NAACP and National Urban League, both of which were very closely associated with the Johnson administration's goals in the antipoverty program and civil rights legislation. National CORE leaders supported the 1965 antiwar march on Washington, sponsored by Students for a Democratic Society, did not participate in the White House Conference on Civil Rights in 1966, and agreed to join the Spring Mobilization movement against the war in 1967.[11] But, increasingly, CORE leaders were wary of the antiwar movement for what they perceived to be its reluctance to link the Vietnam War with racism. And at the local level, the Baltimore chapter was not especially vocal on the war, keeping its paramount focus on civil rights.

Indeed, in the mid-1960s CORE, like a number of other civil rights organizations, was convulsed by turmoil. Newer voices championed Black Power and challenged the interracial nature of the organization. In 1965 James Farmer stepped down from his leadership position. At its 1966 national convention in Baltimore, CORE endorsed the Black Power slogan, abandoned its commitment to nonviolence, abrogated its policy of avoiding condemnation of the Vietnam War, and heard convention speaker Stokely Carmichael assert, "We don't need white liberals." The following year CORE deleted the term "multi-racial" from its constitution, and its commitment to nonviolence continued to fade.[12]

These voices of change were felt locally when in 1966 the national organization made the decision to select Baltimore as a "target city" for programs intended to challenge racism and address more directly the problems of the black poor—rather than seek integration, by now being interpreted as a middle-class goal.[13] A number of local civil rights leaders opposed the choice, fearing it would undermine their own efforts, and Mayor Theodore McKeldin, who felt he had a relatively good record on race, expressed dismay. But probably most disturbed were local CORE leaders, such as Walter Carter, who felt themselves pushed aside by a new, more radical agenda and by outsiders unfamiliar with Baltimore circumstances.

At its inception the Target City program was ambitious in scope—promising to address welfare rights, school opportunity, voter registration, housing, unionization, and community organization—and abrasive in tone. Within a year it had experienced internal difficulties that led to the reassignment of its outspoken director, Danny Gant, said by some to be "abrupt and impetuous."[14] Ironically, its most notable accomplishment had not been radical at all—a partnership with the U.S. Department of Labor and Humble Oil Company to train ghetto school dropouts for jobs as gas station managers. Yet, in a thinly veiled reference to the fear of urban unrest, Gant reported at the end of 1967 that the programs had provided "the foundation for the building of a better city and the prevention of bloodshed and riots, which Baltimore has thus far escaped."[15] In 1968 *Baltimore Sun* reporter James Dilts observed that CORE, which had its origins as an "integrationist" organization, was sounding "closer to the separatism of the Black Muslims."[16]

CORE's Housing Committee ran headlong into the changing political and ideological shifts of the national organization and its local Target City campaign. In the fall of 1965 the local chapter's Housing Committee had continued its campaign for open-occupancy legislation and its protest actions against discrimination in Baltimore-area housing complexes. As the target of sustained demonstrations the group selected Horizon House, a new high-rise apartment building at Calvert and Chase streets in the city's Mt. Vernon district whose owner was president of Maryland's Apartment House Owners Association.[17] In the midst of a series of sustained actions at the complex during May, the national leadership of CORE and its local Target City staff increasingly inserted themselves as spokespersons at the expense of the local chapter members. And when a partial settlement was announced following negotiations with the mayor, the local chapter leadership had been kept in the dark. As dismaying as the power grab was to them, especially troubling was a subsequent press statement by Walter Brooks, Target City director, that "the campaign against the luxury apartments did not focus accurately on the major problems of Negro residents of the inner city. . . . Slum housing, rather than luxury living, is a top priority item in the CORE program."[18] In short, the Housing Committee focus on a broad-based breakthrough on open housing was now being portrayed by the parent organization as irrelevant to the needs of the black poor and the local leadership's direction characterized as elitist. As Barbara Mills reflected subsequently on the meaning of the incident, "As we had known all along, Target City CORE hadn't a clue what our local movement had been about."[19]

Stung by this interference, more moderate CORE members formed a new interracial organization, the Activists for Fair Housing, initially led by Walter Carter, Sampson Green, Fred Jones, and Barbara Mills.[20] Philip Berrigan, a Josephite priest already known for his social activism, had recently arrived in Baltimore and lent his support to the Activists in the fight for housing equality. In an indication of the competing choices among peace and freedom priorities that crisis times compelled, he soon notified the group that he would have to step away to concentrate his efforts in the fight against the Vietnam War.

In 1967 the Activists, still focused on the goal of open occupancy, mounted a campaign against major housing developers to press for voluntary agreements to make their projects available on a nondiscriminatory basis. The group made the decision to target prominent, respected civic leader Joseph Meyerhoff, described by Mills as "the largest builder and financier of middle-income housing in the metropolitan area," a decision based on the strategy that should he respond positively, other builders would follow suit. Though the protests produced little initial response, the following year, one week after the assassination of Martin Luther King, Jr., Congress passed the Fair Housing Act, prohibiting discrimination in rentals, sales, and mortgages. Passage of the act had long been a goal of the civil rights movement and the special focus of both the CORE Housing Committee and its successor, the Activists. As if in vindication of the protest actions the previous year, soon after passage of the act Meyerhoff announced a policy of nondiscrimination for his firm's apartments in the Baltimore area, and his lead was followed by other builders.[21]

Penance marchers in a demonstration along Charles Street designed to confess the "guilt of white racism." (Originally published in the *Baltimore Afro-American*, April 14, 1968. Reprinted courtesy of the *Baltimore News American* Collection, University of Maryland–College Park.)

In 1969–1971 the Activists regrouped to mount a campaign using CORE-style tactics to challenge blockbusting, which was included in the prohibited practices by the 1968 Fair Housing Act. The Activists focused on the Morris Goldseker Company, which they charged had exploited black home buyers by charging exorbitant markups on houses in racially changing neighborhoods in West Baltimore, especially in the Edmondson Village area. In a series of reports, the group used the term "the black tax" to describe the difference between the cost of housing in white neighborhoods and what African Americans had to pay to gain comparable housing in sections where white flight had been triggered by racial fears. However, a civil suit filed against the Goldseker Company eventually was dismissed, leaving the charges unresolved.[22] On July 31, 1971, in the midst of the Activists' campaign against blockbusting, Walter Carter died, and his tragic passing seemed to represent the coda to a significant period in Baltimore's civil rights movement.[23]

In conclusion, CORE as a civil rights organization was born in an ideology of pacifism and committed to nonviolent direct action, and it became one of the more outspoken national groups against the Vietnam War as it escalated. Yet racism and civil rights remained its principal focus.

At the local level of the Baltimore CORE chapter, civil rights activism produced a broad coalition, white and black, and included some—such as Eberhardt, Lewis, and Berrigan—who later played key roles in prominent antiwar actions. Similarly, leaders of the local chapter of CORE such as Walter Carter worked closely with them in civil rights activism; in fact, Carter testified as a character witness for Philip Berrigan at the trial of the Baltimore Four.[24] However, the local chapter of CORE demonstrated little public voice on the war, nor did it express antiwar concerns explicitly in its principal programs and actions. Indeed, in the immediate period leading up to 1968, ideological conflicts over its original interracial and nonviolent commitments, as well as internal struggles, became major preoccupations, overshadowing any explicit antiwar message.

Baltimore Antiwarriors: The Case of the Catonsville Nine

> On May 17, 1968, two women and seven men, three in clerical attire, arrived at the Selective Service office, Local Board 33, located in the Knights of Columbus building in Catonsville, Maryland, a suburb of Baltimore. Entering the second-floor Selective Service office, the raiders brushed past three shocked employees and headed for the filing cabinets along the wall. They seized several hundred I-A draft records, stuffing them into two wire incinerator baskets. Outside in the parking lot, the files were spilled on the ground, doused with homemade napalm, and ignited. Several onlookers, including previously alerted members of the press, gathered to watch the event. As the documents burned, the participants clasped hands near the fire and quietly recited the Lord's Prayer. Their purpose, they said, was to stop the flow of soldiers to Vietnam. "We do this because everything else has failed," said one. . . . The entire action took less than fifteen minutes. The protestors were later identified as Philip Berrigan, Daniel Berrigan, David Darst, John Hogan, Tom Lewis, John Melville, Marjorie Melville, George Mische, and Mary Moylan.[25]

The May 17, 1968, incident in Catonsville was not the first time, and it would not be the last, that a relatively small group of antiwar activists took direct action against the machinery of the selective service system. As the war in Vietnam escalated and the antiwar movement grew in size and diversity, the methods of resistance to the war also began to extend beyond traditional mass demonstrations. The draft became a stationary target of direct actions. Only a week after the October 22, 1967, March on the Pentagon, the largest mass antiwar demonstration in history to that point—made famously ridiculous by the Yippie agenda of "levitating the Pentagon" and famously recorded in Mailer's genre-busting *Armies of the*

Night—Father Philip Berrigan and Tom Lewis led a direct action that represented a radical shifting of strategy in the antiwar movement. Berrigan and Lewis, who would both soon become leading members of the Catonsville Nine, directed their initial antidraft action against the draft board offices in downtown Baltimore's Customs House. Joined by David Eberhardt and Reverend James Mengel, the Baltimore Four, as they would soon become known, entered the building at midday on October 28, 1967, and poured blood—some of which was their own—on cabinet drawers filled with 1-A draft files. Out on bail and awaiting federal trial they began planning a larger, follow-up action.

As it happened, the trial of the Four was set for early April 1968. While one of their primary intents had been to draw attention to issues of racism and urban poverty, it was a letdown and frustration to the Four that their trial did not stir much interest outside of Baltimore. The originality of their largely symbolic action was overwhelmed by the media attention rightfully given to the murder of Dr. King and the subsequent disturbances in cities and campuses around the country, including the extensive unrest in Baltimore. This confirmed, for Berrigan especially, the need for war resistance to move toward more than symbolic actions. They organized to act again and go beyond the symbolism of sprinkled blood, in the process moving the antiwar movement into uncharted territory of draft disruption. At Catonsville their symbol of choice would be fire, and the consequential result would be the actual destruction of several hundred draft files. With this step, the Nine ushered in a new era of "ultra resistance" that inspired many subsequent "hit and stay" actions around the United States, destroying tens of thousands of draft records and ultimately sounding the death knell for the draft. Proceeding from Daniel Berrigan's charge—"If you want to do something big, don't burn your draft card, go burn files"—these antiwar actions evolved to become increasingly effective at actually disrupting the draft.[26] Consider, for example, a single action by the Milwaukee Fourteen that destroyed approximately ten thousand draft files in September 1968, while the Nine awaited their October trial.[27]

The story leading up to the actions of the Four and the Nine mirrors and illustrates the convergences and divergences of the national freedom and peace movements. The prepared press statement of the Baltimore Four included this conjoining of missions: "We charge that America would rather protect its empire of overseas profits than welcome its black people, rebuild its slums and cleanse its air and water. Thus we have singled out inner city draft boards for our actions. We invite friends in the peace and freedom movements to continue moving with us from dissent to resistance."[28] At the trial of the Catonsville Nine in October 1968, Tom Lewis began his personal defense statement by referring to his witness of a civil rights protest that proved transformative for him—the aforementioned 1963 demonstrations against segregation led by Walter Carter and CORE at Gwynn Oak Park. Lewis, a young artist, witnessed two things that day, the ugliness of raw racism and the courageous efforts of civil rights leaders to confront that ugly injustice through direct action. He stood by as a number of local faith and civil rights leaders, including Carter, were cuffed and loaded into paddy wagons.

The connecting thread to his trial with the Nine was direct for Lewis: "Let me speak of an experience that has bearing on why I am here. As you recall some years ago there were civil rights demonstrations at Gwynn Oak Park here in Baltimore. The issue was the right of the Black man to use the park. I went there to do some sketches of the demonstrations. When I arrived they had just arrested some clergymen. You know, I had a feeling that I should be where they were."[29]

Over the next several years Lewis became deeply involved in Baltimore's freedom movement, working with the Catholic Interracial Council and CORE as a civil rights activist. In her memoirs of the civil rights struggle in Baltimore, Barbara Mills described Lewis as "one of CORE's most active demonstrators." That Lewis, who was white, would have such a central and active role in CORE was not extraordinary in the years preceding 1968.[30] As noted previously, CORE demonstrations and direct actions in the early and middle 1960s were marked by their interracial makeup.[31] In fact, this diversity was strategically employed to highlight racial injustice. Tom Lewis frequently played the role of a "white tester" in CORE fair housing actions.[32] It was through these personal experiences of involvement in the civil rights struggle that Lewis moved from being a curious observer to a public demonstrator to the front lines of direct action and civil disobedience. In his trial statement Lewis explained, "I was slowly being educated in the realities around me. . . . It is a shocking thing walking a picket line for the first time sensing the hostility of people—The White people—particularly when we went to suburbia to demonstrate for open occupancy."[33] Lewis's recognition of the shadow side of suburbia was highlighted later in his antiwar activism in the suburb of Catonsville.

Similarly for Father Philip Berrigan, it was his experiences of racial injustice and of civil rights activism that were formative in shaping his worldview and, ultimately, his antiwar activism. Stationed in Georgia as a soldier readying for World War II service, young Berrigan saw sharecropper poverty and Jim Crow racism. In the military he had witnessed the separate and unequal treatment of black soldiers. In his autobiography Berrigan remembers, "Blacks were drafted from a racist society into a segregated army, which treated them like pariahs."[34] After the war Berrigan joined the Josephites, a Catholic religious order with the unique mission of serving African American communities. Berrigan was stationed as a priest in New Orleans in the late 1950s and early 1960s, and there he began to speak out from the pulpit on issues of racial injustice. In a scene foreshadowing the Nine's choice of suburban Catonsville, and also demonstrating the unflinching directness for which he became known, Berrigan remembers, "I was sent on occasion to offer the Eucharist to the all-white parishes that ringed New Orleans. . . . I would offer homilies on racial justice. . . . The parishioners who shouted at me or stormed out during mass were good people. They just didn't want to admit their complicity in our collective oppression of African-Americans. They saw nothing odd about bringing their children to Mass on Sunday, and sending them to segregated schools on Monday."[35]

Before Lewis had started his own activist journey at Gwynn Oak Park, Berrigan, who was by nearly a generation Lewis's elder,[36] had stepped up his activism and himself become involved with CORE, attempting to join national leader James Farmer in an airport integration action in Jackson, Mississippi, in 1962. While in Atlanta to catch a connecting flight, airport officials directed Berrigan to a phone call from his Josephite superior general, who ordered him to return home immediately; this was just one early instance of him pushing the boundaries of his clerical role and expectations.[37] While Berrigan acknowledged that the Josephites were more committed to racial justice and civil rights than most other orders, he continued to challenge the limits of their support with his bold activism against the racial hierarchy in the South. In an effort to remove him from the epicenter, he was sent to teach in the Josephite seminary in Newburg, New York.

In 1965 Philip, along with his brother Daniel, who also would become a leader of the Nine, had answered Dr. King's call for clergy to join in a march from Selma to Montgomery. In his autobiography, Phil remembers feeling the fear and energy of participation in the movement when police surrounded the chapel where they were gathered and stopped the march from happening.[38] By the mid-1960s Dan was a nationally prominent antiwar activist—as early as World War II, in fact, he had asked Phil to reconsider his military service. But now Phil Berrigan too began connecting the messages and actions of the freedom and peace movements. At a talk in Newburg, he recalls, "I asked why we were sending poor African American kids from the Mississippi Delta to kill poor Vietnamese kids in the Mekong Delta? I said the war was an attack on poor people of color."[39] His superiors ordered him to leave New York at once for Baltimore, the order's home base, where he was stationed at Saint Peter Claver parish, which served a predominantly African American section of the city.[40]

By the time Berrigan met Lewis after arriving in Baltimore in 1965, his civil rights passion was already combining with an increasingly vocal and primary antiwar activism. For Berrigan the relationship between poverty, racism, and war was direct and obvious, and it was war that began to emerge as his activist priority. "I concluded that war is the overarching evil in this country. Every other social lesion is related to our willingness to blow up the planet. . . . Racism, discrimination against women, poverty, domestic violence, are connected to this intention."[41] And the war in Vietnam became the most pressing instance of this convergence of issues. "The war in Southeast Asia was our country's paranoia and racism metastasized into genocidal madness. Not a mistake. Not a misunderstanding."[42]

By 1966 Phil Berrigan and Tom Lewis were convinced that direct action was the only approach. There was an urgency to their peace activism born of the life-and-death stakes of war. "We organized seminars, we marched, sang, and chanted; the killing got worse."[43] Phil first heard the idea of raiding draft boards at a Students for a Democratic Society conference brainstorming session in Chicago. He wanted such actions to be pragmatic efforts from the first, but he was persuaded to go ahead with a largely symbolic blood pouring. By the time of the Four in 1967 Phil Berrigan was a recognized, if controversial, leader in Baltimore's peace movement. Along with Tom Lewis and others he founded the Baltimore Interfaith Peace Mission and began considering higher-stakes direct actions against the war. They consistently maintained that war and racism were inextricably related, and they attempted to connect these issues symbolically, by highlighting domestic issues in the urban and suburban settings they chose for their antiwar actions, and explicitly, in their subsequent court statements. While their attempt to interrelate the peace and freedom agendas was sincere and significant, a practical divergence was unavoidable as they became nationally prominent antiwar icons and, perhaps more importantly, as they faced the reality of serving significant time in prison as federally convicted felons.

This practical divergence can be seen in Berrigan's quickly shifting priorities during his early years in Baltimore. Upon settling in the city, Berrigan had immediately accepted an invitation to serve on the advisory board of the Activists, a civil rights organization evolving from CORE and focusing on open-occupancy housing. Barbara Mills described Phil Berrigan to Lewis as being one of Baltimore's most "faithful housing demonstrators."[44] But by 1967 and 1968 Berrigan was increasingly spending his time speaking and acting against the war, locally and nationally. Shortly after the Baltimore Four action, Phil wrote to Mills saying, "I think it would be best Barbara if you dropped me from the Advisory Board. There is not only the ongoing complication of the peace issue, but also every indication that we're going to jail following our trial. . . . You deserve profound respect and commendation. [Signed] Peace and Freedom, Phil."[45] Berrigan's closing phrase "Peace and Freedom" again reflects his dual commitment to the struggles against war and for civil rights but also foreshadows the priority they were taking in his activism. Mills did not give up easily and tried to persuade him to continue his civil rights work: "What difference does it make if we destroy the world if we can't even solve our racial problems here at home?" Berrigan's logic, however, ran the opposite direction, giving primacy to the antiwar agenda, and so, in her words, they "agreed to disagree and parted directions with mutual respect and friendship intact."[46]

Phil Berrigan's and Tom Lewis's narratives of being formatively influenced by their experiences of racial injustice and civil rights activism illustrate the convergences and divergences of the freedom and peace movements. In fact, while their stories are diverse, all of the individuals making up the support teams and direct activists for the Four and Nine actions came to their unflinching antiwar positions and radical methods through formative experiences of human rights violations—domestic or international. None of them had deep or direct connections to Vietnam or its people specifically.[47] They acted in Catonsville not only with Vietnam in mind but to voice their opposition to human injustice in Guatemala (John and Marjorie Melville, John Hogan), in Uganda (Mary Moylan), in Saint Louis (David Darst), and in Brooklyn and Mexico (George Mische). Similarly, for others in the support team—Dave Eberhart, Dean Pappas, and Bill O'Connor—their antiwar activism evolved directly from their work in Baltimore's civil rights movement.

Conclusion

I AM A SOLDIER

I am a soldier and black is my skin,
I must kill a man who could be my friend.
I am fighting for something I don't understand,
Dear God, why am I in this unknown land?
This is my battle, that's what they say,
And I must keep on killing as I am ordered today.
And maybe one day I'll be killed too.
My battle is home, in my native land,
The war that I know, and understand.
Where the black must fight if he wants to be free,
If he wants his civil rights and equality.
This is the kind of war that I am prepared to fight,
The one that will make me equal to the white.
Send me back to the battle at home,
Because this war here is not my own.
It only came about because of some man's greed,
But the war at home will have some man freed.

This poem by twenty-three-year-old Alexander Chin, a marine from Baltimore, was originally published in the *Baltimore Afro-American* on March 2, 1968. Chin was killed in action in Vietnam several days later.

The events following the assassination of Martin Luther King, Jr., in April 1968 provide insight into the dynamics within Baltimore's CORE chapter as it wrestled with the conflicting currents of the civil rights and peace movements. First, the response to the crisis generated very different messages from Danny Gant, director of CORE Target City and a Baltimore outsider, whose first reaction was to call for a militant response, and of local CORE leaders, who sought to calm the situation as rioting spun out of control. When Governor Spiro Agnew convened a meeting of civil rights leaders a week later, he pointedly excluded the national officials of groups he considered too militant, including the national leadership of the Student Nonviolent Coordinating Committee (SNCC) and CORE, as well as the Target City program, but on the invitation list was James Griffin, chair of the local CORE chapter. However, rather than affirm the positive role of Baltimore CORE and other civil rights leaders, many of whom had taken to the streets to try to calm the violence at considerable risk to themselves, Agnew proceeded to criticize them for not standing up to militants and for failing to do enough to prevent the riots—which led many to walk out in protest. In their eloquent statement responding to Agnew, the civil rights leadership indignantly and justifiably rebuked the governor for his accusations and defended the role they had played. But their statement linking the fight for justice at home with the war in Vietnam was instructive: "The people of Maryland, black and white, require leadership of the first order in bringing about those changes for which black men are fighting and dying in Vietnam."[48] The formula was a long-standing refrain in the calculus of civil rights and America's wars: *If* black men are required to fight and die, *then* rights for African Americans must be ensured at home.

The domestic events of April 1968 also came on the heels of dramatic turns in the Vietnam War. The Tet Offensive in January of that year, while technically a military victory for the United States, brought a heightened public awareness of the cost and complexity of the war and a new skepticism about the Johnson administration's approach and honesty. In March President Johnson shocked the nation by announcing he would not run for a second term, and Robert Kennedy entered the race on an antiwar platform that Eugene McCarthy was already popularizing. The complexity of the domestic scene, when weighed against the rising stakes of Vietnam and the possibility of political breakthroughs in the antiwar movement, led Baltimore's antiwarriors to increasingly focus their identity, energy, and actions on the peace movement. While Baltimore's leading peace activists never abandoned the goal of civil rights, a de facto divergence of the movements became increasingly the case by the spring of 1968. The fact that attention to the April trial of the Baltimore Four was overwhelmed by the civil unrest in Baltimore city in the wake of Dr. King's assassination was symbolic of this competing agenda. Phil Berrigan's stepping down from the board of the Activists similarly demonstrates this practical reality. Today, the continued presence of two Catholic Worker houses in Baltimore City, founded in the wake of the tumultuous spring of 1968 by members and supporters of the Catonsville Nine, gives witness to the long-term struggle of this community to keep both the peace and the freedom movements alive and aligned. While there was a practical divergence of the paths taken in the late 1960s, the combined struggle for peace and freedom continues—not as a joined movement, perhaps, but as an interconnected mission in the hearts and minds of these lifelong antiwarriors.[49]

The cases of Baltimore CORE and the Catonsville Nine reflect the convergences and divergences of the freedom and the peace movements nationally through the 1960s. In the early 1960s, with sympathy and public awareness of civil rights issues growing and before the Vietnam War escalated, there was promising cross-involvement of people and issues. CORE had deep roots in peace and nonviolence, and up until about 1966, its racially integrated membership was an ideal as well as a critical strategic component of its open-occupancy activism in Baltimore. The rise of Black Power ideas significantly complicated the role of whites in civil rights organizations such as CORE. Further, while Black Power advocates were often strong in their opposition to the Vietnam War, this antiwar position was not firmly rooted in the nonviolent ideas and methods that had defined the traditional peace movement and the mainstream civil rights movement. Leaders of the Catonsville Nine, such as Phil Berrigan and Tom Lewis, while formatively influenced and deeply engaged in the civil rights movement, began by these same years of 1966–1968 to focus their attention and activism increasingly on stopping the escalating war in Vietnam. While adhering to nonviolence, their methods of direct action against the war became increasingly radical, making continued participation in civil rights actions a practical impossibility even as their role in that movement was becoming less obvious. There is no final and clear verdict to be made from these stories of convergence and divergence. More than anything they reflect the complexity and urgency of these pivotal issues and times as they intersected with the efforts of diverse individuals to engage in the ongoing social struggle for peace and freedom.

NOTES

1. Taylor Branch, *At Canaan's Edge: America in the King Years, 1965–1968* (New York: Simon and Schuster, 2006), 591, 745–746.

2. Simon Hall, *Peace and Freedom: The Civil Rights and Antiwar Movements in the 1960s* (Philadelphia: University of Pennsylvania Press, 2005), 1–2.

3. Ibid., 11.

4. Hall's judgment on the eventual divergence between Black Power advocates and the white-dominated peace movement concurs with the earlier statement by Robert Weisbrot in his history of the civil rights movement that by 1968, "when protest against the war in Vietnam began to draw strong support from liberal Democrats as well as college youths, the ground swell had little connection to black interests or input. By that point the most forceful black critics of the war, once

ardently courted by white radicals, had burned their bridgeheads to the New Left." Robert Weisbrot, *Freedom Bound: A History of America's Civil Rights Movement* (New York: Norton, 1990), 256.

5. Excerpt from a letter from Baltimore CORE's interracial leadership sent to the Baltimore Home Builders Association, the Maryland Association of Real Estate Boards, and to local media on June 17, 1965. Qtd. in Barbara Mills, *"Got My Mind Set on Freedom": Maryland's Story of Black and White Activism, 1663–2000* (Bowie, MD: Heritage Books, 2002), 485.

6. On the history of CORE, see August Meier and Elliott Rudwick, *CORE: A Study in the Civil Rights Movement, 1942–1968* (New York: Oxford University Press, 1973); and for a personal account, see James Farmer, *Lay Bare the Heart: An Autobiography of the Civil Rights Movement* (New York: Arbor House, 1985).

7. This account draws heavily on the memoir by Baltimore chapter CORE staff member Barbara Mills, *"Got My Mind Set on Freedom."* See her account of the chapter's origins (151). Mills, a white woman who moved to Baltimore in 1957, became actively involved as a member and officer of CORE in the mid-1960s and participated in both the chapter's Housing Committee and its successor, the Activists for Fair Housing. *"Got My Mind Set on Freedom"* serves as not only a memoir but also a history that provides insight into the operation of the chapter.

8. The Gwynn Oak action represented the first time the leadership of the National Council of Churches joined a major civil rights demonstration; the protest included demonstrators from nearby cities who joined local organizers, among them members of the CORE chapter, clergy from the Interdenominational Ministerial Alliance, and other area civil rights activists. "393 Integrationists, Many Clerics, Arrested at Gwynn Oak Park," *Baltimore Sun*, July 5, 1963. The amusement park episode in John Waters's *Hairspray* is patterned after the Gwynn Oak demonstrations. Today, Gwynn Oak Park is part of the public Baltimore County Parks system but has been restored as an open-grass and woodlands park. The surrounding residential neighborhoods from which the park draws its many users are nearly 100 percent African American.

9. Mills, *"Got My Mind Set on Freedom,"* 485.

10. Ibid., 502–506.

11. Hall, *Peace and Freedom*, 24–25, 67, 108.

12. Meier and Rudwick, *CORE*, 414–419. Barbara Mills described Farmer's resignation as a "thunderbolt": "I don't think any of us in Baltimore CORE who met and talked so often were even aware of the black/white internecine warfare that was tearing national CORE apart, certainly not how serious it was. That was something we learned about later—much to our horror—when the 'new' CORE invaded Baltimore" (*"Got My Mind Set on Freedom,"* 520).

13. Meier and Rudwick describe the Target City programs as an attempt by the national office of CORE to demonstrate "how the power of the black poor could be mobilized for their own advancement," 409.

14. "CORE Working to Revitalize Target City Project," *Baltimore Sun*, September 29, 1967.

15. Danny Gant, director, "Report on Target City Project, November 4, 1967" (typescript, Maryland Room, Enoch Pratt Free Library).

16. James E. Dilts, "The Warning Trumpet: CORE Is the Only Voice Black People Ever Had," *Baltimore Sun Magazine*, December 1, 1968. Other accounts of Baltimore CORE Target City developments include "Target City: Five-Year

Rights Campaign Contemplated by CORE," *Baltimore Sun*, October 7, 1966; Ben A. Franklin, "CORE's Target City Program in Baltimore Now Hailed for Its Moderation," *New York Times*, April 16, 1967; "It's Job CORE for City," *Baltimore News-American*, April 30, 1967; "Danny Gant Leaving Baltimore CORE," *Baltimore Evening Sun*, August 7, 1968. "Milton Holmes Named Director of Baltimore CORE [Target City Project]," *Baltimore Sun*, October 12, 1968.

17. Mills, *"Got My Mind Set on Freedom,"* 513–518.

18. Qtd. in ibid., 556. Mills noted that she and Sampson Green, cochairs of the CORE Housing Committee at the time, had not been consulted on the settlement agreement (555).

19. Mills, *"Got My Mind Set on Freedom,"* 556.

20. In their history of CORE, Meier and Rudwick wrote that long-time Baltimore chapter members such as Carter "questioned the new focus [of the national leadership] and finally in 1966 seceded to continue their fair housing campaign" (368). In an interview with Edward Orser, June 13, 1981, Sampson Green explained the origins of the group this way: "We [the local chapter of CORE] established a housing committee, and the primary focus of our activities was desegregation of housing at that time, up until '66 or '67, when the national office of CORE came to the city in the form of Target City, and that disrupted the local chapter of CORE considerably, and so a group of us primarily in the housing committee withdrew from CORE and organized the Activists."

21. Mills, *"Got My Mind Set on Freedom,"* 574–576.

22. On the Activists and the Goldseker case, see W. Edward Orser, *Blockbusting in Baltimore: The Edmondson Village Story* (Lexington: University Press of Kentucky, 1994), 133–137; the reports by the Activists included "Communities under Siege" (1970) and "Baltimore under Siege: The Impact of Financing on the Baltimore Home Buyer, 1960–1970" (1971).

23. Chester Wickwire, chaplain at Johns Hopkins University, who was respected locally for his active involvement on behalf of both peace and freedom, penned a poetic tribute to Carter comparing him to a great tree. The poem "Trees That Reach Farthest Upward" (qtd. in Mills, *"Got My Mind Set on Freedom,"* 645, and included here with permission from Mary Ann Wickwire) reads in part:

> *This tree was never quiet*
> *He saw loneliness of the city*
> *He heard cries of laborers*
> *He was angered when he could not break bread with his neighbor*
> *He suffered when justice was denied at the gate . . .*
> *He set a plumb line in the city and we did not measure up.*

24. Murray Polner and Jim O'Grady. *Disarmed and Dangerous: The Radical Life and Times of Daniel and Philip Berrigan* (Boulder, CO: Westview Press, 1997), 201.

25. "Fire and Faith: The Catonsville Nine File," Enoch Pratt Free Library, available at http://c9.mdch.org/ (accessed August 7, 2009).

26. Among the occasions that Dan Berrigan voiced this call to "do something big" included a speech at Towson State College, October 4, 1968 (*Baltimore Sun*, "Police Seize Berrigan in Draft Case," B20).

27. See Jerry Elmer, *Felon for Peace: The Memoir of a Vietnam-era Draft Resister* (Nashville, TN: Vanderbilt University Press, 2005), 80. Other subsequent

Catonsville Nine–inspired actions included the Chicago 15 (May 1969), Women against Daddy Warbucks (New York City, July 1969), the New York 8 (August 1969), and the Boston 8 (November 1969). The methods developed beyond "hit and stay." For example, on July 2, 1969, five women calling themselves "Women against Daddy Warbucks" broke in after hours to a complex housing thirteen draft boards. Rather than stay on-site for immediate arrest, they reappeared two days later at Rockefeller Center tossing homemade confetti made from the shredded draft files.

28. Polner and O'Grady, *Disarmed and Dangerous,* 177.

29. Daniel Berrigan, *The Trial of the Catonsville Nine* (New York: Fordham University Press, 2004), 39–40.

30. In a 1966 visit from CORE national leader James Farmer, Lewis, an artist, presented Farmer with one of his original paintings. Mills records this exchange in an interesting photo ("*Got My Mind Set on Freedom,*" 534).

31. Ibid., 506.

32. As they were awaiting arrest during one sit-in, Lewis remembers, the owner threatened to proceed with his "regular" insect fumigation of the apartment, saying, "The picketing we have no objection to, but the lying around like a bunch of animals we [do]" (Mills, "*Got My Mind Set on Freedom,*" 507).

33. D. Berrigan, *The Trial,* 40.

34. Philip Berrigan with Fred Wilcox, *Fighting the Lamb's War: Skirmishes with the American Empire* (Monroe, MN: Common Courage Press, 1996), 32.

35. Ibid., 55.

36. Philip Berrigan was born in 1923 and passed away in 2002. Tom Lewis was born in 1940 and, perhaps poetically, if prematurely, passed away on April 4, 2008, the fortieth anniversary of Dr. King's assassination.

37. P. Berrigan, *Fighting the Lamb's War*, 59.

38. Ibid., 61.

39. Ibid., 82.

40. Located on Freemont and Pennsylvania avenues on Baltimore's west side. This area was hard hit by the April 1968 disturbances and today remains an area with persistent social and material challenges.

41. P. Berrigan, *Fighting the Lamb's War,* 64.

42. Ibid., 92.

43. Ibid., 87.

44. Mills, "*Got My Mind Set on Freedom,*" 577.

45. Ibid., 578.

46. Ibid.

47. Daniel Berrigan's dramatic POW rescue trip to Hanoi with Howard Zinn did not occur until 1968.

48. Gene Oishi, "Negroes Quit Conference with Agnew," *Baltimore Sun*, April 12, 1968; Mills, "*Got My Mind Set on Freedom,*" 626–627.

49. Both houses have a direct line to the ultraresistance actions of the Four and Nine. Jonah House, founded in 1973 by Phil Berrigan and his wife Elizabeth McAlister, remains a home of peace and center of the peace movement. Viva House, founded in 1968 by Willa Bickam and Brendan Walsh, both support team members of the Nine, has served its struggling West Baltimore community with food and

hospitality with an inspiring and unwavering commitment to justice and human dignity for forty years. In 2008, Brendan was held up at gunpoint near Viva House. He was fortunate to emerge unharmed, and in a September 2 op-ed to the *Baltimore Sun* he decried the social injustices that led to such individual desperation and violence, and he voiced his intent to continue loving and serving his community.

Part III

Consequences for Education, Business, and Community Organizing

9

The Pats Family

Oral History

In 1968 Sidney and Ida Pats were resident owners of Downes Brothers Pharmacy, located in the 800 block of West North Avenue, an area hard hit by the Baltimore riot. When the Patses purchased the pharmacy in 1950, their neighbors and customers were primarily white; by 1968 most white residents had either died or moved away and, in a typical pattern of racial succession, African Americans had came to dominate the neighborhood. In this interview, Ida Pats and her daughters Sharon Pats Singer, who was sixteen at the time of the riot, and Betty Pats Katzenelson, who was thirteen, recall living and working in an urban neighborhood, the looting and burning of their pharmacy during the riot, and family members' subsequent efforts to rebuild their lives. Ida Pats is a retired accountant. Sharon and Betty raised their families in Baltimore's northwest suburbs, where they continue to live. Their outrage at the profound losses they suffered still lingers after forty years; their sense of personal violation remains palpable.

Valerie Wiggins conducted the interview, and Bashi Rose recorded it, on February 20, 2007; both were University of Baltimore students at the time. Also present at the interview were an elderly North Avenue neighbor who wished to remain unnamed; the historian Eric Singer, Sharon Singer's son; Baltimore '68 oral history project director Elizabeth Nix of the University of Baltimore history faculty; and Gadi Dechter, a reporter for the Baltimore Sun.

Sharon Singer: My parents got the pharmacy in 1950. And in 1950 the area, North Avenue, was a white area. The store was in the middle of the block. It was owned by someone else when they bought it, and, in fact, the woman who worked behind the counter, Miss Davis, continued to work there. We lived upstairs. That's all we knew, North Avenue. That was our home.

The store itself was on the first level. At that time it had in it a fountain. The fountain had ice cream and sodas and things like that, really fun kind of things. And then the store had patent goods and medicine; and in the back, the pharmacy was in the back, like an old-time pharmacy. And then as the years went on, the neighborhood did change and it became a mixed neighborhood, let's say. And at some point the fountain became something that was more of a hindrance, and they took it out. And they put in liquor because of the neighborhood change, it was an adaptation to the neighborhood. It was beer in the coolers, and so they took out all the ice cream, like bars and cones and things like that.

The store was a multipurpose kind of place and the people who came in, most of them were regular customers. There was no Rite Aid [pharmacy], there were no big-box stores at that time. This was the place where they could get their prescription drugs, and they could get their toiletries, and it was a place also—even though there was a bank on the corner, which was Union Trust—where they could get their checks cashed, because they did not have accounts at the bank. My mother did the taxes for people during tax season, right in the middle of the store. She would sit there at the little desk, and everybody'd be waiting in line to get their income taxes done.

Betty Katzenelson: And the line would be out the door on check day.

Sharon Singer: What she means by check day is when the people in the neighborhood got welfare checks—not all the people, but whoever did. I mean the line would be out the door to cash the checks. Why they didn't use the bank, I don't really know.

Ida Pats: The banks didn't accept them, and they didn't accept the banks.

Sharon Singer: And they had a trust in my parents, in fact so much so that my parents had a little file box, and in the file box were file cards with people's names on them, and if they didn't have enough money toward the end of the month to buy their toiletries or to get whatever they needed, my parents would write their names down and they would get it on account, and okay, you're good for it. No interest or anything like that; it was just a very trusting kind of system. It was just a neighborhood business.

Let me tell you a little bit about my mother and my father. My mother worked. She got up in the morning and she worked. Before the store even opened, she got us ready for school, did our lunches and all that sort of thing. We'd go downstairs and out the door we would go, and she would open the store for work. Then my father would get up, and he'd come down later. She really was the proprietor of the store, and he was the pharmacist. At eleven o'clock the store would close, at twelve on the weekends.

Their life revolved around everything to do with the store. It was the purchasing, and it was the inventory, and it was the bookkeeping, and everything involved with the running of the store. That was their life.

All I knew growing up was that, that was my home. I would come home from school and go to work in the store. That's what I did. I would be down there waiting on customers and talking to people, and it was great. It was different than your typical upbringing, but I didn't know anything different. And I enjoyed it. The customers were friendly and it was fun. We had people to talk to and things to see and do. I never thought about race as an issue at all.

Ida Pats: They were the customers.

Betty Katzenelson: Just people who lived there.

Sharon Singer: Whether they were white, whether they were black, it never, ever crossed my mind. It was just fun for me. So I think what happened was, when the riots came, I don't think that we really thought that anything bad was going to happen. It was a trusting kind of thing where this was our neighborhood. And they just wouldn't, they just wouldn't do this. It never occurred to us.

And I think that that was true for my father, because I remember before the riots in Baltimore, after Martin Luther King was killed, it was a very tense situation in the country, and one of the women who was working at Lou's bar up the street, a black woman named Brooks, came into the store and came back and said to my father—I was standing there—"You know, you better get out." And he wasn't really listening to that, because he never thought anything was going to happen. And sure enough, the next day—she came into the store literally on that Saturday, and the riot started on Sunday.[1]

I was standing there, and I just wasn't believing what I was hearing. I went to sleep like any other night. I got up. I was driving at that time. I had turned sixteen in December and got my license, and this was April. So, that Sunday morning we went shopping. I was taking my mother in the car, and then after we went shopping, we went to pick up my sister Betty at Hebrew School, all the way out at Park Heights Avenue. And we came down I-83 to go back home—here I'm sixteen, I got this big car, and I'm driving down 83. We turn off at the exit—North Avenue. Make the right to go towards the house—you could see the neighborhood, it's a couple blocks up, right near Mount Royal Avenue. And the whole block was in smoke and flames. That is the point where we freaked out. We didn't know what was going on. My father was sleeping—it was Sunday morning. So, "Oh my God! Is he okay?" At that point I am thinking, I got to get home. The streets were blocked off. There were masses of people in the streets. And masses—all I saw were masses of black people in the streets. That's all I saw.

Soldier–citizen exchange on North Patterson Park Avenue. (Reprinted courtesy of the Lt. James V. Kelly Baltimore City Police Department Collection.)

Betty Katzenelson: And flames.

Sharon Singer: And flames. They wouldn't let us get past. I knew the back roads, and went around and came down through to the Esso station, which was right across the street. There was my father, waiting for us, standing in the Esso station. I will never forget that. He got in the car, and we left.

Betty Katzenelson: Somebody called him and said, "It's burning at the corner." It was that bank. First Union Trust. Somebody called him: "The bank's on fire."

Ida Pats: We picked up the Eisenbergs. They had no car. They had the jewelry repair shop two doors down. Mrs. Eisenberg was in the car with us. She had no transportation. She didn't drive. She had gone shopping with us. My husband and all three of her children and her husband were standing in front of the Esso station.

Sharon Singer: They piled in the car, and we left.

Betty Katzenelson: And then we saw our brother Harvey. Harvey was coming down the street because he had been at Umbec [University of Maryland–Baltimore County, or UMBC]. He had gone to study or something, and he was coming down the street and we hollered, "Harvey! Harvey!"

Sharon Singer: And at that point the house was not burned, when we left. But by the time we came back the next day, the whole house, everything was burned.

Ida Pats: The city said they were watching it. But they didn't; they didn't watch it. The looters were just wild. Everything. Even the store. Everything was out. They looted everything. Everything was empty.

Sharon Singer: There was nothing there. The city said that it was going to be guarded. The National Guard was down there. But they were told they couldn't do anything. They weren't allowed to use guns. But yet—the mayor at the time was [Thomas] D'Alesandro—and in Little Italy they were on the roofs with rifles.[2] That was okay. So. You know. Had we known, maybe we would have done something differently, I don't know, but I think that it was just where this is your community, you know, the community supports you, you support them, and that's the way it should be.

Betty Katzenelson: And it didn't work out that way.

Sharon Singer: And there were people from out of town coming in to organize the, the riots. And so it wasn't just the people in the neighborhood.[3] And so what did we do? We had nowhere to go. Everything we knew was completely gone. My parents went to a motel for a couple of nights. The three of us [kids] went to my aunt's house. And then we all went to live with our uncle. And that was the end of my life as I knew it, let's put it that way. After that, I had nothing. I had no clothes; I had no anything.

Betty Katzenelson: And no income because their source of income was burned.

Sharon Singer: No income. And I think at that point you learn what's important. Number one—besides your family and your life—insurance is important, because my father did not have enough insurance.

Ida Pats: He had insurance, but they said it was coinsurance. They said coinsurance, at that time, so you, you, you're, you are insuring half of it. It was very little.

Sharon Singer: There wasn't enough insurance to cover what was lost in the house and the store. What is also interesting is that before the riots, the city of Baltimore was going through urban renewal, and they were going to upgrade the entire area. Mid-City Development Corporation was going to develop the property across the street, the whole block, and we were going move the store across the street. We were going to have a larger store, and we were very excited about the prospect. And my parents put a lot of money into that, and that was completely lost.

Ida Pats: Mid-City never developed it.

Betty Katzenelson: That's the thing. The city wanted that block demolished anyway. So it was very convenient for them not to help and not to step in and not to stop any of the burning. I mean, how convenient was that? They didn't have to pay for any of our houses. They didn't have to pay for any of us to leave.

Sharon Singer: It was just convenient. People paid money on the Mid-City, and that was all lost and nobody reimbursed anyone. So—it just makes you wonder.

Ida Pats: It never materialized. To this day.

Sharon Singer: So that was just money lost.

Betty Katzenelson: It wasn't just money lost. It was their dream lost. That was what they were going to do.

Sharon Singer: Exactly. But I think that for my parents at that point, it was a survival kind of thing. They have kids that are young, and they have to just go to work, and get on with it. Nobody was giving them anything. Nobody. It's not like now, "Oh my God! Katrina happened! I'm entitled to this, that, and the other."[4] There was nothing like that. The city just completely turned their backs on all this. You know, they weren't responsible. They weren't this, they weren't that. We weren't entitled to anything. So, what do you do? You get up and you go to work. And that's what happened.

Still, it was such a traumatic thing. Everything that they worked so hard to build up from the time they were first married—and here they have three kids to raise—just never materialized. It was gone. Just in one day. And nobody was helping them. The city wasn't helping them. They had no support.

Ida Pats: We had purchased—two years before when they first said there was going to be urban renewal, we purchased a house. But we had tenants in it.

Sharon Singer: Because when they were going move to the new store in Mid-City, they wouldn't be able to live upstairs. So luckily, luckily, they had purchased this house near Reisterstown Road Plaza and were leasing it out. And the riots came and the people were on lease and we couldn't move in. That's why we didn't have a place to go. Eventually that's where we did move.

Ida Pats: In fact, my sisters, they threw a shower, like you're a newlywed.

Betty Katzenelson: Their next anniversary. People brought them blankets. And they gave them dishes, as if it was a wedding shower. That's where my mother still lives to this day.

Sharon Singer: I want to say about going back to school, I only had the one year to go [before graduating]. When we went back to school the following Monday, because I don't even think I stayed out a day of school, I just was going to school like a normal day.[5] I was in a very small A-course class at Western, so it was maybe fifteen girls in that class.[6] And we were all very close because we had been in the same class since ninth grade and never had any kind of racial tension. I mean I went to school with black kids, Chinese kids, white kids. Never. There was never any kind of tension. I walked in that day, and we're in homeroom. And, you know, everybody was kind of removed from the riot situation except me. But they all had two cents to put in—you know, what was going on and this and that. I had a girl in the class, a black girl named Debbie—I won't use her last name—and she was a leader type of a person. She was loud and she was just out there. And she got up and she said—and she was very militant about it—"I want you to know that they got exactly what they deserved!" I started crying. I had to leave the room. I'm crying now. That one thing cut to me like nothing else could cut to me. I was fine until then. I was fine with what I saw, fine with it. And I thought, "What is happening in this world? These are not the people that I thought I knew." It was very traumatic.

Betty Katzenelson: I heard that similar comment, but it wasn't right then. I didn't talk to anybody. I didn't tell anybody in my class what had happened. I was in junior high at Pimlico.[7] I was thirteen in eighth grade. And I didn't say anything to anybody. It wasn't until a year or so later in high school. Same high school; it was at Western, and this girl was, "You know those people exploited, those people who had stores down there exploited the people around." It hit me. It was the first time I had heard somebody just cut like that. And, and they were all talking about how they were so unfair to the blacks in the area. The thing was, "What are you talking about?"

Sharon Singer: This girl was from a middle-class black family, never was subjected to anything to do with the riots, had nothing to do with poverty because she did not grow up in a poor household. Her parents both worked. She was well educated. And for her to be on that side versus this side, I just didn't know where that was coming from. It just didn't make any sense to me. And, you know, the fact that my father and mother had a store and had from nothing, and had this store in a neighborhood that was a white neighborhood, and then just by the sign of the times, it changed, and they stayed down there and were a part of the community, I don't understand how that's an exploitation. The prices came from the price book. It wasn't like we made up the prices. It's what the things cost. I think the people in the neighborhood, the customers, were the ones that really lost out in the end because they had no more stores to go to.

Betty Katzenelson: But I think the hardest thing afterwards was everybody was displaced within the family. My mom was out of her job and what she did. My dad was out of his job and what he did and what we all knew as our house. And nobody, nobody was anywhere near where they had been mentally, physically, emotionally. We were all in different directions and just wondering what the next day would be. It was just—you can't describe—it wasn't turmoil because we just kept going. Like the next day we went to school. It wasn't turmoil at all. But nothing was right. Everything was, nothing was—there was no stability.

Sharon Singer: Nothing was the way it was, was before that, that day. But luckily, thank God, for my parents, they were able to pull themselves up. They had skills, and then my mother went to University of Baltimore when she was maybe close to fifty years old.

Ida Pats: I was fifty.

Sharon Singer: She got her AA degree in accounting. She had never gone to college but was really good with numbers, and she worked for USF&G [United States Fidelity and Guarantee Company] for a lot of years.

Ida Pats: Twenty.

Sharon Singer: And my father, thank God, was a pharmacist. A lot of these people who were grocers and that sort of thing weren't as fortunate in getting jobs. But my father could get a job working in a pharmacy. His parents, who came from the pogroms in Russia, came over to America. They didn't want to be doing the work they were doing, but they did it to support their family and bring them up. Nobody gave them anything. Nobody—they weren't entitled to anything. They just all worked really hard, and they wanted their kids to get a good education. And they demanded that of their kids to get a good education, and they did. Well, the boys anyway.

Ida Pats: The boys for sure. The girls knew they had to go to school and then get a job. Get married, you have your children, and your husband works. But times have changed.

Betty Katzenelson: But it was amazing how it could change so quickly. Because, like Sharon was saying, before that it was just fine, and it was fun, and it was positive, and you weren't scared to walk around. You could just walk through the store or walk up and down the street. There wasn't a sense of "Oh my God! What are we doing here? Everybody went out to the suburbs!" Other people say to me, "You grew up there?"

Sharon Singer: But we never thought of it that way because we were in the community. We lived there. I loved living in the city. I loved it. I loved going out and just going here and there, talking to people. I used to take the bus everywhere. I'd just get on the bus, transfer to wherever I had to go—never thought about anything.

Betty Katzenelson: But to go from it being just fine to suddenly—boom, it's gone and everybody is running and bleeding and burning.

Sharon Singer: It's gone. And everybody's talking about you—you're bad. But we lived there. We lived within the community, and, and we just felt very violated.

Betty Katzenelson: That's a good word for it.

Sharon Singer: Violated. So that's basically the story of the riots, as we, as I saw it. That was it. Life as we knew it was over at that point. That was that, and start anew.

Edited by Linda Shopes

NOTES

1. In fact, rioting in Baltimore had broken out late Saturday afternoon and by nighttime had come within about a mile of the Patses' pharmacy.

2. To avert the large number of fatalities that had resulted from race riots in Detroit and Newark the previous year, federal troops in Baltimore and elsewhere had been ordered not to load their weapons and to refrain from shooting looters. Local police had been ordered not to shoot rioters except in self-defense. Mayor Thomas D'Alesandro had strong family and political ties to Baltimore's Little Italy; however, there is no evidence that either law enforcement officials or private citizens were "on the roofs with rifles" in the community. Police did report some discussion of vigilantism—though not in Little Italy—because of the lack of police protection; and after the riots, several dozen suits were brought against the city for failure to protect.

3. While many believed that outsiders came to Baltimore to instigate or inflame rioters, there is no hard evidence to support this. Most rioters, in fact, lived within ten blocks of the stores they looted and burned.

4. The reference here is to Hurricane Katrina, which caused massive damage along the Gulf Coast in August 2005. Although the timing and extent of federal aid to victims has been much criticized, there was an enormous outpouring of private aid immediately after the storm, in part because of extensive media coverage.

5. Baltimore city schools were closed on Monday, as were city offices, per order of the mayor, who had declared April 8 an official day of mourning for Martin Luther King. Schools reopened on Tuesday, though many students remained out of school for a few days.

6. Western High School is an all-girls public high school in Baltimore, distinguished by high academic standards. Students apply for admission and must meet certain criteria to be accepted.

7. Pimlico Junior High School, now Pimlico Middle School.

10

How the 1968 Riots Stopped School Desegregation in Baltimore

HOWELL S. BAUM

The Supreme Court rejected racially separate schools in *Brown v. Board of Education* on May 17, 1954. The Baltimore school board quickly voted to end segregation and, with black support, adopted free choice as its strategy. Children would select their schools; integration would be voluntary. The policy moderately changed schools' racial makeup. In the 1960s civil rights activity and growing skepticism about free choice led Baltimore to hire integrationist superintendents and consider more active desegregation methods. Thomas D'Alesandro III was elected mayor in 1967 on an integrationist platform. Then, in April 1968, Martin Luther King, Jr., was killed, rioting broke out in Baltimore, and Governor Spiro Agnew attacked moderate black leaders for the violence. Afterward, whites and blacks both pulled away from school desegregation. In 1974 the federal government directed Baltimore to integrate schools, but only a few black leaders endorsed the push while many others resisted. This chapter examines the role of the riots in halting school desegregation.

Portions of this chapter were originally published in Howell S. Baum, Brown *in Baltimore: School Desegregation and the Limits of Liberalism* (Ithaca, NY: Cornell University Press, 2010).

Desegregating Schools in 1954

The Board Acts

Baltimore public school segregation began in 1867 when city government gained jurisdiction over an assortment of private, mostly church-sponsored schools for black students.[1] A 1920 survey of city schools found many in poor condition but "colored" schools conspicuously worse than white.[2] In the late 1930s, the local NAACP branch, revitalized by Lillie May Jackson, and the *Baltimore Afro-American* began campaigning to equalize school conditions. *Afro* publisher Carl Murphy and Jackson's daughter Juanita Jackson Mitchell (wife of NAACP lobbyist Clarence Mitchell) led the initiative. In the late 1940s, they began pushing to desegregate. In the early 1950s, when the Supreme Court took up the school segregation cases, a small group of black leaders organized by Murphy and Mitchell began strategizing to push the school board to integrate as soon as the Court ruled. They presented a plan to school officials.[3]

On May 17, 1954, the Court declared separate schools inherently unequal and hence constitutionally unacceptable. On June 3, Baltimore's board, under the leadership of new president Walter Sondheim, voted unanimously to end segregation. On June 10, the board adopted Superintendent John Fischer's recommendation to continue the open-enrollment policy that went back to the nineteenth century, "except that the race of the pupil shall not be a consideration." White children had been free to attend any white school, and black children had been free to attend any colored school. Now students were free to transfer to any school of their choice, and "no child [would] be required to attend any particular school." Transfer requests could be turned down when schools were overcrowded, and therefore restricted to neighborhood children, and when administrators believed requests contravened students' educational interests.[4]

In short, desegregation would be voluntary. The board refused to assign students and placed responsibility for racial mixing on families. It would no longer pay attention to students' race. Explicitly, it would not discriminate against black children; implicitly, neither would it act on their behalf.

Black leaders celebrated the board's vote to end segregation. The NAACP took credit for board action and adoption of free choice: "The policy statements of the Board issued on June 3rd and June 10th embodied the requests made by the [Baltimore] Branch."[5]

Families Make Choices

Three conditions narrowed the choices truly available. First, many colored school buildings were dilapidated, dangerous, outmoded, and poorly equipped. No reasonable parents, whatever their race or racial views, would choose such schools. Second, the University of Maryland had limited black teacher training by refusing to admit black students. State scholarships to blacks to go to college outside Maryland enabled some to get good educations, but the majority of black teachers had attended Coppin Teachers College, an unaccredited, segregated normal school with meager facilities and few faculty with graduate degrees. Because the school district segregated teachers with students, concentrations of these teachers in historically black schools were unlikely to attract whites. Finally, Baltimore was deeply segregated. Anxiety blanketed racial boundaries and made it unlikely that many parents, whatever their racial views or educational preferences, would feel comfortable choosing schools associated with the other race. The school board did not address any of these conditions.

In 1954, city schools enrolled 144,000 students, 60 percent white and 40 percent black. When schools opened in the fall, a few black students had chosen historically white schools (1,575, or 2.7 percent of 57,000 students), and almost no white students were in formerly black schools (6, or 0.007 percent of 87,000). Enrollment over the next few years showed two trends: slowly growing but moderate racial mixing in the schools and transition from a majority white to a majority black district. As blacks entered white schools, whites left the schools or the neighborhoods.[6]

Baltimore became a majority black district in 1960. That fall, 33 of the city's 143 elementary schools were all white, and 45 were all black. Three of the 39 secondary schools were all white, and 13 were all black. Nearly one-third of black students attended formerly white schools. Secondary schools, because of larger enrollments, were more likely to be mixed.[7]

Blacks participated much more than whites in open enrollment. Black choosers increased from 1,575 in 1954 to 31,983 in 1961; white, from 6 to 86. By the prevailing definition of "integration," that is, including at least 10 percent of students from each race, only 32 of 146 elementary schools and 16 of 40 secondary schools were integrated. In 1954, 4 percent of white students and 3 percent of black were in integrated schools. In 1961 only 35 percent of white students, 19 percent of black, and 26 percent overall attended integrated schools.[8]

The Civil Rights Movement and a New Push for Integration

Playing Out Free Choice

Free choice, ending legal segregation, produced just modest mixing. However, the larger world was changing. The Montgomery bus boycott launched a national civil rights movement, leading to the Civil Rights Act of 1964. Starting in the mid-1950s, a cadre of Baltimore Congress of Racial Equality (CORE) members and Morgan State College, Johns Hopkins University, and Goucher College students demonstrated against discrimination in restaurants, theaters, department stores, and the Gwynn Oak Amusement Park.[9]

In 1963 a group of black and white parents, calling themselves the 28 Parents, presented the school board with a report describing three system practices that maintained de facto segregation.[10] First, the board located new schools in racially homogeneous neighborhoods. Because parents favored nearby schools, these sites made segregation likely. Second, the one exception to free choice, districting of overcrowded schools limiting enrollment to neighborhood children, created segregated schools because housing was segregated. Superintendent George Brain said he also districted schools when neighborhoods started changing from white to black. Third, centrally, administrators handled transfers in ways that made choice anything but free for black families. Some white principals encouraged white parents to transfer their children out when black enrollment grew. Some principals rejected black transfer applications to predominantly white schools. The cumulative result of these practices was to limit black choice and to confine black students to relatively few schools, necessitating shifts and part-time schooling for black children.[11]

The national and local NAACP joined the 28 Parents in demanding the board eliminate discriminatory policies and give parents truly free choice. Over the summer, while the NAACP threatened to sue, the 28 Parents negotiated with the board. In September the board voted to end districting at once (rather than, as planned, in October) and give responsibility for transfers to an assistant superintendent, who would deny transfers only when schools lacked space.[12]

In spring 1964, 59 of 192 schools included at least 10 percent from each race, but 89 schools were at least 90 percent black. The number of all-black or nearly all-black schools had increased by 30 since spring, 1954. Five in six black elementary students and two in three black secondary students attended schools defined as segregated by the 10 percent standard. Two years later, 84 percent of black elementary students would be in such schools, with 92 percent attending majority black schools and two in three white elementary students attending schools at least 90 percent white. Within racially mixed schools, ability tracking put black and white students in separate programs. After a decade of legal desegregation, most children attended class with majorities of their own race.[13]

Open enrollment had not required black and white children to go to school together. Neither had it changed schools' perceived racial identities. Only black students attended historically black schools, and most historically white schools were considered white until some tacit tipping point turned them "black." Few schools had positive identities as racially mixed, and for most, mixing was ephemeral. By the time the board ended practices that limited choices, the desegregation policy had a ten-year history associated in the public mind with continuing segregation.

For all practical purposes, free choice was played out as a desegregation instrument.

Integrationist Initiatives

When Superintendent Brain left in 1964, the board hired Laurence Paquin, New Haven's integrationist superintendent. One of the first superintendents to take on de facto segregation, he had paired black and white schools and initiated busing. In Baltimore he crafted a high school plan with the dual aims of reducing segregation and improving education. The NAACP, Urban League, 28 Parents, and *Afro* endorsed his plan, though CORE criticized it as accommodating white resistance. Some whites attacked it. The board adopted the plan in June 1966. Paquin said ending de facto segregation would require such approaches as school pairing, educational parks, busing, and zoning, but he noted that the city seemed committed to free choice.[14]

Meanwhile, Baltimore CORE chairman Jim Griffin and national CORE director Floyd McKissick announced that CORE would make Baltimore its first Target City in the summer of 1966. It would show what a national civil rights organization could do to fix a city's housing, employment, and education problems. Poor conceptualization and organization would cripple the Target City project, but when it started Mayor Theodore McKeldin created the Mayor's Task Force for Equal Rights, which attacked school segregation. In September 1966 it urged the board to integrate teachers as well as students. In 105 of 155 elementary schools, more than 90 percent of faculty were of the same race, and half of 52 secondary schools had such faculties. The committee requested an assistant superintendent to oversee desegregation.[15]

In June 1967 the task force urged the board to bus students, create educational parks, develop model schools and magnet programs, pair schools, begin integrating middle schools, and improve schools remaining predominantly black. The mayor called for busing more children from inner-city to outer-neighborhood schools. However, by the time the board heard the task force's report in September, Paquin was dying of cancer.[16]

Paquin's initiatives did not advance, but a study he commissioned generated new thinking about desegregation. Johns Hopkins researchers found white movement to the suburbs to be "the most important segregating influence in the metropolitan area" and recommended busing city and county children to educational parks built on the boundaries. The task force promptly proposed busing some black elementary school children to suburban schools, and McKeldin "enthusiastically" gave his support.[17]

Baltimore did not come by these ideas alone. The NAACP and the U.S. Civil Rights Commission increasingly criticized free choice. The 1964 Civil Rights Act created a federal interest in desegregating schools. Title VI declared that no program receiving federal funds could discriminate on the basis of race, under penalty of losing federal funds. In 1966 the U.S. Department of Health, Education, and Welfare (HEW) set up the Office for Civil Rights (OCR) to enforce Title VI for HEW programs, including education. Civil rights activists urged OCR to reject free-choice plans unless they resulted in desegregation.

Baltimore's New Progressive Mayor

Baltimore discussion of these ideas was stimulated by the 1967 mayoral campaign, in which candidates debated busing, metropolitanism, and school improvement. In November voters elected as mayor the city council president, Thomas D'Alesandro III, who had defended busing to relieve overcrowding and to remove children from deficient schools and proposed replacing obsolete schools and building educational parks to draw students from across the region.[18]

D'Alesandro's campaign had involved the first citywide Democratic effort to recruit black support. He prided himself on his racial liberalism. He was also a practical politician who recognized that the city's population was nearly half black. He had introduced civil rights bills as city council president. He worked with the NAACP and the Interdenominational Ministerial Alliance. As mayor, he would appoint the first blacks to several city positions and add blacks to the school board.

At his December inauguration, D'Alesandro rejected despair and white flight and pronounced Baltimore "the city of our hope." He promised "to root out every cause or vestige of discrimination." He would dub Baltimore "Education City, USA." He wanted racially mixed schools and would talk about creating magnet schools to attract white suburban students, but his first task would be to get a bond for constructing adequate facilities.[19]

In D'Alesandro's fourth month as mayor, Martin Luther King was assassinated.

The Riots and Their Aftermath

The Riots and Agnew's Peroration

On Thursday evening, April 4, when the news came, D'Alesandro ordered city flags lowered. When city civil rights leaders urged black workers and students to stay home on Monday to mourn King's death, he ordered city offices and schools closed then and asked businesses also to close. He pledged "to eliminate from every area of public life in Baltimore all forms of injustice, discrimination and inequality" and to create "better schools."

On Saturday D'Alesandro proclaimed Sunday a day of prayer. Five thirty Saturday afternoon, rioting began on Gay Street. City police could not handle matters, and at the mayor's request Governor Spiro Agnew called in the National Guard and imposed an overnight curfew. Quickly the east side and then downtown became sites of fires and looting. Sunday morning, D'Alesandro toured the city in a National Guard convoy. Black leaders from the NAACP, the Interdenominational Ministerial Alliance, CORE, and the Union for Jobs and Income Now (U-JOIN) walked the streets urging calm and order but had little influence with the rioters, many of them young and poor. At Agnew's request President Lyndon Johnson sent 1,900 army troops to the city.

Rioting, looting, and arson worsened and then largely subsided by Tuesday evening. Six persons had been killed, and injuries had reached 600, including 50 policemen. By the end, on Friday, 5,512 people had been arrested, nearly all black, about 1 in every 75 black citizens. There had been 1,208 major fires, and 1,049 businesses were destroyed. Nearly 12,000 troops had occupied the city—1 soldier for every 75 of Baltimore's 900,000 residents.[20]

Agnew invited 100 Baltimore black leaders to meet with him on Thursday at the State Office Building in Baltimore. He identified them as "moderate" black leaders, in contrast with the "circuit-riding, Hanoi-visiting type of leader," the "caterwauling, riot-inciting, burn-America-down type of leader." Yet, he charged, some of them had met with the "reckless" "demagogue" who headed the local Student Nonviolent Coordinating Committee (SNCC) chapter and all had declined to repudiate militants and advocates of violence, such as Stokely Carmichael, who "not . . . by chance" had met with "local black power advocates and known criminals" just three days before the Baltimore riots. "You were beguiled," he told them, "by the rationalization of unity; you . . . were stung by insinuations that you were Mr. Charlie's boy, by epithets like 'Uncle Tom.'" Hence they bore responsibility for the rioting.

As Agnew tongue-lashed them, most walked out. Some drafted an angry rebuttal. "Agnew's actions," they said, "are more in keeping with the slave system of a bygone era." He had taken it on himself to designate legitimate black leaders, separating "good" moderates from "bad" militants. Thus, they said, he sought to divide blacks. Yet if he insisted on tying the moderates to the militants, holding them responsible for the violence despite their efforts to prevent and stifle it, his words, a minister remarked, would have a paradoxical result: "He's forcing us all to become militants."[21]

The Aftermath

Many whites found the riots confirming their worst fears about blacks. While some had sympathized with civil rights activists and could appreciate black anger at King's murder, few could understand looters and arsonists. The unrest seemed to rationalize anxieties about black violence. What many had not said or had kept below the surface they now thought and voiced openly. After Agnew's speech, a hundred telegrams an hour flooded into his office, most from white Baltimoreans, most favorable. They praised his "courage" and his "standing up for the average middle-class American citizen." One said, "Thankful to hear that the white people still have a strong voice in government."[22]

The riots troubled many white liberals. Some shared D'Alesandro's feeling that, after they had been earnest civil rights allies, the riots had violated their trust. It was possible to distinguish rioters from the black leaders with whom white liberals had worked, but the riots bludgeoned the senses. The liberals included many Jews. Jews owned many of the destroyed businesses. A *Jewish Times* editorial, noting this fact, warned against a backlash against all blacks,[23] but many Jews emotionally and physically withdrew from the city.

The riots shocked middle-class blacks in two ways. First, they encountered young blacks who did not regard them as models or leaders—who rejected middle-class civility and discipline because they doubted they could attain middle-class success. Not only would the NAACP have difficulty claiming to speak for all blacks but it was harder to see all blacks as one community. A breach between the middle class and the poor had opened. With industry's departure from the city, black unemployment was growing.

The second shock came from Agnew's peroration and whites' enthusiastic response. The governor had assaulted the black community, and whites had cheered him on. Leaders who for years had painstakingly maintained moderation, tempering their words so as not to upset white officials, found their education and civility counted for nothing; they were just black. Although D'Alesandro and clergy had condemned Agnew's speech,[24] few other whites had joined them. The circle of white allies was contracting, and moderation seemed to bring few returns.

Free Choice for Segregation

Ignoring the Supreme Court

In 1965 the NAACP Legal Defense Fund sued the New Kent County, Virginia, school board over its free-choice plan, arguing that the policy did not satisfy *Brown* because it did not actually desegregate schools. Nearly three years later, the case reached the Supreme Court. Six weeks after the riots, the justices ruled in *Green v. New Kent County* that free choice had to produce results: it had to integrate schools to be constitutionally acceptable.[25]

Baltimore Community Relations Commission director David Glenn asked city solicitor George Russell, Jr., for a legal opinion on *Green*'s implications for the city. Russell, appointed by D'Alesandro, was the city's first black city solicitor. Responding in November, he stated that Baltimore "would appear to have gone as far as it can to bring about integration under a 'freedom of choice' plan. . . . The vestiges of the dual system in effect prior to *Brown* still remain. . . . A new plan is required for students and especially for faculty, until every Negro school child has an opportunity to enjoy his full constitutional rights." The conclusion was clear: "Unless the Board continues to pursue the objective of a fully integrated system and achieve that objective, we do not believe that there is or will be a valid ground for determining that the Board is fulfilling its constitutional responsibilities."[26]

The city's top legal officer had declared the city's desegregation policy unconstitutional. Mayor D'Alesandro, who appointed school board members and had encouraged Russell to render an opinion, ignored the opinion. School board president Francis Murnaghan refused to say whether he agreed with it. Instead, he highlighted obstacles to integrating schools and reaffirmed free choice. He deferred to Superintendent Thomas Sheldon, who had just started in his position on July 1. Two weeks later, Sheldon said he had not yet received the document and would review it when he did.[27] He never acted.

William Donald Schaefer, who had succeeded D'Alesandro as city council president and would follow him as mayor, rejected Russell's opinion. He had no interest in considering the Supreme Court decision and revisiting desegregation, because "immediately the question of race comes in."[28] Schaefer spoke for many Baltimoreans: in the wake of the riots, people did not want to talk about anything tied to race.

Growing Racial Tensions in the School System

In March 1968, a month before King was killed, the school board had hired Sheldon, previously in Long Island, to "shake up" the system. Sheldon understood the board to have given him a mandate to integrate Baltimore schools. He believed busing could help students get better education. His first semester in Baltimore would come right after the riots.[29]

He launched a $133 million school construction program, replacing many dilapidated historically black facilities. He used federal Elementary and Secondary Education Act funds to hire three thousand school aides, many black. He reorganized the superintendent's office and appointed three black associate superintendents and ten other blacks at cabinet level. After a year, the *Afro* approved his performance and exhorted him to be "more aggressive" on integration.[30]

In January 1969 D'Alesandro named two more blacks to the school board. Larry Gibson and Samuel Daniels joined Jim Griffin and Elizabeth

Murphy Moss; with white liberal Philip Macht they formed a five-member majority that pushed for greater black influence over school policy. A January 1970 incident shifted the balance of power. A white teacher at Eastern High School reportedly used a racial slur with a black student. Students protested, and someone called the police, who allegedly mistreated students and eventually arrested eight. Students were sent home, and many went to Baltimore City College High School, where students joined the protest, and City was also closed. At the next board meeting, Sheldon announced he would investigate. At once, Gibson introduced a resolution that the investigation be conducted jointly by a board committee and the superintendent. Murnaghan said the issue was the superintendent's responsibility. Sheldon expressed dissatisfaction with the board's increasing meddling in administration. Gibson, Griffin, Moss, Daniels, and Macht voted for the motion, and Murnaghan resigned.[31]

The mayor, failing to persuade black businessman Henry Parks to take the presidency, tapped lawyer Robert Karwacki. Black board members and civil rights leaders opposed Karwacki because as assistant Maryland attorney general in 1964 he had exonerated city police on charges of beating an arrested black man. As the new president, Karwacki found the "atmosphere so tense you could cut it with a knife. It wasn't only acrimony; it was hatred."[32]

The five-member majority's relations with other board members and the superintendent deteriorated. Increasingly, board members, the superintendent, and the press characterized board meetings as a "circus." In January 1971, when the board rejected Sheldon's nominations for school principalships, he resigned.[33]

While the board searched for a new superintendent, in April 1971 the Supreme Court delivered *Swann v. Charlotte-Mecklenburg*, accepting gerrymandered school districts, mandatory student assignments, and busing as desegregation methods.[34] Baltimore headlines highlighted the approval of busing. However, unlike three years earlier, after *Green*, no one asked the city solicitor for an opinion on the ruling's application to local schools. When the board met two days after *Swann*, no one mentioned it.[35]

In July the board hired Roland Patterson as the first permanent black superintendent. When he arrived in the fall, attacks on him began almost at once. The city was narrowly majority white. The board was split on racial lines. Patterson defined issues racially when criticized. Karwacki resigned in November. Patterson became a focus for racial animosity. Board meetings turned into public spectacles. In the fall of 1973, three white board members resigned. Two black members whose terms had expired at the end of 1972 stayed on without reappointment or replacement by Mayor Schaefer, who disliked Patterson. The new board president, John Walton, a white Johns Hopkins education professor, struggled to manage the board.[36]

The Federal Government Demands Integration

In October 1970, while black board members battled Sheldon, the NAACP Legal Defense Fund sued HEW, charging it was not enforcing Title VI against segregated school districts. On February 16, 1973, Judge John Pratt decided *Adams v. Richardson* for the plaintiffs and gave HEW sixty days to ask eighty-five districts to account for racial disproportions. Patterson got his letter from OCR director Peter Holmes on April 17. Federal law let schools vary 20 percent in racial makeup from the overall district; Baltimore schools, now 70 percent black, thus had to range between 50 percent and 90 percent black, and many did not. Patterson responded on June 4.[37]

Eight months later, on February 5, 1974, Holmes replied. Most of the schools segregated before *Brown*, he said, remained racially identifiable. Open enrollment had not ended segregation. Further desegregation was "necessary and feasible." He told Patterson to submit a plan for fall implementation.[38] On March 14 Patterson appointed a desegregation task force. It met for a month but could not agree on a plan. It sent the board five different, widely ranging proposals. The board discussed the plans on April 25, to conspicuous public opposition to busing. Patterson asked deputy superintendent John Crew to prepare an integration plan.[39]

During this time, task force member Betty Deacon, a southeast Baltimore activist and member of the South East Community Organization, organized neighbors to oppose any plan with busing as a component. She created the Southeast Desegregation Coalition. On April 17, the South East Community Organization convened eight hundred people who opposed every plan with busing. Parents talked about sending children to schools they chose, regardless of what plans said. City councilwoman Barbara Mikulski wrote in a letter to the *East Baltimore Guide* editor, "I AM TOTALLY OPPOSED TO FORCED CROSS-TOWN BUSING." She had urged Schaefer to go to court against HEW.[40]

The *Afro* argued for integration. Baltimore, it said, was defying the law, and busing, accepted by the Court, was necessary to desegregate. It attacked policy makers for putting the putative interests of the minority of white students above the interests of the black majority. The *Jewish Times* supported integration with a story about the Glen Avenue neighborhood, where blacks and Orthodox Jews lived together.[41]

Six hundred people crowded into the May 28 school board meeting to hear Crew present the city's plan. For elementary schools, staff proposed to pair a few predominantly white and predominantly black schools, with students from the paired schools attending different schools for different grades. The proposal included twenty-seven schools enrolling 18 percent of elementary students. Students would attend the school nearest home, with limited transfers. Two possible junior high plans each limited choice. One would cluster schools to produce a racially balanced combined enrollment, with students attending different grades in different schools. The other would create feeder links between elementary and junior high schools, to be implemented one grade per year, starting with one-fourth of junior high students in the fall. The high school plan included seven specialized magnet schools, seven neighborhood schools, four selective citywide schools, and a merger of Carver and Mergenthaler vocational schools. Students could choose within building capacity. The staff plan would move about 10 percent of teachers, mainly through voluntary transfers and reassignment of faculty returning from leave.[42]

The Public Reacts, and the School Board Desegregates Less

Newspapers characterized the plan as "minimal" and "moderate." The *Sun* noted that few students would be affected and that the high school plan was weak and maybe unconstitutional.[43]

In southeast Baltimore, parents with children at General Wolfe, Hampstead Hill, Highlandtown 215, and Highlandtown 237 elementary schools said they did not want their children "fed" into nearly all-black Lombard Junior High, because of the school's poor education, student insubordination, and physical danger. Many southeastern residents resented the designation of Patterson High as a construction trades magnet. Making it a magnet would force many southeastern youths to leave while admitting many blacks from outside. And the nature of the magnet—construction trades—was an insult. Apparently the elite believed working-class children had the ability only for manual labor.

The Southeast Desegregation Coalition organized parents to "pre-register" children at Canton and Hampstead Hill junior highs and drafted a plan to keep Patterson High a neighborhood high school. The day after Crew presented his plan to the board, more than one thousand Patterson students walked out, and five hundred paraded to city hall, chanting, "Hell no, we won't go!" In the next days, two thousand to three thousand students from seven high schools protested at city hall and school headquarters. Over the weekend, two thousand people demonstrated at southeast rallies.[44]

On Tuesday, June 4, Walton opened the board meeting by announcing changes to the plan. Elementary pairings were reduced to seven, involving 9 percent of elementary students. The board chose the feeder plan for junior highs, affecting only the seventh grade the first year. A new high school plan kept Patterson High and four other high schools as neighborhood schools and left Mergenthaler and Carver alone. The staff plan limited teacher transfers. White board members supported the changes; most blacks opposed them.[45]

The *Afro* noted changes in the mood between 1954 and 1974. City officials now defied the law, whereas 1954 officials had supported desegregation.

Business, education, and church leaders no longer supported integration—not even black pastors. Edgar Jones, an *Evening Sun* reporter who had watched desegregation since *Brown*, also contrasted 1974 with 1954:

> The disordered state of race relations in Baltimore was revealed with almost frightening clarity in the past several weeks, as large numbers of white high school students roamed the streets with impunity shouting "Hell no, we won't go." . . . Twenty years ago when a few hundred white students at Southern High School demonstrated . . . nearly every community leader worthy of the name denounced their disregard of law and order. . . .
>
> In those days there was a fairly large reservoir of white goodwill toward Negroes. Many Baltimoreans knew that segregation was wrong and were willing to stand up for the School Board's efforts to eliminate it. In those days, too, the School Board acted unanimously and decisively and without looking to the Mayor for direction. It spoke with confidence for the community.
>
> The past few weeks have shown precious little evidence of white goodwill toward either blacks or the School Board (or school administrators). Except for a few neighborhoods trying to preserve some integration, Baltimore's white residents by and large are buttoned up in their own diminishing sectors. . . . The white kids who hooked school to shout their protests probably quite accurately reflected white parental attitudes, including the disrespect for authority.
>
> But also in slim evidence was support for the School Board from the black middle class and black politicians. . . . The private and parochial schools have a goodly number of middle-class black children, including the offspring of black public school teachers, principals and supervisors.
>
> When there was a need for the white and black leadership to pull together to help bring about a rational school policy, the whites with a few exceptions let their rowdier elements do the yelling, and the blacks with equally few exceptions looked the other way.[46]

Martin Luther King's assassination, the riots, and the aftermath had changed Baltimore.

The Federal Government Moves against Baltimore

The Office for Civil Rights Renders a Verdict

OCR said that Baltimore's plan, which did little in elementary schools and left grades eight through twelve untouched the first year, would not "substantially desegregate" schools. Holmes accepted the plan on an interim basis but directed the city to submit a revised September plan by August 14 and a final plan by November 1. Otherwise, OCR would move to enforcement hearings to cut off funds.[47]

Meanwhile, the school system went into free fall. At the August 8 board meeting, a five-member white majority tried to fire Patterson. His critics charged he was managing poorly. His defenders contended he had become the target for white unease about black power in the schools. The meeting began with a motion to fire Patterson. Hundreds of his supporters rushed the stage; Congressman Parren Mitchell presided over four hours of testimony in Patterson's favor. After reviewing tapes the next day, the city solicitor concluded no vote had occurred.[48]

Five days later, the board approved minor plan changes and sent them to OCR. Holmes rejected the plan and declared there was no alternative to enforcement proceedings unless the city took steps he recommended. With school opening a week away, Patterson stood nearly alone with the plan, and his support was tepid. Mayor Schaefer and city council president Walter Orlinsky attacked the plan. Eventually, Schaefer urged compliance. A biracial group of business and civil leaders appealed for an orderly school opening.[49]

Desegregation affected only 20,000 of 180,000 students, but some parents demonstrated and kept children from assigned schools, often taking them to preferred schools. Parents picketed or held sit-ins at a dozen schools, most in working-class white neighborhoods but also in black East Baltimore. Junior highs were the crucial test, because they involved the most students.

After the first week, white junior high attendance was only 50 percent, much lower than blacks' 78 percent. At the ten schools that had been nearly all black, white attendance was only 20 percent. In southeast Baltimore, eighty parents took their children to Canton, and fifty went to Hampstead Hill, where parents and children took available seats. Over time, most teachers included them in class. Schaefer went to Canton on opening day and met with and praised protesting parents. The next week, he went to a southeast boycott rally, argued for altering school assignments, and urged pressure on HEW.[50]

Four days later, HEW notified Baltimore it would start enforcement proceedings. It charged the city had never taken feasible steps to desegregate and continued "to operate a substantial number of schools which are either one race or substantially disproportionate in student racial composition." In the 1973–1974 school year, HEW reported, approximately 123 of 212 schools were more than 90 percent minority, and 63 were less than 50 percent minority. The district continued to assign faculty in ways that reinforced schools' racial identities.[51]

The School Board Reacts by Desegregating Still Less

On September 19 the board ratified parents' noncompliance by revoking feeder patterns they objected to, allowing students at six junior high schools subject to white boycotts to transfer to their closest or second-closest junior high. Three white members and one black voted for the change; three blacks abstained. The *Sun* decried "desegregation without direction":

> If Baltimore could be said to have had a school desegregation plan for seventh graders, that plan has been disemboweled by the School Board's decision to return to a form of freedom of choice at the six junior high schools where desegregation protests have been heard most strongly. . . . But . . . it should be acknowledged that the feeder system . . . ran contrary to the continuing black interest in preserving a choice of schools and the deep-seated white resentment of having relatively small numbers of white children assigned to overwhelmingly black schools. . . .
>
> Perhaps the most worrisome aspect is the lack of leadership inside or outside the school system on this crucial issue. The School Board is badly divided and at loose ends. . . . School Superintendent Patterson has disowned the desegregation plans, saying they are the board's responsibility, yet the board members can only go as far as professional staff work makes possible. Mayor Schaefer dips in and out, not so much showing leadership as reflecting community indecision.

The *Afro* repeated its call for legal action.[52]

OCR held off enforcement while negotiating. On January 30 a unanimous board approved a working draft of a high school plan. Twelve of seventeen high schools would be zoned. Five schools would stay all black and a sixth would stay 96 percent black, down from nine all-black schools during the current year. Seven high schools would meet federal desegregation guidelines, up from three. Eleven percent of black students would attend majority-white schools, and 44 percent would attend schools at least 96 percent black. Forty-nine percent of whites would attend majority-white schools, and 49 percent would go to schools 50 percent to 90 percent black. Patterson High would be the largest and whitest high school, with 70 percent of 3,400 students white, and the only school on shifts. Many whites supported the plan. Black leaders decried the elimination of open enrollment, contending that zoning would confine black students to schools they did not want to be in.[53]

On March 13 the board responded to protests against the junior high school plan by amending it further. Using zones, it shifted white students from predominantly black into predominantly white schools. Twelve of twenty-three junior high and two middle schools would meet federal guidelines, up from seven under the feeder plan. However, ten would remain more than 90 percent black, and four would be majority white, with Canton whitest. Only 6 percent of black students would attend majority-white schools, and 47 percent would attend schools at least 98 percent black. Thirty-one percent of white students would attend majority white schools, and 67 percent would attend schools 50 percent to 90 percent black.[54]

Now Judge Pratt issued a supplemental order in *Adams*. Faulting HEW for excessive negotiations, he directed it to begin enforcement proceedings against districts such as Baltimore within sixty days. Meanwhile, a new board president, Norman Ramsey, began moving to fire Patterson. Amid that battle, on May 2, Holmes wrote Patterson that Baltimore's plans were unacceptable and that OCR would initiate enforcement hearings. On June 9 the board voted 7–2 to fire Patterson. After court appeals, he was removed on July 17 and replaced by John Crew.[55]

On August 4 administrative law judge Irvin Hackerman convened a prehearing conference to hear Baltimore lawyers' motion to dismiss enforcement proceedings and let negotiations proceed. He ruled that the enforcement hearing should go ahead but postponed it to let the city start up desegregated schools in September.[56]

When schools opened, they remained largely segregated. In a system in which enrollment was 73 percent black, one-fourth of schools still had white majorities, and half were more than 90 percent black. Only one in four satisfied federal guidelines. Two-fifths were 99 percent or 100 percent black. More than fifteen thousand transfer requests in the first two months increased segregation. Middle-class blacks followed whites to suburban schools.[57]

Ramsey quietly resigned after removing Patterson. Schaefer, winning a third term in November, named Mark Joseph the third school board president of the year.[58]

The End

On January 8, 1976, the city sued HEW in federal district court, seeking an injunction against enforcement. Baltimore argued that OCR had treated the city arbitrarily, failing to specify which programs did not comply with federal guidelines, failing to offer specific recommendations for remedies, and halting voluntary negotiations that could have led to compliance. Federal lawyers contended that OCR had followed the law and argued that the court should not halt administrative hearings designed to rule on whether OCR had taken proper procedures and whether Baltimore had complied with the Civil Rights Act. On March 8 Judge Edward Northrop enjoined HEW from continuing enforcement proceedings and required it to provide the city with requested specific information as part of voluntary negotiations.[59]

Lawyers for HEW appealed to the Fourth Circuit Court of Appeals. On August 9, 1977, a 4–3 majority ruled that enforcement proceedings should resume. However, one of the judges in the majority had died before the decision was formally filed, and Baltimore appealed to the court to throw out his vote. On February 16, 1978, the Fourth Circuit ruled that its prior vote had ended in a tie, thus affirming the injunction against HEW.[60]

The Baltimore desegregation battle was over. OCR was stripped of the teeth of sanctions with which to negotiate. The school board, whose lawyers had told the court the city just wanted room to desegregate in ways suited to local conditions, did nothing further to desegregate. Staff at OCR, moving in 1980 into a new Department of Education, devised ingenious but forceless ideas for advancing desegregation in Baltimore. On January 21, 1983, Baltimore and the Department of Education agreed to terminate litigation and continue voluntary negotiations. Finally, on May 12, 1987, the Department of Education wrote Baltimore superintendent Alice Pinderhughes, "OCR has concluded that there are no remaining vestiges of BCPS's [Baltimore City Public Schools'] prior *de jure* school segregation in its student and faculty assignment policies and practices."[61] The letter was not reported at a school board meeting or noted in the press.

When board president Mark Joseph's term expired in 1980, he summarized his accomplishments at a board meeting. "After almost a decade of steady decline, while the system was embroiled in conflict over race, a teachers' strike, and the firing of Dr. Patterson," he reported, test scores were up. The lesson was that "extraneous controversy must be avoided." He did not mention desegregation.[62]

Superintendent John Crew retired in 1982 and addressed the board on that occasion. He did not mention desegregation among his accomplishments. Board president David Daneker lauded Crew for bringing about "an air of harmony, a unity of purpose, and a measure of success which is uncommon to urban school systems." Board member Howard Marshall reiterated, "He brought a good deal of harmony out of a lot of disorder."[63] After years of racial conflict, the board valued peace above much else, including desegregation.

No one ever sued the school board to do more to desegregate. Baltimore stood out from most Southern districts and many big cities in this respect.

Conclusion

Observers contrasted the narrow, mostly black support for integration in 1974 with broad biracial acceptance of desegregation in 1954. In explanation, one might note that desegregation was voluntary in 1954, whereas federal intervention forced the board to require some mixing in 1974.

Moreover, demographic shifts over two decades increased white children's likelihood of attending school with a significant number of black children. Further, many of the whites remaining lacked the resources to get out when desegregation unsettled them.

At the same time, one should note that the school board hired two integrationist superintendents in the mid- and late-1960s, civil rights interests opened public discussion of directive alternatives to open enrollment, and the 1967 mayoral election emphasized biracial cooperation and school improvement. In this context, the refusal of the city's top elected and school officials to consider the Supreme Court ruling that free choice without results was unconstitutional is striking.

Thus one might see the riots and Agnew's attack as abruptly ending Baltimore school desegregation efforts. Many whites backed away from advocating, supporting, or acquiescing in integration. Many blacks turned from hopes of integration to efforts to control an increasingly black school system. However, the riots did not so much cause these changes as catalyze and punctuate shifts already taking place. Here it is useful to think of a well-known optical illusion—a drawing that in one moment appears to be of two faces and becomes a vase in the next. The gestalt shifts. What was background becomes foreground. The riots had the effect of shifting racial gestalts. Ambivalences rebalanced.

Desegregation involved two ambivalences. Whites experienced what Gunnar Myrdal called "an American dilemma." They both espoused the equality of individuals and thought about blacks in ways that could justify discrimination. They might believe in civil rights but simultaneously take a low view of or fear blacks and try to keep blacks down or away. Black ambivalence was expressed in the debate between W.E.B. DuBois and Booker T. Washington. Blacks both believed in integrating into a color-blind society and wanted to maintain a separate society with their own institutions. They might believe in integration but regard whites apprehensively, doubting whites would accept them and worrying that integration would cost them cultural and political power.[64]

These ambivalences were individual, in that many people held both beliefs in some mental and emotional balance. At the same time, they were collective, in that more or less discrete groups within the races held one position more prominently than the other. Thus convention contrasted tolerant whites with prejudiced whites and integrationist blacks with separatist blacks. However, while these distinctions referred to real variations, people could exaggerate differences. For example, whites who wanted to see themselves as tolerant liberals could downplay personal prejudices or fears and attribute racial anxieties to other whites, such as working-class ethnics. Blacks who wanted to find places in a color-blind society could suppress suspicions or fears of whites and attribute separatist impulses to other blacks, such as the less-educated masses.

The riots and Agnew's attack shifted racial sentiments. While civil rights activism encouraged the school board to move more actively toward integration, the same civil rights activity, talk of black power, riots elsewhere, the increase in the city's black population, and black political ascendance threatened many whites' sense of power, status, and security. Increasingly, the whites left in the city were those who had no possibility of leaving.

Paradoxically, the school board's open-enrollment policy probably added to racial anxiety. The essence of free choice was that no one, starting with the school board, was in control of enrollments. Parents could not know what a school's makeup would be when classes started. White families who wanted or were willing to accept some mixing could have no certainty about schools' composition. This uncertainty not only added to anxiety but also made leaving city public schools a choice with a more predictable outcome.

Further, the board's laissez-faire position on race, rejecting responsibility for race relations in 1954, stripped it of authority to manage race relations after the riots. Having assiduously avoided discussing race, the board had neither precedent for nor practice in such talk. Schaefer expressed board anxieties about race in refusing to discuss desegregation after the riots.

At the same time, whites and blacks who once bridged the races in advocating integration had diminished in not only numbers but also authority. White liberals evoked little sympathy among those who had literally or symbolically been burned out by the riots and were retreating from the city physically or emotionally. Black moderates who had counseled cooperation with white officials found little support among younger, poorer, and more militant blacks who saw whites as their adversaries. Agnew's attack showed them powerless to deliver.

This shift caught Superintendent Thomas Sheldon, who represented pre-riot biracial support for integration, watched a post-riot white retreat, and ran into black post-riot interests in taking over the school system. White anxiety about blacks took the foreground over beliefs in equality, and black separatism and independence competed with integrationism. In general, the riots strengthened those who saw the world racially. In particular, they curtailed interest in desegregation. The riots and Agnew's attack scared whites and blacks from further discussing anything tied to race. The well of white support for or acquiescence in desegregation was drying up. Demographically and politically, blacks were gaining in the city. It seemed just a matter of time before they could act without whites.

NOTES

1. Robert Brugger, *Maryland* (Baltimore: Johns Hopkins University Press, 1988), 307–308; James B. Crooks, *Politics and Progress* (Baton Rouge: Louisiana State University Press, 1968), 93–94; Sherry Olson, *Baltimore: The Building of an American City*, rev. ed. (Baltimore: Johns Hopkins University Press, 1997), 187;

Bettye C. Thomas, "Public Education and Black Protest in Baltimore 1865–1900," *Maryland Historical Magazine* 71, no. 3 (Fall 1976): 383.

2. George Drayton Strayer, ed., *Report of the Survey of the Public School System of Baltimore, Maryland*, vol. 1 (Baltimore: Public Improvement Commission, 1921).

3. Juanita Jackson Mitchell oral history interview, McKeldin-Jackson Oral History collection, Maryland Historical Society, OH 8095, July 25, 1975, p. 57; Elizabeth M. Moss oral history interview, McKeldin-Jackson Oral History collection, Maryland Historical Society, OH 8140, July 13, 1976, pp. 22, 24.

4. Baltimore School Board minutes, June 10, 1954, pp. 114–117; "School Board Adopts Policy Erasing Racial Basis for Registration," *Baltimore Sun*, June 11, 1954.

5. "Outstanding Achievements of the Baltimore Branch N.A.A.C.P.," n.d. [1954?], Mitchell family papers, Library of Congress; see also "We Must Learn to Live with It," *Baltimore Afro-American*, June 5, 1954; "Residents of Both Races Happy about School Ruling," *Baltimore Afro-American*, June 5, 1954.

6. "Schools List 140,957-Pupil Enrollment," *Baltimore Sun*, September 17, 1954; "Mixed Classes in 52 Schools, Board Reports," *Baltimore Afro-American*, September 18, 1954; Julia Roberta O'Wesney, "Historical Study of the Progress of Racial Desegregation in the Public Schools of Baltimore, Maryland," (Ph.D. diss., University of Maryland, College Park, 1970), 32, 33, 38; Baltimore City Public Schools, *Informational Materials for Desegregation Task Force* (Baltimore: Baltimore City Public Schools, 1974); "Maryland Board Rulings to Be Appealed to Court," *Southern School News* 4, no. 10 (April 1958); "Desegregation Passes Half-Way Point in Baltimore's Public School System," *Southern School News* 5, no. 9 (March 1959).

7. Baltimore City Public Schools, *Informational Materials for Desegregation Task Force*; "Negro Pupils Outnumber Whites for First Time in Baltimore," *Southern School News* 7, no. 9 (March 1961): 11; "Majority of Baltimore Negro Pupils in Biracial Schools," *Southern School News* 8, no. 9 (March 1962).

8. Joel Acus Carrington, "The Struggle for Desegregation of Baltimore City Public Schools, 1952–1966" (Ph.D. diss., University of Maryland, College Park, 1970), 52; U.S. Commission on Civil Rights, *Racial Isolation in the Public Schools*, vol. 1 (Washington: U.S. Government Printing Office, 1967), Table A3; Parents Committee, *Seven Years of Desegregation* (Baltimore: Parents Committee, 1963), Tables 1, 3.

9. Barbara Mills, *"Got My Mind Set on Freedom": Maryland's Story of Black and White Activism, 1663–2000* (Bowie, MD: Heritage Books, 2002), 147–194; Vernon Edward Horn, "Integrating Baltimore: Protest and Accommodation, 1945–1963" (master's thesis, University of Maryland–College Park, 1991), 75–106; Robert M. Palumbos, "Student Involvement in the Baltimore Civil Rights Movement, 1953–63," *Maryland Historical Magazine* 94, no. 4 (Winter 1999): 449–492.

10. Billie Bramhall, a white parent who valued integration, was upset to find that free choice let her white neighbors opt out of the neighborhood elementary school and leave it predominantly black. Dorothy Sykes, another white parent, was disturbed that free choice made her daughter's elementary school overcrowded and that she had trouble transferring out. They sought other parents who did not like the segregation and overcrowding that resulted from free choice. They called their group, simply, the 28 Parents. Melvin Sykes (unrelated to Dorothy) provided pro bono legal assistance.

11. Parents Committee, *Seven Years of Desegregation*; Parents Committee, *Eight Years of Desegregation* (Baltimore: Parents Committee, 1963); George B. Brain, ed., *Desegregation Policies and Procedures, 1954–1963: Baltimore Public Schools* (Baltimore: Baltimore City Department of Education, 1963), 10–11.

12. Baltimore School Board minutes, September 5, 1963, 181–185, 192–193; Adam Clymer, "School Board Votes to Remedy Effects of Racial Imbalance," *Baltimore Sun*, September 6, 1963; George W. Collins, "Segregation, Overcrowding Target of New School Policy," *Baltimore Afro-American*, September 7, 1963; George W. Collins, "A School Board Talk Sized Up: You Were 'Loud, Clear, Wrong,'" *Baltimore Afro-American*, September 21, 1963.

13. Baltimore City Public Schools, *Informational Materials for Desegregation Task Force*, Table B; "Superintendent Reports Progress in 'Racial Integration' Last Year," *Southern School News* 10, no. 10 (April 1964); U.S. Commission on Civil Rights, *Racial Isolation in the Public Schools*, 4; Carrington, *The Struggle for Desegregation*, 99–100.

14. "NAACP Hails Paquin Plan," *Baltimore Afro-American*, February 5, 1966; Baltimore School Board minutes, June 9, 1966, 131–145; "Paquin Plan Approved with Several Changes," *Baltimore Afro-American*, June 11, 1966; Roger J. Nissly, "Paquin Plan Changing High Schools," *Baltimore Afro-American*, June 18, 1966; *School Desegregation in the Southern and Border States*, monthly report compiled by the Southern Education Reporting Service, February 1966, March 1966, May 1966; Mills, *"Got My Mind Set on Freedom,"* 395–399; School Board minutes, December 16, 1965, 243–245; *School Desegregation in the Southern and Border States*, December 1965; Laurence G. Paquin, *The Senior High Schools in the Years Ahead, 1966–1971* (Baltimore: Baltimore City Public Schools, 1966). Educational parks are campuses that include several elementary and secondary schools and draw students from a large, potentially racially heterogeneous area, thus facilitating integration.

15. Louis C. Goldberg, "CORE in Trouble: A Social History of the Organizational Dilemmas of the Congress of Racial Equality Target City Project in Baltimore (1965–1967)" (Ph.D. diss., Johns Hopkins University, 1970); August Meier and Elliott Rudwick, *CORE* (New York: Oxford University Press, 1973); Baltimore School Board minutes, September 22, 1966, 229–232; Gene Oishi, "Task Force Urges Speed-Up in Integrating School Staffs," *Baltimore Sun*, September 23, 1966.

16. Mayor's Task Force for Equal Rights, "Series of Recommendations on Integration and Quality Education in the Inner City," June 26, 1967; Baltimore School Board minutes, September 20, 1967, 404–409; *School Desegregation in the Southern and Border States*, July 1967; Martin D. Jenkins and Hans Froelicher, Jr., letter to Theodore R. McKeldin (copy in author's possession), July 26, 1967; "Supt. Paquin, Fighter for Quality Education, Succumbs," *Baltimore Afro-American*, October 14, 1967; "Superintendent Paquin," *Baltimore Afro-American*, October 14, 1967; *School Desegregation in the Southern and Border States*, October 1967.

17. Dollie Walker, Arthur L. Stinchcombe, and Mary S. McDill, *School Desegregation in Baltimore* (Baltimore: Johns Hopkins University, 1967); *School Desegregation in the Southern and Border States*, August 1967, September 1967.

18. *School Desegregation in the Southern and Border States*, August 1967; ibid., October 1967.

19. Thomas J. D'Alesandro III, oral history interview, McKeldin-Jackson Oral History collection, Maryland Historical Society, OH 8119, June 17, 1976; Thomas D'Alesandro III, interview by author, November 4, 2003; Peter Marudas, interview by author, December 11, 2003; Dorothy Pula Strohecker, "Tommys Two: The D'Alesandros," in *Baltimore: A Living Renaissance*, Lenora Heilig Nast, Laurence N. Krause, and R. C. Monk, eds. (Baltimore: Historic Baltimore Society, 1982),

232; Mike Bowler, *The Lessons of Change: Baltimore Schools in the Modern Era* (Baltimore: Fund for Educational Excellence, 1991), 12.

20. Stephen J. Lynton, "Mayor Pays King Tribute," *Baltimore Sun*, April 5, 1968; Phillip Potter, "Troops," *Baltimore Sun*, April 6, 1968; Oswald Johnston, "Appeal," *Baltimore Sun*, April 5, 1968; "Unrest Rises in Wake of King's Death," *Baltimore Sun*, April 6, 1968; Robert A. Erlandson, "City to Mark Monday as Day of Mourning for Dr. King; Schools, Offices Will Close," *Baltimore Sun*, April 6, 1968; Stephen J. Lynton, "Baltimore Sad but Peaceful as Negro and White Mourn," *Baltimore Sun*, April 6, 1968; "Guard Called Out in Baltimore Riot; Three Killed; U.S. Troops Sent to Chicago, Bolstered in D.C.," *Baltimore Sun*, April 7, 1968; "1,900 U.S. Troops Patrolling City; Officials Plan Curfew Again Today; 4 Dead, 300 Hurt, 1,350 Arrested," *Baltimore Sun*, April 8, 1968; "Mayor Tours a Scarred City, Seeking to Avert a Second Night," *Baltimore Sun*, April 8, 1968; Edward G. Pickett, "Efficient, Weary Guardsmen Unable to Prevent Looting," *Baltimore Sun*, April 8, 1968; "1,900 More GI's Join Riot Forces as Snipers Peril Police, Firemen; Arrests in 3 Days Rise to 3,450," *Baltimore Sun*, April 9, 1968; "Baltimore's Weary Firefighters Get Help from Two Counties," *Baltimore Sun*, April 9, 1968; Richard Basoco, "West Baltimore Is an Ugly No-Man's Land," *Baltimore Sun*, April 9, 1968, "55,000 Troops, Apparently Most in U.S. History, Are Deployed," *Baltimore Sun*, April 9, 1968; "Today Must End It," *Baltimore Sun*, April 9, 1968; "Backbone of Riot Reported Broken; Return to Normal Could Be Near," *Baltimore Sun*, April 10, 1968; Edward G. Pickett, "Negro Peace Meeting Dispersed by Troops," *Baltimore Sun*, April 10, 1968; John E. O'Donnell, Jr., "600 Treated, 19 Admitted with Wounds from Rioting," *Baltimore Sun*, April 10, 1968; "City Begins Clean-up after Riots; Sightseers Tour Ravaged Areas," *Baltimore Sun*, April 10, 1968; George W. Collins, "City in Turmoil as Rioters Roam," *Baltimore Afro-American*, April 9, 1968; Jewell Chambers and Al Rutledge, "Riot Brings Misery, Suffering to Innocent," *Baltimore Afro-American*, April 9, 1968.

21. Gene Oishi, "Negroes Quit Conference with Agnew," *Baltimore Sun*, April 12, 1968; Robert A. Erlandson, "Mayor, Reacting to Agnew's Remarks, Asks for Restraint," *Baltimore Sun*, April 13, 1968; "Text of Governor Agnew's Statement to Civil Rights Leaders," *Baltimore Sun*, April 13, 1968; "Angry Leaders Walk Out on Agnew," *Baltimore Afro-American*, April 20, 1968; Mills, *"Got My Mind Set on Freedom,"* 625–627; D'Alesandro interview, McKeldin-Jackson Oral History collection, I-2:19; Callcott, *Maryland and America*, 215; Brugger, *Maryland*, 626–628.

22. Gene Oishi, "Telegrams," *Baltimore Sun*, April 13, 1968, B16, B6.

23. Olson, *Baltimore*, 383; "What's the Answer," *Baltimore Jewish Times* 98, no. 9 (April 12, 1968), 8.

24. Robert A. Erlandson, "Mayor, Reacting to Agnew's Remarks, Asks for Restraint," *Baltimore Sun*, April 12, 1968; Weldon Wallace, "Priests," *Baltimore Sun*, April 13, 1968; "Racism Is Good Friday Theme," *Baltimore Sun*, April 13, 1968.

25. 391 U.S. 430, 1968.

26. George L. Russell, Jr., Ambrose T. Hartman, and Blanche G. Wahl to David L. Glenn regarding "Integration in the Baltimore City Schools: Impact of *Green v. County School Board*," Department of Law File no. 118889, November 29, 1968, pp. 4, 6, 8, 9.

27. Alvin P. Sanoff, "Change Denied on Open Schools," *Baltimore Sun*, November 19, 1968; "Murnaghan Poses Two Integration Problems," *Baltimore Sun*, December 2, 1968; Roger J. Nissly, "Baltimore Schools Have No Master Plan for Desegregation," *Baltimore Afro-American*, December 14, 1968.

28. Sanoff, "Change Denied on Open Schools," C24.

29. Richard D. O'Mara, "Dr. Sheldon: A First Impression," *Baltimore Evening Sun*, March 27, 1968; Stephen A. Bennett, "New Yorker Named City School Head," *Baltimore Evening Sun*, n.d. [mid-1968?]; Kay Mills, "New School Chief Maps Poverty Area Push," *Baltimore Evening Sun*; "Dr. Sheldon Takes Over," *Baltimore Afro-American*, August 3, 1968; Bowler, *Lessons of Change*, 11; Kay Mills, "Hempstead Praises Work of Dr. Sheldon, Especially in Community Relations Area," *Baltimore Evening Sun*, April 5, 1968.

30. Bowler, *Lessons of Change*, 11–12; "Dr. Sheldon's First Year," *Baltimore Afro-American*, July 4, 1969.

31. "Racial Tension Blamed for Disruption at Girls' School," *Baltimore Afro-American*, February 14, 1970; "Protests Force School Shut-down," *Baltimore Afro-American*, February 17, 1970; Baltimore School Board minutes, February 12, 1970, 64–67; Joshua Watson, "Murnaghan Threatens to Quit School Post," *Baltimore Afro-American*, February 14, 1970; Allen Feld, "Murnaghan Talks of Future Plans," *Baltimore Afro-American*, February 28, 1970.

32. "TJD Choice Hit for Role in Police Beating Probe," *Baltimore Afro-American*, February 24, 1970; "New School Prexy," *Baltimore Afro-American*, February 28, 1970; Mike Bowler, "Karwacki's 21 Months on Board Helped Avert Disaster, He Believes," *Baltimore Sun*, November 9, 1971, A12.

33. Paul Evans, "TJD's School Board Threat Meets with Fire from Black Community," *Baltimore Afro-American*, January 16, 1971; Bowler, *Lessons of Change*, 1991, 12; Antero Pietila, "Race Issue Foils City's School Plan," *Baltimore Sun*, November 6, 1970; Baltimore School Board minutes, November 5, 1970; Sue Miller, "School Board Head Assails D'Alesandro," *Baltimore Evening Sun*, January 23, 1971; Paul Evans, "To Consult Sheldon on Leaving," *Baltimore Afro-American*, January 9, 1971; Baltimore School Board minutes, January 6, 1971; Sue Miller, "Baltimore School Discord Isn't Unique," *Baltimore Evening Sun*, January 19, 1971.

34. 402 U.S. 1, 1971.

35. Baltimore School Board minutes, June 4, 1971.

36. C. Fraser Smith, *William Donald Schaefer* (Baltimore: Johns Hopkins University Press, 1999); Sue Miller, "Hettleman Is Third Member to Quit City School Board," *Baltimore Evening Sun*, October 19, 1973.

37. 356 F. Supp. 92, 1973; Frederic B. Hill, "Court Tells HEW to Force Schools to Desegregate," *Baltimore Sun*, February 17, 1973; Peter E. Holmes to Roland N. Patterson, April 17, 1973; Roland N. Patterson to Peter E. Holmes, June 4, 1973, in Baltimore City Public Schools, *Informational Materials*, 1974.

38. Peter E. Holmes to Roland N. Patterson, February 5, 1974.

39. Baltimore School Board minutes, March 14, 1974; Glen Fallin, "School Deseg Task Force to Meet," *Baltimore News American*, March 18, 1974; Theodore W. Hendricks, "Task Force Votes 25 to 20 to Send 5 Desegregation Plans to School Unit," *Baltimore Sun*, April 17, 1974; "Desegregation Sentiments," *Baltimore Sun*, April 26, 1974; Antero Pietila, "Placards and Prayer Meld at Desegregation Hearing," *Baltimore Sun*, April 26, 1974; Glen Fallin, "Parents Flay Deseg Plans," *Baltimore News American*, April 26, 1974.

40. "Parents Say 'We're Staying,'" *East Baltimore Guide*, April 25, 1974; "Letters to the Editor," *East Baltimore Guide*, May 2, 1974.

41. "Busing Inescapable," *Baltimore Afro-American*, April 27, 1974; Marc Shelby Silver, "Glen Area—Interracial Stability?" *Baltimore Jewish Times*, May 3, 1974; "The Glen Avenue Area," *Baltimore Jewish Times*, May 3, 1974.

42. Baltimore City Public Schools, *Desegregation Plan for Baltimore City Public Schools* (Baltimore: Baltimore City Public Schools, 1974).

43. Mike Bowler, "School Plan Is Mild Medicine," *Baltimore Sun*, May 30, 1974; Antero Pietila, "Students Protest New Plan," *Baltimore Sun*, May 30, 1974.

44. "Zoning Urged for Patterson," *East Baltimore Guide*, May 30, 1974; "Preregistration Slated for Eastside Schools," *East Baltimore Guide*, May 30, 1974; John Jennings and Glen Fallin, "Students Protest Board's Plans," *Baltimore News American*, May 29, 1974; Sue Miller and Larry Carson, "6 Schools' Students Refuse to Attend Classes in Protest," *Baltimore Evening Sun*, May 30, 1974; Pietila, "Students Protest New Plan"; Edward Colimore, "Mayor Pelted by Busing Protesters," *Baltimore News American*, May 30, 1974; Miller and Carson, "6 Schools' Students Refuse to Attend Classes in Protest"; Theodore W. Hendricks, "Students Cut Class to March," *Baltimore Sun*, May 31, 1974; Kelly Gilbert and Sue Miller, "Students Protest School Plan," *Baltimore Evening Sun*, June 3, 1974; "Desegregation Protest Grows as Pupils of 9 Schools March," *Baltimore News American*, June 3, 1974.

45. Baltimore School Board minutes, June 4, 1974.

46. "After 20 Long Years," *Baltimore Afro-American*, May 4, 1974; "Stop Pussyfooting," *Baltimore Afro-American*, May 25, 1974; Edgar L. Jones, "Where Were Our Top People, while Students Howled?" *Baltimore Evening Sun*, June 14, 1974, A10.

47. Peter E. Holmes to Roland N. Patterson, July 29, 1974.

48. Richard Ben Cramer and Antero Pietila, "Board's Whites Try to Fire Patterson," *Baltimore Sun*, August 9, 1974; Bill Rhoden, "Board for Patterson Scalp," *Baltimore Afro-American*, August 10, 1974; Richard Ben Cramer, "Patterson's Status Unsure following Vote," *Baltimore Sun*, August 10, 1974; Antero Pietila, "Patterson Ouster Seems to Founder," *Baltimore Sun*, August 13, 1974.

49. Richard Ben Cramer, "City Maps School Plan Resistance," *Baltimore Sun*, August 30, 1974; Antero Pietila, "Speak Out on School Plan, Urban Coalition Appeals," *Baltimore Sun*, September 2, 1974; Richard Ben Cramer, "Mayor Bars Changes in School Plan," *Baltimore Sun*, September 3, 1974.

50. Antero Pietila, "School Security Boosted," *Baltimore Sun*, September 5, 1974; Jeanne E. Saddler, "Schools Ask Parents, Teachers: Let's Work Together," *Baltimore Sun*, September 5, 1974; "Pickets, Absenteeism Mark Schools' Opening," *Baltimore Sun*, September 6, 1974; Antero Pietila, "1 in 5 Pupils in City Skips Opening Day," *Baltimore Sun*, September 6, 1974; Mike Bowler, "Student Boycotts Continue; Attendance under Par at Paired Schools," *Baltimore Sun*, September 7, 1974; Mike Bowler, "4 out of 5 Whites Skip Black Jr. High Classes," *Baltimore Sun*, September 10, 1974; "Pickets, Absenteeism Mark Schools' Opening"; Kenneth D. Durr, *Behind the Backlash* (Chapel Hill: University of North Carolina Press, 2003), 166ff; Jeanne E. Saddler, "At the Eye of Picketing, Sit-in Storm, One Calm Canton Teacher Carries On," *Baltimore Sun*, September 7, 1974; Mike Bowler, "Modify Integration, School Board Asked," *Baltimore Sun*, September 12, 1974.

51. Notice of Opportunity for Hearing, Docket No. S-82, September 9, 1974.

52. Baltimore School Board minutes, September 19, 1974; Mike Bowler, "Transfers Allowed at 6 Junior Highs," *Baltimore Sun*, September 20, 1974; "Desegregation Without Direction," *Baltimore Sun*, September 21, 1974, A16; "Time for the NAACP to Act," *Baltimore Afro-American*, September 28, 1974.

53. Peter E. Holmes to Roland N. Patterson, January 8, 1975; Baltimore City Public Schools, *Senior High School Desegregation Plan for Baltimore City Public*

Schools, 1975; Baltimore School Board minutes, January 30, 1975; Mike Bowler, "School Plan Ends Open Enrollment," *Baltimore Sun*, January 22, 1975; "Zone Plan for City High Schools," *Baltimore Sun*, January 22, 1975; Mike Bowler, "It's Back to Zones for the City's High Schools," *Baltimore Sun*, February 2, 1975; "School Board Strives for Feb. 3 Deadline on Deseg Plan," *Baltimore Afro-American*, January 25, 1975; "Desegregation Plan Approved by Unanimous School Board Vote," *Baltimore Afro-American*, February 1, 1975.

54. Jeanne E. Saddler, "Plan to Shift 14,000–16,000 in Junior Highs," *Baltimore Sun*, February 20, 1975; "Junior High Neighborhoods under Anti-bias Plan Listed," *Baltimore Sun*, February 26, 1975; "Gerrymandered Zones for City Schools," *Baltimore Sun*, March 1, 1975; Mike Bowler and Jeanne E. Saddler, "School Plan Passed after Pupil Shift," *Baltimore Sun*, March 14, 1975; "Deseg Plan Improves Jr. Hi Racial Balance," *Baltimore Afro-American*, February 22, 1975; Baltimore City Public Schools, *Junior High School Desegregation Plan for Baltimore City Public Schools*, 1975.

55. *Adams v. Weinberger*, 391 F. Supp. 269, 1975; Mike Bowler, "School Board to Evaluate Patterson Tenure," *Baltimore Sun*, April 18, 1975; Peter E. Holmes to Roland N. Patterson, May 2, 1975; Mike Bowler, "City's School Desegregation Plan Rejected," *Baltimore Sun*, May 3, 1975; Jeanne E. Saddler and Mike Bowler, "Board Votes 7 to 2 to Oust Patterson; Griffin Arrested in Protest at Meeting," *Baltimore Sun*, June 10, 1975; Mike Bowler and Robert A. Erlandson, "School Chief Is Fired," *Baltimore Sun*, July 18, 1975; Mike Bowler, "Crew Is Named to School Post," *Baltimore Sun*, July 19, 1975.

56. Transcript of Proceedings, Prehearing Conference in the Matter of Baltimore City School District, Baltimore, Maryland, and Maryland State Department of Education, Docket No. S-82, August 4, 1975.

57. "Schools Still Segregated," *Baltimore Afro-American*, October 4, 1975; Robert Armacost to Peter E. Holmes, September 9, 1975; Peter E. Holmes to Norman P. Ramsey, November 11, 1975; Jeanne E. Saddler, "School-Transfer Bids Pour In as Headquarters Lifts Freeze," *Baltimore Sun*, September 17, 1975; Portia E. Badham, "Schools Open Peacefully but 2,000 Parents Seek Transfers," *Baltimore Afro-American*, September 6, 1975; "School Transfer Policy May Witness Changes," *Baltimore Afro-American*, November 1, 1975; Mike Bowler, "Lake Clifton Head Asks Transfer Ban, Hints School Plan Is Being Subverted," *Baltimore Sun*, October 27, 1975; "School Figures Indicate Black Flight," *Baltimore Sun*, November 3, 1975.

58. Mike Bowler, "Joseph Well Versed in Urban Affairs," *Baltimore Sun*, December 4, 1975; "Schaefer Turns to School Post," *Baltimore Sun*, November 6, 1975.

59. Transcript of Proceedings, in the United States District Court for the District of Maryland, in *Mandel v. HEW*, Civil Action N-76-1, *Baltimore v. HEW*, Civil Action N-76-23, January 30, 1976; Transcript of Proceedings in the United States District Court for the District of Maryland, in *Mandel v. HEW*, Civil Action N-76-1, *Baltimore v. HEW*, Civil Action N-76-23, February 20, 1976; *Baltimore v. Mathews* (411 F. Supp. 542), 1976.

60. *Baltimore v. Mathews*, 562 F. 2d 914, 1977; *Baltimore v. Mathews*, 571 F.2d 1273, 1978.

61. Lloyd R. Henderson to David S. Tatel, letter, copy in author's possession, November 16, 1978; Roma J. Stewart to secretary Patricia Roberts Harris, January 29, 1980, letter, copy in author's possession; Lloyd R. Henderson to David S. Tatel,

November 16, 1978, letter, copy in author's possession; Roma J. Stewart to Patricia Roberts Harris, January 29, 1980, letter, copy in author's possession; Stipulation and Order, in the United States District Court for the District of Maryland, in *Baltimore v. Mathews*, Civil Action No. N-76-23, January 21, 1983; Alicia Coro to Alice Pinderhughes, May 12, 1987, letter, copy in author's possession.

62. Baltimore School Board minutes, June 26, 1980.

63. Baltimore School Board minutes, September 2, 1982.

64. Gunnar Myrdal, *An American Dilemma*, New Brunswick: Transaction, 2000 (1944); Harold A. McDougall, *Black Baltimore* (Philadelphia: Temple University Press, 1993).

11

Pivot in Perception

The Impact of the 1968 Riots on Three Baltimore Business Districts

Elizabeth M. Nix and Deborah R. Weiner

The events of April 1968 are often used as shorthand in Baltimore City. Residents remember a Baltimore "before the riots," in which the population was stable, race relations were better than in most cities, crime was low, and commercial life was thriving. They believe that "after the riots," the city's population declined rapidly, race relations deteriorated, crime skyrocketed, and businesses left for the suburbs. When the popular imagination assigns this major role to the riots, the city's problems in 2010 of sixteen thousand vacant houses,[1] one of the highest murder rates in the nation, and a dearth of retail become simpler to explain.

However, the actual story of Baltimore in the 1960s is more nuanced. Widespread middle-class flight in residential and commercial areas had already begun. Many were choosing to live and shop outside the city because of real and perceived urban ills, in addition to the temptations of suburbia. The proliferation of suburban shopping centers had taken a toll on the retail life of the city long before the disturbances occurred. Charles Center (opened in 1959) and the Mechanic Theater (opened in 1967) were only two of the highest-profile urban renewal efforts designed to "lure people back to downtown."[2] In 1967 city high school students were found with a variety of weapons, including guns.[3] Even before the streets filled with looters, fear of crime was the "all-encompassing excuse" that many city residents gave when they made the move to the suburbs.[4]

The population of Baltimore City peaked around 1950 and then dropped by ten thousand in the decade between 1950 and 1960, the first-ever decline in the city's history.[5] In 1967 an urban planner wrote in an international journal, "By 1960, Baltimore had almost become a city of low- and low-middle-income people living in spacious apartments with high ceilings for $38 a month. This would have been fine were it not for the fact that upper-income families had moved off the city's tax rolls."[6] In a 1967 interview, William Donald Schaefer, then a city councilman, discussed people who were "staying in or coming back to the city. More are beginning to see the city advantages, but problems such as crime are significant deterrents."[7]

As Schaefer tried to bring middle-class residents back into the city, he also acknowledged the movement of middle-class blacks within the city. In the same interview Schaefer remarked, "Today a Negro in the market for a home can buy one in almost any section of the city if he has the money." The racial desegregation of the city led to increasing concentrations of poverty in the segregated neighborhoods that middle-class blacks left behind, leaving many areas more poverty stricken than they were before desegregation. As a result they were ripe for riot. In 1961 the Baltimore Health and Welfare Council identified "high crime and unemployment rates, social alienation, low level of communication and language skills, poor nutritional and health standards, and limited access to facilities for self-help" as concerns in inner-city neighborhoods.[8] Well before 1968 city leaders had predicted urban unrest and were taking measures to prevent it.[9]

Just as the economic health and population stability of Baltimore before the riots has been exaggerated in the popular imagination, the role of the uprising in the economic downturn the city experienced in the 1970s has also been inflated. Looters and arsonists went to work in fifteen business districts across the city, but they did not destroy the commercial life of those areas. While certain businesses were damaged beyond hope of recovery and never reopened after April 1968, dozens of other stores cleaned up the glass, filed insurance claims, and ordered new inventory. Many of those businesses survived for a number of years until an event such as a fire, a business downturn, or generational succession caused the owners to make the decision to close. Statistics and contemporary news accounts indicate that the riots merely accelerated trends that were already under way and that their tangible effects were not as dire as popular imagination might indicate.

Nevertheless, the events of April 1968 played a major role in changing perceptions about the city. Contemporary accounts and later oral histories testify to the impact the violence had on the way people thought about Baltimore. The city might have already experienced rising crime rates, but in the spring of 1968 the danger suddenly became more tangible, impossible to ignore—and in fact, sometimes overstated. Certain neighborhoods might have been poor, but the chaos illuminated the extremity of their poverty. Shopping districts might have deteriorated, but the gaping holes left by burned-out businesses overshadowed the numerous vacancies that had already occurred. Baltimoreans had previously been able to "pat themselves on the back for the peaceful manner in which integration has been handled,"[10] but after the disturbances they were forced to reexamine race relations.

In the wake of the uprising, no ethnic group wrestled more immediately with its ties to the black community than Baltimore's Jewish community. Dr. Martin Luther King, Jr., outlined the connections between these two groups in an essay published the year before he was assassinated: "The urban Negro has a special and unique relationship to Jews. He meets them in two dissimilar roles. . . . [Some] Jews have identified voluntarily in the freedom movement, motivated by their religious and cultural commitment to justice. The other Jews who are engaged in commerce in the ghettos are remnants of older communities. A great number of Negro ghettos were formerly Jewish neighborhoods; some storekeepers and landlords remained as population changes occurred."[11] In Baltimore and across the nation, the types of neighborhoods that King describes were those hardest hit in the unrest that followed his assassination. Much of the destruction of property occurred to businesses owned and operated by Jewish merchants.

This chapter examines three Baltimore business districts before and after the riots, with particular attention to the black-Jewish relationship. The three districts had distinctive features: Lombard Street, the commercial heart of Baltimore's original immigrant Jewish neighborhood, had undergone racial succession and wholesale urban renewal in the decades before the riots. Pennsylvania Avenue, the African American shopping and entertainment mecca located in the historic center of Baltimore's black community, had been in economic decline since the early 1950s. North Avenue had recently experienced racial succession and was in the midst of urban renewal in the form of highways and new shopping centers. But as the case studies demonstrate, common threads link the three areas. Together, they offer a counterpoint to the popular view of the impact of the events of April 1968. They show that the riots were undoubtedly a watershed event in the city's history, but not exactly for the reasons people think they were.

Lombard Street: "It Was an Open Atmosphere"

The history of the East Baltimore neighborhood that borders the city's downtown reflects the history of America's inner cities in the twentieth century. From the 1890s to the 1920s the district was considered an immigrant slum, crowded mostly with East European Jews who toiled in the city's garment industry. After World War I, Jews began moving up on the economic scale and out to the working- and middle-class precincts of northwest Baltimore, leaving behind a neighborhood of dilapidated row houses that from the 1930s to the 1950s housed the working poor, predominantly white but with a growing black population. This "blight," in the parlance of the day, was subjected to massive urban renewal in the mid-1950s. Virtually the entire housing stock was demolished, and in its place arose one of Baltimore's largest high-rise public housing projects in 1955—a place that started out full of hope but became known for its descent into drugs, crime, and deep poverty.[12]

The housing project, Flag House Courts, was torn down in 2001, making the neighborhood, with its prime location near Baltimore's Inner Harbor, ripe for gentrification. In the footprint of Flag House Courts, a development of mixed-income row houses opened in 2005, known by the fanciful name of Albemarle Square. Where 490 units of public housing formerly stood, there are now 340 homes, around one-third reserved for public housing residents and two-thirds sold at market rates of $300,000 to $400,000.[13]

The 1953–1955 and 2001–2005 transformations of the neighborhood were sweeping, completely making over the neighborhood's housing. But the year 1968 is better known as a marker of change—as the year riots swept through the neighborhood's Lombard Street commercial strip. The impact and meaning of the 1968 destruction varied from neighborhood to neighborhood, depending on the particular character of the local business district and its role in the community. In the case of Lombard Street, perhaps more than for any other Baltimore commercial strip, the symbolic import was more significant than the physical. That is because this four-block stretch of shops already retained a heavy symbolic meaning.

For Baltimoreans, "Lombard Street" has carried the same emotional weight that the terms "Hester Street" and "Maxwell Street" have carried for New Yorkers and Chicagoans. As the bustling early twentieth-century marketplace for Baltimore's Jewish community, its sights, smells, and sounds encapsulated the immigrant experience while providing a vivid sensory link to the old country. In the decades after they moved away, Jewish families made weekly treks to the old neighborhood to shop for the Sabbath or to experience the ethnic foods that were passed down from generation to generation. They were joined by Italians from nearby Little Italy as well as other Baltimoreans in search of ethnic delicacies and local color. From the 1920s through the 1960s, journalists wrote with fascination about the street's mix of people, its exotic ambiance, and its colorful characters.[14]

So in 1968 Lombard Street was more than a nostalgic memory. In the shadow of looming high-rises of its neighbor Flag House Courts, it was a living, breathing, thriving embodiment of Baltimore's immigrant history, especially its immigrant Jewish history. Jewish and Italian merchants, sons and daughters of the immigrants who first set up shop, carried on the commercial tradition with, as one mid-1960s newspaper article put it, "the same spirit, love of life and desire to please."[15] The street was known for its bakeries, delis, fruit and vegetable stores, groceries, dairies, and kosher butchers. The shops crowded each other and their wares spilled out into streets that filled with shoppers on weekends.

The merchants depended for their livelihoods on shoppers coming from across Baltimore, but they also appreciated their local clientele, the residents of Flag House Courts. As former Flag House resident Dorothy Scott put it, Lombard Street was "people friendly." Merchants knew their local customers by name and offered credit in times of need. Some became trusted figures. A pharmacist known as "Doc," for example, "loved the people in the community," Scott said. After filling prescriptions for children, he would call the parents to see how their children were doing.[16]

Flag House Courts began the 1960s with a population that was 65 percent white, and ended the decade with a 97 percent black population.[17] People who lived there during the decade recall a close-knit community of neighbors and decent housing management. There was drug activity, but it was mostly hidden. There was crime, but it was not overwhelming. Housing authority reports show an increase in single-parent households and families on welfare through the decade, but these reports lack the beleaguered tone they would take on after 1968.[18]

From an architectural standpoint, Flag House Courts seemed to turn its back on the neighborhood. Like many public housing complexes built during the era, it was designed to be self-contained, not to interact with the street life around it. Even so, Flag House residents integrated Lombard Street into their lives and the commercial strip became a major part of their community. In fact, their memories of Flag House are bound up with memories of Lombard Street. As former resident Esther Dortch stated in an oral history, "I loved Flag House, tell you the truth, and I loved it that you come down here to these stores, get fresh chickens killed and good fresh eggs." Many stores employed residents of Flag House and other nearby housing projects. One woman recalled, "Some of the African American people that worked with the Jewish people, they knew some of the [Yiddish] words and they would joke and laugh." Residents who worked on Lombard Street welcomed the income, though there were some who felt that a few of the employers exploited or cheated them.[19]

Flag House residents' memories of Lombard Street showed their nostalgia for a time when the project was less isolated, more integrated into the life of the city. As Dorothy Scott said, "Every nationality was on that street. Jews, whites, Italians, African Americans, you name it, they were there. It was just nice, because it was an open atmosphere."[20] Like the journalists and uptowners who came to Lombard Street to soak up the atmosphere, Flag House Courts residents found the place fascinating.

But if Lombard Street helped connect local residents to a larger community, the neighborhood was becoming more isolated in every other way. In the early 1960s, a new highway and related road projects cut the area off from downtown. The area just north of the neighborhood was cleared for an industrial park that never materialized. This project cost two hundred homes and dozens of local jobs, and the land remained vacant until the city built the new main post office in 1970.[21] Like other inner-city neighborhoods in Baltimore and across the nation, the area around Lombard Street was becoming more marginalized as the 1960s progressed. White flight, the movement of middle-class blacks out of inner cities, the concentration of the poor in overcrowded public housing complexes, and the loss of manufacturing jobs—and the opportunity such jobs had formerly provided to escape poverty—all contributed to the growing isolation, frustration, and anger of poor urban black communities.[22]

The looting and arson of April 1968 started on Gay Street, just a few blocks north of Flag House Courts, and Lombard Street was not spared. The *Baltimore Sun* reported on April 7 that "tenants leaned from upper floors of Flag House Courts as they hooted down at firemen responding to a blaze on Lombard Street." An article the next day described how "city police were pinned down behind their cars by two or three snipers firing from the upper floors of the project. Police withdrew under a hail of bottles." A fire broke out at Smelkinson's dairy store, which burned to the ground. One former Flag House resident later claimed this store was deliberately targeted because residents resented what they saw as unfair treatment. But he also said that much of the looting was random and stores that had good relations with residents also were damaged.[23]

Most Flag House residents were trapped inside their apartments, afraid of rioters and law enforcement alike. Esther Dortch recalled that she had her children down on the floor because "the National Guard was out there with guns pointed at the high rises." She also worried that her children might be hit from the stray bullets of snipers within the project. On the other hand, Charles Dingle, who was fourteen at the time, got caught up in the looting. His mother forbade him to go out, but, he said, "I snuck out there anyway. And I'd go in, take a little of this, little of that. But as you get older, you realize now you wasn't doing nothing but hurting yourself. Because we needed those stores." This point was made by several interviewees. As Dorothy Scott observed, "that wasn't what Martin Luther King stood for. That's not what he wanted for us. We only wound up hurting ourselves 'cause those were the mom and pop stores that closed down."[24]

The riots spelled the beginning of the end for Lombard Street—but it did not happen right away. Lombard Street stores suffered only minor damage, aside from the dairy store, two liquor stores, and a small food mart. In fact, during the month after the disturbances, the storeowners' main problem was a lack of customers, not looted stores. Rumors had circulated that the entire Lombard Street strip had burned to the ground, according to a newspaper account, "leaving Baltimore's Italian and Jewish specialty delicatessens almost empty for several days." Business was so bad that "thirteen stores placed a newspaper ad saying, 'We are open and ready to serve you.'"[25] So immediately, perceptions were creating their own reality, a reality at odds with the relatively light damage. Meanwhile, Lombard Street merchants—who knew what had really happened—seemed undeterred by the events of April 7 and 8. A newspaper article reported that they insisted they would "continue the stores started by their fathers and grandfathers," with a meat market owner quoted as saying, "We're here to stay and we'll battle to do it."[26]

Apparently their public relations efforts paid off. Within a month, the street came back to life. A May 6 article noted, "Yesterday, Attman's delicatessen served 400 people and crowds waited in a line 200 feet long at Jack's." One shopkeeper told a reporter that "neighborhood residents were ashamed to return to her store, where many of their children had looted," but soon the locals came back and their relationship with merchants picked up where it left off, say former Flag House residents.[27] Baltimore's Jews returned to patronize the market, as did other Baltimoreans in search of bargains and local color.

Within a year, *Sun* reporter Ralph Reppert described the street almost as if nothing had ever happened. "It survives as a tiny unchanged island, noisy and odorous, of ancient, old world foods, customs, and conversation . . . a milling, pushing gaggle of shoppers talking to storekeepers in half a dozen languages over the noise of blaring automobile horns and squawking chickens." Deep into the article Reppert mentioned a few "gaping storefronts." He did not blame the violent week of April 1968, which he barely mentioned, but "old age, with no younger generation to operate them after the old folks died."[28]

In fact, several factors came together to cause the decline of Lombard Street. The looting and arson did have long-term consequences. "After the riots, it wasn't the same," says Charles Dingle. "The people came but it wasn't as busy." Whites felt less comfortable in the city and blacks felt more isolated than ever. Property crimes such as robbery, vandalism, and petty theft began to plague storeowners. As an Italian fruit dealer told Reppert, "Once, we make up the displays outside. Nobody steal. . . . Now we got to keep somebody at the outside stall every minute."[29] Whether or not increased crime can be directly attributed to the uprising, the change in atmosphere became associated in people's minds with the disturbances of April 1968.

Meanwhile, there was a retail revolution under way in America, with supermarkets, chain stores, and malls drawing customers away from old shopping areas and small businesses. The pull of suburbia had a force of its own, not entirely related to the push of inner-city decline. For the generation of middle-class Jews that came of age after World War II, the professions and the corporate world beckoned. The era of the small family store was drawing to a close, and Lombard Street merchants had an increasingly hard time convincing the younger generation to follow them into the business.[30]

But the final blow came, fittingly, with urban renewal. In 1976 Lombard Street was shut down for major road repairs. The street was impassable for months, causing customers to stay away. The owner of Stone's Bakery complained, "The way the city's busted up the street here, it looks like there's been a war and we've been bombed out." By the end of that year, twelve of twenty-eight stores were vacant.[31] Finally, in the 1980s, boarded-up storefronts outnumbered businesses. By century's end, only a few stores remained.

The 1970s were also difficult for Flag House Courts and public housing nationwide. Major federal budget cuts caused building maintenance, tenant screening, and social services to go downhill. Also, with a growing number of residents on welfare, the "man-in-the-house rule," which dictated that only single mothers with children could receive benefits, added to the loss of an adult male presence.[32] As Dorothy Scott later observed, "It was family oriented when I moved in. There were husbands there. But some families started moving out, and younger mothers, unwed mothers with children were moving in."

It was in the 1980s, said former residents, that "things really started to change." Drugs were the main culprit. By 1993 a *Baltimore Sun* article reported that "together, drugs and guns have transformed Flag House into a place so wretched, where violence and death are so familiar, that it resembles a war zone." By the end of the 1990s, Flag House Courts leaders were advocating for the project's demolition—including some of the people cited previously, who had been so positive about Flag House in the 1960s.[33]

What is the connection between the riots and the deterioration of Flag House Courts? How should the events of 1968 be assessed in relation to the two residential transformations of the neighborhood—the 1953–1955 "slum clearance" and replacement by a massive public housing development, and its 2001 implosion to make way for brand-new row houses whose design deliberately referenced the housing stock that had been torn down to build it? On one hand, April 1968 can be seen, accurately, as a major turning point in the neighborhood's history. Conversely, it would also be accurate to say that the disturbances marked just another point along a continuum—that it is easy to *over*emphasize their importance in the evolution of the neighborhood.

The difficulty of measuring the impact has to do with the interplay between perception and reality. Newspapers of the era, once they got over the tremendous shock of what had happened, seemed to downplay the effect on the street's businesses. That most merchants were determined to keep going in the immediate aftermath lends credence to the view that perhaps the events were not really as important as some people seem to think. And indeed, Lombard Street did manage to survive as a lively ethnic marketplace well into the 1970s.

Yet there's that critical matter of perception. "The riots" occupy that place where perception and reality meet, and this gives them a special meaning. Most people, black and white, *felt* that they were a turning point for Lombard Street, even if their specific recollections indicated otherwise. The riots changed the way people thought about the city. It took a while for reality to catch up with perception, but eventually it did. For Lombard Street, symbol of Baltimore's heyday as an immigrant city, April 1968 served as a powerful reminder that those days were over.

Pennsylvania Avenue: "It Was a Mighty Fine Place to Go"

> Pennsylvania Avenue served as the cultural hub of African-American entertainment in the city from the 1920s until the 1960s, when much of the area was destroyed in the 1968 riots.[34]

Pennsylvania Avenue did indeed serve as Baltimore's African American cultural hub during the mid-twentieth-century. But its demise as a lively shopping and entertainment mecca cannot be blamed on the events of April 1968.

The persistence of this myth, similar to the stories told of other inner-city Baltimore neighborhoods and commercial districts, attests to the power of the riots as a symbol of the city's decline. Certainly the days of destruction that followed King's assassination marked a critical turning point, not only in perceptions of Baltimore residents, white and black, but also in actual, measurable impact on the city's economic and social landscape. But the full story of Pennsylvania Avenue's rise and fall reveals a much more complex picture than the simple equating of riots with urban breakdown.

The Avenue emerged out of the city's racial geography. As late as 1880, African Americans had been widely distributed throughout Baltimore, but as the city grew into a modern industrial center, a pattern of rigid segregation developed. The Old West Baltimore neighborhood surrounding Pennsylvania Avenue became home to fully half the city's black population by 1904. Within its boundaries, middle-class professionals and businesspeople lived on broad avenues in substantial row houses, a growing working class occupied modest homes on the side streets, and the very poor crowded into the alley streets.[35]

By the 1920s this economically and socially diverse population supported a thriving commercial district. Pennsylvania Avenue was the African American expression of a rising American consumer culture, the product of social and residential discrimination combined with black cultural creativity. Though many of its merchants were Jewish, the Avenue was nevertheless an African American space, known especially for clubs and concert halls that showcased America's top black entertainers. "Downtown you couldn't try on a dress or stop and have a snack with a friend," one woman told *Sun* reporter Thomas Edsall in 1967, "but the avenue was ours and, I'll tell you, it was a mighty fine place to go."[36]

But Edsall's article—which appeared almost a year before the cataclysmic events of April 1968—depicted a retail district already struggling, as revealed by its headline, "Pennsylvania Avenue Declining for Generation." Several factors contributed to the pre-riot deterioration of the Avenue and surrounding neighborhood. Racial restrictions had begun to break down after World War II, slowly expanding the shopping, residential, and employment options available to blacks, especially those with some resources. The Supreme Court's 1954 *Brown* decision, and even more so the 1964 Civil Rights Act, greatly accelerated this trend. As a result, Edsall noted, "In recent years middle-class professional and white collar workers have been moving out with a consequent increase in the percentage of very poor people, especially those on welfare."[37]

The Avenue's stores and nightspots were hurt not only by the loss of middle-class residents but also by competition from newly desegregated downtown stores, restaurants, and entertainment venues—and perhaps even more important, by American society's changing consumer patterns, as television and car-oriented shopping malls took business away from downtown and local commercial districts alike. "Stores on Gay Street, Pennsylvania Avenue, West Baltimore Street, which had had a monopoly on the black dollar, they suffered," pointed out longtime Pennsylvania Avenue merchant Herman Katkow in a recent oral history.[38]

Baltimore's shrinking industrial base meant that as opportunities increased for middle-class blacks they decreased for the poor. Edsall reported "large numbers of young men hanging around on the street corners every day. . . . The unemployment rate in the area is very high." Crime worsened and illegal drugs became more and more prevalent. Unfortunately, urban renewal, one of the city's primary tools for combating inner-city blight, only served to add to the problem, as large-scale projects such as the proposed East–West Expressway dislocated residents and businesses. The neighborhood's population "declined 20 percent between 1950 and 1960," Edsall noted, "and this downward trend is continuing as more and more clearance is being done for urban renewal."[39]

The combined effects of middle-class flight, competition from new sources, increased crime, and displacement from urban renewal took a toll on Pennsylvania Avenue merchants throughout the 1950s and 1960s. As Edsall describes, "Stores began to close, theaters became movies and many of the bars began putting in juke boxes to replace live bands." Though still a viable commercial center, by 1967 Pennsylvania Avenue was far from what it once had been. "Both the mood and the physical state of the avenue have changed," Edsall observed. On the lower part of the strip, "about a third of the stores and many of the homes appear empty. Junk-covered vacant lots, broken windows and crumbling buildings combine to give the area an overwhelming aura of decay." Conditions were better in the upper blocks: "Merchants on the hill have less of a sense of defeat than those on the bottom and although they complain, they still seem to think there is the possibility of improvement." Nevertheless, one merchant on the hill, Joseph Rodman, told Edsall that "the crime problem 'gets worse and worse, the streets are dark and there are more and more dope pushers.'"[40]

Rodman, whose hat company had occupied the 1500 block for forty years, was one of the many Jewish merchants with a long-established presence on Pennsylvania Avenue. Also victimized by discriminatory housing practices, Jews had established their own neighborhoods in adjoining northwest Baltimore. "People used to jokingly say, 'Pennsylvania Avenue is the longest road in the world, because it connects Africa to Israel," writes black journalist DeWayne Wickham, whose mother and aunt worked for an Avenue Jewish storeowner, Isidor Cooper, in the 1950s. His comment captures the close relationship between blacks and Jews, whose small family businesses had lined the Avenue as early as the 1910s.[41]

Through the twentieth century, Jewish merchants shared the Avenue with African American business owners and other retailers, including newly emerging chain stores such as an A&P grocery. However, the black middle class was more professional than business oriented. A 1931 survey of neighborhood businesses by the *Afro-American* newspaper found black doctors, dentists, lawyers, barbers, and hairdressers outnumbering whites of the same professions by a wide margin. The pharmacies, restaurants, groceries, clothing, shoe, and hardware stores were overwhelmingly owned by whites, the majority of whom were Jewish. The historian Andor Skotnes notes that in the *Afro-American* in the 1930s, "Pennsylvania Avenue store owners were frequently identified as Jews or Hebrews rather than whites." Even the famed Royal Theater, built in 1921 by black entrepreneurs as the Douglass Theater, was purchased by a Jewish family in 1926.[42]

Like many close relationships, the black-Jewish connection was fraught with complexities. In the 1930s the refusal of Pennsylvania Avenue merchants to hire black employees aroused the ire of local activists, who conducted a "Don't Buy Where You Can't Work" boycott that often referenced the Jewish ethnicity of the storeowners. Although the campaign did succeed in desegregating the Pennsylvania Avenue workforce to an extent, the employment issue remained relevant through the 1950s. Shoppers had other complaints as well. "Some of the Jewish merchants along Pennsylvania Avenue were not well regarded by the area's black residents," Wickham observes. "People complained that their prices were high and their attitudes toward black folks ranged from condescension to outright hostility. Another sore point was that few of the shop owners employed blacks in anything but the most menial jobs." While discriminatory practices were not limited to Jews, the majority of storeowners that African Americans encountered happened to be Jewish, and this led some people to believe that, as Skotnes puts it, "their Jewishness was somehow related to their discriminatory behavior."[43]

Yet individual relationships between customers and merchants, between employees and storeowners, and between black and white merchants often transcended ethnic conflict. Isidor Cooper "was like one of the family," Wickham recalls about the man who employed his mother and aunt. Cooper had an all-black sales force—which may have been unusual in the 1950s but was not completely unprecedented. While some African Americans complained of high prices and exploitative credit practices, many others believed that Jewish merchants provided a valuable service, and that the Jews' experience of oppression made them sympathetic to the plight of blacks. African American interviewees from across Baltimore expressed this sentiment in the oral histories collected by the University of Baltimore. As one woman explained, "For [us], the Jews weren't white. . . . In the Jews' stores, they would give you credit that you could pay once a month. They would let you get what you wanted, milk, butter, eggs, flour, soap, soap powder, stuff like that. You couldn't go into the white stores and say my children need a loaf of bread or a chicken or whatever, and have them give it to you. No way. But in a Jew's store, you could get that. It's interesting because the Jews also have a history of being oppressed. . . . Yes and I think that's why they did for us, because they were also downed people."[44]

Some Jewish business owners became active in community affairs. Herman Katkow, who operated an Avenue women's clothing shop from 1952 to 1977, was a leader of PALMA, the local merchant's association, a multiracial group that sponsored a popular Easter parade, voter registration drives (with store discounts for customers who registered to vote), and other community events. Katkow employed black sales clerks in his store and supported desegregation efforts. In the 1950s he told a recalcitrant fellow Jewish business owner that if he did not desegregate, "I'm going to be on the picket line" with other protesters.[45] The Sussman family, owners of an Avenue pawnshop since 1919, believed that their good relations with customers spared their store during the riots. "We had been here for some fifty years, and we were a part of the neighborhood," stated Seymour

Kerosene fire burning along Lombard Street. (Originally published in the *Baltimore Afro-American*, April 8, 1968. Reprinted courtesy of the *Baltimore News American* Collection, University of Maryland–College Park.)

Sussman in a 2005 article. "People knew that we were not here today, gone tomorrow."[46]

In fact, contrary to popular opinion, Pennsylvania Avenue did not suffer terribly during April 1968. Looting began there late Saturday night, well after other neighborhoods had seen action. Sunday morning was relatively calm, but things heated up late in the afternoon. When police tried to seal off the 1500 to 1700 blocks, "teens circled back to loot liquor stores, with occasional rock and bottle throwing."[47] Soon mobs could be seen the entire length of the Avenue and the side streets were "consumed by looting." But in the weeks that followed, insurance claims were filed on only twenty-five addresses along a thirteen-block stretch, a relatively small number (though it is unknown how many buildings were uninsured). A *Baltimore Evening Sun* article marking the first anniversary of the disturbances reported that "shops along Pennsylvania Ave were looted but not burned," and cited Herman Katkow's opinion that damage was light compared to other parts of the city because of PALMA's community relations program. At the time, 79 percent of Avenue stores were white owned and, by then, 85 percent of employees were African American. One eyewitness, "Little Melvin" Williams, later asserted that only white-owned stores on the Avenue were hit: "It seemed a day that just being white was the wrong

Clothing store dummies left by looters in the 800 block of North Gay Street. Soldiers stand at the ready in the background. (Originally published in the *Baltimore Afro-American*, April 8, 1968. Reprinted courtesy of the *Baltimore News American* Collection, University of Maryland–College Park.)

complexion." However, not enough evidence exists to come to firm conclusions on whether the looting of specific stores was racially motivated.[48]

Nor is it possible to precisely measure the overall impact of the uprising on Pennsylvania Avenue—though it does appear that the immediate loss of business was not very significant. The 1968 Criss+Cross Directory listed 196 businesses on the Avenue between Dolphin Street and North Avenue. Only twenty-eight of those businesses were absent from the 1969 directory. And twelve new businesses were listed that year, so the net loss between 1968 and 1969 was only sixteen. It must be kept in mind, as well, that not all of the business closings can be directly attributed to the riots. Given the deteriorated state of the Avenue as described by Edsall in 1967, some of them might have closed anyway.[49]

Baltimore directories show an annual acceleration of business closings in the five years following the riots. Forty-five businesses disappeared from the directory in 1970 and thirteen new businesses were added: a net loss of thirty-two businesses between 1969 and 1970, twice the loss of the previous year. By 1973 there were 124 businesses listed on the street, a 37 percent drop from 1968.[50] While some of these closings may have been a delayed effect of the riots, again, many of the shuttered businesses might have succumbed to the factors mentioned earlier, such as displacement from urban renewal, even if the riots had not occurred.

A direct consequence of the riots, but also difficult to measure, was the storeowners' increased focus on security. PALMA hired a private security firm to patrol its members' stores at night. At the time, Herman Katkow headed a citywide merchant's group in addition to his leadership of PALMA. He told the *Sun* in 1969 that he knew of "many merchants who now keep guns on their premises." Stores began to resemble fortresses. For some merchants, especially whites, the urban unrest fed rising concerns about crime that shaded into a greater distrust of their customers and of the surrounding neighborhood.[51]

Yet the uprising did not provoke a wholesale abandonment of Pennsylvania Avenue by storeowners. Katkow and many other PALMA members, black and white, remained committed to staying and recovering. The events undoubtedly intensified problems that had been present earlier, but the street also continued to suffer from problems that had nothing to do with them. "We continued in business, but the area itself went downhill," Katkow observed. "And I think it was unrelated to the riots, it was more because the opening of one shopping mall after another." He persevered until 1977, when his store and two others were destroyed by a fire caused by a worker building the nearby subway. "He hit a live gas line. We were in business for 27 years, and we were out of business in 27 minutes." The Royal Theater closed in 1970, but its demise was made permanent only by the hasty decision to tear it down for an urban renewal project in 1971.[52]

Pennsylvania Avenue's oldest business probably belonged to Deaver Smith, whose Smith Punch Base Coffee and Tea Company opened in 1908 as the third black-owned store on the Avenue. By 1972 his son had joined him, but at age eighty-one Deaver Smith was still going strong. That year he told a reporter he had been "robbed so many times that it's useless to call the police." Unlike other merchants, his response to increased crime was less security, not more: his safe stood empty, with a door that did not close, and he kept only a few coins in his half-opened cash register. According to Smith, most of the robberies had occurred "shall we say, since the revolution," which the reporter interpreted as an indictment of black militancy, not just April 1968. However, Smith blamed much of the decline of the Avenue on poor city services caused by city officials' discrimination against blacks. He and his son had no intention of leaving, though their business was scheduled to be displaced by a planned urban renewal project. A 1977 city directory, however, shows the company still hanging on.[53]

The Sussmans remain on the Avenue to this day. Their Northwestern Loan Company proudly advertises on their website that it is "one of Maryland's oldest and largest pawnshops . . . [and] under the same family ownership at the same location since 1919." Customer service remains a hallmark: "We have a long-standing tradition of treating our customers with fairness and dependability. We take great pride in saying that, like us, many of our customers are third and fourth generation."[54]

Like the Sussmans, city officials and neighborhood activists have determined to build on the Avenue's historic legacy. Reflecting current trends in urban planning, recent renewal efforts have focused on preservation and renovation rather than tearing down and rebuilding. Pennsylvania Avenue was declared an official city Heritage Area in 2001 and a Pennsylvania Avenue Heritage Trail walking-and-driving tour now showcases the street's remaining historic sites (a Royal Theater Marquee Monument substitutes for the real thing). The events of 1968 are missing from the trail brochure.[55]

West North Avenue: "These Are Not the People That I Thought I Knew"

The section of North Avenue that runs west from Charles Street to the edge of the city is yet another business district that, in the recollections of many Baltimoreans, was bustling and vibrant in the years before April 1968 but declined rapidly afterward. However, the disturbances were just another in a long list of factors that contributed to the loss of business activity along this major Baltimore artery, joining racial succession, urban renewal, and unpredictable fires. West North Avenue was the commercial strip of the Eutaw Place and Lake Drive neighborhoods on Baltimore's west side. Prominent German Jewish families began to settle there in the 1870s, moving out of their downtown neighborhoods and into the elaborate mansions along Eutaw Place south of North Avenue. Four synagogues followed their congregants uptown in the late 1800s, and by the late 1910s Eutaw Place and the blocks adjacent to it north of North Avenue were filling up with less prosperous German Jewish families and more recent Russian Jewish immigrants. The Eutaw Place–Lake Drive neighborhood, now known as Reservoir Hill, was predominantly Jewish by the 1930s.[56]

Many of these Jewish residents shopped along a fifteen-block stretch of West North Avenue, and beginning in the 1920s the eastern end of this commercial strip became part of one of the most desirable shopping districts in the city. Baltimore boosters envisioned a new commercial center for the city on the strip of North Avenue east of the Jewish neighborhoods and separated from them by a bridge that spanned an extensive set of railroad tracks.[57] In 1928 the North Avenue Market, the city's most modern environment for food shopping, opened at the corner of West North and Maryland avenues. This indoor facility provided each of its 254 merchants with a sanitary stand complete with running water and refrigerated display cases. The enterprise offered home delivery and used technological advances to reduce the smell of fish. In addition to buying fresh meat and produce, shoppers could enjoy a meal at the restaurant, mail a letter at the post office, pick up a prescription at the drug store, and even get some exercise at the second-floor bowling alley.[58]

The opening of the market ushered in the economic heyday for the street. Lawrence Goldbloom moved his clothing store from Baltimore Street downtown to the corner of Charles and North in 1932.[59] By 1939 the *Baltimore News Post* stated, "Few Baltimore neighborhoods have changed more in recent years than the vicinity of North Avenue and Charles Street. . . . Today with the North Avenue Market, four movie theaters and half a dozen palatial lunchrooms, North avenue and Charles street is the hub of one of the busiest sections of the city."[60]

Farther west, in the 900 block of West North Avenue, another Baltimore institution opened during the 1930s. Nates and Leons, the twenty-four-hour deli that became famous in Baltimore's Jewish community, served monstrous sandwiches to rival those of Corned Beef Row, downtown.[61] In the blocks between the market and the deli and farther west along North Avenue, shoppers could find in the first floors of row houses barber shops, hardware stores, automotive supplies, liquor stores, dry cleaners, and even a doll hospital. In the apartments above, shopkeepers and tenants raised families throughout the twentieth century. Sidney and Ida Pats were typical Jewish shop owners, buying the Downes Pharmacy in 1950. Their daughters recall that the business in the 800 block originally had a soda fountain, an ice cream counter, and the pharmacy in the back. The girls and their brother grew up in the rooms above, coming home from school, working in the shop until it closed at 11:00 P.M., then getting a late-night snack at Nates and Leons. Sharon Pats Singer remembers, "It was different from your typical childhood. But I enjoyed it because the customers were friendly and fun, and we had people to talk to and things to see and do. I never thought about race as an issue at all."[62]

But race was becoming an issue in the surrounding neighborhood. The demographics of the West North Avenue corridor changed dramatically in the years after the Pats family moved in. This shift could be traced to several factors. First, the highway system placed a major entrance and exit of the new Jones Falls Expressway in a three-block area between the North Avenue Market and Nates and Leons. About thirty blocks of land bounded by Druid Hill Park and the shopping district were taken over by the massive ramps that combined with an existing set of railroad tracks to effectively cut off the western area of the avenue to pedestrians coming from the Charles Street corridor.[63] The highway opened in early 1968, but in the same decade that the highway plans were made public and construction began, blockbusting hit the area, just as it did in many other neighborhoods in Baltimore and across the nation.[64] Blockbusters used less-than-ethical techniques to prey on white residents' stereotypes of race and class, causing rapid turnover in the Reservoir Hill area north of West North Avenue and driving down property values, sometimes to less than half their former value.[65] When the whites sold at low prices, the speculators were able to sell at a substantial profit to blacks eager to move to a neighborhood that had formerly been closed to them. In 1967 an urban planner wrote that "when Negroes expanded into white neighborhoods, the residents did not try to stop them; they just left. Druid Hill, a huge, exquisitely maintained park with a superb English-style zoo, is now surrounded by Negro districts. White people no longer go there."[66]

The residential changes brought about changes for the surrounding businesses. The owners of Goldbloom's estimated that between 1964 and 1974 their customer base went from 95 percent white to 95 percent black. Goldbloom's stayed and reported more profits than ever, but beginning in the early 1960s many other businesses fled and property values declined.[67] North Avenue Market was sold in 1961 for $1 million less than it had cost to build it three decades earlier.[68] Nates and Leons closed in 1967, and the property was sold at auction, but only after the auctioneer told the bidders to "hold back your tears."[69]

The Pats family decided to stay. Sharon Pats Singer says that she barely registered the racial change: "They were the customers, just people who lived there, whether they were white, whether they were black, it never, ever crossed my mind. It was just fun for me." But her parents made some changes in the pharmacy. During the 1960s they took out the soda fountain and brought in rows of liquor bottles. Beer replaced ice cream in the coolers. The store began cashing checks, becoming a source of credit to the neighborhood. Sharon Pats Singer remembers, "My parents had a little file box, and in the file box were just file cards with people's names on them, and if they didn't have enough money to buy their toiletries or to get whatever they needed, my parents would write their names down and they would get it on account. . . . It was just a very trusting kind of system."[70]

In some communities the credit system of corner stores engendered resentment among neighborhood residents, but many African Americans saw the necessity and even the benefits of this particular lending practice, sometimes called "the book." Yvonne Hardy-Phillips explains the ambivalence: "In our neighborhood there were mostly Jewish stores, and of course, you know, they kept . . . a book that would allow people to have credit. And . . . some people may have suspected that they always didn't get treated honestly, . . . or something was tacked on. You figured, well, at least I could get credit because I didn't have money for the kids to eat last week, so, I mean, that's just the price you pay."[71] Larry Wilson, an African American, remembers that the Jewish store owners in his neighborhood "did not live in the neighborhood, but they came in every morning and they opened the store and they provided credit to black people, you know, and I'm not saying they're trying to be buddies or pals with you. They were business people, but, that's where you went . . . and when you got paid you'd go pay them off and something and maybe you'd have to pay a little extra fee, but . . . we didn't resent those people."[72] Barbara Gaines also views the credit extended by corner stores in a positive light. In her neighborhood she remembers owners who "were good to our people. They had running tabs."[73] Ruth Stewart agrees: "Now the Jews, they were the ones that would give us credit in their stores so we could eat. . . . They were looking out for us. . . . Because if it wasn't for them, some of us wouldn't be here."[74]

Where shop owners and customers saw relations built up over dozens of exchanges over time, city planners saw check-cashing liquor stores in declining neighborhoods. West North Avenue became a target for urban renewal well before the disturbances of 1968. The Mid-City Development Corporation had contracted with the city in 1965 to build a major shopping center on an eight-acre site across West North Avenue from Downes Pharmacy.[75] The Pats family had been included in the planning and remember that they were "going to have a larger store, and it was a very exciting kind of prospect." The new shopping center would be zoned commercial, however, and the family would have to leave their apartment on West North Avenue. In preparation, they had bought a house in the suburb of Pikesville, just northwest of the city line. The family's intimate day-to-day interaction with their customers and the traditional mix of commercial and residential uses of the street was coming to an end even before the looting in April 1968.

The days after Martin Luther King's assassination are vivid in the mind of Sharon Pats Singer. As unrest began in other parts of the city, she and her family remained convinced it would not touch them. Even when they were specifically warned on the evening of Saturday, April 6, they remained in denial:

> One of the women who was working at Lou's bar up the street, a black woman named Brooks, came into the store and said to my father—I was standing there—"You know, you'd better get out." And he wasn't really listening to that, because he never thought anything was going to happen. And sure enough, the next day . . . I'm driving down [Interstate] 83 [returning from an errand]. . . . We turn off at the exit—North Avenue. Make a right to go towards the house—you could see the neighborhood—and the whole block was in smoke and flames.[76]

Newspaper reports confirm that around noon on Sunday, April 7, looting began in the 900 block of West North Avenue, one block west of the Patses' store. Later they hit Sagel's Market in the 800 block. The radio and TV shop, hardware store, jewelry repair store, and two liquor stores on the Patses' block made tempting targets. The block was filled with flames and smoke; the street was filled with people. Sharon Pats found her father across the street, picked him up, and drove away. "And that was the end of my life as I knew it," she states.

When they returned the following day, they took photos of their looted business and apartment.[77] The next day their store, the apartments where they lived upstairs, and all of their belongings were burned. Perhaps the prospect of destroying "the book" had been too strong for the arsonists to resist—or perhaps whoever torched the store simply got carried away in the fever of the events. Whatever the motivation, the end was the same. Singer was right; her life as she had known it did end that Sunday. By 1970 all of the businesses in the 800 block of West North Avenue would be gone.

But of course, urban renewal had already determined that the life of this block would in fact change, maybe not so abruptly, but certainly in the coming months. Her family's store, their customers, and her neighbors had already changed. So what aspect of the events was so arresting that she felt that these events marked the point where nothing would ever be the same again? Singer's stories powerfully evoke her family's pivot in perception regarding their relationship with their neighbors and customers, people in the surrounding black community. She comments, "I don't really think that we thought that anything bad was going to happen. It was a trusting kind of thing where this was our neighborhood, and it just wouldn't happen, they just wouldn't do this, and it never occurred to us."

The trust that she had assumed in her neighbors had either been betrayed or had never existed in the first place. She was forced to reevaluate her understanding of her childhood, her parents' life work, and the reality of her city. She remembers that despite the physical loss, the family trauma, and financial uncertainty, the most disturbing aspect of the week was her encounter with a black classmate at school in the days that followed the riots:

> I was in a very small A-course class at Western, so it was maybe fifteen kids in that class. And we were all very close because we had been in the same class since ninth grade and never had any kind of racial tension. I mean I went to school with black kids, Chinese kids, white kids. Never. There was never any kind of tension. I walked in that day, and we're in homeroom. . . . I had a girl in the class, a black girl . . . she got up and she said—and she was very militant about it—"I want you to know that they got exactly what they deserved!" I started crying. I had to leave the room. I'm crying now. That one thing cut to me like nothing else could cut to me. I was fine until then. I was fine with what I saw. . . . And I thought, "What is happening in this world? These are not the people that I thought I knew."[78]

"What is happening in this world? These are not the people that I thought I knew." This realization struck this Jewish girl, a participant in the first generation of mandated educational desegregation and a lifetime resident of an integrated neighborhood, as the most significant change. An idealistic youngster who had "never had any kind of racial tension," and who had "never, ever" registered the race of her parents' customers as significant now had to confront the prospect that a racialized urban landscape had taken the place of what she had understood to be a trusting network of postracial relationships.

The Pats family left West North Avenue for their new home in the suburbs. Even though they had been planning a move away from their residence above the store for some time, the destruction of their building and business led to a major upheaval in their lives. Sidney Pats had been an entrepreneur for almost two decades. He had been looking forward to a new facility and expanded business in collaboration with the city and Mid-City Development. Overnight he went from being an independent businessman with a bright future to a man with no source of income and no equity in his business. He took a job as a salaried pharmacist for E. J. Korvette's. After the family's pharmacy was destroyed, Sidney's wife, Ida, was no longer a partner in the family business. She used the skills she had developed in tax preparation and bookkeeping to earn her accounting degree at the University of Baltimore. Four decades after April 1968, not only has she forgotten the riots themselves but she cannot remember any of the events of her eighteen years on West North Avenue. She has blocked out the years in which she and her husband built a business, raised a family, and became part of the community.

Outside of the 800 block, the neighborhood itself remained remarkably stable in the late 1960s. As they did on Lombard Street and Pennsylvania Avenue, the disturbances marked an important point on a continuum, not a complete upheaval. For the next five years many of the same businesses operated in their same locations along West North Avenue. A much more mundane event took a far higher toll on the district. On August 28, 1968, an accidental fire began in the Woodlawn Lunch counter of the North Avenue Market and quickly grew to a six-alarm event. Smoke and water damage affected the entire forty-year-old complex. Despite assurances from the owners that the market would reopen in a week, or during the following year, the building sat vacant until discount stores occupied the space starting in 1974.[79]

Farther down the street, the grand schemes of Mid-City Development did not materialize. In 1969 city officials announced they had down scaled the project "in favor of a smaller shopping center combined with town houses for low income families."[80] By 1971 even those modest plans had fallen by the wayside, replaced by designs for subsidy rental housing under a new program in which Baltimore's Department of Housing and

Community Development consulted neighborhood residents as they set their priorities for new projects.[81]

Along West North Avenue one bright spot did appear after the destruction of 1960s urban renewal. In 1969 the Amalgamated Clothing Workers Union created "the first trend upward for West North Avenue"[82] when it broke ground on a state-of-the-art children's center that took up the entire 600 block. The $1 million Hyman Blumberg Day Care Center was designed to care for the children of working parents who paid just $1 a day for their children to participate in a cognitive learning program based on the research of Jean Piaget. Under the guidance of professional educators, preschoolers engaged in art, science, and housekeeping, learned to cook, and played on their $100,000 playground.[83] The photograph accompanying a 1973 profile of the center shows a white boy and a black boy enjoying the swings together.

Conclusion

The lasting physical impact of the 1968 riots across Baltimore cannot be denied. The Riots Driving Tour recently created by the University of Baltimore highlights the damage inflicted during the uprising, offering dramatic evidence that many inner-city business districts remain in the distressed condition in which they found themselves on April 9, when Baltimoreans awoke to a changed city. Shortly after the violence, a police department study reported that one thousand stores had been damaged or destroyed. A 1969 *Evening Sun* article marking the first anniversary found that one-third of those stores were still boarded up or were completely gone.[84]

And yet such statistics can be deceiving. Indeed, the 1969 anniversary article, while lamenting the physical destruction, added that "some merchants changed their minds" about leaving "when they found themselves operating profitably again." The article also correctly pointed out that many of the vacant stores might have closed anyway. Assessments of the riots often ignore the preexisting conditions that had already produced decline—and they also do not address the factors that have prevented many areas from recovering in the years that followed. The continued physical impact of April 1968 is due not so much to the event itself but to the failure to solve these underlying problems, such as concentrated poverty combined with a lack of opportunity, disinvestment combined with misguided urban renewal policies, and institutional racism. The riots themselves remain a potent symbol of these failures.

This is not to downplay the importance of the events of April 1968. As these case studies show, the uprising played a pivotal role in how Baltimoreans perceived their city and the changes it was going through. These perceptions had an impact that was just as critical as smashed windows and looted stores. One major effect concerned relations between blacks and whites. Another *Sun* anniversary article delved into this topic. In it, Rabbi Abraham Shusterman observed, "There is a tension between the races. There seems to be more of a polarization than a year ago." The "loss of person-to-person relationships . . . set us back a quarter century. It will take another generation to overcome." Councilman Robert L. Douglass expressed the frustration African Americans felt at the failure of whites to understand the root causes. "Baltimore is still two societies, very far apart, and a lot of white people have no idea what we're talking about." Black merchant Gardie Williamson reflected on how the disturbances affected African Americans. "In the black community, we're faced with more of a separatism now. The seeds were there before, but the riot brought it out. . . . Children are much different since the riot. They are looking at the white man altogether differently than they used to. . . . There's hate and violence in their eyes."[85]

Root causes were not uppermost in the minds of many Jewish merchants whose stores were damaged or destroyed. Some, like Herman Katkow, were able to put the disturbances into perspective and rebuild. For others, the personal pain and anguish overshadowed all else, and they withdrew from the city. In their eyes, decades of inner-city decline became collapsed into this one event. "The riot and Baltimore's rising crime rates have become inextricably linked in the minds of many inner-city businessmen," stated Harry Goldberg, spokesman for a businessman's organization, in 1969. "Baltimore is a sick city. In fact, it's worse. It's a dying city. And the riot speeded up the disease. The riot really sent the city to hell. . . . Every day some businesses close up, or leave, but nobody ever hears about them. They're scared out."[86]

Such sentiments only grew with the passage of time. Frank Bressler's dry cleaning store in lower Park Heights survived the violence in part because of defensive action taken by the area's business association. As he put it in a 2007 oral history,

> After the riots nothing was the same. . . . Most of the business in the inner city just never opened up again. It wasn't worth it. . . . If you were in business you lost everything that you spent a lifetime building up. You're never gonna forgive anybody for it. . . . Crime moved in, drugs came in, . . . businesses didn't rebuild and so the result after the riots is where Baltimore is today. . . . People have moved out of Baltimore and the people that live in Baltimore live in fear. . . . I may go all the way around the Beltway to get there but I wouldn't drive through the city anymore.[87]

Bressler's comments reflect the views of not only Jewish merchants but many white Baltimoreans.

Today all three neighborhoods profiled in this chapter have hopes for renewal. The community around Pennsylvania Avenue is building on its heritage as an African American cultural center. Lombard Street merchants hope to benefit from the recent development of Albemarle Square and nearby Harbor East. The corner of North Avenue and Charles Street is the hub of Baltimore's Station North arts and entertainment district where storefronts house a fledgling group of avant-garde theater troupes, community arts organizations, and trendy restaurants. Meanwhile, perceptions created by the 1968 Baltimore riots linger in the minds of many. While the events should not be forgotten or ignored, perhaps the passing years will enable Baltimoreans in these and other inner-city neighborhoods to once again change their perception of their city and the meaning of its history.

NOTES

1. "One House at a Time," editorial, *Baltimore Sun*, November 5, 2010.

2. "50 Years in Store and Never a Sale," *Baltimore Evening Sun*, May 1, 1967.

3. "Hard-Core Troublemakers Bring Knives, Brass-Knuckles, Guns, Clubs to School," *Baltimore Evening Sun*, April 9, 1967.

4. "Exodus of Whites Seen as Damaging," *Baltimore Evening Sun*, January 25, 1967.

5. U.S. Census. This trend was seen in other American cities during the 1950s. See Kenneth T. Jackson, *Crabgrass Frontier: The Suburbanization of the United States* (New York: Oxford University Press, 1985) and Thomas Sugrue, *The Origins of the Urban Crisis: Race and Inequality in Postwar Detroit* (Princeton: Princeton University Press, 1996).

6. David Jacobs, "Running in Place: Baltimore: Regeneration Requires More than a Renewal of the Physical City," *Interplay of European/American Affairs*, November 1967, 50.

7. "Councilman Schaefer Expresses His Views on City's Problems in Housing Field," *Baltimore Evening Sun*, February 8, 1967. Schaefer went on to serve as mayor of Baltimore from 1971 to 1987 and governor of Maryland from 1987 to 1995.

8. William Boucher, executive director of the Greater Baltimore Committee; Harold Edleston, director of the Health and Welfare Council; and Richard Steiner, director of the Baltimore Urban Renewal and Housing Agency (BURHA), Health and Welfare Council of Baltimore, "A Letter to Ourselves" 1961. Available at Baltimore '68: Riots and Rebirth (hereafter BSR), University of Baltimore (UB), http://archives.ubalt.edu/bsr/archival-resources/reports.html (accessed September 5, 2009).

9. "Negro Community Leaders Joining Officials in Effort to Avert Trouble," *Baltimore Evening Sun*, September 2, 1964; Floyd Miller, "How Baltimore Prevents Riots," *Reader's Digest*, March 1968, 109–113, condensed from the *Baltimore Sun*.

10. Jacobs, "Running in Place," 50.

11. Martin Luther King, Jr., *Where Do We Go from Here: Chaos or Community?* (New York: Harper and Row, 1967), 92.

12. Deborah R. Weiner, Avi Y. Decter, and Anita Kassof, eds. *Voices of Lombard Street: A Century of Change in East Baltimore* (Baltimore: Jewish Museum of Maryland, 2007).

13. Ibid. Flag House Courts was named for the nearby historic house where the Star Spangled Banner was made in 1814.

14. See, for example, "Baltimore Has Colorful Old-World Market," *Baltimore Sun*, April 13, 1924; "Queer Shops Found on East Lombard Street," *Baltimore News-Post*, November 22, 1946; Lloyd B. Dennis, "Lombard Street Stores Offer Old World Variety," *Baltimore Sun*, August 12, 1964; Ralph Reppert, "Where Old World Flavors Linger: East Lombard Street Is an Island of Foreign Foods and Customs," *Baltimore Sun*, January 5, 1969.

15. Dennis, "Lombard Street Stores Offer Old World Variety."

16. Dorothy Scott oral history, February 27, 2006, OH 680, Jewish Museum of Maryland (JMM).

17. "Dislocation and Relocation, Past and Future: Baltimore, Maryland," Baltimore Urban Redevelopment and Housing Agency (BURHA) Staff Monograph, 1965; *U.S. Census of Housing, Maryland—Block Statistics*, 1970.

18. Scott oral history; Ann Faulkner Evans oral history, January 10, 2007, OH 705, JMM; Esther Dortch oral history, December 13, 2006, OH 702, JMM; Charles Dingle oral history, January 17, OH 706, JMM; BURHA, "Types of Families Living in Baltimore's Low-Rent Projects, 1951–1964," unpublished report, 1965; Baltimore City Department of Housing and Community Development (HCD), *Baltimore Public Housing*, 1973 annual report.

19. Dortch oral history; Julia Matthews oral history, July 3, 2006, OH 693, JMM; Dingle oral history.

20. Scott oral history.

21. Deborah R. Weiner, "From New Deal Promise to Postmodern Defeat: Two Baltimore Housing Projects," in *From Mobtown to Charm City: New Perspectives on Baltimore's Past* (Baltimore: Maryland Historical Society, 2002): 198–224.

22. Sugrue, *Origins of the Urban Crisis*. On Baltimore public housing, see Rhonda I. Williams, *The Politics of Public Housing: Black Women's Struggles against Urban Inequality* (New York: Oxford University Press, 2004). On urban disinvestment see, for example, Jackson.

23. *Baltimore Sun*, April 8 and 9, 1968; Dingle oral history.

24. Dortch, Dingle, and Scott oral histories.

25. David Friedman, "Trouble Plagues Lombard Corned Beef Belt," *Baltimore Sun*, April 24, 1968.

26. "Corned Beef Makes a Comeback," *Baltimore Sun*, May 6, 1968.

27. Ibid.; Scott, Dortch, and Dingle oral histories.

28. Reppert, "Where Old World Flavors Linger."

29. Ibid.

30. In the postwar era, a decline in anti-Semitism led to expanded opportunities for Jews in the professions and corporate America. On these new opportunities, suburbanization, and the changing demographic and economic profile of American Jewry, see, for example, Edward S. Shapiro, *A Time for Healing: American Jewry since World War II* (Baltimore: Johns Hopkins University Press, 1992).

31. Joyce Price, "Lombard Merchants' Beef: Road Repaving Hurts Sales," *Baltimore News-American*, October 11, 1976; Tracie Rozhon, "Fix-Up Stirs Lombard Street," *Baltimore Sun*, November 11, 1976.

32. *National Journal*, July 1, 1972; HCD, *Baltimore Public Housing*, 1973 annual report.

33. Michael A. Fletcher, "No Way to Live," *Baltimore Sun*, May 9, 1993; Michael Anft, "Half Staff: Facing the End at Flag House Courts, the City's Last High-Rise Project," *Baltimore City Paper*, December 22, 1999.

34. "Proposals Sought to Redevelop Historic Sphinx Club on West Side," *Baltimore Sun*, July 24, 2009.

35. Karen Olson, "Old West Baltimore: Segregation, African-American Culture, and the Struggle for Equality," in *The Baltimore Book: New Views of Local History*, E. Fee, L. Shopes, L. Zeidman, eds. (Philadelphia: Temple University Press, 1991), 57–80. Olson defines Old West Baltimore as bounded by North Avenue (N), Franklin Street (S), Madison Street (E), and Fulton Street (W).

36. Thomas Edsall, "Pennsylvania Avenue Declining for Generation," *Baltimore Evening Sun*, May 10, 1967.

37. Ibid. See also Christina Royster-Hemby, "Street of Dreams," *Baltimore City Paper*, a two-part article on Pennsylvania Avenue that appeared on February 2 and 9, 2005, available at http://www.citypaper.com/news/story.asp?id=9603.

38. Royster-Hemby, "Street of Dreams"; Herman and Ethel Katkow oral history, BSR, UB, available at http://archives.ubalt.edu/bsr/oral-histories/index.html.

39. Edsall, "Pennsylvania Avenue Declining."

40. Edsall, "Pennsylvania Avenue Declining." See also Royster-Hemby, "Street of Dreams." Edsall defines Upper Pennsylvania Avenue as starting roughly north of Lafayette Avenue, though he notes that "geographic definitions vary."

41. DeWayne Wickham, *Woodholme: A Black Man's Story of Growing Up Alone* (New York: Farrar, Straus, and Giroux, 1995), 12; Royster-Hemby, "Street of Dreams," part 1.

42. "Don't Spend Your Money Where You Can't Work," *Baltimore Afro-American*, January 10, 1931; "ASCO Stores Name Two Clerks to New Posts," *Baltimore Afro-American*, October 21, 1933; Andor Skotnes, "'Buy Where You Can Work': Boycotting for Jobs in African-American Baltimore, 1933–1934," *Journal of Social History*, Summer 1994: 754; Royster-Hemby, "Street of Dreams," part 1, pp. 5–6 of printed online version.

43. Skotnes, "'Buy Where You Can Work,'" 754–755; Wickham, *Woodholme*, 22. On tensions between Jewish merchants and black activists, see Olson, "Old West Baltimore," 72; Royster-Hemby, "Street of Dreams," part 1, p. 6 of online printed version.

44. Wickham, *Woodholme*, 22–23; Ruth Stewart oral history, BSR, UB, available at http://archives.ubalt.edu/bsr/oral-histories/oral-histories4.html. See also oral histories of Juanita Crider and Harold L. Knight in the archive.

45. Katkow oral history; quote is from Royster-Hemby, "Street of Dreams," part 1, p. 6 of printed online version. PALMA stands for Pennsylvania Avenue–Lafayette Market Association. It remains active today.

46. Royster-Hemby, "Street of Dreams," part 2, p. 2 of printed online version.

47. UB timeline of Baltimore 1968 riots, available at http://archives.ubalt.edu/bsr/timeline/index.html.

48. UB 1968 timeline; Paul Samuel, "Inner City Small Business Find Crime More a Concern," *Baltimore Evening Sun*, April 1, 1969; Peter Levy, "Buildings Damaged during the Riots," database available at http://archives.ubalt.edu/bsr/archival-resources/reports.html; Edsall, "Pennsylvania Avenue Declining," on the racial makeup of storeowners and employees; Melvin Douglas Williams oral history, BSR, UB, available at http://archives.ubalt.edu/bsr/oral-histories/oral-histories4.html.

49. Stewart Criss+Cross Directories, Baltimore, 1968–1969.

50. Stewart Criss+Cross Directories, Baltimore, 1968–1973.

51. Samuel, "Inner City Small Business."

52. Katkow oral history; Royster-Hemby, "Street of Dreams," part 1, p. 2, and part 2, p. 3 of online printed version.

53. John C. White, "Cobblestones, Brick Walks and a Back Yard Privy," *Baltimore Evening Sun*, February 21, 1972.

54. Available at http://www.nwpawn.com/home.htm (accessed August 27, 2009).

55. Royster-Hemby, "Street of Dreams," part 2, p. 4 of online printed version; available at http://www.pennsylvaniaavenuebaltimore.com/; "Proposals Sought to Redevelop Historic Sphinx Club," *Baltimore Sun*, July 24, 2009.

56. Isaac M. Fein, *The Making of an American Jewish Community: The History of Baltimore Jewry from 1773 to 1920* (Philadelphia: Jewish Publication Society of America, 1971); Gilbert Sandler, *Jewish Baltimore* (Baltimore: Johns Hopkins University Press, 2000), 49–51.

57. For early history of North Avenue, see Emily Emerson Lantz, "Do You Know the Street on Which You Live? North Avenue," *Baltimore Sun*, March 9, 1924. For opinions about the development prospects of North Avenue at Charles Street, see "North Avenue Area Rich in Historic Tradition: Growth Ousts Landmarks of Old Section," *Baltimore Home News*, June 29, 1939, "Streets-Baltimore-North Avenue" vertical file, Maryland Department, Enoch Pratt Free Library.

58. A photograph and more detailed description of the interior of the market in 1928 are available at Maryland Digital Cultural Heritage, http://collections.mdch.org/cdm4/item_viewer.php?CISOROOT=/mdaa&CISOPTR=341&CISOBOX=1&REC=9.

59. Earl Arnett, "Where It's an Effort to Keep the Spirit of Christmas Alive," *Baltimore Sun*, December 20, 1974.

60. *Baltimore News Post*, October 12, 1939.

61. Sandler, 188. The civil rights leader Rev. Marion Bascom recalls regularly sitting down with deli owner Nates Herr before the disturbances. Rev. Marion Bascom oral history, BSR, UB, available at http://archives.ubalt.edu/bsr/oral-histories/oral-histories1.html.

62. Sharon Pats Singer, Pats Family oral history, BSR, UB, available at http://archives.ubalt.edu/bsr/oral-histories/oral-histories3.html.

63. Carleton Jones, "The Outlook from North Avenue," *Baltimore Sun*, December 12, 1971, "North Avenue" vertical files, Maryland Department, Enoch Pratt Free Library, Baltimore.

64. For the classic description of blockbusting that details a neighborhood just a few miles west of this area, see Edward Orser, *Blockbusting in Baltimore: The Edmondson Village Story* (Lexington: University Press of Kentucky, 1997).

65. Jones, "The Outlook from North Avenue."

66. Jacobs, "Running in Place," 50.

67. Arnett, "Where It's an Effort to Keep the Spirit of Christmas Alive."

68. "North Avenue Market Is Sold," *Baltimore News-Post*, July 28, 1961. The buyer paid $850,000 for it in 1961. The *Baltimore Sun* of November 16, 1928, reported that the market cost $1,850,000 to build.

69. Sandler, *Jewish Baltimore*, 133.

70. Sharon Pats Singer, Pats Family oral history.

71. Yvonne Hardy-Phillips oral history, BSR, UB, available at http://archives.ubalt.edu/bsr/oral-histories/oral-histories3.html.

72. Larry Wilson oral history, BSR, UB, available at http://archives.ubalt.edu/bsr/oral-histories/oral-histories4.html.

73. Barbara Gaines oral history, BSR, UB, available at http://archives.ubalt.edu/bsr/oral-histories/oral-histories2.html.

74. Stewart oral history.

75. "North Avenue Plans Are Revised," *Baltimore Sun*, May 27, 1969.

76. Sharon Pats Singer, Pats Family oral history.

77. Pats Family oral history.

78. Sharon Pats Singer, Pats Family oral history.

79. *Baltimore Sun*, August 29, 1968. James D. Dilts, "A Market Returns to North Avenue," *Baltimore Sun*, September 29, 1974. At the turn of the twenty-first century the North Avenue Market found itself at the center of a newly designated arts and entertainment district. The City of Baltimore offers tax incentives for artists to locate their businesses there, and one bookstore took up its offer in the spring of 2009.

80. *Baltimore Sun*, May 27, 1969.

81. Jones, "The Outlook from North Avenue."

82. Ibid.

83. Norman Wilson, "Union-Run Day-Care Center Not Just Babysitter Service," *Baltimore Evening Sun*, August 3, 1973.

84. "One Sad Year After," *Baltimore Evening Sun*, April 1, 1969.

85. "1968 Riot Assessed by Officials, Civic Leaders," *Baltimore Sun*, April 7, 1969.

86. Samuel, "Inner City Small Business."

87. Frank Bressler oral history, BSR, UB, available at http://archives.ubalt.edu/bsr/oral-histories/oral-histories1.html.

12

"Where We Live"

Greater Homewood Community Corporation, 1967–1976

Francesca Gamber

When Martin Luther King, Jr., was assassinated on April 4, 1968, the scenes of civil disturbance that stretched from Washington, D.C., to Chicago to Detroit to Minneapolis were upsetting but not unfamiliar.[1] From Birmingham, Alabama, in 1963 to Newark, New Jersey, in 1967, Americans were getting used to seeing these flare-ups in the street, whether in their own cities or on television. Even the federal government had taken on the task of analyzing why black uprisings in particular had become more frequent in 1966 and 1967 by convening a National Advisory Commission on Civil Disorders. The Kerner Commission, as it was more commonly called, laid the blame for civil disturbance among inner-city African Americans squarely on "the racial attitude and behavior of white Americans toward black Americans." Despite the legislative victories achieved by the civil rights movement in the Civil Rights Act of 1964 and the Voting Rights Act of 1965, the Kerner Commission shrewdly observed that there could be a great distance between what was on the books and what was happening on the ground. It found at the root of black resentment "frustrated hopes" caused by "the persistent gap between promise and fulfillment." In Newark, historian Kevin Mumford asserts, the riot that erupted in 1967 is not easily dismissed as a mere function of poverty-induced desperation. African Americans in Newark rioted in 1967 because, even though civil rights activists were making progress in Congress, the city's political leadership continued to neglect black leaders and their appeals for more resources in their communities. The riot, Mumford writes, was the product of an "intransigence" that "ignor[ed] reasonable grievances and refus[ed] to negotiate."[2]

Baltimore, of course, was not without its own "reasonable grievances" in the spring of 1968. City school officials had accepted the *Brown v. Board of Education* decision in 1954 without the resistance that characterized other Southern states, and both former mayor Theodore McKeldin and current mayor Thomas D'Alesandro III had reputations as "champion[s] of civil rights." Nonetheless, African Americans in Baltimore continued to face daily discrimination in employment and housing as well as the general distrust of "others" that was common to many of the city's fiercely ethnic neighborhoods. For many black Baltimoreans who were not politically active and who had responded to white racism for generations by building their own institutions, white hostility was often just a fact of life. "You knew it, it was everywhere, you felt the pressure, you felt the double standards, but it was almost like it [was] something you couldn't do nothing about," recalls Nate Tatum, who was born in north Baltimore's Barclay neighborhood in 1954. "It was a condition of living." At the highest levels of city government in 1968, there was hope that Baltimore's black residents would be less restive than their counterparts in Newark and Detroit. Mayor D'Alesandro heard news of King's assassination and held his breath. "My hope, at that time, was that if we could have made it to Sunday morning when . . . the black churches would be opened for services . . . then we would have made it," he recalled. City council president William Donald Schaefer was eating dinner at a restaurant in Baltimore County's bucolic Greenspring Valley when the evidence of D'Alesandro's dashed hopes became apparent on April 6: "I could see into the city . . . it looked hazy and smoke was coming out of the city."[3]

Although the riot took the mayor and the president of the city council by surprise, a small group of activists working in north Baltimore was well aware of the inequality and resentment that fueled it. In 1966 officials within Johns Hopkins University (JHU) had begun investigating the social and economic conditions of the neighborhoods surrounding the school's main Homewood campus. Ross Jones, a JHU alumnus who returned to work in university administration in the early 1960s, was among those who "began to recognize more clearly than ever before the obvious sense of rapid deterioration" of those neighborhoods. Jones and others were noticing a decline in the quality of housing, an increase in the number of "absentee landlords," and "the continued flight of middle-class Whites to the newer suburbs"—a phenomenon that, as we will see, intensified after the 1968 riot. The Greater Homewood Community Project (GHCP) was born in 1967 to study these concerns and the university's response to them in an area that was demarcated by Cold Spring Lane to the north,

Twenty-fifth Street to the south, the Jones Falls Expressway to the west, and Greenmount Avenue to the east. Two years later, the GHCP became the independent Greater Homewood Community Corporation (GHCC). Although GHCC was no longer part of JHU, the university remained committed to the organization's work and continues to serve as a crucial source of funding, volunteers, board members, and other support.[4] GHCP and GHCC clearly saw a relationship between neighborhood stability and addressing the racial inequalities faced by African Americans in the Homewood area. Unlike the civil rights movement, however, GHCP and GHCC did not make racial equality their organizing principle. The civil rights movement operated from the assumption that all Americans, regardless of color, would be persuaded by the moral imperative of ending discrimination. By the late 1960s, legislative achievements and a rising tide of black nationalist rhetoric were draining the civil rights movement of both direction and support. Community organizers in Greater Homewood instead took "where we live" as their organizing fulcrum. The shift in focus allowed GHCP and GHCC to address racial inequality as part of a package of problems, enabling interracial cooperation around a set of issues faced by everyone who lived in Greater Homewood. Within the context of the late 1960s and early 1970s—when the last interracial civil rights groups were fragmenting, when the civil rights movement appeared to be over—GHCP and GHCC developed a means of organizing that allowed them to sidestep many of the obstacles that undid civil rights groups. It was a tactic shared by many civil rights movement veterans in a landscape changed by black nationalism and urban unrest. This shift in approach gave GHCC a way to tackle a broad range of racial and economic concerns that has survived for more than four decades.

Community Organizing after the "Beloved Community"

The setting in which GHCP matured into GHCC hardly seems supportive of an organizing approach that downplayed race. Baltimore's 1968 riot was immediately received in distinctly racial ways by black and white Baltimoreans—and, not surprisingly, in ways that set black and white in an oppositional relationship to each other. Martin Luther King's vision of an interracial "beloved community" seemed to die with him as blame was traded in the riot's aftermath. For African Americans, King's murder was the last straw as far as nonviolent cooperation with white people in the slow progress toward racial equality. "That was it," says Nate Tatum. "You've gone too far, was the attitude. That's just it. All bets are off. Turning the other cheek ain't working." Black rioters and looters turned their attention to white- and Jewish-owned businesses in their neighborhoods that they perceived as unfair or unscrupulous, while black business owners hastened to hang flags reading "Soul Brother" outside their windows. "There were several white people that owned stores up and down Pennsylvania Avenue and it seemed a day that just being white was the wrong complexion," remembered the infamous Baltimore hustler Melvin "Little Melvin" Williams.[5]

For Maryland governor Spiro Agnew, it was not white racism but black leaders themselves who were responsible for the riot. About a week after the disturbance began, Agnew summoned about eighty black leaders to a meeting and reprimanded them for not taking a stronger stand against the forces that were transforming groups such as the Student Nonviolent Coordinating Committee (SNCC) into black nationalist organizations. It was no "coincidence," he asserted, that SNCC leader Stokely Carmichael was in Baltimore on April 3 and "was observed meeting with local black power advocates and known criminals." Agnew was convinced that moderate civil rights leaders had not done enough to stop Carmichael. "You were stung by insinuations that you were Mister Charlie's boy, by epithets like Uncle Tom," he accused. Black residents feared that the National Guardsmen called in to patrol the city after the riot would similarly collapse any distinction between black militants and those who were simply coming and going from work or shopping. Nate Tatum was accustomed to joining his father, a contractor, at different work sites but stayed inside after the riot for fear of "the establishment confusing us . . . going to a job site with being someone in a truck going to loot."[6]

Fear following the riot exacerbated the physical separation of white from black in Baltimore. Many looted businessmen refused to rebuild in the city. "Pay us and give the businesses to the people who destroyed it," demanded one man at a meeting with Mayor D'Alesandro. White flight ensued throughout the city. Between 1970 and 1980, 120,000 people left Baltimore, as did 35,000 jobs between 1969 and 1980. The signs of white flight were evident beyond the inner city, in areas such as Greater Homewood, as well. In the section of Guilford Avenue in Barclay where Nate Tatum lived, neither of the Jewish entrepreneurs who owned corner stores that were damaged during the riot returned. In Waverly, almost as soon as African Americans began moving below Thirty-third Street, white residents moved out. Harwood, a section of southern Charles Village, was also acquiring a larger black population.[7]

From GHCP's perspective, it was not the prospect of black neighbors that was troubling. The Hoe's Heights neighborhood, which is sandwiched between the mostly white neighborhoods of Roland Park and Hampden, had been almost entirely African American since the 1880s. When housing went from owned homes to rental properties, however, the likelihood increased for a deterioration in the local housing stock and general neighborhood well-being because of inattentive landlords (whether this was done intentionally or because they now lived in far-flung counties from which regular monitoring of their properties was more difficult is unknown). In May 1969 JHU professor Robert Crain warned Ross Jones that the concentration of apartments and other rental properties in Greater Homewood made the area less attractive to middle-class African Americans who could afford single-family homes in neighborhoods on the west side of the city such as Park Heights. The people who were moving into Greater Homewood were increasingly African American renters who were vulnerable to the economic predations of absentee landlords. But beyond the economic issues, GHCP was also invested in what Crain called "a stable pattern of integration in the area." Unlike the white residents who left the city, GHCP organizers were not afraid of having black people move in. They believed in the value of integration, and this was precisely the reason why they sought to keep white people from moving out. GHCP's former director Dea Kline noted in the fall of 1969 that two elementary schools in the southern end of Greater Homewood, Margaret Brent and Barclay, already had majority-black student enrollments. "If we are to maintain a community with young, well educated black and white families, we must assure these parents that the schools are as good, or better, than those they can find further out in the City or in the counties," she advised.[8]

GHCC approached racial integration from the imperative of neighborhood stabilization rather than taking integration as its own organizing principle. This tactic is the essential point of difference between civil rights organizing and the community-organizing discipline to which GHCC belonged. Civil rights organizing involved a good deal of convincing hostile white Southern communities and apathetic Northern white communities that racial equality was their concern. Community organizing, by contrast, worked to help the rural and urban communities generally left out of decision-making processes identify their own interests and develop the means to advocate on their behalf. As Chicago community organizer Saul Alinsky puts it in his foundational text *Rules for Radicals* (1971),

> The organizer knows . . . that his biggest job is to give the people the feeling that they can do something. . . . The organizer's job is to begin to build confidence and hope in the idea of organization and thus in the people themselves: to win limited victories, each of which will build confidence and the feeling that "if we can do so much with what we have now just think what we will be able to do when we get big and strong."[9]

Most historians of community organizing date its beginnings back to the settlement houses of the early twentieth century, where Progressive and increasingly professionalized case workers looked to neighborhood stabilization as a means of combating poverty. During the Great Depression, social scientists launched projects that were also designed to improve conditions within neighborhoods. The Chicago Area Project dispatched young male "curbstone counselors" to tough neighborhoods to mentor boys prone to gang membership. Saul Alinsky was one such curbstone counselor. His work with the Chicago Area Project found him in the Back of the Yards neighborhood in 1938, where he first practiced the community organizing principles for which he would become renowned. Alinsky worked with community leaders to create the Back of the Yards Neighborhood Council (BYNC), an umbrella organization of existing local groups that pursued issues defined and voted on by community members. The BYNC promoted neighborhood economic development by encouraging entrepreneurs to hire local workers. It also lobbied decision makers, from city government to federal agencies, for more and better benefits. Alinsky established the Industrial Areas Foundation (IAF) in the 1940s to spread this model of community organizing to other cities. In Baltimore, IAF-inspired groups included the Northeast Community Organization (NECO), founded in 1970, and Baltimoreans United in Leadership Development (BUILD), created in 1977.[10]

By the advent of the civil rights movement, there were several models of community organizing in addition to IAF projects. Thanks to the urging of community-minded staffers such as Ella Baker, the Southern Christian Leadership Conference (SCLC) and the NAACP were driven to civil rights protest in the 1950s and 1960s in part at the prompting of local associations of black Southerners that were mobilizing against discrimination in their communities. The 1955 bus boycott in Montgomery that propelled Martin Luther King to national prominence, for example, began as a campaign of the locally formed Montgomery Improvement Association. The SNCC, whose creation was heavily influenced by Baker's community-centered approach, took pains to organize rural black communities in Georgia, Mississippi, and Alabama, operating from a democratic ethos that eschewed organizational hierarchies and sought to avoid the class resentment that often developed between the NAACP and working-class black Southerners.[11]

In addition, the ability of community organizing to broaden concerns beyond de jure equality to include poverty and economic parity was becoming increasingly attractive to civil rights activists during the 1960s. SCLC launched its Operation Breadbasket program, which threatened businesses with boycotts if they refused to hire more black employees, in Atlanta in 1962; the program had spread to Chicago by 1966. On the eve of his death, King unveiled his Poor People's Campaign, which called on Congress for $30 billion to fight poverty, legislation promising jobs and income for every American, and a commitment to build affordable housing every year. Students for a Democratic Society (SDS) also expanded into urban antipoverty and hiring concerns in 1963 with the establishment of their Economic Research Action Project (ERAP). Even the federal government was adopting localized strategies for fighting poverty. In 1964 the Johnson administration created the Community Action Program (CAP), which distributed funds through local Community Action Agencies (CAAs) for antipoverty and youth programs. Federal regulations mandated a robust community presence in the CAAs, empowering low-income residents to make budgetary decisions based on their own priorities.[12]

The community organizing that GHCP and GHCC promoted took its cues from the people. Rather than foisting a radical agenda on them, community organizers encouraged local people to determine their own demands and to focus their energies on local change—to "take power to power," as veteran Baltimore organizer Joe McNeely puts it. The community organizing that GHCP and GHCC represented shared Alinsky's emphasis on local empowerment and goal setting. Yet as Robert Fisher, a chronicler of community organizing, notes, Alinskyite organizations ultimately wanted to create a "locally-based national movement to pressure and change the system, perhaps even to develop a populist political party which could wrest power from the current, corporate-dominated ones." By contrast, organizations such as GHCP were "development-oriented" and sought to stabilize local communities "by working in, maximizing benefits from, and even accepting the restraints of the existing political and economic system." Around the time GHCP was created, for example, Baltimore's Southeast Community Organization (SECO) made its name by organizing mostly white ethnic neighborhoods against the extension of Interstate 83 into Fells Point. Despite the radical potential of the highway battle, SECO's goals in the wake of that fight were for community development rather than systemic change. By 1973 SECO had become a Ford Foundation grantee to develop infrastructure and public health projects. In early 1975 the organization remade itself into the Southeast Development Corporation. One of SECO's lead organizers, Barbara Mikulski, went on to become a longtime U.S. senator from Maryland.[13]

Likened to the Populists of the 1880s and 1890s, these organizers emphasized economic issues rather than racial or gender equality. Poverty was a cross-cutting issue that appealed not only to urban African Americans but also to urban white ethnic groups that had stayed out of the civil rights movement. Community organizers in Baltimore fought hard to keep working-class white residents in the city. The riot in 1968 "scared the hell out of people," McNeely recalls. Community organizing "wanted to create an alternative to fleeing for people for whom those riots represented a horror." Groups like those created by the IAF were touted by national commentators such as those in *Time* magazine precisely because of their ability to avoid intensifying racial antagonisms seen in 1960s-era civil disturbances.[14]

For GHCP, and later for GHCC, the interracial nature of its catchment area meant that organizers' task went beyond appealing to white residents and stopping white flight. Organizers were also aware of the racial inflection of many of their neighborhoods' economic concerns. GHCP organizers would have been well aware of the underlying pressures that boiled over in Baltimore in the spring of 1968. In the fall of 1967, GHCP director Dea Kline and Ross Jones traveled to New Haven, Connecticut, to study the relationship of Yale University to the city and the attempts to promote "group cooperation and development of community leadership crossing race, religious, and socioeconomic barriers." Their trip came about three months after New Haven, which had been hailed as a "model city" and awarded $120 million of federal urban renewal money, experienced its own riot of black and Latino residents when a white businessman shot a Puerto Rican man.[15] For Ross Jones, Baltimore's riot pointed up the racial inequalities behind the neighborhood destabilization that the GHCP was fighting. Johns Hopkins, he told the university's Woman's Club about six weeks after the riot, must "do more for urban America. . . . We must do more than we have ever done to understand the needs of Negro Americans nationally and in Baltimore, finding ways . . . to help them meet problems of self-identification, political determination, increased economic stature, and equality, generally."[16]

There was, then, more to GHCP's interest in stopping white flight than simple neighborhood stabilization. The ethos behind the project was integrationist, to be sure, even if the specific issues it tackled were code enforcement and beautification. Project organizers included among their early priorities "involving black and lower income residents in programs" and "coming to grips with spoken and unspoken white racism." GHCC's "objectives" included "racial integration" and "encourag[ing] communication and interaction among persons of all ages, religions, races, and socioeconomic levels." This was more than just official boilerplate. Records indicate an intent to provide "enrichment programs which are consciously drawn to provide maximum involvement of a cross section of the community." In the summers of 1968 and 1969, the project sent a group of twenty children, "both black and white youngsters, girls and boys," to a swim camp at the Ruxton home of Mrs. William Richardson. A registration flyer for another GHCC-run summer camp in 1968 pointedly contains illustrations of both a black child and a white child. As the new GHCC recruited its board of directors, it solicited members from "the Greater Homewood black community" and got one in Frank DeCosta, then dean of the graduate school at Morgan State University.[17]

Ironically, a shift in focus toward community organizing in the late 1960s found JHU much more deeply engaged with the bread-and-butter civil rights issues of the day than it had been during the civil rights movement of 1955 to 1964.[18] While direct-action civil rights protests awakened a generation of students across the country in the early 1960s, Johns Hopkins remained very much the genteel Southern university, taking cautious steps toward incorporating more African American students. "It was slow. It was slow," Ross Jones remembered of the progress of integration at the university. Individual students, faculty, and staff members, however, constantly worked to push the university toward a commitment to integration. Jones recalled working with one of JHU's first African American graduates to create a scholarship fund for black students and to recruit black undergraduates. Chester Wickwire, who came to JHU in 1953 to run the Levering Hall YMCA chapter on campus, became legendary in Baltimore's civil rights community. He orchestrated the city's first interracial jazz concert in 1959 at the Fifth Regiment Armory, created the Tutorial Project in 1958 to involve JHU students in serving the city's children, was arrested and jailed during a protest to integrate Gwynn Oak Park in 1963, and brought dozens of controversial speakers to campus.[19]

Wickwire's activities inevitably ran afoul of certain administrators of both Johns Hopkins and the YMCA. Wickwire, for example, suspected that JHU president Milton Eisenhower was not entirely supportive of a letter, written by Ross Jones on the university's behalf, instructing landlords who rented to students that they could no longer discriminate between black and white renters. (Jones recalled that this "was the only time in my life I ever got hate mail at home—'nigger lover' and that sort of thing.") "I liked Milton Eisenhower. He was a good man," Wickwire noted years later, "but he had trouble with coming into the twentieth century with race." He and Baltimore Neighborhoods, Inc., promised to call the media if Eisenhower backpedaled. Although Eisenhower and Wickwire were often at odds, Wickwire and his social justice initiatives appear to have had a friend in Ross Jones. In 1968 the YMCA turned its JHU campus office at Levering Hall and Wickwire's position over to the university, which also made Wickwire its chaplain. Almost immediately after that, students accused JHU of depriving Wickwire's office of the funds it needed to accomplish its work. The issue worsened by 1971, when Wickwire suspected that JHU was hampering fundraising for his office because of its work in draft counseling, which was perceived as anti–Vietnam War. Jones, who was by now vice president for university affairs, personally signed a fundraising appeal on behalf of Levering Hall. "I always thought it was important to have someone like Chester, a burr under the saddle," Jones said in 2006.[20] In fact, both Wickwire and Jones shared a sense of the university's responsibility to the community around it.

Changing the Conversation

By the early 1970s GHCC was no less invested in creating a sense of community among the racially and economically varied neighborhoods in its footprint—from the grand mansions of Guilford to the modest row homes of Barclay and Harwood. The context in which GHCC worked, however, had changed. Most of the locally based antipoverty initiatives would not survive the 1960s. Although we cannot know for certain what would have happened to Operation Breadbasket and the Poor People's Campaign if King had lived, SDS closed down its ERAP by 1968. Historians have cited a number of reasons for its failure, but principal among them was ERAP's ultimately impractical anticapitalism. "As a consequence," concludes Jennifer Frost, "not enough New Left organizers understood or appreciated community organizing on its own terms, as the slow, undramatic, and long-term process of helping people develop their powers." In fact, Alinsky himself had been critical of ERAP's philosophizing. At the federal level, CAP's emphasis on local priority setting fell victim to partisan maneuvering when Richard Nixon succeeded Lyndon Johnson. New regulations emerged subjecting community representatives serving on CAAs to new standards and requiring that funding be spent on a handful of national initiatives such as Upward Bound. And the civil rights organizations that pursued an interracial society were either eclipsed (in the case of SCLC and the NAACP) or subsumed (in the case of the SNCC) by the turn to black nationalism after 1965.[21]

White activists in these groups were instructed to focus on organizing white communities. The rioting that followed King's assassination only underscored the apparent wisdom of decisions such as the one the SNCC made in 1967 to eject the last of its white members. "As long as it's a white person telling a black person what to do, you're not changing the power equation," explains McNeely of the SNCC's new approach. "It cannot by definition be empowerment." Many white former civil rights activists found new causes in the antiwar, feminist, and gay liberation movements; others made their way to community organizing. In southeast Baltimore, Joe McNeely took the SNCC's advice and worked in mostly white neighborhoods with a few pockets of black residents. He quickly discovered that the racialized lexicon of the civil rights movement was no longer appropriate among his Italian, Irish, Polish, and Greek constituents. "White people do not sit around and talk about race . . . so you didn't organize around that," he recalled. The *New York Times* took note of community organizing's "delicate" work of "retaining the white working class . . . without at once excluding blacks" in southeast Baltimore, rehabbing row houses while remaining "aware that they would lose substantial credibility with the community if the residents of the restored rowhouses turned out to be 90 percent black."[22]

The maturation of conservative Republican politics in response to the civil rights movement and the rising tide of black nationalism spelled further trouble for organizing around integration. As early as 1964, the presidential campaign of Barry Goldwater appealed to white conservatives who opposed what they perceived as a socialistic civil rights agenda that expanded federal authority and spending. By 1968 the specter of gun-toting

Black Panthers made federal intervention into the economic inequalities faced by African Americans increasingly unpalatable to conservative voters. In that presidential election, the South overwhelmingly voted for Republican Richard Nixon over Democrat Hubert Humphrey. At best, Nixon's victory was a sign of white discontent with the transformation the government had undergone as a result of the civil rights movement; at worst, it represented the same resistance to racial equality that had been only held at bay by the Kennedy and Johnson presidencies. What was certain was that the majority of voters were losing patience with the language and liberalism of the civil rights movement.[23]

In Greater Homewood, GHCC continued to stress "where we live" as its organizing principle. There is less overt reference to "race" or "integration" in its documents during the first half of the 1970s; language is instead more concerned with the nuts and bolts of neighborhood work. Yet as it had in the late 1960s, GHCC's leaders knew that achieving, if not interracial harmony, at least interracial tolerance was essential to that work. They remained acutely aware, as former executive director Dick Cook puts it, that "the issue in the community was often the issue of race."[24] The visual means that GHCC used to represent its neighborhoods and advertise its work in the 1970s are indicative of this consciousness. The Greater Homewood coloring book, assembled in 1972, features a deliberate inclusion of people of color in many illustrations, as seen in the use of stippling or hatching in the skin tones of some of the figures. The same tactic is used in drawings in issues of *Key Notes*, GHCC's newsletter, and in a promotional brochure. Each of these pieces uses multiracial crowd scenes to underscore Greater Homewood's ethnic and racial diversity. "Just like the larger city . . . this complex area of Baltimore contains people of all income levels, all races, many ethnic groups," the brochure explained.[25]

There were at least two incidents in the course of Cook's tenure at GHCC in which the organization had to confront racial tensions between neighborhoods. In 1973 GHCC joined neighborhood leaders in Remington, Hampden, Woodberry, and Tuscany-Canterbury to complain to the director of Parks and Recreation, Doug Tawney, about the condition of Wyman Park. At the time, the park was in poor shape, polluted on its eastern end by runoff from JHU chemistry labs and on its western end by neighborhood trash. Schooled in what Cook calls a "confrontational organizing model" learned from the 1960s, the coalition demanded that the city clean up the park. Tawney agreed with the group that Wyman Park was a "stinking sewer," so bad that he claimed he "wouldn't walk [his] dog through that park." But Tawney blamed "the neighborhood people" for "dumping their trash there" and challenged them to clean it up before the city would "spend one cent." GHCC organized a summertime cleanup project in response, staffed by about eight Youth Corps workers from Hampden and Remington who worked in interracial teams.

Although the workers "bonded over the summer," the black workers were frequently harassed on their way home from work by local rowdies from the neighboring Hampden community, a mostly white community with a well-established reputation for racial hostility. "It actually got a bit dicey at one point and we had to get the neighborhood association presidents to walk alongside the kids as they left work," Cook remembers, "and on one occasion we had to get the police involved." Nonetheless, there is no evidence that GHCC ever considered replacing the interracial work teams with all-white teams.[26]

The second incident also took place in Hampden. In 1971 the Supreme Court ruled in *Swann v. Charlotte-Mecklenburg* that public school districts needed to do more to fulfill the desegregation ruling handed down in *Brown v. Board of Education* seventeen years earlier. In many cities, doing more meant busing black students from their neighborhoods into white areas to attend school. In Baltimore, busing was implemented around 1976 to desegregate Hampden's Robert Poole Middle School. The plan involved transporting black students north from the Harwood neighborhood in south Charles Village. The practice threatened to rock Robert Poole, which one longtime teacher described as a place "that didn't change. You had the same names, you had the same families sending children." Black parents also feared for their children's safety, especially given Hampden's reputation. Whenever Nate Tatum and his friends rode bicycles through Hampden, for example, neighborhood children would throw rocks at them—which is why Tatum and his friends tended to ride in groups of ten or more if their path would take them through Hampden.[27]

As busing loomed, GHCC sent organizers into both Hampden and Harwood, the latter walking the black students through the line of angry white parents who formed a picket in front of the school. But when GHCC was able to facilitate conversations between both sets of parents, "the parents discovered that they were being played off against each other by the principal at Robert Poole," says Cook. "The principal had a short career after that." Cook credits GHCC's community-organizing approach with effecting this coalition between black and white parents in one of Baltimore's most racially hostile neighborhoods. "It was a matter of gaining trust one on one with people in the community. . . . If you come in spouting what you think people should do, they're going to treat you a certain way," he says. In southeast Baltimore, Joe McNeely was experiencing a similar phenomenon: despite all of the bad press that white urban ethnics were getting in the 1970s around a much more violent busing crisis in Boston, McNeely found that it was not so difficult to build coalitions between them and African Americans:

> By starting with people's experience and developing organizing, then they come to understand that, "hey, we're being, we're being,

> our schools are being undermined by exactly the same kind of things that the black schools are being undermined by. We ought to get together." The factories are closing, and white employees and black employees alike are losing their jobs. Now, we can fight over each other and say, "Oh, the blacks are taking our jobs," when there's two jobs left, or we can say, "How come there's only two jobs left?"

In fact, the *New York Times* agreed, in a 1976 article about SECO, that it was "probably the most thoroughly integrated protest since the early civil-rights days—more so, since it is integrated out of common self-interest rather than the limousine liberalism of upper-middle-class white support groups."[28]

In the end, it was GHCC and not black nationalist groups, such as the SNCC and the Black Panthers, that succeeded in forming sustainable organizations that empowered their constituents. Community organizing is not without its critics. Sidney Plotkin warns that the "enclave consciousness" wielded by community organizing can allow "community" to "become a euphemism for racial and ethnic hatred, loathing of the poor, or contempt of the 'other.'" Taking a community as it is and beginning with its self-identified self-interest temporarily restrains the community organizer from challenging his or her constituents on whatever latent (or not so latent) racism they might possess. But as McNeely argues, "Any organizer that's good is only starting with people's narrow self-interest as a start. As you get broader, you've got to develop a group of leadership who are capable of more sophisticated analysis" and who can identify their points of shared interest with communities that do not share their racial, ethnic, or religious characteristics.

GHCC, whose geographic boundaries have expanded since 1969 to include Roland Park, Barclay, and parts of Station North, continues to encourage these varied communities to consider themselves neighbors invested in each other's struggles. Given Baltimore's famed neighborhood loyalties, it's not an easy struggle; it never was, especially because these loyalties are often tied to racial identity. But ultimately, the coalitions that GHCC built (and continues to build) between the affluent neighborhoods in its northern end and the neighborhoods in its southern end are more enduring than the civil rights movement's reliance on Northern white donors to funnel money to the Deep South. It is a means of organizing that privileges commonality and proximity over difference, that values diversity but seeks to put it to use for the common good—that believes there is, in fact, a common good.[29]

Studying community organizing in the 1960s, 1970s, and into the 1980s tells a different story about America at that time than we usually hear. Instead of urban communities mired in economic downturn and movement fatigue, we see dedicated groups of activists—black and white—doing the unglamorous work of holding meetings, running the mimeograph machine, and raising money. They pursued an organizing model that was different from the one used in the civil rights movement but was concerned with the same questions of democracy and equality. In the aftermath of riots, black nationalism, and Nixon's Southern Strategy, groups such as GHCC discovered a different way to ask those questions.

NOTES

1. This chapter uses terms such as "riot" and "civil disturbance" interchangeably to avoid repetition. Some scholars of and participants in these events express preference for one of these terms for different reasons. Opponents of "riot," for example, argue that its connotation of irrationality obscures the very real discontent that motivates civil uprisings. Opponents of "civil disturbance" worry that the term drains these events of their revolutionary potential. Using a variety of terms to refer to what happened in cities throughout the United States from 1963 to 1968 reflects my belief in the impossibility of assigning a single definition to these events and in the much more important task of understanding why they happened. For more on riot terminology, see Vincent Jeffries, Ralph H. Turner, and Richard T. Morris, "The Public Perception of the Watts Riot as Social Protest," *American Sociological Review* 36, no. 3 (1971): 443–451; Barry Carter, "What You Call the Events Depends Largely on Where You Were in '67," *Newark (NJ) Star-Ledger*, July 11, 2007, p. 8; and Max Herman, "Summer of Rage: Newark and Detroit in the Summer of 1967" (draft manuscript, 2008). I thank Max Herman for sharing his manuscript chapter with me.

2. *Report of the National Advisory Commission on Civil Disorders* (New York: Bantam Books, 1968), 38–108, 203–205; Kevin Mumford, *Newark: A History of Race, Rights, and Riots in America* (New York: New York University Press, 2007), 98–122, 191.

3. Nate Tatum, interview by the author, tape recording, Baltimore, MD, November 26, 2007; Thomas D'Alesandro III, interview by Fraser Smith, May 22, 2007, available at http://archives.ubalt.edu/bsr/oral.htm (accessed April 2, 2008); William Donald Schaefer, interview by Fraser Smith, n.d., available at http://archives.ubalt.edu/bsr/oral.htm (accessed April 2, 2008). On school desegregation in Baltimore, see Matthew Crenson, "The Elephant in the City," *Urbanite*, November 2006; and David Taft Terry, "'Tramping for Justice': The Dismantling of Jim Crow in Baltimore, 1942–1954" (Ph.D. diss., Howard University, 2002). As Howell Baum notes in Chapter 10, Baltimore's embrace of school desegregation was rather toothless, leading to a retrenchment of de facto segregation in the years that followed the *Brown* decision.

4. Ross Jones, foreword, *Greater Homewood Community Project Final Evaluation Report, June 15, 1968–August 15, 1969*, iv, ix, Office of Community Affairs (OCA) papers, subgroup 1, series 3, box 1, folder "Greater Homewood Community Project: Final Evaluation Report (copy 2), 1969," Special Collections, Milton S. Eisenhower Library, Johns Hopkins University; "Copy I," n.d., OCA papers, subgroup 2, box 3, folder "Greater Homewood Community Corporation Press Releases, 1967–74." For evidence of JHU's continued participation as a funder and

supporter of GHCC, see the organization's most recent annual reports at http://www.greaterhomewood.org/about_us/annual_reports (accessed August 12, 2009).

5. Tatum interview; Melvin Douglas Williams, interview by Sunni Khalid, 2007, available at http://archives.ubalt.edu/bsr/oral.htm (accessed November 29, 2007).

6. "Agnew Angers Negroes," *New York Times*, April 12, 1968, p. 20; "Agnew Raps Top Negroes for Silence," *Washington Post*, April 12, 1968, A1; Tatum interview. After the incident with Agnew, at least one black leader—John Compton of the City Hall Youth Council Committee—spoke out against Stokely Carmichael; see Joe Nawrozki, "Negro Youth Leader Scores Militants," *Baltimore News American*, April 17, 1968, 2B–3B.

7. "Businessmen Shout: 'Want Protection!'" *Baltimore News American*, April 18, 1968, 1A, 4A; Stephen Kiehl, "When Baltimore Burned," *Baltimore Sun*, March 30, 2008; Tatum interview; Tom Chalkley, "For Better or For Worse," *Baltimore City Paper*, January 1, 2003; Donald E. Meserve, "Planning with the Community: A General Look at the National Neighborhood Movement and an Evaluation of a Case Study in Neighborhood Planning" (master's thesis, University of North Carolina–Chapel Hill, 1980), 38–39. Meserve was an AmeriCorps VISTA at GHCC in the mid-1970s.

8. *Hoe's Heights: A Neighborhood Plan* (1979), Greater Homewood Community Corporation archive, Baltimore, MD (hereafter GHCC archive); Robert L. Crain to Ross Jones, May 13, 1969, OCA papers, subgroup 2, box 2, folder "Greater Homewood Community Corporation, 1967–75"; Dea Kline, memorandum to Ross Jones, October 22, 1969, OCA papers, subgroup 2, box 2, folder "Greater Homewood Community Project Education Sub-Committee, 1968–72."

9. Saul D. Alinsky, *Rules for Radicals: A Pragmatic Primer for Realistic Radicals* (New York: Vintage Books, 1971), 113–114.

10. On the early history of community organizing, see Robert Halpern, *Rebuilding the Inner City: A History of Neighborhood Initiatives to Address Poverty in the United States* (New York: Columbia University Press, 1995), 29–39, 50–56; and Neil Betten and Michael J. Austin, eds., *The Roots of Community Organizing, 1917–1939* (Philadelphia: Temple University Press, 1990). On NECO and BUILD, see Antero Pietila, *Not in My Neighborhood: How Bigotry Shaped a Great American City* (Chicago: Ivan R. Dee, 2010), 245–247; and Harold A. McDougall, *Black Baltimore: A New Theory of Community* (Philadelphia: Temple University Press, 1993), 126–135. BUILD is still operating; see http://www.buildiaf.org (accessed July 19, 2010).

11. David J. Garrow, *Bearing the Cross: Martin Luther King, Jr., and the Southern Christian Leadership Conference* (New York: William Morrow, 1986), 223, 462, 595–596; Barbara Ransby, *Ella Baker and the Black Freedom Movement: A Radical Democratic Vision* (Chapel Hill: University of North Carolina Press, 2003), 113–114, 273–298.

12. Jennifer Frost, *"An Interracial Movement of the Poor": Community Organizing and the New Left in the 1960s* (New York: New York University Press, 2001), 27–47; Robert Fisher, *Let the People Decide: Neighborhood Organizing in America*, ed. Irwin T. Sanders (Boston: Twayne, 1984), 110–116; Halpern, 106–115.

13. Joe McNeely, interview by the author, tape recording, Baltimore, MD, March 5, 2008; Fisher, *Let the People Decide*, 142–148. On SECO, see Kenneth Durr, "The Not-So-Silent Majority: White Working-Class Community," in *From Mobtown to Charm City: New Perspectives on Baltimore's Past*, Jessica Elfenbein, John R.

Breihan, and Tom Hollowak, eds. (Baltimore: Maryland Historical Society, 2002), 225–249; Joe McNeely joined SECO as an organizer in 1970.

14. See Frances Fox Piven and Richard A. Cloward, *Poor People's Movements: Why They Succeed, How They Fail* (New York: Pantheon Books, 1977); Harry C. Boyte, *The Backyard Revolution: Understanding the New Citizen Movement* (Philadelphia: Temple University Press, 1980); Gary Delgado, *Organizing the Movement: The Roots and Growth of ACORN* (Philadelphia: Temple University Press, 1986); Andrew Sabl, "Community Organizing as Tocquevillean Politics: The Art, Practices, and Ethos of Association," *American Journal of Political Science* 46, no. 1 (2002): 1–19; and McNeely interview.

15. "Schedule for Visit of Mrs. Dea A. Kline, Mr. Ross Jones, Mr. Victor Dates, Friday, November 10"; Dea A. Kline, memorandum to Ross Jones, October 18, 1967; and Dea A. Kline, memorandum to Ross Jones, August 31, 1967, all in OCA papers, subgroup 2, box 2, folder "Homewood Community Project, 1967–9." On the New Haven riot, see Ralph Blumenthal, "New Haven Arrests 165 in 2d Night of Disorders," *New York Times*, August 21, 1967, pp. 1, 26; and "New Haven Riots Hit 'Model City,'" *New York Times*, August 21, 1967, p. 26.

16. Ross Jones, "A Commitment to Urban Affairs," speech to the Johns Hopkins University Woman's Club annual meeting, May 15, 1968, in *Homewood Community Project Final Evaluation Report, June 15, 1967–August 5, 1968*, pp. 94–95, OCA papers, subgroup 1, series 3, box 1, folder "Homewood Community Project: Final Evaluation Report, 1968."

17. "Case Study Highlights Presented to National Seminar on the University in Urban Community Services," University of Maryland, October 2–4, 1968, in *Greater Homewood Community Project Final Evaluation Report, June 15, 1968–August 15, 1969*," p. 97; "Revised Prospectus for Greater Homewood Community Corporation, April 2, 1969," p. 3, OCA papers, subgroup 2, box 1, folder "Greater Homewood Community Corporation Board of Directors—Committee: Education, 1969–70"; Edward J. Hinman, M.D., memorandum to All Sub-Committee Chairmen of the Community Services and Facilities Committee, n.d., OCA papers, subgroup 2, box 2, folder "Greater Homewood Community Project Community Services and Facilities Committee, 1967–70"; Dea A. Kline to Mrs. William Richardson, June 4, 1969, OCA papers, subgroup 2, box 3, folder "Swim Program, 1968–69"; "Members and Nominees, Board of Directors, Greater Homewood Community Corporation," November 28, 1969," OCA papers, subgroup 2, box 1, folder "Greater Homewood Community Corporation Board of Directors—Committee: Executive, 1969–1977"; "*Vita* of Frank Augustus DeCosta," OCA papers, subgroup 2, box 1, folder "Greater Homewood Community Corporation Board of Directors—Biographies, 1969."

18. My periodization of this phase of the civil rights movement begins with the 1955 Montgomery bus boycott and ends with Freedom Summer and the Civil Rights Act of 1964—a period of nonviolent, integrationist activism around legal equality that was followed by a more radical turn toward black nationalism in groups such as the SNCC. See Deborah B. Balser, "The Impact of Environmental Factors on Factionalism and Schism in Social Movement Organizations," *Social Forces* 76, no. 1 (1997): 214–218, 221.

19. Ross Jones, interview by Mame Warren, transcript, Baltimore, MD, June 18, 1999, Johns Hopkins Oral History Collection, box 3, folder "Jones, Ross—Transcript," pp. 33–34, Special Collections, Milton S. Eisenhower Library, Johns Hopkins University. On Chester Wickwire, see "Reflections: Chester Wickwire,"

Johns Hopkins University Center for Social Concern, available at http://csc.jhu.edu/OLD/reflections_wickwire.html (accessed August 16, 2009); "Obituary: Chester Wickwire, Chaplain Emeritus and Social Activist, Was 94," *JHU Gazette*, September 8, 2008, available at http://www.jhu.edu/~gazette/2008/08sep08/08wickwire.html (accessed August 16, 2009); Jessica Elfenbein, "Chester L. Wickwire and Levering Hall," available at http://archives.ubalt.edu/clw/index.htm (accessed August 16, 2009); and C. Fraser Smith, *Here Lies Jim Crow: Civil Rights in Maryland* (Baltimore: Johns Hopkins University Press, 2008), 147–153. On the university's deliberations over community engagement, see John C. Schmidt, *Johns Hopkins: Portrait of a University* (Baltimore: Johns Hopkins University, 1986), 54–55, 64.

20. Ross Jones, interview with Mame Warren, 34; Chester Wickwire, interview with Mame Warren, transcript, Baltimore County, MD, July 9, 1999, Johns Hopkins Oral History Collection, box 7, folder "Wickwire, Chester—Transcript," pp. 10–12; Smith, 151; "The Levering Protest," *Johns Hopkins News-Letter*, April 25, 1969, Johns Hopkins Oral History Collection, box 7, folder "Wickwire, Chester—Research"; Weldon Wallace, "Levering Issue Is Aired," *Baltimore Sun*, May 10, 1971, Johns Hopkins Oral History Collection, box 7, folder "Wickwire, Chester—Research."

21. Frost, *"An Interracial Movement of the Poor,"* 71–72, 148–161, 174; Fisher, *Let the People Decide*, 117–119.

22. Central Committee meeting, notes and decisions of May 1967, *Student Nonviolent Coordinating Committee Papers, 1959–1972* (Sanford, NC: Microfilming Corporation of America, 1982), reel 3; McNeely interview; Bob Kuttner, "Ethnic Renewal," *New York Times*, May 9, 1976, 177 ff.

23. On Goldwater and Nixon, see Lisa McGirr, *Suburban Warriors: The Origins of the New American Right* (Princeton, NJ: Princeton University Press, 2001), 55–186.

24. Dick Cook, roundtable of former GHCC executive directors, GHCC Annual Meeting, October 24, 2006, DVD.

25. Greater Homewood Coloring Book, 1972; *Keynotes*, March 1973; and "People are the Key to Greater Homewood" brochure [1970s?], GHCC archives.

26. Dick Cook, interview with Michael and Margaret Beer, August 25, 2004, GHCC archives; Dick Cook, interview by the author, March 28, 2008.

27. "The Nixon Busing Bills and Congressional Power," *Yale Law Journal* 81, no. 8 (1972): 1542–1573; Margaret Doyle, interview by Susan Hawes, August 16, 1979, Hampden Community Archaeology, Center for Heritage Resource Studies, available at http://www.heritage.umd.edu/CHRSWeb/AssociatedProjects/hampden/doyleoh.htm (accessed March 28, 2008); Tatum interview.

28. Cook interview, August 25, 2004; Cook interview, March 28, 2008; McNeely interview; Kuttner, "Ethnic Renewal." For a similar assessment of integration in IAF organizations, see William Julius Wilson, "Rising Inequality and the Case for Coalition Politics," *Annals of the American Academy of Political and Social Science* 568 (2000): 95–96.

29. GHCP and Wickwire's Tutorial Project are examples of university engagement by Johns Hopkins at its best. A much more contentious community engagement process continues in East Baltimore, where the university's medical campus has set its sights on constructing an $800 million biotech park. Unlike the north Baltimore Homewood campus, whose largely forested land was donated to JHU in the 1910s, the expansion of the medical campus in the early twenty-first century

involves the seizure through eminent domain and demolition of about eight hundred residences. Most residents of this neighborhood, known as Middle East, are working-class African Americans; despite the perception of Middle East as a community riddled with drugs, crime, and vacancy, many worry about what will happen to their community after development. The Save Middle East Action Coalition (SMEAC), a community group, continues to negotiate with the nonprofit East Baltimore Development, Inc., (EBDI) to protect residents' interests on matters ranging from dust and debris during construction to access to rehabilitated homes and compensation for neighbors whose homes are slated for demolition. "People of color have always been viewed as sub-standard individuals. When we were poor and didn't have anything and this land wasn't worth anything, they didn't bother us at that time. . . . But after four generations . . . they decided, 'I [JHU] want their land.' . . . It's a sad thing when a medical institution that is supposed to save lives, can't save this community," said SMEAC president Donald Gresham at an October 2008 rally. "It is important that there is an organized expression from the community, and SMEAC is that. They have been extremely valuable and extremely constructive in being that organized voice in a depopulated community," EBDI's Chris Shea said in 2008. On Johns Hopkins and East Baltimore, see Charles Cohen, "A Bitter Pill," *Baltimore City Paper*, November 12, 2003, available at http://www.citypaper.com/news/story.asp?id=3317 (accessed August 16, 2009); Melody Simmons, "A High-Tech Center Moves into Baltimore, and Residents May Be Driven Out," *New York Times*, June 17, 2007, available at http://www.nytimes.com/2007/06/17/us/17baltimore.html?_r=1 (accessed August 16, 2009); Charles Cohen, "Danger Zone," *Baltimore City Paper*, March 16, 2005, available at http://www.citypaper.com/news/story.asp?id=9754 (accessed August 16, 2009); and Adam Rothstein, "Rebuilding the Middle East (Neighborhood in Baltimore)," *Next American City*, August 28, 2008, available at http://americancity.org/daily/entry/1001/ (accessed August 16, 2009). Donald Gresham, qtd. in Nick Petr, "East Baltimore Residents Tired of Broken Promises," *Baltimore's Indypendent Reader*, available at http://indyreader.org/content/east-baltimore-residents-tired-broken-promises-%E2%80%94-nick-petr-photo-andy-cook (accessed August 16, 2009). Chris Shea, qtd. in Michael Rogers and Lena Denis, "Despite Improvements, Residents in East Baltimore Remain Disgruntled," *Johns Hopkins News-Letter*, March 13, 2008, available at http://media.www.jhunewsletter.com/media/storage/paper932/news/2008/03/13/NewsFeatures/Despite.Improvements.Residents.In.East.Baltimore.Remain.Disgruntled-3268820.shtml (accessed August 16, 2009). On JHU's acquisition of the Homewood campus, see Schmidt, *Johns Hopkins*, 20.

13

Planning for the People

The Early Years of Baltimore's Neighborhood Design Center

MARY POTORTI

During the October 1968 national convention of the American Institute of Architects (AIA), Whitney Young, Jr., executive director of the National Urban League, chastised his audience of some four thousand architects for their "thunderous silence and . . . complete irrelevance." He insisted, "You share the responsibility for the mess we are in, in terms of the white noose around the central city. We didn't just suddenly get in this situation. *It was carefully planned.*"[1] Complicit in urban abandonment by designing to the whims of white contractors and influential citizen lobbies, the nation's architects had, in Young's mind, willfully neglected those most in need of their expertise. While the notion of community design had been introduced with some success four years prior, Young's speech infused members of the profession with a new sense of urgency and social responsibility.[2] The AIA swiftly encouraged local chapters to reorient toward "advocacy in architecture" by donating time and services to initiate efforts in blighted communities.[3] Within the year, AIA chapters were actively investigating the potential for and merits of sponsoring community design centers in cities across America. By 1971 eighty-four community design centers sprouted across the country in cities including New York, San Francisco, Philadelphia, Washington, Los Angeles, Cleveland, Minneapolis, Atlanta, Little Rock, and Lexington. Notable among these was Baltimore's Neighborhood Design Center (NDC), one of the earliest, most successful, and enduring organizations to emerge from this movement for community-driven, asset-based planning.

The ambiguous concept of community design itself complicated this work from the start. In essence, community design aims to facilitate the active involvement of residents in the politics of their neighborhoods by making the services of professional architects, planners, and designers available to communities unable to afford them. The explosion of professional interest in this principle during the late 1960s and early 1970s stemmed from two major realizations. First, the fury and aggravation evidenced by large-scale rioting demonstrated the destructive potential of citizens who felt ignored by local leaders and exploited by outsider entrepreneurs, particularly white ethnic merchants and property owners. Countless acts of looting and arson revealed that many residents felt excluded from the process of planning and policing their streets. From this stemmed a second, related understanding: outsiders alone could not save the cities. Without the input of community stakeholders who possessed a deep understanding of the needs and character of specific neighborhoods, drives for change would be fleeting, if not counterproductive. Of course, resident activism was not a new phenomenon in American cities; however, as broader societal conflicts unfolded, much local energy had become haphazard and misdirected. The Philadelphia chapter of the AIA observed that most criticisms offered by residents "succeed only in bringing projects to a halt . . . [for] they are seldom able to generate positive action which brings concrete results." In theory, then, community design centers would serve as a link between residents and city hall, bridging what the Philadelphia Architects' Workshop termed the "severe communications gap" between those who lived in the city and those who mapped its future.[4]

The driving objective of community design is to enhance and promote the health and productivity of neighborhoods and communities, mandating a procedural structure propelled by civic dialogue and community participation. To that effect, "advocacy planning" rapidly gained momentum among chapters of the AIA. In many cases, such efforts tapped into an existing undercurrent of volunteerism among architects, as well as simmering public agitation, particularly within African American communities.[5] To utilize these conditions to their advantage, many early organizers believed community design centers should be located in the low-income neighborhoods they targeted. This would enhance their visibility and accessibility in a way that would involve residents to the greatest extent possible. An architect from the University of Maryland School of Architecture surmised, "If the center appears to be just another governmental or charitable agency, the people will distrust its efforts and be antagonistic toward it. If the people establish and run it themselves, they will use it, trust it, and benefit from it."[6]

The Philadelphia Architects' Workshop was the predominant model for community design centers. Established in January 1968 under the auspices of AIA Philadelphia, the organization's primary task was "translating the residents' desires into the language of the agency bureaucrat and/or professional planner." Toward that end, an executive director trained in social work managed a staff of about twenty, primarily trained but unregistered students and interns monitored by licensed architects and planners. The University of Pennsylvania supported the enterprise with office space and the director's salary. A steering committee determined which projects would be accepted, while an advisory committee was responsible for identifying ways the workshop could be more useful to those it served. The workshop recognized its place in "a city of neighborhoods . . . and of . . . neighborhood associations" that exhibited "a vital concern with the physical improvement of their neighborhoods." AIA Philadelphia may as well have been describing the situation in Baltimore, noting, "Increasingly these organizations are becoming outspoken about their needs . . . and increasingly frustrated when these are not met."[7] Within a year, requests for assistance far exceeded the workshop's capacity. A need had been identified. The nature and extent of that need, however, had yet to be defined.

In 1970 affiliates of several young community design centers met in Washington, D.C., to share concerns and to brainstorm possible courses of action. Grady Poulard, a civil rights activist, AIA member, and future cofounder of the National Organization of Minority Architects, stressed the need for immediate action in lieu of public posturing. "We know how we feel," he reminded his colleagues. "We all feel that we live in a racist society. We all feel that the AIA and the OEO [Office of Economic Opportunity] have not done what they said they were going to do . . . [and] that perhaps they aren't serious anyway." Nonetheless, he concluded, "the important thing is that the skills exist. The money exists. The structure exists—they ain't performing but they exist. The possibilities are there. . . . [But] there's one thing that's been missing all these years. It's the will, the commitment, to do something about the problems we are all concerned about."[8] While Poulard highlighted the need for unwavering commitment backed by timely follow-through, Jack Bailey, director of the San Francisco Community Design Center, emphasized the importance of mobilizing communities. In his mind, the real responsibility of architects was not to devise schematics or contract for construction. "The problems that we are dealing with," Bailey pronounced, "are how public or social resources are allocated. . . . So, what it boils down to . . . what we're really doing . . . is trying to build a *political movement*."[9] Despite ongoing debate over process and approach, conference attendees largely agreed on the central premise of community design to make the services of architects and planners available to those unable to pay for them. As one Atlanta architect graphically affirmed, "The people who fight the day-to-day battle of rats and roaches—they're going to make the determination of what they are going to live in."[10]

In 1976 the *AIA Journal* reflected on the diversity of this movement for "social architecture." "Despite their many similarities," it commented, community design centers "differ widely from one another. Each is a local product, reflecting local problems and priorities."[11] One such product was NDC in Baltimore, conceived and loosely formed in 1968 and incorporated as a nonprofit organization in 1970. Born at the dawn of what one historian has termed "the Decade of the Neighborhood," NDC hoped to channel and further galvanize grassroots efforts to remodel the city by assisting community organizations in a budding campaign to take back their streets.[12]

The organizational foundation for community design in Baltimore was laid by two white architects, Charles Lamb, a founding partner of the city's premier architectural firm RTKL, and David O'Malley, a newcomer to the area. A Chicago native and West Coast transplant, O'Malley arrived in Baltimore in the early 1960s to open an office for the California-based firm of Victor Gruen Associates, whose architects were working with the Rouse Company developing shopping malls in the metropolitan region. He was quickly unnerved by the state of the city. When Martin Luther King, Jr., made an appearance in Baltimore shortly thereafter, O'Malley was startled by the hostile response of many whites watching King's passing motorcade. He then understood what the city was up against.[13] "I realized I was really in the South," said O'Malley. "But I thought there were others like me who probably shared a certain level of concern" and that by using "our architectural design skills or organizational skills, we could do things that . . . would maybe make a difference." After the violent response to King's assassination, O'Malley and others knew they could wait no longer.

Aware that many of the federal programs designed to benefit impoverished areas were not accessible to the people who needed them, O'Malley and Lamb discussed "creating an entity that would provide some of the services that would enable those communities or neighborhoods to apply for those funds."[14] According to Al DeSalvo, a member of the Baltimore City Planning Department who joined the NDC board of directors in 1971, "One of the big obstacles just generally in Baltimore for any kind of community-based action was to try to change the mentality of both the people living in the neighborhoods and the mentality of City Hall from . . . listening to the old-line political hacks and the ward leaders to listening more to what's good for the neighborhoods."[15] To expedite the process and secure funding, the task of establishing a community design center in Baltimore was conducted through the official channels of the AIA. Chaired by Lamb, the chapter's Urban Design Committee (UDC) formulated a proposal for a community design center that drew heavily on the models of San Francisco and Philadelphia, the latter of which "more closely parallel[ed] Baltimore's potential."[16] However, unlike many others around the nation, Baltimore's design center would not be directly affiliated with a university architecture program, nor would it be an extension of a private firm. Rather, it would operate as an independent nonprofit entity. Emphasizing the importance of "public faith" in programs initiated by the AIA under the banner of public interest, the UDC's memo to the executive committee stressed caution in moving forward.[17] With O'Malley serving as director, NDC focused its inaugural efforts in West Baltimore.

The theory of community design encountered two significant complications in Baltimore. First, given the demographic makeup of those working with and for NDC, early affiliates were wary of appearing as crusaders imposing their own ideas in areas they hoped to uplift. Thus, from the beginning NDC required that community groups approach the center with an issue or idea. One early brochure explained that NDC volunteers "assisted on community projects which were generated by the residents themselves, in response to their own expressed needs, and at a level which they defined."[18] These stipulations increased the likelihood not only that accepted projects would be supported by at least a small group of core constituents but also that the implemented changes would have a lasting effect in the neighborhoods where they were instituted, because residents themselves had played an integral part in the process. Additionally, to maintain communities' trust, the center soon came to realize the vital importance of ensuring that projects could be funded and completed within a reasonable time frame without overextending the resources of volunteer professionals or frustrating clients who might be anticipating immediate results. Peter Swensson, an early NDC member of Volunteers in Service to America (described later), outlined this philosophy in the fall 1973 issue of *Planning Comment*, explaining that while "morale is high enough so that volunteers are unlikely to wander away in despair after a setback . . . community groups cannot have their expectations unrealistically encouraged by staff members only to be disappointed by their unfeasibility."[19] Quite simply, the center intended to undertake projects that were *possible*.

A second major concern was that the professional architectural community might view NDC as competition, giving away free labor and expertise, devaluing services, and thus detracting from potential business. To avoid such accusations, NDC provided services only to community groups unable to afford them. If a group's financial standing improved to a point where they could pay for the services NDC provided free of charge, the center would refer stakeholders elsewhere and hand back the project. In this way, board members rationalized, the center might actually cultivate new clients in underserved areas. Moreover, to prevent conflicts of interest, volunteer architects and designers were ineligible to accept any paid contracts that stemmed from their contributions. With these aims in mind, NDC eventually limited its involvement to the conceptual and schematic phases of grassroots projects, thereafter advocating on behalf of groups and educating them to maneuver the political system on their own.[20]

As discussions concerning NDC's purpose, role, and policies carried on, the need to acquire funding for paid staff to answer phone calls, schedule meetings, and interact with members of the community became critical. The national AIA urged chapter presidents to seek federal funding through the OEO's Volunteers in Service to America (VISTA) program, established in 1964 as part of President Lyndon Johnson's War on Poverty. Arguably the most progressive of the administration's antipoverty programs, VISTA deployed individuals for a year of service in the nation's most destitute communities. Rather than provide direct aid such as medical care or food assistance, VISTA aimed to build capacity from within to help disadvantaged groups learn to help themselves. Their duty, as President Johnson reminded the first cohort of volunteers, was "to encourage the downtrodden, to teach the skills which may lead to a more satisfying and rewarding life. No aspect of the War on Poverty will be more important than the work you do."[21] In the AIA's estimation, the primary role of VISTA would be to "assist in the development of relevant two-way communication between the community and the professionals." Moreover, the AIA reasoned that by living in the communities they served, VISTA workers could "help the professional to better understand the emotional, psychological, and cultural implications of the community environment" and, in doing so, "help in the difficult process of translating the needs and demands of the ghetto resident into design programs that have real significance to him."[22] In 1969 NDC was first awarded VISTA support for three full-time volunteers. NDC VISTA workers, each formally trained in a relevant field, began work the following year. Additionally, in 1970 the Baltimore chapters of the AIA and the American Institute of Planners contributed $5,000 and $2,000, respectively, toward the costs of hiring a community director and renting office space, first on Park Heights Avenue, then on East Biddle Street, and ultimately, in the basement of the Christ Episcopal Church at 1110 Saint Paul Street. By 1971 NDC was allotted ten individuals through the VISTA program.[23]

In this way, NDC was infused early on with the vigor of the New Left student movement, as most early VISTA workers were fresh from college campuses. A letter from one VISTA hopeful summarized the sentiments of other students. "After spending five years in higher education," the young man explained, "[only now have] I . . . become aware of contradictions between how we are taught to design for people and what people actually want and need. . . . Frankly, I am anxious to become involved, fully involved, because direct citizen and community participation is the only way by which we can make our living environment a fulfilling one."[24] An early NDC VISTA worker explained the effect: "The staffs on design centers across the country were young and idealistic, because . . . we were only paid twenty-six hundred dollars a year as VISTAs. . . . And the idea was . . . that you would be living basically under the same conditions and [with] the same money as the people you were helping."[25] NDC thus benefited from the labor of aspiring professionals while cultivating the talents and approach of a breed of architects and designers geared to partner with the community in the course of planning.[26] In addition, the VISTA program supplied NDC with a small salary for someone to supervise its volunteers.

Those funds were soon used to pay a woman many remember as the "heart and soul" of the fledgling organization, Doris Johnson, who came to NDC in 1969.[27] A seasoned and well-respected community leader in her northeast Baltimore neighborhood of Homestead-Montebello, Johnson quickly emerged as the natural candidate to guide the center in its mission. O'Malley recalled, "She was a neighborhood activist, one of these marvelous people who represented community issues and understood the political process." Johnson brought invaluable connections with neighborhood leaders and a particular passion for community health concerns, as her husband had died in a city hospital emergency room while awaiting treatment.[28] Moreover, as the lone African American woman in an organization dominated by white male professionals, she lent the center much-needed credibility among its clientele. Johnson mirrored the personalities and strategies of the activists with whom she collaborated, for as an NDC VISTA worker later noted, "the neighborhoods . . . tended to have a couple of very strong, usually women, African American leaders. And they were really the ones that were trying to salvage the neighborhoods." O'Malley believed Johnson fit that model perfectly. "She's a real tiger," he recently remarked, ". . . capable of being aggressive and forceful." This was no minor asset as several NDC affiliates promptly confronted racial hurdles in connecting with black leaders and residents, long suspicious of the intentions of ostensibly well-meaning white liberals.[29]

By the early 1970s NDC instituted a formal operational structure involving four key players: community organizations, the NDC community coordinator, VISTA workers, and volunteer professionals. Once NDC accepted an official request for assistance from a legitimate organization, the community coordinator (a role filled by Johnson until early 1976) met with the group to define what the community needed so as to ensure that the project would "fairly represent the interests of most of the people" who lived there.[30] Johnson often led these meetings, with VISTA workers assigned to the project also present to ensure a smooth transfer of responsibility once Johnson's task was accomplished. According to one NDC VISTA worker, Johnson "wouldn't turn anybody loose in the community if she wasn't confident, because she didn't think the point of all this was for the communities to be . . . laboratories for young architects and planners. . . . That would have offended her. . . . The whole idea was to help make these services available to empower the communities."[31]

Once the needs of the group had been identified, the NDC team came together to determine the specific services required. Johnson and the VISTA workers then selected a volunteer architect or planner with time, interest, and expertise to devote to the project and introduced that professional to the community. After the original objective was achieved, Johnson again met with community members to assess the project's accomplishments and alter or extend its goals.[32] Throughout this process, the community coordinator bolstered NDC's relationship with participating communities, while the daily legwork, scheduling, and organizing performed by VISTA workers gave the center an air of professionalism and stability. The long-term viability of NDC, however, depended on its volunteer professionals, as more intricate projects such as multipurpose centers and large-scale planning schemes could take years to complete. In that regard, area architects, planners, and designers—those who had helped to get NDC off the ground—were essential in sustaining a consistent central mission and a constructive relationship with the neighborhoods of Baltimore. NDC volunteer professionals eagerly tackled the first test of their ability to adapt to the needs and nuances of specific neighborhoods, assisting a young community organization in an operation that would prove most visionary and challenging.

In early 1968 a formidable organizing entity known as the United Western Front (UWF) surfaced in southwest Baltimore, an area then replete with boarded-up buildings and vacant lots.[33] Characterized by James Dilts of the *Baltimore Sun* as "a militant black organization," the UWF boasted almost 450 dues-paying members, led by a thirty-year-old retired electrician, local resident, and father, Neyland Vaughn.[34] Advocating for self-determination in the fashion of the Black Panthers, the UWF, which had already organized a football team, youth group, and women's auxiliary, sought to convert the empty Capitol Theater building at 1518–1532 West Baltimore Street into a dynamic community center.[35] Preliminary goals included locally owned stores, entertainment facilities, and a recreation program. "The idea," asserted Vaughn, was "to keep the money in the community."[36] Skeptical of city hall's motivations, Vaughn and others sought practical guidance from Echo House, a community center located at 1705 West Fayette Street. The center's objective to help "people to discover and fully use their own internal resources as well as those of the community" meshed perfectly with the outlook of the UWF, which began holding meetings in the Echo House basement.[37] UWF members soon teamed with students from the University of Maryland School of Architecture on a spatial layout and plan for securing city support. Armed with $10,000 from the Archdiocese of Baltimore, the UWF worked with more than a dozen young members of the local AIA. In addition to the Capitol Theater plan, the organization sought to purchase and renovate seven houses on Bruce Street to be sold at cost to families on welfare. The UWF wanted neighborhood residents to be trained to do much of the manual labor themselves. Prospects, however, were daunting. The cost of purchasing the theater alone would be $40,000.[38]

Given the nature of the project and the fervently local focus of the UWF, professionals from outside the neighborhood toiled to win the community's confidence. In an interview with the *Baltimore Sun* Vaughn proclaimed, "We don't want planners comin' in here tellin' us what we want. . . . We know what we want. We're planners too. We want City Hall to help us with our plans. We'll buy up the houses and fix 'em up ourselves if that's what it takes. We don't want conflict. We just want to be left alone to run our program."[39] Many observers noted flaws in the UWF approach. Dilts reported, "There is even a set pattern: initial enthusiasm over a plan that sounds good on paper, some 'seed money,' internecine feuds in the black community, confrontations with the powers downtown, charges of misspending of funds, disillusion on everybody's part."[40] After a funding application was rejected by the Model Cities Policy Steering Board, Vaughn and others approached the federal Department of Housing and Urban Development (HUD) for a Neighborhood Facilities Grant. To be considered, the UWF first needed to prove its legitimacy by producing a design that could be taken seriously.

Attempting to jump-start the project, Walter Lively, a well-known and respected civil rights leader and community organizer arrested during the riots in April 1968, brought NDC's O'Malley to a UWF meeting. At the head of the group, "sitting there on a throne with a robe on and a walking stick and . . . animal fur around his neck" was Neyland Vaughn. Remembered O'Malley, "Walter wanted me to help that group do something . . . [and] this guy sitting up in the front was really challenging." Architect Harry Hess, also in attendance, explained, "These guys basically said, 'Okay Whitey, what are you doing here? What do you want? What are you up to?' . . . They were very suspicious." In Hess's estimation, the meeting was crucial to forging a cooperative relationship between the groups, as it allowed NDC to convey its intentions "to try to broach the differences between City Hall and the white power structure" and city residents. O'Malley recalled a more specific intervention: "Walter Lively told this guy [Vaughn] to shut up. He said, 'You listen to O'Malley and he can . . . teach you how you can take one brick out of a building and it will fall down. You don't have to burn the buildings down.' And all of a sudden all the dynamics of the meeting changed and . . . we started working together." Lively's allusion to the potential for strategic application of expertise to upset the traditional balance of power was vivid and persuasive. NDC had its first client.

The UWF found itself in a difficult position with few natural allies. The Black Panthers and other groups accused the UWF of being led by whites, while many conservative organizations and city agencies viewed it as dangerously separatist. To sidestep such controversy, the Capitol Theater plan was folded into an Echo House proposal for a new multipurpose complex. Ron Kreitner, then a member of the Baltimore City Planning

Department, explained, "Echo House leadership came up with this concept of getting . . . city services and state services and federal services . . . to locate in the neighborhood by developing a . . . set of facilities to accommodate them [that] would be neighborhood-owned and operated." The crux of the vision was to remove urban blight and institute such services simultaneously through the adaptive reuse of vacant buildings.[41] From the start, HUD was unconvinced that community groups should or could operate such a complex. As a result, Workers Allied toward Cultural Unity (WATCU), an umbrella association chaired by a female African American community leader from southwest Baltimore, was incorporated as the legal entity responsible for the project. Its goals were ambitious, as the UWF's community center was only one component of the proposed Echo House complex, slated to consist of six neighborhood buildings restored and renovated for community use.[42]

Embedded in the buildings that would house WATCU was a history of West Baltimore itself, a community transformed in the postwar years by racial turnover fueled by the insidious practice of blockbusting by real estate agents seeking to exploit white fears of residential integration.[43] The site of the proposed cultural center, an empty church building at 101 South Mount Street, offers a revealing example. Founded in 1869 to serve a growing German-speaking population in the western part of the city, the parish of Fourteen Holy Martyrs began construction of a church and school in 1902 at the corner of Mount and Lombard streets.[44] While Fourteen Holy Martyrs served an active parish community during the early decades of the twentieth century, by the mid-1940s the shifting racial demographics of West Baltimore took a toll. As wartime industries boomed, demand for housing became pressing, particularly among African Americans with limited options.[45] Until 1945, Fulton Avenue, two blocks west of Mount Street, rigidly divided an expanding black population from a white community immediately west. As African Americans inched closer, the white working-class membership of the Fulton Improvement Association turned to church leadership for support and guidance, and area Catholic churches held meetings to organize opposition against black movement into the community. Despite initial vows to remain and fight for their homes, white residents began moving out following the so-called Fulton Avenue Breakthrough of African Americans across that line in 1945, leaving hundreds of properties open to new black residents. The 1950s saw residential turnover in most of west and northwest Baltimore, and by 1960 the racial demographics of those areas largely morphed from white to black. Church leaders' fears came true as their congregants left the community, and by 1964 the dwindling white Catholic population could no longer sustain a parish at Fourteen Holy Martyrs. Signifying the area's racial transformation, the empty church and school buildings were eventually leased by the Archdiocese of Baltimore for use as WATCU's planned cultural center, a potent symbol of what Vaughn and others hoped would be a black renaissance of West Baltimore.[46]

Though momentum was building before NDC became directly involved, its participation was crucial in producing working schematics for the facilities and in securing federal funding for WATCU. With NDC's assistance, WATCU submitted a Neighborhood Facilities Grant application to HUD and was finally awarded $811,000 in 1971.[47] Several donated buildings, together with services rendered by professional architects under NDC, accounted for a large portion of WATCU's $405,000 required match. Hess believed that, more importantly for NDC, WATCU "was the first real chance to put . . . money, resources, and something where our mouths were to try to give substance to what otherwise may have just been a verbal exchange."

By the mid-1970s, NDC volunteers oversaw the completed renovation of five of the buildings. However, despite federal funding and the moral support of city government, the sixth component of the WATCU complex—the community center so ardently championed by the UWF—was ultimately dropped. Kreitner reflected on the project nearly forty years later. "Components of it were successful," he contended, as it showed "a big commitment to . . . a large community that had been left out of a lot of things, a community that was really struggling in many respects." Given these realities, "professional architects working with neighborhood people very directly as they did was a pretty significant thing." While several buildings served the area for a number of years, the project was perhaps too grandly envisioned, particularly for a community in the early stages of organizing and for a design center taking on its first coordinated project. "It may have been a flawed concept," Kreitner, now an executive with the Westside Renaissance Corporation, has admitted. "It was just . . . a huge reach for the architects in terms of . . . the extraordinary commitment . . . of volunteer time and resources. . . . [And] it was a real reach in terms of community responsibility in administering the complex."

Despite these shortcomings, WATCU offered several indispensable lessons to NDC. The WATCU complex remains the largest and most elaborate project in NDC's history. Thereafter, the volunteer-driven organization generally restricted itself to the conceptual phase of complicated technical projects, usually assisting only long enough to secure outside funding. Moreover, while the majority of the WATCU complex was eventually built, even a dedicated core of activists could not sustain it over the long haul. The community center imagined by Vaughn and the UWF was rather symbolic. Its completion was the UWF's driving vision and its primary goal in aligning with WATCU. The unrealized dream of the theater renovation typified the limitations of spirited groups such as the UWF in striving to remodel their physical community without input from all parties.[48] The prospect of community-managed social service programs, for example, relied on a partnership with social workers and other outside professionals. Kreitner explained, "There was resentment . . . [among] a number of professionals over the years who really had trouble with the . . . sense of role reversal . . . that went on." Despite the relatively short life span of WATCU's facilities, Kreitner nonetheless concluded, "[the] project was probably one of preventing or slowing the loss of community fabric in Southwest Baltimore and . . . I think it was very important and very worthwhile in that regard."

As the WATCU venture dragged on, NDC shifted attention elsewhere, taking on a number of smaller projects. Founded on the conviction that the city's residents knew best the needs of their neighborhoods, NDC was soon approached by several community groups seeking to turn empty lots into communal playgrounds. As a result, "tot lots" (in NDC parlance) began sprouting around the city.[49] Their popularity stemmed from Baltimore's dearth of areas for safe, structured recreation; a plethora of unsightly vacant lots in some areas (a problem exacerbated by the riots); and, not least, the relative ease of construction. By 1974 at least four NDC tot lots had been constructed and no fewer than five others were in the works.

One of the earliest was the East Twenty-eighth Street tot lot, completed in 1971 in Doris Johnson's neighborhood of Homestead-Montebello.[50] Collectively requested by several neighborhood associations, the Twenty-eighth Street playground, more than two years in the making, was a shared ambition. The park was designed with assistance from NDC volunteers, built with materials donated by local businesses and salvaged by residents, and supported financially by neighborhood churches, city council president William Donald Schaefer, the city police department, and proceeds from a neighborhood bake sale. The Public Works Department agreed to install wooden posts to protect the area from motor traffic, and the Parks Department donated wood chips to make the ground safe for play. NDC VISTA workers supervised construction, which was carried out primarily by twenty-six soldiers enrolled in a program designed to ease their transition from active duty to civilian life. The *Stars and Stripes* reported that the GIs had grown tired of classroom instruction and wanted to apply their skills and energy to something practical, tangible, and meaningful. While the soldiers performed the bulk of the manual labor, neighborhood children cleared debris and raked the soil. The completed playground included swings, a sandbox, several climbing structures, and a sliding board.

Products of a national playground movement that took shape during the 1960s, tot lots reflected citizens' recognition of the potential for education, socialization, and community building during recreation.[51] Their creation also addressed the problem of litter-strewn and abandoned lots, havens for children and teenagers engaged in a variety of objectionable diversions, including sexual activity, substance abuse, and street fighting. The community of Homestead-Montebello called attention to the perils of drugs and gun violence in particular, dedicating the Twenty-eighth Street tot lot in honor of a city police officer killed while pursuing a narcotics suspect. Exhibiting a long-term commitment to urban youth, tot lots also served a deeper, more immediate purpose by providing NDC a chance to demonstrate its efficacy in otherwise skeptical neighborhoods. According to one NDC VISTA worker, once communities "developed some leadership around . . . [a tot lot] and some goals, then the neighborhoods could start to really look broader at bigger things. . . . Oftentimes, after meeting with them a few times, the goals would become much greater. We'd start them with a tot lot and we'd convince them what they really needed was a community plan."[52]

More than technical expertise, the most forsaken areas of the city needed proponents familiar with politics, city codes, and constituents' concerns. Something as simple as a tot lot, for example, was a low priority for the 2,400 residents of the predominantly African American Fairfield community in South Baltimore, likened by an NDC VISTA worker to "a small rural area in the city."[53] Housed on land zoned for industrial use, Fairfield residents had for years demanded standard public services and amenities such as trash collection, sidewalks, paved streets, and drainage systems. Facilities were so obsolete that by 1970 one in six residences still used an outhouse. The head of the Fairfield Improvement Association described the situation to Doris Johnson, stating simply, "We are in need of many things for our community, and we are without funds to acquire professional aid."[54]

NDC polled the citizens of Fairfield—over half of whom were homeowners—and found that 90 percent did not want to move. A mortgage banker volunteering with NDC then conducted a land and housing survey and presented three possible courses of action. Fairfield homeowners could keep their land values high by remaining zoned for industrial use and thus forfeit the right to public services, meet the costs of bringing their houses up to residential codes to reap the benefits of those services, or pool their land as a jointly held package for industrial sale. The community resolved to fight for residential zoning, and after the conditions in Fairfield were widely publicized in early 1972, the district's councilman petitioned city hall for the zoning change. Architectural historian Phoebe Stanton wrote of NDC's role, "This is an example of the meaning of 'architectural advocacy,' for industrial zoning made sense if you did not consider the preferences of the residents who lived in Fairfield. They did not wish to leave their homes. Then NDC had informed, not directed, opinion."[55] In such cases, NDC's most innovative contributions helped enable marginalized communities to define and defend their own best interests.

Later in 1972 the Planning Department, the Planning Commission, and the Board of Municipal and Zoning Appeals endorsed the zoning change, but the city council failed to vote on the measure before adjourning for summer recess. In NDC VISTA worker Peter Swensson's estimation, the council had made a calculated move and, considering strong industrial opposition, "tabled the bill to let the fires burn themselves out."[56] By the time Fairfield's councilman withdrew the bill the following year, the enthusiasm needed to sustain the effort had dissipated. Though residents were ultimately forced to relocate, NDC's involvement demonstrated that even the most disenfranchised communities did not have to fight alone. Neighborhood associations and advocacy groups such as NDC can help bandage the physical wounds of urban decay, but their greatest potential for facilitating community development is their ability to help infuse citizens with a sense of empowerment and a stake in the health of their neighborhoods. In 1975 O'Malley commented on the relationship between NDC and communities such as Fairfield. "Their demands have become sophisticated," he said, "but it is a sophistication that is not imposed. It is one that grows out of their own desires."[57]

In retrospect, the scope of NDC's involvement was remarkable. From 1968 to early 1974, the center participated in more than 140 community projects. It helped design, construct, or renovate more than ten city playgrounds, three recreation centers, and twenty-three buildings tailored for community use, and it sponsored several workshops to educate city residents about urban planning and strategies for neighborhood improvement. Countless other local undertakings received city or federal funding due in part to NDC. Promotional material drafted by the center advertised that "by 1976 the estimated value of construction that had been generated exceeded $7 million, 60 projects had been completed, or were near completing, and NDC could boast a roster of over 100 volunteer professionals that had actually provided some form of assistance to such projects."[58] If not for these endeavors, areas of west and northeast Baltimore might today be far worse for wear.

As with most movements for social change, NDC's achievements have been influenced and inhibited by external factors emblematic of broader historical shifts. If the idealism of the 1960s made a reimagining of the social order possible, soaring rates of unemployment and inflation during the 1970s ultimately put public programs targeting poverty and discrimination squarely on the fiscal chopping block.[59] President Richard Nixon's dismantling of OEO in 1973 presaged the end of broad national investment in programs designed to foster equality for all Americans, and by early 1976 federal VISTA support for NDC ceased almost entirely.[60] With these grim developments looming, NDC's youthful undertakings were imperative in safeguarding Baltimore's future prospects as a vibrant, livable city.

Truth be told, though early NDC clients such as WATCU and the community of Homestead-Montebello waxed after the civil unrest of 1968, the neighborhoods they sought to revitalize have since largely waned. All facets of the WATCU complex have folded. Most are now surrounded by undeniable signs of abandonment; some are even boarded up.[61] Across town in northeast Baltimore, vestiges of the Twenty-eighth Street tot lot remain, as surveillance cameras monitor students at local high schools in an attempt to curtail rising rates of youth violence.[62] In 2010 Doris M. Johnson High School (a subdivision of the former Lake Clifton Eastern High School, dedicated in 2004 to the late community leader) was among five schools scheduled for closure by a Baltimore City school system desperate to improve overall performance.[63] These realities underscore the inauspicious state of formerly tenacious communities like Johnson's beloved Homestead-Montebello. And as some neighborhoods continue to struggle, Old Fairfield and others have been deserted or condemned. Once rallying points for community action, the remnants of these projects attest to the myriad challenges faced by many industrial cities in the twenty-first century.

Despite numerous obstacles, NDC has outlived many of its peer institutions and continues to work with the people of Baltimore. After weathering a severe funding crisis in the mid-1970s, NDC flourished during the 1980s and expanded in 1993, establishing a satellite office in Prince George's County, Maryland, a largely African American suburb of Washington, D.C. Because a sickly economy has in recent years again drained government support from many nonprofits, foundation grants and corporate and private donations have become crucial to NDC's livelihood. These, too, are often elusive. With its Baltimore office currently down to a staff of two paid professionals, NDC nevertheless remains dedicated to community outreach and neighborhood development, touting the value of smart design for crime prevention and community revitalization. In 2007 the center launched its greeNDC initiative, which focuses on promoting sustainable design and construction practices, energy efficiency, improved air quality, and the overall health of the urban environment.[64] In addition to reconceptualizing best practices for direct project assistance, greeNDC emphasizes civic education to enable citizens across the socioeconomic spectrum to act locally with consideration for global issues. Such priorities and programs mirror many of the center's preliminary efforts. In this way NDC stimulates small but significant improvements in the quality of city life propelled by engaged citizens open to the premise and the promise of community design. In light of these achievements, NDC's unremitting existence is perhaps its greatest feat. Though much of the energy once directed toward neighborhood revitalization must now focus on the preservation of the center itself, NDC nonetheless survives as an apparatus for activists laboring to strengthen and stabilize their communities.

Other relics of the late-1960s push for community design remain as well, but the achievements and longevity of local efforts have been uneven. The Community Design Center in San Francisco is still in operation, but the movement's other prototype, the Philadelphia Architects' Workshop, foundered in the late 1980s when financial scandal called into question the motives of its leadership.[65] That setback notwithstanding, Philadelphia remains a hotbed of progressive urbanism, and in 1991 AIA Philadelphia sponsored the inception of the Community Design Collaborative to promote the adaptive reuse of vacant spaces and the restoration of small-business building exteriors to enhance commercial vitality. On a broader scale, coalitions geared toward participatory planning such as Planners Network, the Association for Community Design, and the Mayors' Institute on City Design have, since 1975, emerged to stimulate national conversation about how to approach and remedy the deterioration of parts of urban America. The guiding ideology, if not the spirited ardor, of the community design movement persists.

Ultimately, because some of the nation's most neglected areas require a systemic redistribution of resources before long-term recovery is possible, structural factors underlying the racialization of poverty must be addressed—a strenuous mission to be sure. Nearly four decades after Whitney Young lambasted the primarily white architectural profession in 1968, Augustus Baxter, longtime director of the Architects' Workshop, reported with frustration, "Afro-American architects are [still] not getting a fair share of business opportunities. . . . There is a wall of exclusion."[66] Considering the disproportionate number of African Americans living in underserved inner cities, this truth threatens attempts to spark and execute community projects truly representative of residents' interests. The wisdom of an early NDC VISTA worker continues to ring true: "Although the problems of race and poverty are no longer chic, they are still with us, making the need for community design centers as great as ever."[67] The work goes on, and there is still much to be done.

NOTES

Acknowledgments: I thank the following individuals for participating in the oral history component of this project: David Albright, Jim Arnold, Tom Carlson, Al DeSalvo, Sally Digges, Harry Hess, Ron Kreitner, Charles Lamb, David O'Malley, Phyllis Sachs, Jay Steinhour, David Tufaro, and Norm and Ilene Tyler.

1. Whitney Young, speech at 1968 National Convention of the American Institute of Architects, Portland, Oregon (October 1968), qtd. in Robert Traynham Coles, "Black Architects: An Endangered Species," *Journal of Architectural Education (1984–)* 43, no. 1 (Autumn 1989): 60; emphasis added. According to Coles, of the four thousand architects in attendance (including Neighborhood Design Center cofounder Charles Lamb), no more than five were African American.

2. The idea of involving residents in the design of their communities first took root in 1964 with the establishment of the Architects' Renewal Committee for Harlem (ARCH). Funded by the New York chapter of the AIA, the Office of Economic Opportunity (OEO), and private grants and commissions, the committee was composed of young African American planners, architects, and lawyers who believed

that only professionals with roots in a community could adequately respond to residents' needs and desires. Priscilla Tucker, "Poor Peoples' Plan," *Metropolitan Museum of Art Bulletin*, n.s., 27, no. 5 (January 1969): 266; "Community Design Centers: Practicing 'Social Architecture,'" *AIA Journal* (January 1976); Richard Hatch, "Planning for Change: Towards Neighborhood Design and Urban Politics in the Public Schools," *Perspecta* (Yale School of Architecture) 12 (1969): 43; "Social Content in Teaching and Design: Max Bond Interviewed by Paul Broches," *JAE* 35, no. 1, With People in Mind: The Architect-Teacher at Work (Autumn 1981): 53.

3. Qtd. in Phoebe Stanton, "Architects' Revolution in the Neighborhoods," *Baltimore Sun*, February 2, 1975, sec. D.

4. Philadelphia chapter AIA, internal documents, NDC archives, June 25, 1968.

5. Richard C. Hatch, "Giving Form to Life," *Architectural Record*, December 1979, 96.

6. Rurik Ekstrom (University of Maryland School of Architecture) to Charles Lamb (RTKL), "RE: Design Centers Program for State of Maryland," memo, NDC archives, December 17, 1968.

7. Philadelphia chapter AIA, internal documents, NDC archives, June 25, 1968.

8. Qtd. in James B. Pettit, Jr., ed., "CDC Conference Proceedings: Howard University, 13–14 March 1970," newsletter, NDC archives, p. 1.

9. Qtd. in ibid., 2; emphasis added.

10. Paul Cheeks, qtd. in ibid., 4.

11. "Community Design Centers: Practicing 'Social Architecture,'" *AIA Journal* (January 1976).

12. Suleiman Osman, "The Decade of the Neighborhood," in Bruce J. Schulman and Julian E. Zelizer, eds., *Rightward Bound: Making America Conservative in the 1970s* (Cambridge, MA: Harvard University Press, 2008), 106.

13. Though O'Malley suggested that this incident occurred before King's famous speeches in Washington during 1963, it most likely occurred on October 31, 1964, when King visited Baltimore to address issues of housing, segregation, poverty, and unemployment in time for the upcoming election. His motorcade route included North Gay Street, near the Saratoga Street office of Rouse Company.

14. N. David O'Malley, telephone interview with author, tape recording, July 30, 2007. All quotations from O'Malley are derived from this source, unless otherwise noted.

15. Albert DeSalvo, telephone interview with author, tape recording, July 24, 2007.

16. See James B. Pettit, Jr., ed., "CDC Conference Proceedings: Howard University, 13–14 March 1970," newsletter, NDC archives, p. 4.

17. Baltimore AIA Urban Design Committee, "Report: Proposal for Baltimore AIA Community Design Center," NDC archives, n.d.; NDC, "Neighborhood Design Center, Inc.," informational packet [1974?], NDC archives.

18. NDC, "Introduction," *Neighborhood Design Center Inc.*, brochure, NDC archives, 1972.

19. Peter Swensson, "A Case Study of Advocacy Planning: The Baltimore NDC," *Planning Comment* (Fall 1973): 12.

20. Andy Leon Harney, "Community Design Centers in the '70s: A Status Report," *AIA Journal*, November 1978, 55.

21. Qtd. in Marvin Schwartz, *In Service to America: A History of VISTA in Arkansas, 1965–1985* (Fayetteville: University of Arkansas Press, 1988), 10.

22. AIA, "Help in Sight for Community Design Centers," memo to AIA chapter presidents, NDC archives, April 14, 1969.

23. Charles E. Lamb, "Baltimore Chapter, NDC," memo to AIA chapter presidents, NDC archives, November 4, 1969.

24. Russell Braun to Doris Johnson, letter, NDC archives, June 15, 1976. This letter was written just after NDC's VISTA funding was cut. For more on student activism, see Terry Anderson, *The Movement and the Sixties* (New York: Oxford University Press, 1995).

25. Jim Arnold, telephone interview with author, tape recording, July 23, 2007.

26. Harney, "Community Design Centers," 54.

27. Jim Arnold and Sally Digges, telephone interview with author, tape recording, July 23, 2007. Most respondents expressed similar sentiments.

28. Ibid.

29. Both O'Malley and Hess described these encounters in interviews with the author. In contrast, not a single VISTA worker reported experiencing any racial tension during service. Harry Hess III, interview with Irene Poulsen (NDC) and author, tape recording, Baltimore, MD, July 6, 2007. All quotations from Hess are derived from this source.

30. NDC, "Process," brochure, NDC archives, 1974.

31. Arnold, interview.

32. This process is outlined in many NDC brochures. See, for example, "Neighborhood Design Center, Inc.," brochure, NDC archives, 1972.

33. NDC, "United Western Front," internal documents, NDC archives, October 22, 1968.

34. A workplace accident had disabled Vaughn, forcing his early retirement. James D. Dilts, "Advocates for Baltimore: United Western Front," *Baltimore Sun*, November 10, 1968, D1.

35. Harry Hess suggests this connection. According to Vaughn, however, the Black Panthers were suspicious of UWF's cooperation with white architects. See James D. Dilts, "Not Quiet on the Western Front," *Baltimore Sun*, September, 28, 1969.

36. James D. Dilts, "Advocates for Baltimore: United Western Front," *Baltimore Sun*, November 10, 1968, D1.

37. Echo House Foundation, Inc., "Efforts of the Community Helping Others," promotional material, NDC archives, n.d.; "About Us: History," *Echo House*, available at http://www.echohouse.org/about/aboutus.html (accessed August 9, 2009).

38. Dilts, "Not Quiet on the Western Front."

39. Qtd. in Dilts, "Advocates for Baltimore."

40. Dilts, "Not Quiet on the Western Front."

41. Ron Kreitner, interview with author, tape recording, Baltimore, MD, July 10, 2007. All quotations from Kreitner are derived from this source.

42. The plan included a social services center, health center, cultural center, halfway house, and block daycare. The community center sought by the UWF rounded out the plan. Rehabilitation costs were estimated at nearly $737,000. NDC, "Project Summary," internal documents, NDC archives, July 1970, pp. 3–5.

43. For the definitive work on this topic, see W. Edward Orser, *Blockbusting in Baltimore: The Edmondson Village Story* (Lexington: University Press of Kentucky, 1994).

44. *The Catholic Church in the United States of America*, vol. 3, sec. 1 (New York: Catholic Editing, 1914), 64–65.

45. Kenneth D. Durr, *Behind the Backlash: White Working-Class Politics in Baltimore, 1940–1980* (Chapel Hill: University of North Carolina Press, 2003), 85, 87, 101.

46. Jack Carr (Archdiocesan Office of Planning and Development) to George Kostritsky (RTKL), letter, NDC archives, July 8, 1970.

47. Details on plans for construction and renovation are drawn from internal NDC documents unless otherwise noted. NDC, "Design Assistance for Echo House Multi-Purpose Complex Center Discussion" and "NF 120 Description of Proposed Facility," Construction documents, NDC archives, n.d.

48. Several articles from the *Baltimore Sun* mention dissent among some black residents, including suspicion and threats of violence from the Black Panthers and other radical groups.

49. Public concern about the influences of the urban environment on child development have deep historical roots in the United States, dating back to Progressive-era reformers at the turn of the twentieth century.

50. Unless otherwise noted, information about the construction of the Twenty-eighth Street playground is derived from the following: Barry Rascovar, "In Baltimore, Too, the GI Helps Children," *Baltimore Sun*, August 6, 1971; Antero Pietila, "Army-Built 'Tot Lot' Is Opened," *Baltimore Sun*, August 12, 1971; "GI 'Scroungers' Build a 'Tot Lot,'" *Stars and Stripes* 30, no. 112 (August 8, 1971).

51. Richard Dattner (AIA), *Design for Play* (New York: Van Nostrand Reinhold, 1969), 134. Similar projects in cities including New York were termed "pocket" or "vest-pocket" playgrounds.

52. Arnold and Digges, interview.

53. This description of the Fairfield predicament is derived from the following sources unless otherwise noted: James D. Dilts, "Chief City Engineer Tells Fairfield Residents Long-Delayed Sewers Await Federal Approval," *Baltimore Sun*, November 21, 1972, D8; Phoebe Stanton, "Architects' Revolution in the Neighborhoods," *Baltimore Sun*, February 2, 1975, D1; Peter Swensson, "A Case Study of Advocacy Planning: The Baltimore NDC," *Planning Comment*, Fall 1973, 16–17; David Albright, interview with author, tape recording, Baltimore, MD, July 5, 2007.

54. Jennie Fincher (president of Fairfield Improvement Association) to Doris Johnson, letter, NDC archives, February 7, 1971.

55. Stanton, "Architects' Revolution."

56. Swensson, "A Case Study of Advocacy Planning," 16.

57. Qtd. in Stanton, "Architects' Revolution."

58. "Neighborhood Design Center: Then and Now," promotional material (draft), NDC archives, January 1980.

59. See Bruce J. Schulman, *The Seventies: The Great Shift in American Culture, Society, and Politics* (Cambridge, MA: Dacapo Press, 2001).

60. Larry Carson, "Design Center Group Merely Dormant Now," *Baltimore Sun*, August 25, 1976, F19; Ed Blume (Church Women United/VISTA) to VISTA sponsor (NDC), letter, NDC archives, March 26, 1976. Blume noted that proposed cost-sharing measures that would require local projects to raise about $4,000 to fund a volunteer "could seriously destroy the poverty emphasis of VISTA."

61. These descriptions come from personal observations of the author made primarily in August 2007.

62. Sara Neufeld, "10 More City Schools to Get Surveillance," *Baltimore Sun*, October 20, 2006; Sara Neufeld and James Drew, "Attack Highlights 'Chronic Problem,'" *Baltimore Sun*, April 13, 2008.

63. Hassan Giordano, "Education Watch: Baltimore City Schools to Be Transformed/Closed," *Baltimore Examiner*, March 2, 2010, available at http://www.examiner.com/independent-in-baltimore/education-watch-baltimore-city-schools-to-be-transformed-closed (accessed August 14, 2010).

64. "greeNDC," *Neighborhood Design Center*, available at http://www.ndc-md.org/GREENNDC.htm (accessed August 14, 2010).

65. For more about director Augustus Baxter's ethics violations, see Michael Sokolove, "Vanity Tagged Questions Drive Architects' Workshop to Return Vehicle to City," *Philadelphia Daily News*, November 7, 1986, local edition, p. 12.

66. Linn Washington, Jr., "Op-Ed: Black Architects Face a Wall of Exclusion," *Philadelphia Tribune*, November 4, 2003.

67. Swensson, "A Case Study of Advocacy Planning," 17.

14

Robert Birt

Oral History

Robert Birt was fifteen years old at the time of the 1968 riot and living with his mother and sister in the Latrobe Homes public housing project in the heart of the East Baltimore riot area. Birt went on to become a professor of philosophy and a member of the faculty of Bowie State University in Maryland. Here he gives a close-up view of the riots and assesses the long-term impact of King's assassination and the subsequent rioting on his own personal philosophy, as well as on Baltimore as a whole.

Nyasha Chikowore and Maria Paoletti, students at the University of Baltimore at the time, interviewed Birt on July 7, 2007.

I was fifteen in 1968 and I lived in the Latrobe Projects, the 900 block to be exact. It's in East Baltimore, bounded by Madison, Eager, Greenmount, and Aisquith. I was a student at Mergenthaler High School[1] at the time. I was somewhat of a precociously dweebish or nerdish kind of kid because I did used to read, which was—I wouldn't say nobody did it, but it wasn't the most popular activity in my neighborhood. It rarely is, in very poor neighborhoods. But for me it was something that gave me a world outside of my environment and also enabled me to look at my environment differently. And particularly after King was shot, I started reading his books, and I think that partly contributed to my getting involved in what you might call the life of the mind. He's the first philosopher I ever read.

Mergenthaler at that time was still predominantly white. So I had a bit of interaction with white students. But the African American part of the student population was growing. And there were some black teachers there. They were a minority, but they were definitely there, and there were enough of them for me to notice them. Of course, now it's predominantly black, like what has happened throughout much of the city. In the beginning, we'd make an appearance, and there'd be a few of us, and then gradually the whites or their parents would start pulling them out, and then the school would become predominantly black. Even in the schools that were in some sense mixed, unfortunately they didn't stay that way.

Prior to high school, my frame of reference was the neighborhood and, of course, it was a black neighborhood. There just weren't that many white people around, and the ones that were, were people like the store owners, the police, and a lot of folks that most people didn't like very much. But in high school and then in college is when I developed some significant number of friends who were white and eventually Latino and Asian.

The racial mood in Baltimore before the riots was more or less like the mood in most communities during the sixties. Civil rights was large enough for everybody to know about it. People were talking about what was happening in the South. Kids talked about things, too. Dr. King had come to Baltimore. He came to the Civic Center, and I think it was around '66 or '67. It would have been after Birmingham, Selma, and all that.[2] I wasn't there when King spoke, but I remember being in a group of teenagers, we were about thirteen or fourteen, and we had gone skating. On the way back, we took a wrong turn or something, and we ended up in this clearly predominantly white area, which—let's put it mildly—was not very friendly. We started getting catcalls; we were called porch monkeys and niggers and what have you. We had girls with us, and we're teenage guys, thinking, well, we have to at least get the girls out of here and get ourselves out as soon as we could. Rocks were thrown, but fortunately we were at enough distance that nobody connected. Once we had gotten safely out of their range, one kid, I think he was called Pretty Boy Norman, says, "Well, they'd better not cross this track. If they do, their asses are ours." And he says, "By the way, I heard it was a very good talk he gave at the Civic Center, but I'm not so sure I believe in Dr. King's nonviolent program." So, we were aware of things.

Baltimore wasn't as mobilized as Bull Connor's Birmingham, where you had children facing police dogs.[3] And of course the authorities here weren't quite as extreme as in the Deep South. I don't think Baltimore had the extreme racial tension that some cities had. It was there—it still is there—but it seemed sort of undercover, so maybe that's the reason why there was—I don't know if it's civility, but there was something. But the tensions were there. And there had been activism here. Some churches were involved, and there were activists in communities who were always telling you to get off your butt and fight for your rights. The activists, at least the—I wouldn't call them career activists, but the ones that were the most persistent, were usually not the majority, although at times significant numbers of people could be drawn into something. But not everybody was always on the barricades. That's the image of the sixties that's a little naive. But there was an attitude that was at least receptive, at least sympathetic with the activists, because after all they're supposed to be for us. But everybody wasn't an activist.

I recall that King was assassinated on the fourth of April. It was a Thursday, and it was somewhere in the neighborhood of 6:00 P.M. That I do remember. I think it was Walter Cronkite who announced it on television, and my mother broke down and cried. She broke down and cried. And I said this is something I will never forget. I even remember what the weather was like. It was warm—I remember that. I told my mother, "I'll never forget they killed King."

Baltimore, if I remember, did not immediately erupt as some cities did. But you could feel something in the air. It seemed that almost anything might trigger something. There was school Friday, although my mother wasn't sure whether she wanted me to go because everybody felt that something wasn't right. But I did, and students were talking about it at Mergenthaler. I started noticing a certain uneasiness in the interaction between black and white students, more so than usual. Everybody knew what the deal was, but nobody really wanted to talk about it, but it would come out anyway, and then emotions would blow up in classrooms, and teachers would have a difficult time just trying to keep things civil.

I remember '67.[4] That had been everywhere. Troops were on television, with their bayonets. And people were talking about it. My mother said she was talking about it at her job, students were talking about it, kids were talking about it. People saying people in Detroit, they've had enough of this. Another group didn't think that it was a good idea. But when King was assassinated, there was just this funny kind of feeling just everywhere. And some people had lowered flags. Some people wore black. There were people who threatened that any white businesses in the neighborhood that didn't show some sort of remorse would be torched. I actually heard people saying that if they didn't wear something black or lower a flag or something and they operated in our neighborhood, they shouldn't be here.

I seem to remember it was Saturday that it happened. It was as if people had two days of mourning and then a day or two of rage. It was a weird thing because Saturday, I think it was Mayor D'Alesandro[5] who got on the radio or on television and made a nice liberal speech about mourning the loss of this great American. He said he thought that it was commendable how black citizens of Baltimore in this trying time didn't resort to an explosion of mass anger. And I remember he was saying that just as I started noticing some things were happening. It's almost as if the riot was beginning as he was commending us for not doing it.

I had gone to the store. Coming back, I bumped into some people and was talking with them. Eventually I found myself around by Eager and Asquith streets. There were people standing around, but there were people standing around everywhere. Then suddenly a group of young guys came up, and they were saying things like "They killed King so we're gonna burn them out." And there was a store there run by a middle-aged or elderly white couple, and they attacked the store. "We're going to make them pay for this." And just as this was happening, somebody had turned on a little transistor radio, and some white official, I think it was D'Alesandro, was commending the black community for its dignified restraint in this time of sadness. And people laughed because the riots were just starting. And one person says, "Well, I guess white folks got confused." I don't think D'Alesandro or whoever it was had any sense for what people were feeling.

I stayed out for a while, and then I went home. My mother was having a fit because by this time it was on the news. "Where were you all this time? You know they're going to send in the National Guard. They'll start shooting people." But I said, "As far as I'm concerned, they started it." That is, I regarded the riots as a reaction. To be quite frank, I was not unsympathetic to the people who did riot because I thought we had to do something. I know people who said that we ought to take out some of their leaders, maybe the mayor, or a governor, or even the president. "They killed ours. Let's kill theirs." People said things like that. But a lot of it was just people venting. But I didn't believe that the persons who did these things were criminals. And I know that some of them were my neighbors. So I said, "Well you know, Mom, they started it."

There's no telling what started it. I heard that police were driving around saying, "What are you people doing on this corner?" This was very bad timing. That was fairly common in those days—they would order you off the corner. They were known to be quite abusive, and the police—I would guess the police force in those days was maybe 80 to 90 percent white—many of them had an in-your-face attitude.[6] I don't know whether one of those incidents was the spark that provoked the rioting, but that's one of the things I heard that happened. And there were cases where a person would throw rocks at police cars.

One guy I know claimed that he was in the Oldtown Mall[7] when rioting there started. Now, Baltimore was fortunate insofar as we didn't have organized gangs like the Cripps and the Bloods, like they have in California. We didn't have that sort of thing. However, what you sometimes did have was confrontation between people who came from different projects. So some guys from Latrobe might have a tiff with some guys from Lafayette. Say one guy would see a guy with a girl from the projects that's he's from, he wants to know why he's dating this person. Or when guys from Lafayette and guys from Latrobe bump into each other, something often happens. Or Somerset project and some other group, Flag House, what have you. The guy I know said that he saw some people from our project, Latrobe, and some young toughs from Lafayette projects meet at the Oldtown Mall. And, of course, very often that meant a dispute, if not an outright fight. But he said that everybody was so taken up with Martin Luther King's assassination that it didn't happen. They formed a kind of common bond. They decided instead of fighting each other, they were going to loot these stores. And one person—my friend tells me—from our project actually gave one of those power signs to a person from the other project. They reciprocated, and instead of the usual gang fight, they teamed up against the white merchants and started tearing up their property and looting things. Now that's hearsay, but it was hearsay from a friend who says he was there.

I didn't go back out on Saturday. And very shortly, if not the next day, the National Guard came to town, and then they imposed curfew. Then parents started pulling their kids off the streets for fear they might have a fatal encounter with the National Guard. Eventually, though I had a difficult time at the time distinguishing one from the other, some detachment of the regular military arrived with all their paraphernalia. Of course they had their weapons. We would see them with their bayonets. I didn't have all the words I might use for it now, but on a certain emotional level, I just saw them as an occupation. They were here to defend white property and to enforce white law.[8]

In the house we turned on the television and there were films of people out in the streets. They even had pictures of people here in Baltimore. It was kind of weird because I was thinking to myself, wait a minute, the camera's there, but the cops aren't there. In fact, I think the National Guard had actually arrived in town, but they didn't stabilize the whole place all at once. They probably got control of some places before they got control of other places. I remember seeing some black ladies on television going into a store and trying on dresses and other clothes. It was like they were shopping, but of course they weren't paying for it. Somebody had even brought a shopping cart, and she went shopping, basically. I guess even then sisters had fashions on their minds.

I don't remember seeing that kind of thing on the street as it was happening. What I saw on the street were some people smashing windows and burning some things, but I didn't see them taking things. In fact, I get the impression that even in the riots there was a gender difference in what happened. That is, the physically violent parts were mainly carried out by young guys. They smashed in the store windows, threw things out, threw the owner out, and made him watch his store being burned. I don't think there were a lot of cases where women physically confronted the police or directly threw Molotov cocktails. Everybody that I saw doing that were guys. But sometimes females would be cheering what the guys were doing, and after they broke into a store, they would come in and do their shopping. I guess they figured that it was the guys' responsibility to do the war part. We'll take care of the commodities. I did notice that.

I was aware that people in my neighborhood got arrested. Some of our neighbors got arrested. There were a good number of people whom you didn't see for a while. They hadn't been killed, and I didn't think all of them were just penned up in their homes. Some of them had probably gotten arrested because they might have got caught taking something out of a store or may have just got arrested because they were out after the curfew.

The fact that the riots happened should give you a clue to the mood in my area. Everybody was hurt and angry about what had happened to Dr. King. I even heard one person, I think it was a minister, of all persons, say something to the effect that while he's not happy about the riots, if we didn't do something, then they would think they could get away with anything, and we'd be back to the days of our parents and grandparents, when they could just take you out and hang you whenever they felt like it. I've heard some older people who remember lynching say, "At least now they know there is but so much we will take from them." I've heard people who didn't want to condone this activity also say that it was provoked by the other side and that they have to know that there is a limit to what we'll put up with. So, I think even people who were unfavorable towards the riots often had that addendum they'd add to it: it's unfortunate, but they provoked it.

Of course, school was out for a while. I know schools would have been officially closed, but I don't remember for how long. Could it have been a couple of weeks before it started up again? I know it wasn't the same week, and it wasn't the week after that, so at least two weeks had to have passed before I went back to school and maybe before school was reopened. But I don't remember exactly.[9] But when some people began returning to classes, then the riots themselves became part of the conversation. Like I said, at that time at Mergenthaler, the student population was still majority white, so you got to listen to the white students trying to talk about this. One guy says, "This is terrible. My father says that they are a bunch of criminals. They ought to lock them all up and shoot them." And another guy says, "Well, I don't know. Because my father said that if he was colored, he'd probably do the same thing." So I started observing the divisions of opinion among whites, which was interesting, because you could easily think that whites all thought the same way about things, that they all regarded us as inferior. Some black people felt that way.

Then somebody said, "Nobody's asked any of the 'coloreds'"—a lot of people still used the word 'colored' even then—"in the class what they think." So the teacher asked whether any of us had anything to say. And I said, "We didn't start the riots. You did." People had very different reactions to that. One said, "How did we make you go out and do this?" I said, "The last thing you did was kill Dr. Martin Luther King. And that's just the last thing you did." "But I didn't do it!" And I said, "Some of your people did." I started telling them things my parents talked about, that whites were always messing us around. They grew up in the South. They talked about that, because there was a lynching on both sides of my family, I was told. What happened in families was just part of the lore of the time. So I said, "Y'all started it. You're always starting it, and this time you just have to pay for it." I was angry about this.

Eventually tensions between the white students and the black students got back to normal in that the tensions weren't right at the surface. But there was a certain sense in which something had changed, even when it was no longer being talked about. The volume of the tension subsided, but it was there on a lower frequency, you could put it.

The school then started trying to do things like introducing little elements of sanitized black history into the curriculum. Some teachers started trying to talk a little more about Africa, but nobody was really prepared. People were reacting to this crisis. But there was also pressure, because the black student population was demanding more in the line of black studies. That was happening in other schools, too.

I sometimes wonder how my life would have developed if King hadn't been murdered. I eventually went to college, and I studied philosophy, of all things, the subject Dr. King had studied in Boston. The first piece of philosophical literature that I ever read was his famous "Letter from a Birmingham Jail."[10] I read that maybe a year or two after his assassination. I was very impressed by it because it talked about the moral grounds of what we then called civil disobedience and the whole idea that law in and of itself is not sacred, but that justice is what is sacred. The law is justified as an expression of justice.

I hate to think of it this way, but in a certain respect what happened to King and the whole tragic situation at the time precipitated my entering into what might be called intellectual life. I wanted to find out who all these names that King kept mentioning in this letter were. Who's Martin Buber? Who's Nietzsche? Who's Augustine? Who are all these people? I was wondering about King—what led him—so I read the things that he kept mentioning.

After the riots, I also began thinking more about the way I was treated by other people. For example, were I stopped by the police for some reason, even if it was just to ask a question, I now had another attitude about this. Of course, the police were never the most favorite people in the neighborhood, but it was something that had always existed. And now I sometime took an attitude of questioning or challenging what right do you have to stop me, on what grounds, for what reasons. I developed an attitude of being less accepting towards authority. Initially, less accepting towards white authority and after a while, less accepting of authority, period. I began to think it was very important for people to think for themselves. I don't mean that everything goes, but I developed this attitude that there's too much respect for authority, which is one of the reasons—aside from force and violence—that things like Jim Crow lasts this long. It's one reason why we're in Iraq.[11] People are too accepting. They don't question things.

At this time you also had the beginning of people talking about black consciousness. A lot of people began taking stock: This is serious. If they can kill King, we need to know what's happening. So black consciousness started developing. It began to make its appearance in some churches. Certain students were talking about it, and it did make me more sensitive to racial issues. I started reading Malcolm, also writers like Baldwin, Richard Wright, others.[12]

The Black Panther Party also managed to establish a presence here in Baltimore, and after the assassination of Dr. King, they found some people were willing to listen to them. They had a certain influence. I was reading more of their literature. My mother, of all people, had started buying their newspapers, and one of the Panthers who worked in the neighborhood became friends of the family. This is not very well known, but the fortunate thing is that where the Panthers had an influence, one of the things they did was link racial and economic justice. The problem of economic injustice then connects you with a lot of folk besides black people who have to deal with the matter of poverty or economic injustice. So, that partly contributed to my thinking evolving in a certain way. There was a misconception that the Panthers were an antiwhite group. They weren't, but there were a lot of them like that who were, I can tell you that. I remember all of them. There were some black nationalist groups for whom the white man was the enemy, plain and simple—and not just the Nation of Islam. But the influence of the Panthers and their writings and their papers made me ask, "What is the relationship between racial injustice and economic injustice?" Or they would often say more bluntly, racism and capitalism. They would often talk about international issues. So, you could say that the assassination of Martin Luther King helped prepare the way for my becoming radicalized in a certain way. It prepared me to renegotiate how I viewed these things, you know.

After the riots Baltimore went through the kinds of changes a lot of cities went through. It was after '68—well, who knows when it really started—that a sizable white flight got to be noticeable. I think it was after '68 that the city became predominantly black. When I was growing up, it was, I'm told, 60 percent white, 35 percent, 40 percent black, something like that. I remember shortly after the riots, a teacher, a white teacher, said that the city was about half and half. I don't know how accurate her figures were, but that's what she said. But going to the seventies, more white people left the city. This is before the black middle-class flight, of course. And gradually a number of the schools that were in the city that had been predominantly white became predominantly black, or if they were predominantly black and had a sizable white population, then the white population became less sizable. And obviously, the complexion of some neighborhoods changed.[13] I didn't notice this so much in my neighborhood—it was already black. There were a few white people who lived there. Are there any now? I don't know—there may be. I was driving through yesterday, and I saw something that you did not see in those days. And that is interracial couples. I can remember a time when that was a real eye stopper. When I was coming up, it just didn't happen—maybe it was illegal. But then during the seventies, that became more noticeable, at least in certain parts of town.[14]

As for the businesses in my neighborhood, buildings that were destroyed were boarded up, and some of them were never rebuilt. There was one Jewish store owner on Eager and Valley streets; that's a block or two down from the one on Asquith Street that I saw attacked. They, I understand, had been attacked too, but not damaged as much. They recuperated, remained for awhile, but eventually retired in the seventies, maybe early eighties. There was a place—I think they were said to be German—up on Madison or Monument Street. They were demolished, they never returned. When it reopened, some black guy who had married a Korean woman took it over.

There were a number of businesses that began to take on the cultural symbols of black consciousness or black nationalism. Some would have the red, black, and green insignia in their stores. A number of barbershops would have pictures of distinguished black people, whether it was the Kings or Malcolm or Angela Davis. There was a barber shop which appeared where what is now the Oldtown Mall. You'd go in the barber shop and see pictures of Marcus Garvey and Malcolm X.[15] One of the outcomes of this is that eventually most of the white businesses, at least the store owners, disappeared from the area. The larger ones near Oldtown were able to hang on, I guess because they had more capital, but they eventually reopened with black owners.

Of course, there are a lot of places boarded up now, but that can't be explained by '68. That's something else that's going on. In the area where I grew up, they've torn down most of the buildings. The market's gone, the stores that were there are all gone. There are fewer businesses there now than there were after the riots. I suppose it has to do with things like gentrification, and probably small or medium-size businesses being edged out by larger chains. I remember there were more small businesses around, regardless of their ethnic mix. There were more movie houses around. There were movie houses in even the poorest neighborhoods. And there were all sorts of movie houses all over downtown, which I heard had been segregated.[16] But they were there until sometime in the eighties. I'm reluctant to say that the riots exactly caused these businesses to leave because much of that has happened quite a bit of time after that. I'm not sure whether 1968 helped it along, but it doesn't explain it. Maybe indirectly, white flight has something to do with it.

King's assassination was an event that changed a lot of people. In a way it changed all of us. For some people, it was the beginning of their awakening. For some people, it might have been the beginning of their radicalization. It created a situation where there's no going back. One thing, of course, is that I, unlike most of my contemporaries, did end up going to college and eventually even to graduate school.[17] Graduate school meant a predominantly white, very upper-class, private school in the South, which wouldn't have happened without the civil rights movement. Pursuing an education affects ways in which you view the world. While in the universities I met not only, of course, white people but people from different countries, people from the Middle East, from Latin America. I've met people whose families were refugees from El Salvador because of that mess that happened down there in the eighties. I've met people in the seventies who had been in Soweto during the fight with apartheid.[18] Over time you could say my view of the world became more globalized, both by meeting people and just by studying. My understanding of the world became a bit more complex.

So, for example, now I tend to look at things like the institutional basis of power, rather than saying it's simply the white man. Things aren't quite that simple, particularly when I look at things like social and economic justice. One of the things made possible no doubt by the 1960s is that there are some black people, mainly from the elite, who are also involved in the game of injustice. So you've got to reexamine things.

We're naturally sensitive to the injustice we experience, but it's important we realize there's a lot of injustice, and it's all over the country and all over the world. There's a certain sense in which I'm always rooted in the African American community and African American experience, but I also think of injustice in a global way. Beginning with that experience and dealing with that, I eventually got to a point where I could be sympathetic to the situation of people in Latin America, for example. I've had people ask me about El Salvador, "Are they black people?" Well, there are some black people there. The thing is that there's injustice there. As Dr. King says, "Injustice anywhere is a threat to justice everywhere." That's a saying of his which has become part of my conviction.

Could it happen again? Of course, it could happen again. I wouldn't look forward to it happening again. One thing that I'm thinking about more and more now is Dr. King's Poor People's Campaign—that's what he was involved in before he was killed.[19] He was working toward certain things he wanted to present to the government as necessities. One was going to be an economic bill of rights, because there's a Bill of Rights, but it's not an economic bill of rights. And this would obviously have an impact on the black community, with the high rates of poverty, but he thought that he could unify a large part of the American population around this idea, because there's no group that doesn't have to deal with poverty or economic injustice. Since I mentioned the Panthers—this is an unlikely parallel, but it's interesting that the Panthers also were opposed to rioting. People don't know that, oh yeah, but for a different reason. Actually, Huey Newton[20] and Martin Luther King both agreed that at the end of the day, unless something, some new initiative, comes out of it, it turns out to be fruitless. If nothing in terms of either organizing or mobilizing or conscientizing or politicizing or educating, if nothing comes out of that, then it's useless and people die for nothing. And so King thought that riots were fruitless. The Panthers weren't exactly committed to the philosophy of nonviolence; they simply thought undisciplined, disorganized violence is ineffective. If you have a riot and then you go home and things go back to the way they were, at least in the sense of the objective conditions of people's lives, then we haven't gotten very far. Now some people may have been inspired by the riots of the sixties to try to do some things. And that's fine, but riots in and of themselves produce very little. You know, there has to be the long-term commitment to community and the fight for social justice.

Edited by Linda Shopes

NOTES

1. Mergenthaler Vocational–Technical Senior High School is a public high school and trade school in Baltimore. Before the Supreme Court's 1954 *Brown v. Board of Education* ruling that segregated school systems were illegal, it was a whites-only school. Although integrated after the *Brown* decision, its student body remained mostly white for at least two decades; its black student body increased only as the city itself became increasingly African American.

2. King visited Baltimore several times between 1953 and 1966. Birt is probably referring to his visit of April 22, 1966, when he spoke to Methodist clergy at the Baltimore Civic Center. Birmingham and Selma, Alabama, had been key sites of the struggle against racial segregation and for civil rights in the early to mid-1960s.

3. Theophilus "Bull" Connor (1897–1973) was police commissioner in Birmingham, Alabama, during the civil rights movement. He employed fire hoses, attack dogs, and other extreme measures against civil rights protesters. During the Southern Christian Leadership Conference's 1963 Birmingham Campaign, he authorized the use of these methods against demonstrating children and young people.

4. In the summer of 1967, deadly race riots broke out in both Newark, New Jersey, and Detroit, Michigan. Birt is referring to the Detroit riot, which began in

the early morning of July 23, after police raided an after-hours drinking club in a predominantly black neighborhood, arresting dozens of patrons. At the end of five days of rioting, 43 people were dead, 467 were injured, and more than 7,200 had been arrested. More than two thousand buildings were burned.

5. Thomas J. D'Alesandro III (1929–) was the Democratic mayor of Baltimore from 1967 to 1971.

6. Although Peter Levy in Chapter 1 notes that "Baltimore's police department, unlike those in nearly all other cities, was making strides toward overcoming the racial divide" (p. 15), there is no doubt that in 1968 the racial divide, rooted in a history of segregation within the police force and antagonistic relations between police and the African American community, remained firmly in place.

7. The pedestrian-only Oldtown Mall was developed in the mid-1970s, on the site of the old commercial corridor along East Baltimore's Gay Street. Many stores on Gay Street were looted and burned during the 1968 riot, and the incident Birt is describing likely took place on or near Gay Street.

8. Governor Spiro Agnew activated the Maryland National Guard shortly after 10:00 P.M. on Saturday, April 6, two hours after he had declared an official state of emergency. On Sunday, April 7, President Lyndon Johnson authorized the use of federal forces to join the National Guard. In all, nearly eleven thousand troops were deployed in the city over a period of approximately a week. An initial curfew was imposed from 11:00 P.M. on Saturday, April 6, to 6:00 A.M. Sunday, April 7. A 4:00 P.M. curfew was in effect on Sunday, April 7, and Monday, April 8. On Tuesday, April 9, the curfew was relaxed, starting at 7:00 P.M. and ending at 5:00 A.M. Wednesday, April 10. The curfew was lifted on Thursday, April 11.

9. Baltimore city schools were closed on Monday, April 8, as were city offices, per order of the mayor, who had declared that day an official day of mourning for Martin Luther King. Although schools reopened the next day, Birt's memory of "being out for a while" probably reflects the fact that he, like many students, remained out of school for some days. Or perhaps in retrospect, the enormity of events leads him to think he must have stayed out of school for some time, when, in fact, he did not.

10. King wrote this open letter on April 16, 1963, after being arrested and jailed during nonviolent civil rights protests in Birmingham, Alabama.

11. Birt is referring to the Iraq War, begun on March 20, 2003, when U.S. troops led an invasion of Iraq on the grounds that it possessed weapons of mass destruction. The war was ongoing at the time of the interview, despite evidence that the country did not, in fact, possess such weapons.

12. Malcolm X (né Little, 1925–1965) was a minister and national spokesman for the Nation of Islam and, after becoming disaffected with that organization, his own Muslim Mosque. James Baldwin (1924–1987) and Richard Wright (1908–1960) were African American writers whose work addresses both racial and sexual themes.

13. As Peter Levy in Chapter 1 of this volume suggests, white flight and racial change in Baltimore were well under way by 1968, and the impact of the riots on these processes is unclear. In 1950 blacks composed just under one-fourth of the city's population (19.3 percent); in 1960, just over one-third (34.7 percent); in 1970, almost half (46.4 percent). During the same twenty-year period, the population of surrounding Baltimore County more than doubled, while the number of African Americans remained nearly stable; the percentage of black residents in the county therefore declined from 6.6 to 2.7 between 1950 and 1970.

14. Maryland law prohibited blacks, Filipinos (Malays), and Asians from marrying whites until 1967, when the law was repealed.

15. Angela Davis (1944–) is a scholar-activist who was active in the Black Panther Party in the 1960s and 1970s and, most controversially, in the Communist Party. Marcus Garvey (1887–1940) is best known as the founder of the Universal Negro Improvement Association and African Communities League, which advocated black nationalism and Pan-Africanism in the early twentieth century.

16. By the late 1950s, most Baltimore movie theaters were open to black patrons, although seating may have been segregated. In 1963 the Maryland General Assembly enacted an open accommodations law, outlawing segregation by race in public places, including theaters, in Baltimore and twelve of Maryland's twenty-three counties. In 1964 open accommodations were extended to the remaining counties.

17. Birt received his doctorate in philosophy from Vanderbilt University in Nashville, Tennessee.

18. Civil war waged in El Salvador between 1980 and 1992, pitting the right-wing military government against a coalition of rebellious left-wing militias. More than seventy thousand people, many of them noncombatants, were killed during the war, many by government agents in brutal violation of their human rights. Soweto was a designated black township near Johannesburg, South Africa, during that country's apartheid regime. Home to many antiapartheid activists, it was the site of numerous protests against apartheid, including the Soweto Uprising in June 1976, in which black students and their supporters protested the government's policy of requiring instruction to be conducted solely in Africaans and English.

19. Martin Luther King and the Southern Christian Leadership Conference initiated the Poor People's Campaign in late 1967, seeking, as Birt explains, a biracial, multiethnic movement for economic justice. Its economic bill of rights called for a federal jobs program, unemployment insurance, a fair minimum wage, better housing, and education for the poor. The campaign continued after King's assassination, culminating in a march from Mississippi to Washington, D.C., where participants demonstrated and lobbied federal agencies for more than a month. Resurrection City, a makeshift settlement of tents and shacks along the Mall, housed the demonstrators. There they ate, slept, strategized, and made visible the plight of poor people in America. The campaign exacted some small concessions from the federal government, but its broader call for economic justice was unheeded.

20. Huey Newton (1942–1989) was a political activist and cofounder, with Bobby Seale, of the Black Panther Party in 1966. He served as the party's minister of Defense.

Epilogue

History and Memory

Why It Matters That We Remember

Clement Alexander Price

I am delighted to contribute to this important volume, generated by new and old colleagues and friends who have made such a uniquely Baltimore contribution to historical literacy and civic culture through their efforts.

This anthology, and indeed the series of initiatives that together comprise Baltimore '68: Riots and Rebirth, at once an example of public intellectual work and civic engagement, was easier imagined than accomplished. Such public assemblies and the lasting scholarship they generate require a great deal of planning, even as the customary academic and civic duties of the planners go forward.

Funding, always a challenge, is hard to come by. To be sure, programs such as this one require a blend of civic fearlessness and civic courage. Not everyone wants to walk through the past, especially when the past is riddled with anxiety, destruction, and fire bells in the night.

When the Newark campus of Rutgers University, where I have taught for many years, got involved in establishing a credible public platform for scholarship and civic engagement, funding was scarce (it still is), and few members of the faculty imagined themselves to be public scholars.

Thinking out loud about the riots in the public sphere at the time was discouraged, especially so by the corporate elites and, interestingly enough, by black elected officials, all of whom surely knew that their ascent in public life was in large part attributable to the upheavals of the late 1960s.

The Baltimore phase office of the Poor People's Campaign, at 604 Mosher Street, in mourning. (Originally published in the *Baltimore Afro-American*, April 9, 1968. Reprinted courtesy of the *Afro-American Newspapers* Archives and Research Center.)

The works in this volume build on an obvious turn in the fortunes of higher education and its role in the civic sphere. What was accomplished over the course of the three-day public convening of Baltimore '68 in April 2008 could not, would not, have been possible a generation ago, at least not in most American cities.

We are witnesses to a transformation in American memory. First and foremost, the memory of conflict in American history and race relations is now a part of the normal rhythm of scholarship. We expect that when historians, humanists, activists, and journalists interrogate America's past they will find what Thomas Jefferson observed many decades ago: that democracy is messy.

By April 4, 2008, the fortieth anniversary of Dr. King's death and of the spasm of violence that followed, we were arguably better prepared than ever to look into the past without shielding our eyes from its harsh realities.

Not unlike previous generations of Americans, we are living through a period in which the need to remember, in both personal and collective terms, is in high relief. In the past, Americans remembered, often agonizingly so, the nation's wars, its cyclical episodes of democratic momentum, its monumentalized leaders, and especially, its episodes of social unrest.

As a historian, my thinking about the past was as much influenced by the civil rights movement as it was by the rise of the so-called new American history. Much of my career has considered the remembered narrative of slavery, the great migration of blacks from the South to imagined promised lands in the North, the civil rights movement, and more recently, the articulation of race and blackness in American history in the public sphere.

The centrality of memory in American culture and history has never been as evident as it is now. Our times are exceptional for what Yale

Maryland National Guardsmen thanking residents of Baltimore for their cooperation. (Originally published in the *Baltimore Afro-American*, April 14, 1968. Reprinted courtesy of the *Baltimore News American* Collection, University of Maryland–College Park.)

historian David Blight calls the "memory boom." At a conference at Rutgers in February 2007, Professor Blight argued that the slaughter-filled twentieth century, the general enhancement of education among a huge swath of Americans, the intensity of Holocaust studies, the new American history's emphasis on the lives of ordinary people, and the ascendancy of African American historical scholarship accounts for the boom in our memory, or in our quest for it.

To Blight's list, I add accessibility to new technologies in communication, especially in making more widely available still and moving images of Americans in the modern age. Images encourage memory. Images preserved over time can hasten reconsideration of old memories.

Consider, for example, the role of coaxial cable in documenting the life and times of Dr. King and the modern civil rights movement. More to the point, Henry Hampton's magisterial documentary film *Eyes on the Prize* has had an extraordinary impact on American public memory. It generated scholarly interest in the movement and stirred memories of America's domestic battlegrounds and the sadness associated with human deprivation and loss.

How do the memories of Americans unfold? To what purpose can they be placed? Private memories are sacrosanct—"Don't mess with my momma's memory," as David Blight has said. Historians David Thelen and Roy Rosensweig have shown that private memories—enshrined in remembered conversations with elders, in family photos, and in other aspects of private life—connect us, not to history as such, but to an intimate past that belongs to the individual, not to the historian.

Baltimore '68's public convening was a time when private memories swirled around our communities, especially for those who bore witness to the life and times of Dr. King. Many of that generation remembered their private sadness, others their rage and confusion over what the future might look like without Dr. King. For my part, I remember the news as if it were yesterday. For nearly two weeks, I had very little to say to my white classmates at the University of Bridgeport. While I knew they were not responsible for Dr. King's death, I also realized that they did not know—how could they?—how deeply painful his death was to me and to the other black students on campus.

Public memory is negotiated over time. It is sustained and often overly embellished by commemoration. The historian John Bodnar argues that for the longest time, especially in the twentieth century, public memory was grandly constructed. It sought to foster patriotism, social order, and public discipline. Public memory seeks social control.

Public memory is always in a state of flux. It is negotiated and contested, often an extension of the conflicts out of which it arises. As examples, consider the controversies surrounding the Smithsonian Institution's Enola Gay exhibition and the initial reception given Maya Lin's Vietnam Veterans Memorial.

On the local level, public memory seems to be more navigable. On the community level, the scale of what is remembered by residents is manageable. A locale can reconcile past differences as a part of marketing its virtues and its past, as happened, for example, after the Atlanta race riot of 1906 and the so-called Liberation of Conklin Hall at Rutgers University–Newark, when, on February 24, 1969, two dozen black students barricaded themselves in a classroom building and made demands that ultimately forged a closer relationship between the university and a city that was well on its way to becoming predominantly black and brown.

Public memory is increasingly challenged by scholarship and by the democratization of memory. We are far more concerned than ever before over what might be called our segregated memories. My Newark colleagues journalist Brad Parks and sociologist Max Herman have shown us that when it comes to the civil disorders—the riots—in Newark in 1967, the memory of those days, and that era, is predicated on race, neighborhood, and the perception of civic propriety.

The chapters included here give us an opportunity to confront the dif-ulty of remembering civil unrest and the racial discord that lay at the root of what happened in Baltimore and other cities forty-plus years ago. They represent the contested territory that is history and memory.

Congresswoman Maxine Waters observed on April 30, 1992, on NBC's *Today Show*, "Whether we like it or not, riot is the voice of the unheard." That statement, made soon after the Rodney King riots in Los Angeles, probably angered far more Americans than it encouraged, and yet the congresswoman may have a point. When we don't hear the voices from the past, especially those voices at the margins of society, our perception of history is skewed. For over a generation, historians have persuasively argued that all voices from the nation's historical narratives ultimately matter, especially during periods of conflict or tragedy or when the nation attempts to confront a common crisis or objective.

My first public foray into community memory and its discontents came more than ten years ago, during the thirtieth anniversary of Newark's 1967 riots, known to some as the Newark rebellion. At the inaugural program of Memory and Newark, July 1997, the Rutgers Institute on Ethnicity, Culture, and the Modern Experience assembled an audience of over four hundred citizens from throughout the greater Newark metropolitan area. In short, those proceedings revealed how, over time, personal and civic memories are both contextualized and marshaled into a call for reconciliation.

Long before the nearly catastrophic events of the late 1960s, civic memory was being shaped by transformations in the daily rhythms of ordinary people and in the buildup of American cities. The reshaping of private and public lives—which included the physical and social devastation of old neighborhoods—was symptomatic of the decline of cities and the reconfiguration of contemporary metropolitan territories. Increasingly, after World War II the American city became contested territory, framed over time by more complicated memories by blacks, ethnic whites, and those entrusted with public policy.

One's race, generation, social class, and civic vantage point all contribute to the making of civic memory. Civic memory emerges out of the social landscape of the community writ large. It acknowledges that citizens and settlers usually remember what is most important to their personal lives and to the emotional fabric of their own families and neighbors.

Civic memory is not immediately encumbered by scholarly scrutiny. It is best sustained and burnished in local institutions—libraries, museums, colleges, universities, and so on—though I for one would be pleased if an American city would create a mayor's commission on memory. Such a body, it seems to me, would help its city hall pay better attention to the rhythms of civic life and the way that memory frames local discussion about the legacy of urban renewal, demographic transformation, and alas, the city's awkward relationship with surrounding suburbs. Short of such a commission, I am delighted that this anthology has taken shape so well.

Bringing the memories of a cross section of citizens into the public sphere is important and increasingly necessary for communities and cities to be able to move forward. We need to account for the memories of nearly invisible citizens and settlers, those from whom we have heard too little. Their memories help challenge their invisibility in the past. Their memories also pry open our civic imagination as to how memory can shed light on what cannot be known through traditional modes of historical inquiry. Memory matters in reconciling civic discord.

As an example, at Memory and Newark, July 1997, Paula Bornstein remembered that a group of inner-city black men on Hawthorne Avenue protected her parents' tailoring shop, standing outside it while many buildings along the street were looted and burned. It mattered that Abram and Ida Bornstein, survivors of the Holocaust, came to Newark, willing to live in a black neighborhood and willing to treat black patrons with respect. Mostly, Paula Bornstein remembered, her parents "feared Hungarians, not Negroes."

Civic memory takes us deeply into the realm of community emotions, into the essence of what people feel most deeply about. In February 2008 the Rutgers Institute of Ethnicity, Culture, and the Modern Experience mounted a day-long conference in Newark, "Private Grief, Public Mourning in African American Life and History." In planning the conference we were primarily interested in exploring, in a public setting, how the private grief that followed the death of Dr. King and other far more anonymous civil rights movement martyrs mattered in contemporary American life. Bernice Johnson Reagon delivered the keynote lecture. Her presentation focused not so much on Dr. King's death and the sadness unleashed forty years ago. Primarily, she narrated the meaning of lives well lived in the struggle for social justice and the swift inevitability of death. In word and song juxtaposing life, death, and memory, Dr. Reagon turned an audience of over five hundred into citizens galvanized by the memory of private grief—grief over Dr. King, of course, but also private grief displayed openly. For my part, I saw something I have not seen in quite a while: whites, blacks, and browns weeping together in a public space.

Civic memory may indeed embolden a community's search for what can unify disparate interests. Our memories of what we saw in the late 1960s, or thought we saw, are repeated again and again, giving traction to convictions about then-young lives, the aspirations of those years, and for many of us, the collapse of those aspirations.

Sigmund Freud once observed that memory becomes less efficient with age. But civic memory, navigated over time by a cacophony of citizens, enhances the efficiency of public work. This volume, containing those unheard voices who were heard by the authors here, is a testament to this fact.

Contributors

Howell S. Baum is a professor in the Urban Studies and Planning Program at the University of Maryland–College Park. He has conducted research on Baltimore school desegregation, race, and community action for school reform. His most recent book is Brown *in Baltimore: School Desegregation and the Limits of Liberalism* (2010).

John R. Breihan has taught history at Loyola University Maryland since 1977 and is a coeditor of *From Mobtown to Charm City: New Perspectives on Baltimore's Past*. Among his interests are planning history, aviation, historic preservation, and British history.

Alex Csicsek, a Baltimore native, holds a bachelor of arts degree in history from the University of Maryland–College Park, where he studied Maryland history. He lives and works in the United Kingdom.

Jessica I. Elfenbein is an associate provost and professor of history and community studies at the University of Baltimore. She directed the prize-winning Baltimore '68: Riots and Rebirth project and is the author of *Civics, Commerce, and Community: The History of the Greater Washington Board of Trade, 1889–1989* and *The Making of a Modern City: Philanthropy, Civic Culture, and the Baltimore YMCA*. She is also a coeditor of *From Mobtown to Charm City: New Perspectives on Baltimore's Past*.

Francesca Gamber is a Baltimore native who earned her doctorate in historical studies at Southern Illinois University–Carbondale. Her research focuses on nineteenth- and twentieth-century African American history, and her work has been published in *Slavery and Abolition* and several edited collections. She is the AmeriCorps coordinator for the Community Art Corps at Maryland Institute College of Art, where she is also an adjunct faculty member.

Howard F. Gillette, Jr., a professor of history at Rutgers University–Camden, specializes in U.S. urban history with an emphasis on planning and issues of social justice. His most recent publication is *Civitas by Design: Building Better Communities, from the Garden City to the New Urbanism* (2010).

Thomas L. Hollowak is associate director for Special Collections at the University of Baltimore's Langsdale Library. He created and maintains the Baltimore '68: Riots and Rebirth website and is the author of *University of Baltimore* and a coeditor of *From Mobtown to Charm City: New Perspectives on Baltimore's Past*.

Peter B. Levy is chair of the History and Political Science Department at York College of Pennsylvania, where he teaches courses on recent America and the civil rights movement. He has published nine books, including *Civil War on Race Street: The Civil Rights Movement in Cambridge, Maryland* and *The New Left and Labor in the 1960s*. He was a scholar in residence at the University of Baltimore in 2007, where he worked on the Baltimore '68: Riots and Rebirth project.

Emily Lieb earned her doctorate in history from Columbia University. Her dissertation, "Row House City: Unbuilding Residential Baltimore, 1940–1980," was nominated for the Bancroft Dissertation Award. She lives in Seattle and teaches at Seattle University.

Elizabeth M. Nix is an assistant professor in the Division of Legal, Ethical, and Historical Studies and director of the Community Studies and Civic Engagement program at the University of Baltimore. She teaches courses on public history and the history of race relations in America and oversaw the collection of oral histories for the Baltimore '68: Riots and Rebirth project.

W. Edward Orser is a professor of American studies at the University of Maryland–Baltimore County. He is the author of *Blockbusting in Baltimore: The Edmondson Village Story* (1994), *The Gwynns Falls: Baltimore Gateway to the Chesapeake Bay* (2008), and numerous articles on community and the environment, particularly in the Baltimore area. During the spring 2008 semester, he and Joby Taylor team-taught a course on the civil rights and the peace movements in the 1960s, which resulted in the chapter that they contributed to this volume.

Mary Potorti is a doctoral candidate in American and New England studies at Boston University, where she teaches courses in women's and American studies. She is a native of Baltimore and a graduate of Catonsville High School and the University of Maryland, Baltimore County.

Clement Alexander Price is Board of Governors Distinguished Service Professor of History and director of the Institute on Ethnicity, Culture, and the Modern Experience at Rutgers University–Newark. An authority on the history of African

Americans in New Jersey, Price is the author of *Freedom Not Far Distant: A Documentary History of Afro-Americans in New Jersey* (1980) and numerous other scholarly works. He has received many awards for academic and community service.

Linda Shopes is a freelance developmental editor and consultant in oral and public history. She has written widely on both fields. Currently, she coedits Palgrave Macmillan's Studies in Oral History series and is a coeditor of *Oral History and Public Memories* (2008) and *The Baltimore Book: New Views of Local History* (1991), both published by Temple University Press. She has also served as president of the U.S. Oral History Association.

Joby Taylor is director of the Shriver Peaceworker Fellows Program and an affiliate faculty member in the Language, Literacy, and Culture Program at the University of Maryland–Baltimore County. He is the author of *Metaphors We Serve By: Critical and Constructive Play with the Discourses on Service, National Service, and Service-Learning*, a collection of essays investigating the history and future of service-learning. He teaches courses across a number of disciplines, applying strategies of place-based learning and service-learning to engage students in Baltimore communities.

Deborah R. Weiner is research historian at the Jewish Museum of Maryland in Baltimore, where she curates exhibitions and edits publications on Baltimore Jewish history. She has taught classes in public history and American Jewish history at the University of Baltimore and the University of Maryland–Baltimore County. She is the author of *Coalfield Jews: An Appalachian History* (2006).

Index

African Americans: black nationalism, 210, 217, 221, 253–254; businesses, 4–5, 43, 190, 194, 210; civil rights, 27, 36, 76, 80, 90, 125, 156, 172, 210, 247, 255, 260; Governor's Youth Council, 72; militants, 16–18, 76, 80, 91, 103, 160, 211, 255; professionals, 190; socioeconomic conditions, 12–14, 18–20, 35, 39, 51, 66, 72–73, 77, 128, 181, 183–184
Afro-American newspaper, 26–30, 66, 72, 135, 155, 158, 162, 164–165, 168, 190; George Collins, 30–31; Washington edition, 29
Agnew, Spiro T., 7, 16, 19–21, 37, 96, 136, 154, 159–161, 171–172, 211
Alinsky, Saul, 213–214
American Civil Liberties Union (ACLU), 125
American Institute of Architects (AIA), 226–228, 230–231; Philadelphia chapter, 227–228, 241; Urban Design Committee, 229–230
American Institute of Planners, 231
Archdiocese of Baltimore, 233, 235

Bailey, Troy, 77
Baily, Jack, 228
Baker, Ella, 213
Baltimore: Board of Municipal Zoning Appeals, 238; Canton, 35, 167, 169; Capitol Theater plan, 233–234; central, 210–212, 215–216, 218–220; Charles Center, 180; Civic Center, 9, 56, 247; Community Action Commission (CAC), 15; Community Relations Commission, 11, 13, 15, 161; Department of Housing and Community Development, 200–201; Downtown Committee, 54–56, 60; East, 3–4, 7–9, 16, 18, 28, 71, 93, 105, 159, 182, 246, 249; ethnic groups, 28, 86–88, 90, 150–151, 183–185, 199, 217, 235, 254; Fairfield, 239–240; Greater Baltimore Committee, 60; Guildford, 216; Hampden, 218–219; Highlandtown, 28; Housing Authority, 40–42, 44, 65; Inner Harbor, 39, 183; Little Italy, 149; Mechanic Theater, 180; mid-town, 128, 147, 237, 239–240; northeast, 240; northwest, 26, 92, 104, 147, 183; Oldtown Mall, 249–250, 254; Park Heights, 212; Pigtown, 86; Pilot Program, 104–107; Planning Commission, 52, 54–56, 238; Planning Department, 234–235, 238; Rosemont,

Baltimore (*continued*)
52, 57–59, 61–66; South, 40, 238; southeast, 165; southwest, 235, 237; urban renewal, 4, 16, 54, 56, 60, 65, 104, 107, 194; Waverly, 211; West, 4, 7–8, 109, 129, 150–151, 187, 188–193, 211, 235–236
Baltimoreans United in Leadership Development (BUILD), 213
Baltimore County, 32, 72, 78–79, 150, 209; Board of Zoning Appeals, 78; Gwynn Oak Park, 81, 125–126, 132–133, 157; Human Relations Commission, 80, 82
Baltimore Four, 131, 136
Baltimore Sun, 45, 52, 71, 127, 138, 141, 187, 233–234
Baxter, Augustus, 241
Berrigan, Daniel, 130–131, 133
Berrigan, Philip, 128, 130–135, 137
Black Panthers, 91, 220, 233–234, 253
Black Power movement, 16, 103, 117, 123–124, 127, 137, 172, 211, 218
Bowie, William B., 79
Bowie State College, 18, 30–32, 35–36, 52, 54, 56–59, 63, 81–82, 246. *See also* University of Maryland
Bradby, Robert, 3, 16–17
Brain, George, 157–158
Bresler, Charles, 75, 81
Brown, H. Rap, 77, 91
Brown, James, 9
Buckley, William, 16

Carmichael, Stokely, 16–18, 75, 77, 127, 160, 211
Carter, Walter, 124–131
Catonsville Nine, 123, 130–132, 135, 137
Cherry Hill, 8, 18–19; Cherry Hill Homes, 40–42, 43; Cherry Hill Protective Association, 43; Cherry Hill Shopping Center, 39, 43, 45; Cherry Hill Village, 40; homeownership rates, 40–41, 44; liquor stores, 42–43
Chin, Alexander, 135
CIA, 33
Civil disturbances. *See* Riots
Community Design Center, San Francisco, 228, 240
Congress of Racial Equality (CORE), 16–17, 91, 123–130, 132–137, 156, 158, 160; Target City program, 127–129, 136, 158
Cook, Richard, 218–219
Crain, Robert, 212
Crew, John, 164, 169–170

D'Alesandro, Thomas, III, 7, 16, 64–65, 96, 149, 159, 161–162, 209, 211, 248–249
Daneker, David, 170
Daniels, Samuel, 162–163
Darst, David, 130, 135
DeSalvo, Al, 229
Dilts, James D., 52, 57, 127, 233–234
Dobson, Vernon, 113
Dortch, Esther, 184–185

Eberhart, David, 135
Echo House, 233–235
Edsall, Thomas, 189–190, 193
Eisenhower, Milton, 216

Fairfield Improvement Association, 238
Fair housing, 126, 128, 129, 132
Farmer, James, 127, 133
FBI, 17, 33
Federal Housing Administration (FHA), 65
Fischer, John, 155

Gant, Danny, 127, 136
Gelston, George M., 8, 15, 32, 72, 74–75
Gibson, Larry, 162–163
Glenn, David L., 13, 161
Goldwater, Barry, 17
Grady, J. Harold, 58
Grant, Daniel, 17, 136
The Greater Homewood Community Project (GHCP), 209, 211–212, 214–215
Griffin, James, 136, 158, 162–163

Hackerman, Irvin, 169
Harris, William "Box," 8, 15–16
Health, Education, and Welfare, Department of (HEW), 159, 164, 166–170
Hess, Harry, 234
Highways: East-West Expressway, 189; Interstate 83, 214; Jones Falls Expressway, 196, 210
Hogan, John, 130, 135
Holmes, Peter, 164, 167, 169
Housing and Urban Development, Department of (HUD), 234–236
Hughes, Langston, 18
Humphrey, Hubert, 218

Interdenominational Ministerial Alliance, 79–80, 159

Jackson, Lillie May, 77
Jackson, Viola, 105
Jews, 10, 161, 164, 182, 195; businesses, 4, 10, 19, 115, 145–147, 151, 182–187, 189–191, 195–200, 202, 211, 254, 264
Johns Hopkins University, 209–210, 212, 215, 218
Johnson, Doris M., 232–233, 237–238, 240
Johnson, Lyndon B., 7, 16, 20, 124, 126, 136, 160, 214, 217–218, 230
Johnson, Max, 74
Jones, Ross, 209, 212, 215–216
Joseph, Mark, 169–170

Karwacki, Robert, 163
Katkow, Herman, 189, 191–193, 202
Kennedy, John F., 33, 98, 218
Kennedy, Robert F., 28, 33, 136
Kerner Commission, 6, 16, 19, 21, 80, 82, 112, 115, 208
King, Martin Luther, Jr., 11–12, 37–38, 71, 90–91, 96–97, 122, 133, 162, 185, 210, 247, 252, 254–256, 261–262; assassination, 3, 5, 17–19, 21, 28, 33, 39, 62, 79, 91, 99, 103, 112, 117, 123–124, 128, 131, 135–136, 147, 154, 159–160, 166, 208–210, 213, 217, 229, 246, 248–254, 260, 262, 264; March on Washington, 125; Poor People's Campaign, 13, 33, 115, 122, 213, 217, 255
Kline, Dea, 212, 215
Kreitner, Ronald, 234–237

Lamb, Charles, 229
Lewis, Thomas, 130–135, 137
Liss, Solomon, 16–17
Lively, Walter H., 13, 17, 234

Macht, Philip, 163
Marshall, Howard, 170
McCarthy, Eugene, 136
McKeldin, Theodore R., 55, 61, 127, 158, 209
McKissick, Floyd, 158
McNeely, Joseph, 214, 217, 219–220
Melville, John and Marjorie, 130, 135
Meyerhoff, Joseph, 128
Mid-City Development Corporation, 4, 149–150, 198, 200
Mikulski, Barbara, 164, 214
Mills, Barbara, 124–125, 128, 132, 134
Milspaugh, Martin, 104
Mische, George, 130, 135
Mitchell, Clarence, 70, 155
Mitchell, Clarence, III, 8
Mitchell, Juanita Jackson, 77, 155
Mitchell, Parren, 15, 65, 167
Model Cities Program, 12, 234
Moore, Robert, 13, 17
Morgan State College, 27, 114–115, 125, 156, 215
Moses, Robert, 55–58
Moss, Elizabeth Murphy, 162–163
Movement against Destruction (MAD), 61
Moylan, Mary, 130, 135
Mumford, Kevin, 208–209
Murnaghan, Francis, 162–163
Murphy, Carl, 155
Myerberg, Edward and Julius, 40, 43

NAACP, 40, 74, 77, 80, 91, 124, 126, 155, 157–161, 164, 213, 217
Nafzinger, Clyde, 111–112
National Guard, 4, 6–10, 15, 19, 29, 32, 44, 63, 72, 75, 93–96, 149, 160, 185, 211, 249–250, 261
National Organization of Minority Architects, 228
National Urban League, 40, 124, 126, 226
Nixon, Richard M., 20, 73–74, 82, 217–218, 221, 239
Northeast Community Organization (NECO), 213
Northrop, Edward, 169

O'Connor, William, 135
Office of Economic Opportunity (OEO), 228, 231
O'Malley, David, 229, 232, 234, 239
Orlinsky, Walter, 167

Pappas, Dean, 135
Paquin, Lawrence, 158
Patterson, Roland, 163–164, 167, 169–170
Pennsylvania Avenue–Lafayette Market Association (PALMA), 191–193, 205
Pinderhughes, Alice, 170
Pomerleau, Donald, 7
Poulard, Grady, 228
Prince George's County (MD), 240
Provident Hospital, 4–5
Public housing projects: Flag House Courts, 183–187; Lafayette, 250; Latrobe Homes, 246, 249–250. *See also* Baltimore; Cherry Hill

Ramsey, Norman, 169
Relocation Action Movement, 61
Riots, 263; Atlanta, 262; Chicago, 3, 19, 208; Detroit, 9, 51, 92–93, 208–209, 248; Harlem, 51; Los Angeles, 263; Louisville, 51; Minneapolis, 208; Newark, 51, 209, 262–264; Washington, D.C., 3, 5–6, 29–30, 92–93; Watts, 9, 51
Roemer, John, 125–126
Rouse, James, 104, 229
Russell, George, 16, 161–162

Schaefer, William Donald, 61, 162–164, 167–169, 172, 181, 209, 237
School desegregation: *Adams v. Richardson*, 164; *Brown v. Board of Education*, 4, 14–16, 154, 161–162, 164, 166, 189, 209, 219; busing, 164; *Green v. New Kent County*, 161–162; Southeast Desegregation Coalition, 164–165; *Swann v. Charlotte-Mecklenburg*, 163, 219
Scott, Dorothy, 184–185
Sheldon, Thomas, 162–163, 172
Singer, Sharon Pats, 196–197, 199
Sondheim, Walter, 155
South East Community Organization (SECO), 164, 214, 220
Southern Christian Leadership Conference (SCLC), 213
Stanton, Phoebe, 238
Student Nonviolent Coordinating Committee (SNCC), 13, 16–17, 91, 136, 160, 211, 213, 217, 220
Students for a Democratic Society (SDS), 126, 134, 213, 217; Economic Research Action Project (ERAP), 213, 217
Sussman, Seymour, 191–192, 194–195
Swensson, Peter, 230, 239

Tatum, Nate, 209–211, 219
Tawney, Doug, 218

Union for Jobs and Income Now (U-JOIN), 13, 17, 160
United Church of the Brethren: Brethren Volunteer Service (BVS), 104–106, 109, 113–116; Fresh Air program, 107–113; Pilot House, 105–107, 109–110, 113–117
United Western Front (UWF), 233–234, 236
University of Baltimore, 200–201
University of Maryland, 156; Baltimore County (UMBC), 86, 90, 148; School of Architecture, 227, 233
University of Pennsylvania, 228
Urban Coalition, 13
Urban Design Concept Team (UDCT), 62, 64
U.S. Army, 5–6, 10, 15, 30, 44, 94, 99, 132, 160

Vance, Cyrus, 10
Vaughn, Neyland, 233–234, 236
Vietnam War, 14, 33, 90, 97–98, 115, 122–124, 126–128, 130, 133–137; veterans, 72, 262
Volunteers in Service to America (VISTA), 230–233, 237–239, 241

Walton, John, 163, 165
Ware, Gilbert, 74, 79
Washington, Clarence, 13
Welcome, Verda, 77
Weschler, Stuart, 17
Westside Renaissance Corporation, 236
Wickham, DeWayne, 43, 190–191
Wickwire, Chester, 216
Wilkins, Roy, 80, 124
Williams, "Little" Melvin, 8, 15, 192, 211
Wilson, Larry, 197–198
Workers Allied toward Cultural Unity (WATCU), 235–237, 240

York, Robert, 7
Young, Whitney, Jr., 124, 226, 241